*PERSONAL
FINANCE*

PERSONAL FINANCE

VIRGINIA BRITTON

formerly University of Maryland

AMERICAN BOOK COMPANY

New York • Cincinnati • Atlanta • Dallas • Millbrae

Preface

Each family and individual has many choices to make in getting and using income. Only the consumer unit can make the decisions that are most appropriate for itself. Family welfare requires, therefore, an understanding of the financial problems that may arise during the life cycle, decisions to be made, and alternatives available.

Changes in socioeconomic conditions, in the stage of the family life cycle, and in the singular needs and resources of individuals provide an endless procession of financial experiences. Each family has a unique array of concurrent experiences. The tremendous variety of ways of obtaining income and of spending, saving, and sharing it has greatly increased the number of decisions to be made and the complications in making them.

This book has, therefore, been written to aid the family in working on its financial plan and budget. While it has been prepared as a textbook for college courses on family and personal finance, it should also be useful to families and individuals who are working independently on their budgeting problems. The discussion assumes little previous information on the subject so that it can be used by the beginning student as well as the more experienced one. The book is oriented primarily to family interests because most people spend most of their lives as family members; however, the material is adaptable to the needs of the individual.

The book includes a number of subjects not generally discussed in texts on family and personal finance. It presents basic facts and principles, sources of reliable information, and methods of analysis that are valuable to families and individuals in their personal lives and in helping them to consider similar problems of other families. The book seeks to avoid both over-simplification and profusion of details while attempting to serve as a foundation for more detailed study of topics of individual interest. The social, political, and economic institutions of the country are accepted as the framework within which the family operates in its financial management.

Attention is given to them as they affect family problems and decisions.

The topics dealt with are those about which each family or individual must make decisions, consciously or unconsciously. The book is divided into three parts. Part One, Your Family Finances, includes a discussion of financial experiences of families, the family's income, the budgeting process, prices of consumer goods, consumer credit, and income taxes. Part Two, Your Expenditures, includes sections on family expenditure patterns, the food budget, the clothing budget, the shelter budget, the automobile budget, the medical care budget, and other expenditures. Part Three, Your Investments and Long-Run Protection, discusses the family's savings program, savings systems and savings bonds, social security, life insurance, retirement annuities, investments in business, and wills distributing property.

For their collection and analyses of data used in this book, gratitude is particularly due the Bureau of the Census, the Bureau of Labor Statistics, the Consumer and Food Economics Research Division, the Department of Agriculture, the Office of Business Economics, the Board of Governors of the Federal Reserve System, the Federal Housing Administration, the Treasury Department, the National Center for Health Statistics, the Social Security Administration, the Health Insurance Institute, the Institute of Life Insurance, Household Finance Corporation, E. H. Boeckh and Associates, Incorporated, and Standard & Poor's Corporation.

Gratitude is also due numerous undergraduate and graduate students, families, and colleagues at the University of Maryland, Pennsylvania State University, the University of Akron, Kent State University, and the Vermont Agricultural Experiment Station. Their probings during the past three decades of college teaching and research in family economics have been a constant source of stimulation resulting in the preparation of the materials contained herein.

V. B.

Contents

x / *Contents*

Part One

Your
Family
Finances

Financial Experiences of Families / 1

- PREVALENCE OF BUDGET PROBLEMS
- FINANCING THE FAMILY'S LIFE CYCLE

Today many of us feel that we have budget problems because prices and taxes are too high and incomes are not high enough—not high enough, that is, for us to procure all of the desirable goods and services attractively advertised and displayed on the market. Frequently we think that getting more income would be a simple solution to these problems. In many cases it would help. But there are indications that more dollars is not a cure-all.

The family's needs change during its life cycle and continuous effort is required to obtain money for family support. Decisions must be made as to how this income will be used for current living, future needs, and the assistance of others. It would be simpler if some omniscient authority would tell us exactly what to do to ensure success in our financial decisions, but who would accept such dictation? These decisions are important in determining the quality of our lives and not many of us are willing to allow someone else to make them for us. However, we need all the information possible on which to base our decisions, in the hope of making the wisest ones for our families.

PREVALENCE OF BUDGET PROBLEMS

The family with an unemployed father or a child requiring expensive medical care is well aware of its acute budgeting problems. But the average family also finds that it has to manage carefully in order to supply its needs. Providing a college education for the children sometimes strains the budget even of a family with higher income.

Even families in the top tenth income group report budget problems. Some years ago *Fortune* printed an article titled "$25,000 a Year: A.D. 1948," and described it as follows: "This is how seven families in seven U. S. metropolitan areas are not quite managing to live on that income. And how one other is not doing much better with almost double the money." Through the years several articles on the same theme have appeared in the *Ladies' Home Journal:* "Broke but happy on $11,200 a year;" "We have no children, a split-level home and overspend on $18,000 a year;" "We can't live on $25,000 a year;" and "How it feels to earn $200,000 a year."

Recently an actor filed a bankruptcy petition after earning $12 million in 30 years of show business. He listed debts of almost $500,000 and assets of only $500 in clothes and household goods. To cite another case: When a movie star whose pictures grossed more than $200 million died, she had only $4,800 in the bank. She had recently purchased a $75,000 home with a $5,000 down payment and a 20-year mortgage, and had furnished it sparsely.

What can be the explanation for these situations when income is high? First, one must realize that some families are caught in circumstances that require high amounts of dollar income to provide basic necessities. There may be an unusually large number of members in the home to be supported; the family may have large, necessary medical expenses or other uninsured losses to meet; it may have to contribute to the support of relatives outside the home. Or the family may live in a community where the costs of ordinary consumer goods are exceptionally high.

But the reasons may also be connected with the family's ideas of its necessary level of living. Desires for goods and services may increase as fast or even faster than income does. One couple that was regularly climbing into higher and higher income classes remarked that it was strange that they never felt any better off—for every extra $1,000 the husband got they already had plans to spend $2,000. But why does this occur? Perhaps it is exposure to even higher levels of living among one's acquaintances. Perhaps one feels that a more expensive level is necessary for advancement. Or there might be a feeling of insecurity about one's job or social position or personal relationships. Perhaps the family has had a higher income in the past so that it feels deprived at its present income level. Of course, "talking poor with a full mouth" might be protective covering from the importuning of relatives and friends, of charitable and cultural organizations, and from tax inroads by legislatures.

But how do these families manage to spend their high incomes so easily? First they mention the high income taxes they must pay, then the contributions they must make to relatives and worthy organizations. There are many temptations to have more varied foods and beverages, more expensive clothing, and a bigger house and grounds which involve larger utility bills, household help, and sizable quantities of more expensive durable goods. In addition, they have expenses for country club dues, entertainment of guests at home and at clubs, recreation, travel, private education and special lessons for the children, and probably more expensive medical care. At the same time they feel they should have large insurance and savings programs. So they feel poor.

At any rate, it seems clear that budgeting problems are not eliminated by a higher income. In certain respects they increase, since a wider range of choice is opened, requiring broader consideration and knowledge.

FINANCING THE FAMILY'S LIFE CYCLE

In planning its budget, the family tries to foresee and take into account the likely course of its life cycle, with its changing needs, goals, and resources. Family living is the prevailing way of life in this country where 93 percent of us live as members of families (defined as two or more persons related by blood, marriage, or adoption, and residing together [1]). Of the total 48 million families, 87 percent are headed by a husband and wife, 11 percent by a widowed, divorced, or separated person, and 2 percent by a single person.

While families vary in their life cycles, much can be learned from consideration of average patterns.[2] The following discussion of the life cycle draws on statistical data to present a picture of the

---

[1] U. S. Bureau of Census, *Current Population Reports,* Series P–20, Nos. 159 and 164, 1967 (1966 data).

[2] For individual histories reflecting changing socioeconomic conditions, see Virginia Britton, "Case Studies of the Economic Experience of Selected Families During Their Life Span" (unpublished doctoral dissertation, U. of Chicago, 1950).

family at various stages. The discussion deals in general terms; later chapters include details on income, savings, and needs for food and other items throughout the life cycle.

The Beginning Family · The beginning family is usually composed of the young couple alone. This stage continues a year or two, on the average, until the birth of the first child. To illustrate the average situation, we might consider Allan and Ann Amos who were married when he was 23 and she was almost 21, median ages at first marriage in recent years. This contrasts with 26 for men and 22 for women in 1890.

At marriage Allan had a car, a little insurance, and small savings. Ann had a sizable wardrobe and some house furnishings. They received gifts of household items. Some young couples begin marriage with premarriage debts, perhaps for education or a car, but Allan and Ann were lucky to be free of debts. While half of the young men have begun employment by the time they are 18,[3] Allan started later. He earns $90 a week, which is more than many young workers earn.[4] He hopes to become a supervisor at a higher wage. To help them set up housekeeping before they have a family, Ann is continuing at her office job where she earns $60 a week. About half of the young wives work at paid jobs the first year or two of marriage.[5]

Their needs for food and clothing are low. They need small and inexpensive private quarters. Their medical needs are probably low, and their recreation needs moderate. During this period some couples seek to complete their education or repay premarriage debts. Allan and Ann are trying to accumulate furniture and equipment toward the establishment of a home and to make cash savings for emergency expenses. Beyond this, they want to start health and life insurance programs for the next period, and wish to save toward the purchase of a home.

The Expanding Family · The expanding stage includes the childbearing, preschool, and grade-school years, and lasts about 13 years, until the oldest child reaches adolescence. Let us look at another hypothetical family to illustrate the average situation at this stage. Ben and Barbara Boguslavsky were 24 and 22 years old when their

[3] U. S. Bureau of Labor Statistics, *Employment and Earnings and Monthly Report on the Labor Force,* April 1967.
[4] U. S. Bureau of Census, *Current Population Reports,* Series P–60, No. 51, 1967 (1965 data).
[5] U. S. Bureau of Labor Statistics, *Marital and Family Characteristics of Workers,* Special Labor Force Report No. 64, 1966 (1965 data).

first child was born. Their third and last child was born some 8 years later. (See Figure 1–1.)

Like most mothers, Barbara did not take paid employment while she had preschool children. Thus the family depended almost entirely on Ben's earnings during the expanding stage. Fortunately he had greater experience and business conditions were good, so he was able to earn about $125 weekly, about a third more than the young husband.

Food and clothing needs of the family are increasing throughout this period as the children progress from the preschool through the grade-school years. There are likely to be high medical expenditures for birth of the children, preventive care for them, and child-

FIGURE 1–1. Family Life Cycle With Three Children

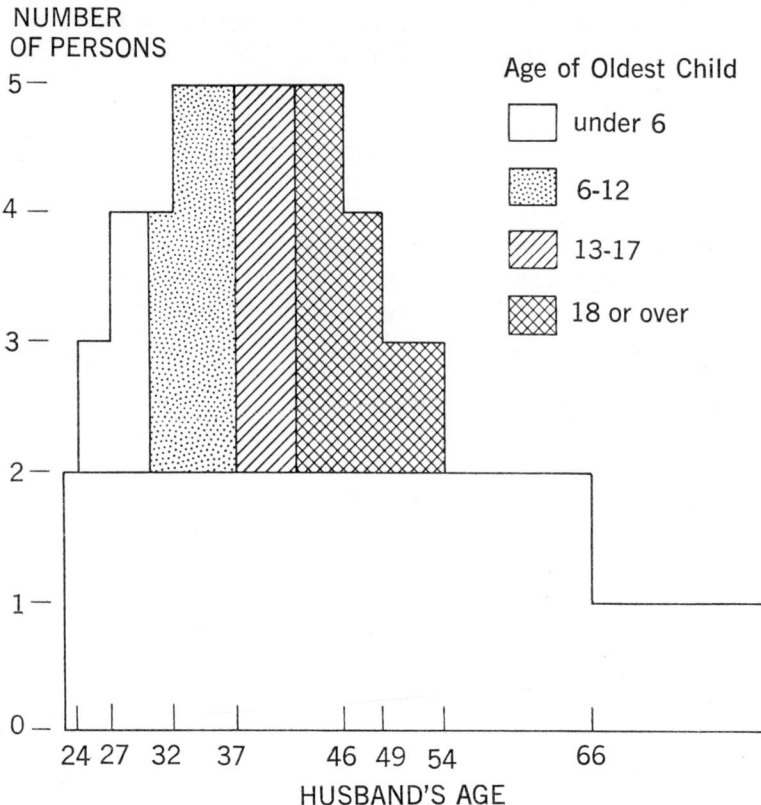

SOURCE: Estimates based on Paul C. Glick and Robert Parke, Jr., *Demography*, 1965, pp. 187–202.

hood diseases as the first child starts to school. The family's shelter needs are increasing as it requires more space in a place where children are permitted and which is close to schools and other community facilities.

Recreation outside the home is probably negligible, although some should be provided, especially for the mother. But play equipment is needed for the children and perhaps TV. Since the mother's duties are heavy at this stage, provision needs to be made for the purchase of labor-saving equipment, extra household help, or the use of outside services. Early in the period the couple needs to purchase baby equipment and, as the children start to school, there are rising costs for school supplies and special lessons.

Through the period as children are born, the parents need to increase their life insurance program and to include the children in health insurance programs. They may be purchasing a home or saving toward its purchase, and they need to save toward the future education costs of the children, which will be high in the next period.

The Launching Family · In this stage the family is concerned with completing the formal education of its children and launching them on their careers. It begins when the first child reaches adolescence and presumably ends with the marriage of the last, a period of about 17 years on the average. The median situation might be illustrated by Carl and Cynthia Cohen. They were 37 and 35 years old when their first child reached 13. Carl was 42 when the first child reached 18 and 46 when the first child married. Their last child married by the time Carl was 54 and Cynthia 52.

If the family is fortunate, it has accumulated some savings by the beginning of this period, but savings are likely to total no more than a few thousand dollars. The family is still largely dependent on the father's earnings, although an increasing number of mothers and children make contributions as the children progress through the high-school and later years. Other things being equal, family income may be about a tenth higher than during the expanding stage. The burden of the expensive high-school and college years is eased for the family if this stage coincides with a period of general prosperity, but the burden is intensified when this stage coincides with a depression.

During this stage of the life cycle, food, clothing, recreation, and shelter needs are high and increasing. Education expenses increase as the children progress through high school and, especially, if they continue into college or graduate work. The family may help the children start in a business or profession and start their homes, including the provision of weddings. During this period some families also have to help their elderly parents who are retired.

The Middle-Age Family · The middle-age family is again composed of the husband and wife after the marriage of their children and before retirement or widowhood. While the children are now generally self-supporting, the parents may have some children living with them, particularly early in the period. On the average, the period lasts about 11 years, beginning when the husband is 54 years old and the wife 52 at the marriage of their last child, and ending when the husband is about 65.

Parents who have reared and educated a family probably do not have much financial accumulation at the beginning of the period. The family is still primarily dependent on the husband's earnings, although the wife may take paid work to help prepare for old age or to occupy her time. Other things being equal, family income is likely to decline somewhat from the peak income of the previous period.

During this period, the parents' needs are low for food, clothing, and shelter. Entertainment, particularly of their children, may add to their food and housing costs. During these years, their medical needs are likely to be rising. Recreation expenses rise as they engage in more social activities, travel, and develop wider interests for the retirement years. In addition, they may need to help their elderly parents. They will seek to replace worn-out durable goods, repay debts, complete payment of insurance premiums, and increase savings for old age when income will decrease and medical and death costs will rise.

The Old-Age Family · The period of old age might be considered to begin with the retirement of the husband or the death at about that time of one of the spouses. For half of the couples, marriage is broken by death of one of the spouses by the time the husband is 66 years old. Since the wife is more likely to be the survivor because of her younger age at marriage and the greater longevity of women, she will probably be a widow for a number of years. But at present half of the parents have some years together after retirement starts.

Their income from their investments and retirement programs is likely to be only about half that of their peak years, other things being equal, so that they will be fortunate if they have some accumulation of financial assets on which to draw. Furthermore, they may wish to revise their insurance programs to maximize provision for their own current needs. While their income is limited, they probably have more time and ability for careful shopping and home production of goods and services than do younger families. Thus they are able to make the most of the money they receive, at least as long as health permits.

Their needs are low for food, clothing, and shelter. Recreation needs are moderate, including social activities, hobbies, and perhaps travel. But medical needs may be high and growing as chronic illness develops, and there may be increasing need for household help.

Abnormal Cycles · For some people, the life cycle differs considerably from the foregoing description. Among men 27 years old, 17 percent are single, and by 45 years of age 4 percent may still be single.[6] Among women 27 years old, 10 percent are single, and by 45 years of age 3 percent may still be single. While some start their families late, others who never marry live with related persons, unrelated persons, or alone. In any case, they may aid in rearing children or supporting elderly parents.

For many people, the family life cycle is more complicated, since the first marriage is not always the only marriage. At age 27, approximately 5 percent of the men and 7 percent of the women have been married more than once.[7] By age 40, remarriage figures climb to 12 percent for men and 14 for women.

Divorce is more important in the dissolution of marriage in its early years, and death is more important in the late years. Among older generations, death allowed the survivor to remarry, but today's greater longevity for both men and women makes this freedom less common. Divorce has somewhat replaced it. Landis summarizes the situation this way: "If we accept the estimate that one in six spouses today has realized a second marriage following divorce, which is a conservative estimate, it is clear that 'sequential polygamy' is more common in our society than polygamy is in some societies of polygamous cultural norms." [8]

Median age at remarriage of divorced persons (three-quarters

6 Robert Parke, Jr., and Paul C. Glick, "Prospective Changes in Marriage and the Family," *Journal of Marriage and the Family*, May 1967, pp. 249–256.

7 U. S. Bureau of Census, *Current Population Reports*, Series P–20, No. 122, 1963 (1962 data).

8 Paul H. Landis, "Sequential Marriage," *Journal of Home Economics*, 1950, pp. 625–628.

of those remarrying) is 36 for men and 32 for women.[9] Average age at remarriage of widowed persons is 58 for men and 49 for women. Remarried couples tend to be worse off financially than the once-married with regard to annual income and increase in income with years of marriage.[10] Financial problems are particularly serious at divorce or widowhood when children are involved. Fortunately, death rates of parents are low during the child-rearing years. But divorce is more frequent. The father's income then needs to be divided to support the mother and children in one household and himself in another—a much more expensive arrangement. If he later remarries and establishes a second family, the financial difficulty is compounded.

In one example, the young wife of a factory worker learned when they needed a larger apartment for their expected child that her young husband had been previously married and had monthly payments to make toward the support of his child and former wife. The financial situation worsened progressively and the husband finally went into military service.

Another family's situation started differently. When his three children were in their early twenties, Jack D., a 50-year-old executive, was divorced. He retained half of the couple's property and was ordered by the court to make monthly alimony payments. He then married a woman of 30 who bore three children. He has found it difficult to meet his financial obligations although his income is good, and he has made no savings since remarriage. When he retires at 65, the family will have to depend on his retirement benefits and small savings plus any earnings of the mother, then 45, to support the children through the expensive high-school and college years ahead.

Support payments set by the courts are generally modest from the point of view of the mother trying to take care of the family. For example, the court recently awarded a former beauty queen $15 weekly support from her husband for their year-old daughter. But to the father the payments may become more and more onerous as time goes by and he withdraws from personal involvement with the children and especially as he establishes another family. Even a good income becomes small when divided. Therefore, it is not unusual to find the father becoming more lax in payments and the mother striving to find ways to eke out income. Newspapers recently carried an account of the divorced wife of a millionaire who had been evicted

---

[9] U. S. National Center for Health Statistics, *Vital and Health Statistics: Marriage Statistics Analysis, United States, 1962,* Public Health Service Publication No. 1000, Series 21, No. 10, 1967, p. 18.
[10] Paul C. Glick, *American Families* (New York: Wiley, 1957), p. 120.

from her home and was seeking a job to support their daughter, 16, and son, 13. She said that her husband had been ordered to pay $700 a month for support of the family, but that he was paying only $100. An uncontested divorce with no property to divide may cost $2,000, mostly for the lawyers representing the two parties. Minimum fees for each party range from about $100 in some counties in the Southwest to $500 in some New York counties and "actual fees frequently exceed the minimum." [11] A poor man may thus be forced to resort to desertion.

Life Cycle and the Population · While a family is in one stage of the life cycle, other families are in other stages. The 37 percent of the 197 million population that is now 20–49 years old has major responsibility of caring for the 40 percent that is younger.[12] Fourteen percent of the population is 50–64, and 9 percent is older. The population remembering socioeconomic conditions before the postwar period is fast being outnumbered. Only about half remember World War II, and a third remember the Great Depression. Census projections for a population of 300 million by 1990 envision children and child-rearing adults as comprising slightly larger proportions, the middle-aged stage comprising a smaller, and the elderly remaining about the same proportion.

QUESTIONS

1. What types of financial problems and decisions do families face? How would you evaluate them as to relative importance? What problems should be studied?
2. Why doesn't increased income serve as a cure-all for financial problems?
3. What are the important characteristics of each stage of the normal family life cycle?
4. Explain the meaning of a "median."
5. How would you name and describe the major stages of the life cycle for a person who never marries?
6. How does early dissolution of a marriage affect the course of the family life cycle? How does remarriage affect it?

---

[11] *Washington Post*, Parade, June 4, 1967, pp. 34–35.
[12] U. S. Bureau of Census, *Current Population Reports*, Series P–25, No. 359, 1967 (1966 data).

SUGGESTIONS FOR FURTHER READING

Carter, Hugh, and Glick, Paul C. *Marriage and Divorce: A Social and Economic Study.* Cambridge: Harvard U. Press, 1968.

U. S. Bureau of the Census. *Current Population Reports,* Series P–20, P–25, and P–60, latest reports.

U. S. Bureau of Labor Statistics. *Employment and Earnings and Monthly Report on the Labor Force,* latest reports.

————. *Special Labor Force Reports,* latest reports.

"You yourself are much condemn'd
to have an itching palm."
—JULIUS CAESAR

The Family's Income / 2

- SOURCES OF GOODS AND SERVICES
- FAMILY EFFORTS TO INCREASE EARNINGS
- HOMEMAKERS' CONTRIBUTIONS TO INCOME
- EFFECTS OF SOCIOECONOMIC CONDITIONS
- SIZE OF MONEY INCOME
- AID FOR FAMILIES IN DISTRESS

Most of us share a deep interest throughout our lives in money income—whether it is in dollars, pounds, pesos, francs, lire, or beaver skins. We want it to be large and regular. Maybe we are greedy at times. But we are not likely to be miserly. We see few of the dollars we receive and accumulate limited amounts. We want money because of the things it will buy—necessities, decencies, and luxuries, for the present and for the future, for ourselves and for others. The earner, the homemaker, and others strive to increase family income. Their success is affected both by individual situations and by socioeconomic conditions. Sometimes, in a financial crisis, the family is forced to seek outside aid.

SOURCES OF GOODS AND SERVICES

Goods and services for family support may be obtained directly or through the use of money resources.

Money Resources · Current income is the most important source of money for family support. It includes earnings for services in wages, salary, commission, or bonus, as well as net income from self-employment in a private profession or business, nonfarm or farm. It also includes investment income in the form of interest from savings accounts and similar items, dividends from stocks, profits from unincorporated enterprises, and net rentals from property. A family may have other sources of income such as benefits from Social Security, the Veterans Administration, Workman's Compensation, Unemployment Compensation, public assistance, annuities, pensions, and alimony. These are generally termed "transfer" income, that is, transferred from one person or group to another.

The great importance of currently earned income is shown by the aggregate figures for all persons in the United States. Almost seven-tenths of gross income comes from wages, salaries, and other labor income, and a tenth is proprietor's income.[1] More than a tenth comes from rentals, dividends, and interest, and less than a tenth from transfer payments, as follows:

ITEM	BILLIONS OF DOLLARS, 1965	PERCENT
Gross personal income*	548	100
Wages, salaries, other labor income ...	377	69
Proprietors' income	56	10
Rental income of persons	18	3
Dividends	19	3
Personal interest income	38	7
Transfer payments	40	7

* Before personal contributions for social insurance and personal tax and nontax payments.

Almost half of all families have currently earned income only.[2] Somewhat less receive other types of income in addition to current earnings, and a few have no earnings at all. Median income is highest for those with current earnings plus other income and lowest for those with no current earnings, as follows:

SOURCES OF INCOME	FAMILY INCOME BEFORE TAXES, 1965	PERCENT OF FAMILIES
All sources	$6,900	100
Current earnings only	6,900	48
Current earnings plus other income (investment or transfer)	7,800	44
No current earnings	2,400	8

[1] U. S. Department of Commerce, *Survey of Current Business,* July 1966.
[2] See U. S. Bureau of Census, *Current Population Reports,* Series P–60, No. 51, 1967. (Unless otherwise noted, all data on family and individual income quoted in this chapter are from *Current Population Reports,* 1965.)

At low income levels, a sizable proportion of the families have no current earnings. At middle income levels, the majority have current earnings only. But at high income levels, the majority have both current earnings and other income. For example, the percentage of families with various sources of income at three income levels is as follows:

| | FAMILY INCOME BEFORE TAXES, 1965 | | |
SOURCES OF INCOME	$1,000–$1,499	$6,000–$6,999	$15,000–$24,999
All sources	100	100	100
Current earnings only ..	29	59	31
Current earnings plus other income	33	40	68
No current earnings	38	1	1

In addition to current income, a family may have other money resources for family support. It may use credit for the purchase of goods and services, that is, draw on future income, as many young families do. On the other hand, it may draw on its accumulation of savings, using up its principal, as many elderly persons do.

Some families have windfall receipts from gifts, lump-sum inheritances, or insurance policies. Some receive money from the sale of their own property, such as stocks, bonds, a house, or car. Such money is counted as an exchange of one asset for another. In any case, the money usually passes first into the family's bank account. It may then be used as part of the accumulation of savings that is withdrawn for family support. Or it may be invested or reinvested so as to add to investment income in later periods.

Nonmoney Income · Many families have additional goods and services for which they do not pay out of current money resources. Sometimes these constitute large additions to real income. The family may receive goods and services as gifts, charity, pay, or prizes. Gifts from individuals and organizations include everything from baby-sitting services by a friend to surplus foods distributed by the government. Farm laborers and ministers are among the groups that frequently receive housing as part of their pay. According to the Survey of Consumer Expenditures 1960–61 (by the U. S. Bureau of Labor Statistics and the U. S. Department of Agriculture), the value of free items averaged $206 for urban families of two or more persons, two-thirds of the value being in clothing, medical care, and housing, and for farm families averaged $135.

The family may home-produce many items for its own use. For example, the value of garden and farm-furnished food averages $460 for farm families of two or more persons, according to the 1961 survey. This contrasts with averages of $66 for rural nonfarm families and $7 for urban. In addition, the family may service many of the repairs around its own home. The mother may perform the house-keeping tasks. When these are totalled, the value of home-produced goods and services often makes a substantial contribution to the family's level of living. The value is estimated on the basis of what it would cost to purchase similar items on the market.

Some families have services available from their owned durable goods, such as a home, car, and household equipment. A family with a $3,000-income and no durable goods is in quite a different position than another family with the same income and a large stock of equipment. Frequently this is a basic cause of difference in the level of living of a newly-married couple and a retired couple.

In addition, the family may obtain sizable nonmoney income in the form of services that are provided wholly or largely at community expense, such as education, parks, museums, libraries, and religious services. A family may add greatly to its level of living by taking advantage of these services, which would be exceedingly expensive if purchased privately.

FAMILY EFFORTS TO INCREASE EARNINGS

During its life cycle, the family may try to enlarge money earnings by various means, such as multiple jobs, multiple earners, increased education, mobility, and choice of industry and occupation. The family may be aided or frustrated in attempts to increase earnings by personal characteristics of the earner as well as by general socioeconomic conditions.

The frequency of some efforts to increase earnings is indicated by recent data showing 5 percent of all employed persons holding multiple jobs.[3] Typically, the person is a family man between 25 and 44 years old, holding a full-time job and working an average of 13 hours a week on his secondary job in an industry or occupation different from his first job.

[3] U. S. Bureau of Labor Statistics, *Multiple Jobholders in May 1965*, Special Labor Force Report No. 63, 1966.

Almost half of all families have more than one earner. Among nonfarm families, median money income currently varies from about $6,300 for those with one earner to $8,100 for those with two earners, and to $10,600 for those with three or more. These figures probably understate the additions made by supplementary earners who are more common where the income of the primary earner is low.

Education · Many families see education as a means of increasing earnings; this has been at least part of the reason for the increased educational attainment of the population. Among men now 25–29 years old, 17 percent have completed college, an additional 13 percent have had some college, and 41 percent have completed high school, but gone no further.[4] Thus, 71 percent have at least a high-school education, about twice as large a proportion as in 1940. The top projection for 1985 is 77 percent.

Data show men 25–34 years old with a high-school education receiving 37 percent more income than those with elementary education, and men with college education receiving 22 percent more than those with high school (Table 2–1). In the peak earning years, 45–54, those with college education received 70 percent more than those with high school. Obviously, education pays, but how well it pays in comparison with other investments is not so easily determined. Estimating the average rate of return on the investment in a college education is a complicated matter, requiring estimates of both costs and future income.

Private costs of a college education include the direct costs of tuition, fees, books, supplies, and any extra living expenses that would not otherwise be incurred, as well as the indirect costs of earnings foregone while attending college. Income through the working years is affected not only by the individual's educational level, but simultaneously by his advancing age, the availability of employment, productivity gains, and progressive income taxes. Furthermore, the income is received through the years, and $1,000 received in 20 years is worth considerably less than $1,000 received today. Estimates of the average rate of return on money spent on a college education indicate that it may approximate 12 percent a year.[5] Gains by individuals may be greater or less, depending on many circumstances.

---

4 U. S. Bureau of Census, *Current Population Reports*, Series P–20, No. 158, 1966 (1966 data), and Series P–25, No. 305, 1965 (projections).
5 Gary S. Becker, *Human Capital* (New York: National Bureau of Economic Research, 1964), p. 128.

TABLE 2–1. Median Money Income Before Taxes for Males, by Education and Age

| | SCHOOLING COMPLETED | | |
AGE	ELEMENTARY (8 YEARS)	HIGH SCHOOL (4 YEARS)	COLLEGE (4 OR MORE YEARS)
25 to 34 years	$4,475	$6,151	$7,474
35 to 44 years	5,219	7,040	10,460
45 to 54 years	5,430	6,957	11,835
55 to 64 years	4,893	6,626	9,593
65 years and over	2,171	2,882	5,000

SOURCE: U. S. Bureau of the Census, *Current Population Reports*, Series P–60, No. 51, 1967 (data for 1965).

Whether investment in a college education pays better than other investments is another matter.

Miller cautions that it is not inevitable that money invested in education will pay dividends or that the rate of return will be constant over time.[6] Higher incomes of those with more schooling may be due partly to differences in intelligence, home environment, and family connections. While college graduates are more likely to have some income in addition to earnings, the amount of nonearned income is relatively small and tends to be underreported in surveys.

Mobility · Mobility is a chief means of increasing earnings for the individual worker. It may also be a stimulating experience for the worker and his family. Mobility includes a change in employer, occupation, industry, and geographic location. But the new job opportunity must be available, the worker must learn of it, he must have the necessary skills and ability, and he must be willing and able to move. Consequently, the young, the educated, the informed, and the unemployed are the most mobile.[7]

Emotional ties, pension plans and other fringe benefits, and the costs of moving—transportation of the family and its household goods, loss on sale of its home, loss of earnings during the move, expenses of establishing the family in a new location—all tend to decrease the worker's mobility. But they surely have not immobilized

[6] Herman P. Miller, "Annual and Lifetime Income in Relation to Education: 1939–1959," *American Economic Review*, 1960, pp. 962–986.
[7] U. S. Bureau of Census, *Current Population Reports*, Series P–20, No. 156, 1966 (1966 data).

TABLE 2–2.   Median Years on Current Job

MEN		WOMEN		
			YEARS ON CURRENT JOB	
AGE	YEARS ON CURRENT JOB	AGE	SINGLE WOMEN	MARRIED WOMEN
20–24 .... 1.0		14–24 .... 1.6		.9
25–34 .... 3.2		25–34 .... 3.5		1.7
35–44 .... 7.8		35–44 .... 8.9		3.3
45–54 .... 11.5		45 and over 15.5		6.4
55–64 .... 15.8				
65 and over 15.5				

SOURCE: H. R. Hamel, "Special Labor Force Report: Job Tenure of Workers, January 1966," *Monthly Labor Review*, January 1967, p. 33 (Report of Supplement to Current Population Survey in January 1966).

the American worker. On the average, employed men remain at a job 5 years, but young men change jobs more frequently (Table 2–2). Only those men 55 and over average 16 years on their current job. Single women stay on one job as long as men, but married women stay shorter times, usually because of maternity and family responsibilities.

A worker's mobility may be important in determining how well he participates in the gains from the nation's economic growth and productivity. Miller's study of the 1950 and 1960 censuses indicated that the young male worker participated much more fully in the gains from economic growth than did the mature worker of equal education.[8] The greater mobility of the young worker may be the major reason. Furthermore, the college-educated young worker, in probably the most mobile group, participated more fully in the gains than did young workers with less education. Among older workers, those with college education appeared to participate somewhat less fully in the gains from economic growth than did those with less education. It may be that their specialized education, experience, and seniority rights immobilized them more than less educated workers.

Industry · Earnings differ importantly by industry, because of the average level of skill required, union activity, and other factors.

[8] Herman P. Miller, "Lifetime Income and Economic Growth," *American Economic Review*, September 1965, pp. 834–844.

Among the thirteen major industry groups, median earnings for year-round full-time male workers in 1965 ranged from $7,200 in professional and related services and in finance, insurance, and real estate down to $3,000 in agriculture, forestry, and fisheries, as follows:

Professional and related services; finance,
    insurance, and real estate $7,200
Public administration; manufacturing;
    transportation, communication, and other
    public utilities; mining; wholesale trade . . $6,900–$6,600
Construction; business and repair services . . . . . $6,300–$6,100
Entertainment and recreation services; retail
    trade . . . . $5,900–$5,700
Personal services $5,000
Agriculture, forestry, and fisheries $3,000

Manpower needs of industry by 1975 are expected to be a quarter higher than in 1964, assuming full employment, the continuation of economic and social patterns and relationships, no cataclysmic war or other event, and approximately the same size of the armed forces as at present.[9] Expected manpower needs by 1975 as compared with 1964 vary from industry to industry, and may be summarized briefly as follows:

INDUSTRY	EXPECTED CHANGE IN MANPOWER NEEDS BY 1975
Agriculture	Decline
Mining	May decline
Bituminous coal mining	Decline
Contract construction	Increase a third
Manufacturing	Increase a fifth
Durable goods industries	Increase more than a fifth
Nondurable goods industries	Increase less than a fifth
Petroleum refining, tobacco, textile-mill products	Grow little or decline
Wholesale and retail trade	Increase nearly a fourth
Government:	
Federal	No increase
State and local	Increase two-thirds
Finance, insurance, and real estate	Increase a fourth
Transportation and public utilities	Increase little
Railroad transportation	Decline slowly

9 Howard Stambler, "Manpower Needs by Industry to 1975," *Monthly Labor Review,* March 1965, pp. 279–284. This article contains material originally presented in the Secretary of Labor's Report on Manpower Requirements, Resources and Training submitted to the Congress March, 1965, together with considerable additional detail.

INDUSTRY	EXPECTED CHANGE IN MANPOWER NEEDS BY 1975
Air transportation and motor freight transportation and storage	Increase
Communications, electric, gas and sanitary services	Change little
Service and miscellaneous industries	Increase a half
Medical and health services	Grow rapidly
Business services (e.g., advertising, accounting, computing, collecting, maintenance)	Grow
Educational services	Grow very rapidly

The economist sees high salaries as useful in attracting workers into growing industries, and low salaries as useful in repelling them from declining industries. But, as R. A. Lester points out:

> The structure of compensation (wages and fringe benefits) may also be a barrier to movement out of labor-surplus and into labor-shortage industries and occupations. In large sections of the economy, wage-benefit levels are the reverse of what they should be for labor mobility purposes. They are high for unskilled and semiskilled workers in mass-production industries, mining, and railroading, in which such employment has been declining, and relatively low in expanding service lines like schools, hospitals, and hotels and restaurants.
>
> Wage structures seem to be rather insensitive to changing manpower needs. . . .[10]

Occupation · Fortunate choice of occupation helps greatly to increase earnings. Of course, freedom of choice is limited by the skills and other characteristics of the worker and the availability of jobs, as well as his knowledge of opportunities and his willingness and ability to accept the job. Table 2–3 shows median earnings for males ranging from $8,500 for professional and technical workers and $7,900 for managers, officials, and proprietors down to $2,300 for farm laborers and foremen.

Earnings are higher for professional workers who are self-employed, particularly those in medical work, than for professional workers who are salaried. Engineers and technical workers comprise the highest paid group among the salaried professional workers. In

10 Richard A. Lester, "The Adaptation of Labor Resources to Changing Needs," *Monthly Labor Review*, March 1966, p. 247.

contrast, earnings are higher for managerial workers who are salaried than for those who are self-employed, largely because of the number of self-employed who are in retail trade where reported earnings are lower. While earnings average $7,200 for male sales workers, $6,800

TABLE 2–3. Median Earnings for Year-Round Full-Time Workers 14 Years Old and Over, by Occupation of Longest Job

OCCUPATION GROUP, 1965	MALE	FEMALE
Professional, technical, and kindred workers	$ 8,500	$5,500
Self-employed	11,800	..
Medical and other health workers	13,700	..
Other self-employed workers	10,200	..
Salaried	8,300	5,500
Engineers, technical	10,400	..
Medical and other health workers	7,400	5,100
Teachers, elementary and secondary schools	7,100	5,700
Other salaried workers	7,900	5,800
Farmers and farm managers	3,100	..
Managers, officials, and proprietors, except farm	7,900	4,200
Self-employed	6,800	2,200
In retail trade	6,000	..
Other self-employed workers	7,400	..
Salaried	8,500	4,700
Clerical and kindred workers	6,300	4,200
Secretaries, stenographers, and typists	..	4,400
Other clerical and kindred workers	6,300	4,100
Sales workers	7,200	2,900
In retail trade	6,100	2,800
Other sales workers	7,700	..
Craftsmen, foremen, and kindred workers	6,800	3,800
Foremen	7,700	..
Craftsmen	6,600	..
In construction	6,700	..
Other craftsmen and kindred workers	6,600	..
Operatives and kindred workers	5,800	3,300
Manufacturing	6,000	3,400
Durable goods	6,100	3,900
Nondurable goods	5,600	3,100
Other operatives and kindred workers	5,500	2,700
Private household workers	..	1,200
Service workers, except private household	4,900	2,700
Waiters, cooks, and bartenders	4,900	2,300
Other service workers	4,900	2,900
Farm laborers and foremen	2,300	..
Laborers, except farm and mine	4,700	..

SOURCE: U. S. Bureau of the Census, *Current Population Reports*, Series P–60, No. 51, 1967.

for craftsmen and foremen, $6,300 for clerical, and $5,800 for factory operatives and kindred, there is considerable variation among their subgroup averages.

Recent estimates of earnings in the major professions indicate differences that the young person might note as he plans a career: [11]

PROFESSION	MEDIAN	BEGINNING	SUPERVISORY
Accountants		$6,400	$10,000–$16,000
Architects (graduate)		$4,700–$6,200	....
Dentists (private practice)	$16,000	....	....
Engineers (bachelor's degree)		$7,400	$14,500
Lawyers		$7,200	$24,000
Librarians (graduate)		$5,900	$10,000–$16,000
Nurses (registered)		$4,500	$9,300
Physicians (private practice)	$19,000	....	....
Teachers:			
Elementary	$6,000	....	....
Secondary	$6,500	....	....
College	$8,500	....	....

Women might well compare the earnings in the "women's professions" with estimates of $2,800–$4,000 for beginning typists and $3,100–$5,000 for senior typists, and estimates of $2,600 for beginning sales clerks in retail stores and $4,200 for experienced clerks.

Manpower needs by 1975 as compared with 1964 also vary from one occupation to another, and may be summarized as follows: [12]

OCCUPATION	EMPLOYMENT IN 1964 (MILLIONS)	EXPECTED CHANGE IN MANPOWER NEEDS BY 1975
Professional, technical, and kindred workers	8.5	Increase two-fifths
Teachers:		
Elementary and secondary	1.8	Increase a fifth
College	.2	Increase two-thirds
Engineers and natural scientists	1.3	Increase a half

11 U. S. Bureau of Labor Statistics, *Occupational Outlook Handbook: Career Information for Use in Guidance, 1966–67 Edition*, Bulletin No. 1450 (Washington, D.C.: Superintendent of Documents, 1966).

12 Howard Stambler, "Manpower Needs in 1975: Part II. Detailed Projections of Occupational Requirements in the Next Decade," *Monthly Labor Review*, April 1965, pp. 378–383.

Technicians in engineering and science	.8	Increase two-thirds
Managers, officials, and proprietors (except farm)	7.5	Increase a fourth
Clerical workers	10.7	Increase a third
Sales workers	4.5	Increase a fourth
Craftsmen, foremen, and kindred workers	9.0	Increase a fourth
Operatives and kindred workers .	13.0	Increase a sixth
Industrial laborers	3.6	Change little
Service workers	9.3	Increase two-fifths
Farm occupations (managers, foremen, and laborers)	4.4	Decrease a fourth

Replacement needs for workers who are promoted, retire, die, or leave the work force may exceed the net growth in manpower requirements by 1975. Replacement needs are higher than expansion needs in some occupations, particularly those where large proportions of women are employed. These include elementary-school teachers, stenographers, typists, telephone operators, and sales clerks.

Stambler points out that the overall effect of the changing occupational structure of the work force and the differing growth rates of industries will be toward a rising demand for workers with a high level of education and training, and a relative lessening of opportunities for the less skilled and less educated. A college degree or a graduate degree is now being required by employers for more and more professional positions. Higher than average education is required for managerial positions and some types of clerical work.

Personal Characteristics · The success of the earner's efforts to increase income may be affected by his personal characteristics. Earnings which are usually low for the young person, increase with age to a peak in the middle years, then decline thereafter. The averages for males with different amounts of education, shown earlier, indicate age differences. It should be noted that such data cannot be used to estimate income through the life cycle, even for the average person, because of changing socioeconomic conditions. Probably most men who were in their sixties in the 1940's received the highest incomes of their lives at that time.

The differences in earnings of men and women workers in an occupation are sizable. For example, male clerical workers average $6,300, whereas women average $4,200; male operatives average $5,800 and women average $3,300. Median income for nonwhite workers is about two-thirds that for white workers, considering only year-round full-time workers.[13]

	MALE	FEMALE
White	$6,700	$4,000
Nonwhite	4,200	2,800

HOMEMAKERS' CONTRIBUTIONS TO INCOME

The homemaker may extend the family's money income by careful planning of family expenditures, using free community services, and wise buying of items for the family. She may conserve income by care to avoid waste in the use of items in the home—by herself and by others. Or she may enlarge the family's nonmoney income through home production by making items such as pastries or children's clothing, or performing services for the family members, such as laundering or cutting the children's hair.

On the other hand, the homemaker may enlarge the family's money income by taking a full- or part-time job, working in the family business, or working at home for pay—baking bread, typing manuscripts, giving piano lessons. About 35 percent of married women with a husband present are in the labor force, including those employed or seeking employment and those working 15 hours or more a week in the family business.[14] Of these wives, 3 percent are employed in agriculture; 70 percent are employed full-time (35 hours or more a week) in nonfarm occupations, and 22 percent part-time; and 5 percent are unemployed (contrasting with 3 percent for married men).

Four of 10 employed wives are clerical and sales workers; 2 are service workers and laborers; 2 are operatives, craftsmen, and foremen; and 2 are professional and technical workers, managers, and proprietors. The proportions are the same for all employed women as for employed wives. In contrast, only 3 out of 10 men are in the first two groupings—the lower-paid ones. Among women in the professional and managerial class, the majority are public-school teachers and nurses.

---

[13] These disparities are related to differences in skill and education and the industry in which the individual is employed, as well as to the worker's sex and color, which may affect the particular level of job assigned him as well as his level of pay in that job.

[14] U. S. Bureau of Labor Statistics, *Marital and Family Characteristics of Workers*, Special Labor Force Report No. 64, 1966 (1965 data).

In general, a married woman is more likely to be employed when the husband's income is lower than average, the wife is younger, and she has no preschool children, other conditions being equal. Labor force participation rates vary with age for married women with husband present according to the ages of their children. The comparisons are as follows:

PERCENT OF MARRIED WOMEN IN LABOR FORCE

AGE OF WIFE	ALL MARRIED WOMEN	NO CHILDREN UNDER 18 YEARS OLD	CHILDREN 6–17 YEARS OLD	SOME CHILDREN UNDER 6 YEARS OLD
25–34 years	32	69	44	24
35–44 years	41	60	44	23
45–54 years	44	48	41⎱	23
55 years and over ...	22	22	32⎰	

Labor force participation rates generally increase slightly with the wife's educational level, but more at the top educational level. For example, at 25–34 years of age, participation rates are under three-tenths for wives with less than 8 years of schooling, slightly more for those with 8 years up to 3 years of college, but four-tenths for those with 4 or more years of college.[15] While more attractive employment opportunities are available to the wife with more education, the higher income of her husband lessens her urge toward employment.

Should the Wife Take Paid Work? · Many problems are involved in trying to answer the question of whether the wife should take paid work. If one says, "No," many families would find themselves facing hardships. If one says, "Yes," many other families would find themselves in difficult positions. Various conditions need to be considered carefully in making the decision; and the decision may need to be reviewed several times during the family's life cycle.

The first problem is to learn what the financial gain would be from the job the wife is able to obtain in the community. The second is to consider how necessary this financial gain is to the family—in its present situation and through its life cycle. Will her earnings help to provide long-run security in case of emergency expenses or loss of the

---

15 U. S. Bureau of Labor Statistics, *Educational Attainment of Workers, March 1965*, Special Labor Force Report No. 65, 1966.

husband's earnings? For one family, her earnings may be necessary to pay the rent; for another, they may be needed to purchase a car or educate the children.

Next, it is important to consider the personal characteristics of the wife. Does she prefer paid work to being a full-time homemaker? At the same time, does she have the energy for the long work week of 60 to 70 hours and consequent lack of leisure?

The family situation and attitudes also need to be taken into account. How does the husband feel toward his wife's job? If there are children, the important problems are how they will be cared for, the acceptability of the method, and the cost. How will the housework be done, how acceptable will the substitutes be, and what will be the cost? Special situations need to be taken into account: for example, how will household emergencies such as sickness in the family be met? In addition, hospitality as well as participation in community activities may become excessive burdens.

Women make up a third of today's labor force and account for most of its increase in the postwar years.[16] A special study of women who took jobs in one year showed that most (73 percent) did so primarily for financial reasons (clear or probable), which were stated as financial necessity, earn extra money, husband lost job, woman was widowed or divorced, or woman finished school or training. Sixteen percent took jobs primarily for personal satisfaction, 8 percent because they were offered jobs or their help was needed in the family business, and 4 percent for other reasons.

It is not surprising that married women with a husband present were less likely than other women to take jobs primarily for financial reasons. At the same time, financial reasons were especially strong when jobs were taken by wives with a husband making less than $100 a week and by wives with preschool children.

Among the married women who stopped working during the year, 43 percent did so primarily because of pregnancy, 14 percent because of family responsibilities, 13 percent because of illness, and 30 percent for other reasons. Pregnancy was much more important among wives under 35 than among those older. Family responsibilities were much more important for wives 25–44 than for those younger or older. Both illness and "other reasons" (being laid off, retirement, or no longer needing to work) were much more important for wives 45–64 than for younger age groups.

16 U. S. Bureau of Labor Statistics, *Why Women Start and Stop Working: A Study in Mobility*, Special Labor Force Report No. 59, 1965 (1963 data).

Financial Gain From Wife's Job · The net financial gain to the family from the wife's paid work will depend on the income she is able to earn and the costs of her job. Certain costs are required by the job, such as additional income taxes, Social Security taxes, retirement contributions, and additional insurance. The wife may have extra personal expenses that she would not have as a full-time homemaker—extra clothes, personal care, lunches, transportation, contributions. There may be extra costs at home for household help, outside services, more highly processed items, and extra household equipment. Decreases in homemaking standards, such as mending of garments, may result in increased costs. The employed homemaker may not have the time to shop as economically as she otherwise would.

While each family needs to estimate the net financial gain in its own situation, certain data are available for consideration. A large study in four small cities in Georgia included 365 wives, each with a husband employed full time.[17] Half were working wives who earned an average of $2,200 a year. Half worked full time and half worked part time, but at least 1,000 hours. The wife's earnings increased after-tax income of these families from $3,400 to $5,200, whereas the average income of families with nonemployed wives was $4,200. The increased costs of working wives averaged $903, including $614 for job-related expenses, $184 for extra hired help, and $105 for extra clothing and personal care, thus making a net gain of $1,297, less than three-fifths of gross earnings. Wives with preschool children netted about half of their earnings. The wife's percentage gain was also lower when her husband's income was high, largely because of higher income taxes.

A similar study of 750 urban and open-country families in Ohio showed like results, though the wives earned about $2,900. The wife's net income was about three-fifths of her gross income when there were no young children, but about half when there were preschool children. Again, her percentage net gain was lower when her husband's income was high. Similar conclusions were shown by a related study in North Carolina, where wives' earnings averaged $2,600.

The effects of income taxes on a couple may be indicated by assuming standard deductions. The estimates for some situations are as follows:

[17] Emma G. Holmes, *Job-Related Expenditures and Management Practices of Gainfully Employed Wives in Four Georgia Cities*, Home Economic Research Report No. 15, U. S. Department of Agriculture, 1962; . . . *Ohio*, Report No. 27, 1965; . . . *North Carolina*, Report No. 34, 1967.

HUSBAND'S EARNINGS, 1965	WIFE'S NET EARNINGS AFTER TAXES WHEN SHE EARNS—		$4,000 (PERCENT*)	$8,000 (PERCENT)
	$4,000	$8,000		
$4,000	$3,358	$6,582	84	82
$10,000	3,126	6,132	78	77

* Percent of wife's gross earnings

When the wife earns $4,000, her net earnings after subtracting the additional family taxes paid by the couple are 84 percent of her gross earnings when the husband earns $4,000, but 78 percent when he earns $10,000. Also, the higher the wife's gross earnings, the lower her percentage gain after taxes. In each case, other job expenses and taxes, extra personal expenses, and extra household expenses would also be deducted before calculating the wife's net addition to family income. If such expenses approximate $25 a week for the wife earning $4,000 and $50 a week for the wife earning $8,000, her net addition to income would be as follows:

HUSBAND'S EARNINGS, 1965	WIFE'S NET ADDITION WHEN SHE EARNS—		$4,000 (PERCENT)	$8,000 (PERCENT)
	$4,000	$8,000		
$4,000	$2,058	$3,982	51	50
$10,000	1,826	3,532	46	44

EFFECTS OF SOCIOECONOMIC CONDITIONS

A family's efforts to increase income may also be furthered or frustrated by general socioeconomic conditions—primarily by the levels of technology, production and employment, and government and investment expenditures. Family efforts may be affected also by activities of labor organizations and by minimum wage laws, kinds of tax programs, agricultural policy, welfare programs, and fair employment practices. Prices of consumer goods affect the value of the income.

Technological Improvements · Let us concentrate on the basic conditions—the most spectacular of which is our high and increasing level of technology. Technological improvements have brought dislocations for workers displaced by machines or by competing products—coal miners, railroad workers, and farmers in recent years. At the same time, technological advance has brought tremendous increases in productivity per man hour worked, providing a greater quantity of all sorts of goods and services (for consumption, government, and investment) and reduced hours of work. In the postwar years, productivity per man hour worked has increased on the average about 2.5 percent annually over the previous year.[18] At this rate, output per man hour would be about 2.4 times as high by the end of the century as in 1965.

Production and Employment · In order to get maximum goods and services from technological advances, high-level production and employment are essential. This means that all parts of the economy (consumption, government, and investment) can share a bigger pie. Our growth rate has been averaging about 3.5 percent a year since World War II,[19] partly because of technological advances and partly because of a larger labor force and plant capacity.

Full employment of manpower and plant capacity would have increased the growth rate of total production. In the postwar years, an average of about 5 percent of the civilian labor force has been unemployed, and some persons have worked less than full time. This is decidedly lower than the 25 percent unemployed in 1933, but it is above 1 percent in 1944.

Unemployment may continue to average about 4–5 percent in the coming decades, primarily because of adjustments required by rapid technological change, but also because of other changes—seasonal work, relocation or bankruptcy of the employer, or declining demand for a particular product. While we want to believe that unemployment will never again be as high or production as low as in the depression years, we need to guard against unduly sanguine expectations—or undue pessimism in any depressed period that may occur.

Government and Investment Expenditures · While technological advance plus a high level of production serve to increase the production of goods and services, what the consumer gets depends importantly on what government needs. A sizable part of national production—a fifth in the postwar years—has been channeled into government goods and services. This has been used for national defense and for all other services of government at all levels—federal, state, and local. While this is a small proportion in comparison with 50 percent for government needs, especially defense, in 1944, it is still a sizable share and decidedly larger than the 11 percent so used in 1929.

18 Based on data of the U. S. Bureau of Labor Statistics and the Council of Economic Advisers.
19 Based on U. S. Department of Commerce data on gross national product in dollars of constant value.

Government needs for goods and services constitute a prior claim on national production and will be met by reductions in consumption and investment items if they are not met by greater production. No longer does anyone laugh at Hitler's slogan, "Guns before butter." It is only fair to note, however, that sizable parts of the expenditures of governmental bodies provide "free" consumer goods and services—public schools, libraries, parks, museums, highways, police and fire protection. Some authorities believe it is imperative that these be expanded.

Another large part of production is not available for current consumption. This includes gross private domestic investment in business structures and equipment and in residential structures, change in business inventories, and net exports of goods and services. These investments have averaged almost a fifth in the postwar years. The figure was about the same in 1929, but was only 2 percent in 1944.

While the investment items do not result in consumer goods and services currently, they enlarge future possibilities. Residential construction provides housing for the future. Business construction and increased equipment provide for future increase in production of consumer goods and services, as well as government and producer goods.

Consumer Goods and Services · Personal consumption expenditures almost tripled from 1946 to 1965, increasing from $143 billion to $428 billion. Population has increased about 38 percent, while prices of consumer goods have increased about 62 percent. As a result, personal consumption expenditures per person in dollars of constant purchasing power have increased about 41 percent. This gives a rough measure of the increase in the individual's level of living. The annual growth rate has averaged about 1.75 percent. If such a rate should continue to the end of the century, the increase would amount to about 84 percent above the 1965 level—a tremendous amount, it hardly need be emphasized.

SIZE OF MONEY INCOME

Socioeconomic conditions and personal efforts have resulted in increased incomes of families through the years. Knowledge of the size and distribution of income and its long-run trend aids the family in attaining perspective on the present situation, estimating future prospects, and improving financial decisions.

Median total money income of the 49 million families in the U. S. was $7,400 before taxes in 1966. The median was $7,600 for nonfarm families and $4,800 for farm families, who comprised about 6 percent of all families. These figures include earnings, investment, and transfer income, as previously defined, of all family members. The figures do not include other money resources used for family support, or any items of nonmoney income.

The distribution of families by total money income shows 9 percent with incomes of $15,000 or over and almost 2 percent with incomes of $25,000 or over (Table 2–4 and Figure 2–1). On the other hand, 8 percent had incomes under $2,000. A large proportion of the latter families were aged families and farm families. For some, their financial problems were moderated by special circumstances. The aged families are generally small in size and some have financial

FIGURE 2–1.   Distribution of Families By Income*

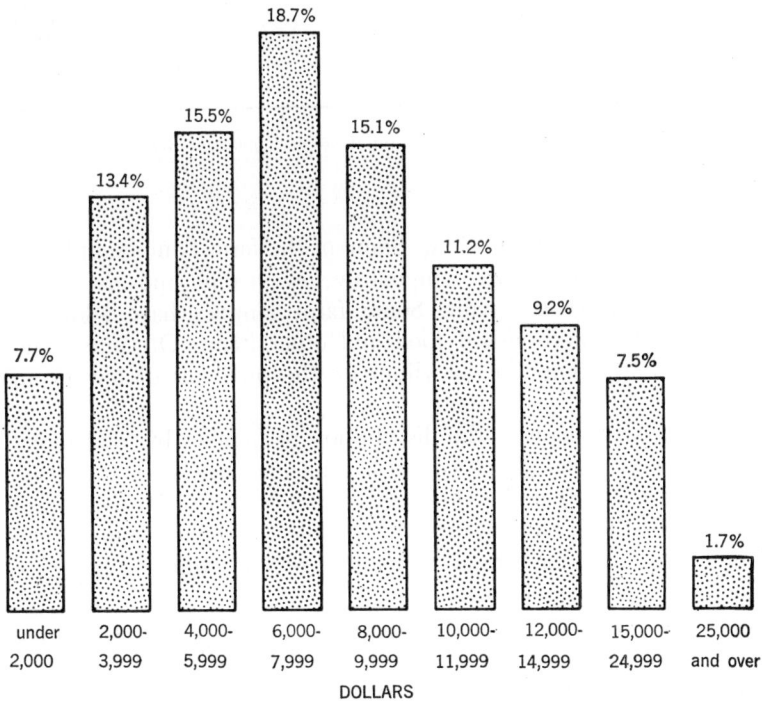

* Total money income before taxes, 1966
SOURCE: U. S. Bureau of the Census

TABLE 2–4. Distribution of Families by Total Money Income

TOTAL MONEY INCOME BEFORE TAXES	1965 DATA	1966 DATA
Percent of families	100.0	100.0
Under $1,000	3.0	2.3
$1,000 to $1,999	6.1	5.4
$2,000 to $2,999	7.4	6.6
$3,000 to $3,999	7.8	6.8
$4,000 to $4,999	8.0	7.1
$5,000 to $5,999	9.3	8.4
$6,000 to $6,999	9.3	9.4
$7,000 to $7,999	9.7	9.3
$8,000 to $8,999	8.1	8.1
$9,000 to $9,999	6.3	7.0
$10,000 to $11,999	9.7	11.2
$12,000 to $14,999	7.6	9.2
$15,000 to $24,999	6.1	7.5
$25,000 and over	1.5	1.7
Median income, all families	$6,880	$7,400
Nonfarm families	$7,060	$7,600
Farm families	$4,120	$4,800

SOURCE: U. S. Bureau of the Census, *Current Population Reports*, Series P–60, No. 52, 1967.

assets on which they can draw. Some of the farm families and other low-income families have temporarily low income and are able to use their savings or credit. Some farm families have additional amounts of farm-furnished food and other items. Of course, such individual situations do not eliminate the problems of low-income families.

Looking again at the distribution of families by total money income, we see that about a third had incomes below $5,600, a third had $5,600–$9,500, and a third had $9,500 or more. This is a simple way of classifying families into low, middle, and high income groups. But it does not take into account differences in family size, stage of the life cycle, and residence.

For some purposes it is desirable to look at the percentage share of aggregate family income received by each fifth of families ranked by income. The Census Bureau found that there has been almost no change in the relative proportion received by the fifths in the postwar period. Latest Census estimates are as follows:

INCOME RANK OF FAMILIES	PERCENTAGE SHARE OF AGGREGATE INCOME BEFORE TAXES, 1965
Total	100
Lowest fifth	5
Second fifth	12
Middle fifth	18
Fourth fifth	24
Highest fifth	41
Top 5 percent	15

FIGURE 2–2. Trend of Family Income*

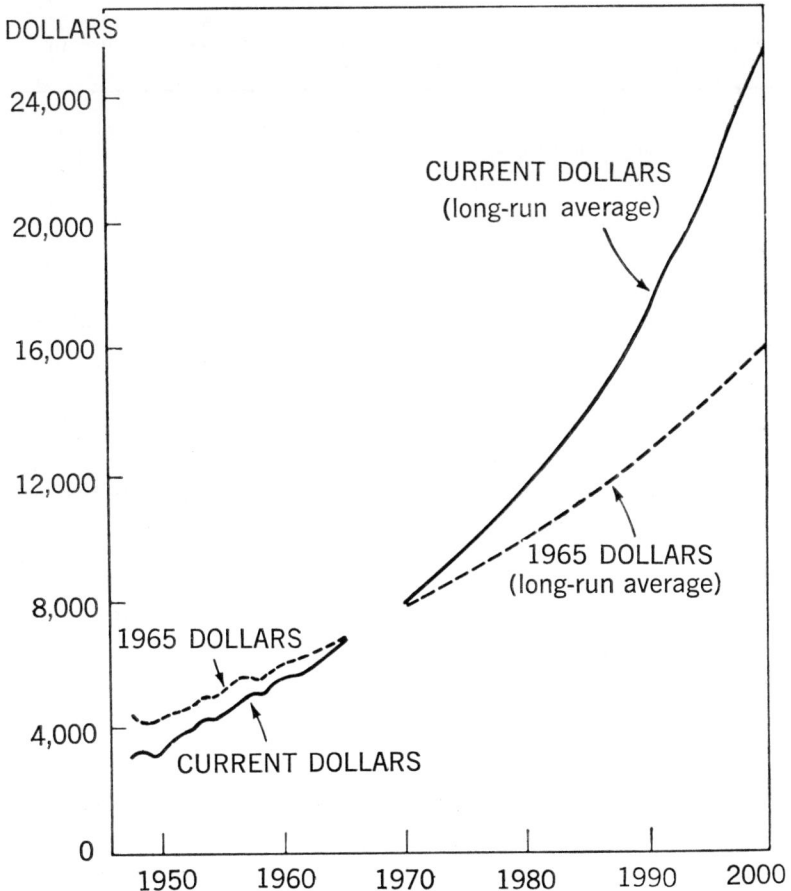

* Median total money income before taxes.
SOURCES: U. S. Bureau of the Census. Long-run estimates by the author.

YEAR	CURRENT DOLLARS	1965 DOLLARS**	YEAR	CURRENT DOLLARS	1965 DOLLARS**
1947	3,031	4,275	1959	5,417	5,856
1948	3,187	4,180	1960	5,620	5,991
1949	3,107	4,114	1961	5,737	6,054
1950	3,319	4,351	1962	5,956	6,220
1951	3,709	4,504	1963	6,249	6,444
1952	3,890	4,622	1964	6,569	6,676
1953	4,233	4,991	1965	6,957	6,957
1954	4,173	4,889	1966	7,436	7,226
1955	4,421	5,223	1970	7,917	7,777
1956	4,783	5,561	1980	11,705	9,979
1957	4,971	5,554	1990	17,366	12,732
1958	5,087	5,543	2000	25,802	16,310

** Adjusted for price change by use of Consumer Price Index, 1957–59 = 100.
[Checked p. 3 of P–60, No. 52 and p. 2, P–60, No. 51.]

In evaluating these figures, account should be taken of graduated income taxes, which decrease the share of net income going to families with highest incomes. Also, average family size tends to be higher at higher income levels, which moderates the increase in income per person.

Income Trends · Trends in income are also important to families in their financial plans. Median money income before taxes has more than doubled in the postwar years—from about $3,000 in 1947 to $7,400 in 1966 (Figure 2–2). Because of the rise in consumer prices, income in dollars of constant purchasing power has increased by 69 percent.

An estimate of future trends of income may be helpful to the family as it considers its future financial plans. If average productivity per man hour continues to increase through the long run at about 2.5 percent a year, median family income in 1965 dollars might approximate $10,000 by 1980 and $16,000 by the year 2000. In current dollars, assuming average upward movement of the price level, the figure might be around $12,000 in 1980 and $26,000 in the year 2000. Such estimates indicate simply the general trend. Realized income might depart considerably from the trend in any depression or other unusual period. Of course, the income of an individual family may increase more or less than average.

AID FOR FAMILIES IN DISTRESS

While most people strive to be self-supporting, it is not always possible to manage. Unemployment; loss of the earner due to death, divorce, or desertion; old age; loss of investments; disability or illness; and disasters such as floods, tornadoes, and fires, may reduce income or increase costs beyond the ability of the family.

For those in financial distress, with no legally responsible relatives who are able to assist sufficiently and with inadequate contributions from others, a number of assistance programs have been established. These include state-federal programs such as Aid to the Blind and Disabled, Aid to Dependent Children, and Old Age Assistance. Local agencies provide supplementary assistance. State and local institutions are available for the care of the indigent elderly, the orphaned, and certain disabled persons.

Clinic care and assistance in dealing with certain illnesses are available from the appropriate health agency, such as the National Foundation for Infantile Paralysis, the American Heart Association, the American Cancer Society, and the National Tuberculosis and Health Association. The Red Cross, the Salvation Army, churches, and other organizations also provide assistance. Families and individuals lacking funds for their support may apply to the appropriate organization. Families needing legal assistance which they cannot afford may contact a local Legal Aid Society.

The social security programs, which do not require proof of destitution, have helped many families meet calamities without having to seek public assistance. Such programs include Old-Age, Survivors, and Disability Insurance, Medicare, Unemployment Compensation, and Workman's Compensation.

QUESTIONS

1. What are the major sources of money income for family support? Give examples of each. Which are most important?

2. What additional money resources may a family use?

3. What are the important types of nonmoney income of families? Give examples of each. What types of families are most likely to have each?

4. What are some of the methods a family uses to enlarge its earnings? How effective does each appear to be?

5. What are some personal characteristics of the earner that seem to affect income and in what direction? Why?

6. In what ways may a homemaker contribute to income or help to conserve it?

7. What are the characteristics of employed married women and their families?

8. Should a wife take a paid job? What conditions need to be considered?

9. What is the likely financial gain from the wife's paid work?

10. What effect does each of the following have on the family's income: technological improvements, production and employment levels, and government and investment expenditures?

11. Speculate on the effect on the family's income of some of the other socioeconomic conditions.

12. How has the individual's level of living changed since World War II?

13. What was median money income for U. S. families in 1966? How did it differ for farm and nonfarm families? What is the meaning of a median?

14. Obtain the latest data on family incomes and compare with the 1966 situation.

15. The lowest third, middle third, and top third of families by income had what amounts?

16. How has median family income changed from 1947 to 1966? What influenced these changes?

17. Speculate on future trends in income in the long run. What about the short run?

18. What conditions cause financial distress of families? Where can they turn for assistance?

19. How does this discussion of the family's income help the family in making its long-run financial plan for its support?

SUGGESTIONS FOR FURTHER READING

Economic Report of the President, together with The Annual Report of the Council of Economic Advisers, latest reports.

U. S. Bureau of the Census. *Current Population Reports,* Series P–20 and P–60, latest reports.

U. S. Bureau of Labor Statistics. *Employment and Earnings and Monthly Report on the Labor Force,* latest reports.

————. *Monthly Labor Review,* latest issues.

————. *Occupational Outlook Handbook: Career Information for Use in Guidance,* latest edition.

————. *Special Labor Force Reports,* latest reports.

U. S. Department of Commerce. *Survey of Current Business,* latest issues.

"Men at some time are masters of their fate.
The fault, Dear Brutus, is not in our stars
But in ourselves that we are underlings."
—JULIUS CAESAR

The Budgeting Process / 3

- · THE FINANCIAL PLAN
- · FINANCIAL GOALS OF THE
  BUDGET
- · CONSTRUCTION OF THE BUDGET
- · ATTITUDES TOWARD MONEY

The family's determination of its general financial objectives places detailed financial decisions in proper perspective. The budgeting process involves, first, creation of a comprehensive, long-range financial plan; second, determination of specific budget goals; third, construction of the budget; and fourth, development of wholesome attitudes toward money.

THE FINANCIAL PLAN

The family's financial plan includes general plans and expectations through the family's life cycle for raising a family (or not, as the case may be), educating the children, and obtaining income through choice of occupation and number of earners. It also involves plans for the family's way of living, savings and investments, and contributions to others. The financial plan is in general terms and for the long-run period, including changes to be made through the life cycle.

For instance, a young couple may plan that during the first few years of marriage, while the husband is getting started in business, the wife will work and they will live simply in order to save money toward the acquisition of a home and the rearing of children.

Through the child-rearing years, they may expect the wife to concentrate her efforts at home, anticipating some increases in income for the husband. They may plan that later, if the husband's income does not increase sufficiently, the wife will take a part-time job during the children's high-school years and perhaps a full-time job during their college years. She may work for a while thereafter to help prepare for retirement or support their aged parents.

Use of Time · What to do with time is the basic decision for a family and for each member since it determines the quality of life. All people are alike in having twenty-four hours a day, though they differ in the number of days in their lives. Because people differ in abilities, financial resources, needs, and values, their decisions on the use of time may differ.

The family decides, first, what part of its time shall be devoted to work that will produce income for the support of the family and what part shall be kept as nonworking time. Nonworking time may be devoted entirely to personal activities and recreation, or it may be used for personal development, religious service, and community service. For many people with routine jobs, the quality of life depends importantly on the uses made of free time.

Working time may be used partly for paid work, partly for household production of goods and services for the family's own use, and partly for job-centered leisure activities, such as the entertainment of prospective clients. As the individual selects his paid work, he may have to choose between a position with a higher income and one that follows his occupational interest. Or the possibility of choice may be between income, on the one hand, and the family's way of living, on the other. Some jobs require that the earner travel constantly or the family move frequently. Some require living in a big city or in a foreign country. Some jobs involve a supervised personal life.

The income created through paid work, home production, and job-centered leisure can be used to support a single individual, a couple, or a family. What part of the family's income shall it devote to having more children, "the most desired of all consumer goods," as one writer commented? What part of the income shall be spent for goods and services; what part saved; and what part shall be shared with those outside the home? The next step is to determine what shall be spent on specific classes of items, how the savings shall be invested, and what kind of sharing program shall be devised. Figure 3–1 shows graphically the various levels of decision.

FIGURE 3–1. Choice in Use of Time and Resultant Income

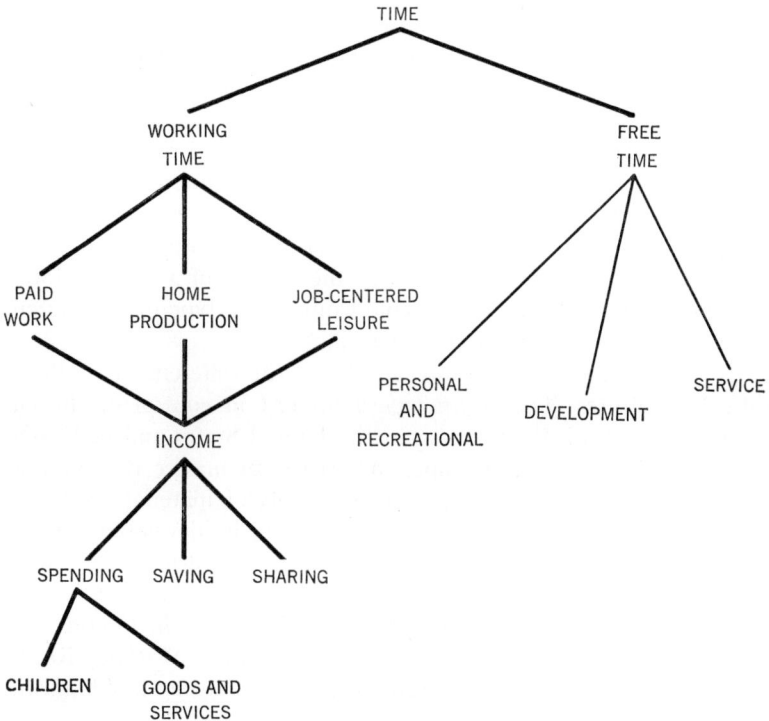

Expression of Interests · In his apportionment of time between working and nonworking hours, in occupational choice, in free-time activities, and in allocation of his income, an individual uses his resources to express his interests. Thereby he shows what values are most important to him.

Elizabeth Hoyt's classification of interests, used fruitfully over a period of time to analyze economic choices, provides exceptional help for the family in improving its own choices. Thoughtful consideration of the classification may be highly beneficial.[1]

Interests are divided into two major categories: the primary and the secondary. Primary interests are found everywhere in all cultures and are always strong. They include the *sensory* interest in the satisfaction of the needs of hunger, thirst, warmth, exercise, and sex. They keep us alive as individuals and as a genus. Consumption

---

[1] Elizabeth E. Hoyt, *Consumption in Our Society* (New York: McGraw-Hill, 1938), pp. 16–30.

of food, clothing, and shelter is at least partly for satisfaction of sensory interests.[2]

The primary interests also include the *social* interest in being with a group and being a part of a group. Most of us enjoy our meals more if we eat them in the company of other people. Probably movies and TV are enjoyed more when there are others in the audience. A frequent complaint by the homemaker and the paid worker is that housework is lonely. We show our social interest also in the way we identify ourselves as a member of a group—the buttons and pins as badges of membership, the Bermuda shorts and battered sneakers worn by college students in the middle of a snowy winter, the spike heels worn by fashionable women, the type of car chosen, the kind and timing of the food we eat.[3]

The secondary interests are found in different strength in different cultures. The *technological* interest in control of the environment is particularly strong in the United States and in Russia, as well as in Western Europe. We strive to master the physical environment; we pursue an increasing supply of material goods; we bend the plant and animal worlds to our will by developing hybrid corn and specially bred beef cattle. The environment to be controlled includes also the human worlds of society and business.[4] Consider the implications of such famous titles as *How to Win Friends and Influence People* and *How to Succeed in Business Without Really Trying*. All in all, Huxley's *Brave New World* seems less fantastic every year.

The *intellectual* interest in control of one's mental powers is strong in some individuals. Attendance at school or college is not always due to intellectual interest, but may be strongly vocational and, therefore, technological in nature. Some few have high intellectual curiosity, as do some teachers, research workers, and inventors. While few people are intellectually creative, all may express intellectual interest by reading and listening thoughtfully.

The *aesthetic* interest involves creation or appreciation of the beautiful. Vincent Van Gogh was creative in painting and Frank Lloyd Wright in architecture. Beethoven and Victor Hugo enriched the worlds of music and literature. Great performers such as Judith Anderson, the actress, and Wanda Landowska, the harpsichord player, are also creative. Most of us have insufficient talent for such creativity, but we can express our aesthetic interest by learning to

---

[2] Comfort, health, and cleanliness are fundamental values related to this interest.
[3] Companionship, cooperation, conformity, and prestige are related values.
[4] Power, efficiency, abundance, and security are related fundamental values.

appreciate the beauty of nature and of man's creations. Opening our eyes as we walk or ride along the street, visiting museums, listening to music, reading great literature—these ways are open to all. We may express our aesthetic interest also in the clothing we wear and the decoration of our homes.

The *empathetic* interest, the sense of relationship of oneself to the cosmos, may be expressed in regard to religion or nature or humanity. It includes religious service, contemplation of nature, community welfare activities, and direct help to relatives.[5]

A combination of interests may be expressed in a given use of a family's economic resources. For instance, dinner served to a group satisfies hunger and provides companionship. The technological interest may be expressed in the use of modern equipment to prepare the meal. The beauty of the table service and the dining area may give aesthetic satisfaction. Provision of dinner for foreign students may be an expression of the empathetic interest. The conversation may be on intellectual subjects.

Church activities which are thought of as entirely religious may serve other interests. The comfort of the arrangements, the pleasure in being with a congenial group, the beauty of the church and the music, modern housekeeping and recreational facilities, stimulating lectures—all may represent interests other than religious.

Maximizing Satisfactions · Individuals seek to attain maximum development of the human personality and to maximize their satisfactions from the use of their time and money and related resources. The most obvious way is by getting more—the typical American approach. More free time comes with shorter hours of work and longer vacations. Improved health and longevity also increase free time. More income from working time comes with greater productivity and mobility. More goods and services for the money come with better planning and buying.

Another means of maximizing satisfactions is choice of what gives most satisfaction in itself. Does the person feel that teaching is a more satisfying occupation than carpentry? Is a small town a better place to live than a metropolis? Is a baseball game or a visit to the natural history museum a more satisfying use of a free afternoon? Would you choose a new car or a trip to London?

Discriminating choice requires knowledge of the alternatives available and the satisfactions to be derived from them. It involves

---

[5] Reverence, love, concepts of human worth, and personal freedom are related values.

putting first things first in order to obtain the most wanted satisfactions, not frittering away time and money on nonessentials. The most lasting sources of satisfaction rather than ephemeral ones need to be emphasized. A single woman, questioning her expenditure on foreign travel, was told by an elderly friend, "Go on—build memories for your old age." Balancing choices among different interests generally optimizes satisfactions. One could be a "clothes horse" or a bookish recluse. But a well-balanced selection among a variety of sources of satisfaction is desirable for most people.

One may also increase satisfactions by expanding his appreciation for what he has already chosen. He may learn to have more delight in his food and in his growing children. He may find renewed joy in his work because of its skillful performance and social implications. Visits to museums and sessions with classical records help develop greater appreciation in the arts.

Early in the Industrial Revolution, philosophers thought that the eventual gains of greater productivity would be the freeing of mankind from continual grubbing for the means of subsistence so that time could be spent in developing the intellect, the arts, and philosophy—in other words, the fullest expression of human abilities. Results have not fulfilled the expectations. Much of the gain has been taken in more goods and services and more armaments. Some of the gain has been taken in increased leisure from paid work, but it is questionable how much of this free time is used for the higher pursuits that the philosophers had in mind.[6]

Each person must consider his values carefully before getting down to the specific job of planning a budget, in the hope of avoiding one man's summary of his life: "I was part of that strange race of people aptly described as spending their lives doing things they detest to make money they don't want to buy things they don't need to impress people they don't like."

FINANCIAL GOALS OF THE BUDGET

In contrast with the family's long-range, general financial plan, the budget is a relatively definite plan for the use of expected income in the next period to support known dependents, and for saving and sharing.

---

[6] For classic discussions, see Hoyt, pp. 32–70, 343–365, and 380–390; Hazel Kyrk, *The Family in the American Economy* (Chicago: U. of Chicago Press, 1953), pp. 373–393; and Kyrk, *Economic Problems of the Family*, (New York: Harper, 1933), pp. 389–395.

In order to prepare a definite budget, one must set up specific financial goals. A number of the goals which families seek to attain need, therefore, to be considered. First they seek to provide for daily necessities—food, clothing, shelter. These costs are recurrent and reasonably predictable. Families also seek to provide for the costs of unexpected emergencies, such as repairs, illness, death, loss of property, and liability for damages inflicted by family members on the persons or property of others. Provision for periods of reduced income due to the illness, death, or unemployment of the earner is another goal. Reduced income may also result from the earner's desire to change jobs or go into business for himself. Or the wife may quit her paid job to raise a family.

In addition, the family probably wants to provide for some daily comforts and luxuries, above the necessity level. It also seeks to provide for large expenditures which it anticipates with pleasure, such as furniture and education. Furthermore, the family needs to be thinking of providing funds for its support in old age. While the elderly wish to be self-supporting, the goal is more likely to be achieved by planning and working toward it before old age arrives. The family also wants to help others outside its own immediate household. This may include needy relatives and friends, organized charity, and public causes. For some families, an immediate financial goal is the repayment of debts previously incurred. For others, there is a desire to make investments to increase income or simply to build a fortune.

The family's budget, then, should provide for current spending, for saving for the near and far future, and for sharing with others outside the family.

Choice of Current Goals · Because of many circumstances, a family may be unable to pursue all its goals concurrently. Circumstances change, and they differ from one family to another. A primary factor affecting goals is the hierarchy of family values, the relative importance of the sensory, social, technological, intellectual, aesthetic, and empathetic interests. Is the family most eager to keep up with the Joneses by having as good a house and car? Does it place a high value on security so that it can live happily in simpler circumstances in order to build a nest egg for the future? Is the family willing to reduce expenditures in order to help others less fortunate? Does the family place higher value on the home or education for the children? For many people, all goals cannot be achieved simultaneously, so choices must be made.

Values may differ from one family or individual to another because of many individual differences.[7] However, it is unwise to overestimate the strength of these differences in affecting consumer use of economic resources. Mass production, mass communication, and advertising are powerful in "democratizing consumption," so that outsiders see Americans as seeking the same general way of living, although, because of circumstances, some achieve it less completely than others. To what extent are the values of the intelligent, the educated, the religious, the professional person different from the values of other people? Perhaps they should be higher, but the important question is whether or not they are.

The family's income in relation to family size has an important effect on choice of current financial goals. A low-income family may have to concentrate its efforts on the most immediate and pressing goal, such as the provision of daily necessities, whereas a high-income family may be able to work toward many goals simultaneously. When asked what financial plans they are making for the education of their children or for their own old age, some parents say they have none, that the best they can do is to take care of present needs and the future will have to take care of itself.

Of particular importance is the family's *real* income, that is, the value of its money income plus its nonmoney income. Regularity of income, the contributors to it, and expectations of future changes also affect family choices of goals. The claimants on income comprise not simply a count of family members, but also consideration of the composition of the family with regard to age and sex of members.

Special needs of family members add decidedly to daily expenditures. A crippled child or invalid grandparent in the home may result in major drains on income for medical care and related items. Occupations of family members may necessitate special clothing. The climate may require expensive heating or cooling equipment for minimum comfort. Residence in a suburb may necessitate ownership of an automobile.

The family's accumulation of financial assets or debts affects its choice of current financial goals. A family with a large amount of investments might consider its provision for the future adequate and concentrate on current living. A family with similar current income but no investments may limit current living in order to make

---

[7] Such as those in intelligence and its use, energy, personality, sex, and age as well as education, religion, urbanization, ethnic background, region, and occupation.

savings. Another family with heavy indebtedness may need to concentrate its efforts toward repayment.

Personal expectations of future emergencies with increased costs or decreased income affect the family's choice of financial goals. In general, such expectations probably increase with age and experience.

The stage of the family life cycle is also important. While each stage places daily necessities foremost, the newly married couple may concentrate on setting up a home, whereas an older couple, with their children reared, may concentrate on providing for retirement.

CONSTRUCTION OF THE BUDGET

Establishment of a general financial plan and clarification of specific financial goals are preliminary steps to construction of the family's budget, which is the plan for use of expected income in the next period.

A good budget helps the family maximize satisfactions from use of income through requiring careful consideration of various alternatives. This means that the budget must be tailored to fit the individual family's values, needs, and resources. It gives appropriate consideration to the family's short-term and long-term financial goals. When changes occur in any of these areas, the budget requires readjustment. The seemingly easy way is to use suggested percentages in a budget book, but this is a delusion. At best, such figures can be only a starting point. Outsiders may be helpful in suggesting ideas for consideration, but they can never be in a position to know a family well enough to construct its budget.

A good budget helps achieve financial peace of mind by matching expenditures to receipts. It must start with realistic income expectations. The budget includes reasonably definite and practical plans for spending, saving, and sharing. It spreads big expenses and provides that money for them be accumulated regularly each week or month. At the same time, the budget provides some flexibility for unexpected expenses. Young couples with modest incomes and heavy indebtedness have little flexibility, which may cause some anxious moments. The charge that we bring on many of our own troubles is as true in our money management as in other areas of life.

A good budget increases family cooperation and lessens friction in regard to money. In this country today, a budget probably works

TABLE 3–1.   Check List of Budget Items

I. Required as Worker or Citizen
  A. Taxes (involuntary)
    Income: Federal, state, local
    Social Security
    Wage or occupation
    Poll or head
  B. Job expenses (involuntary)
    Tools, technical books, journals
    Protective clothing, uniforms
    Unreimbursed travel expenses
    Union or professional dues
    Charities, flower funds
  C. Insurance premiums (involuntary)
    Retirement plan
    Life insurance
    Health insurance
II. Contractual Obligations
  A. Other taxes
    Real estate
    Poll or head (voluntary)
    Assessments on real estate
    Personal property
  B. Debt repayment
    Home loan
    Auto loan
    Installment payments
    Personal loan
  C. Other insurances (voluntary)
    Life
    Health
    Annuities
    Home
    Auto
    Furniture, equipment, etc.
III. Expenses (not in I and II above)
  A. Food
    Eaten at home
    Board at home or at school
    Meals, snacks away from home
    Meals while traveling
  B. Clothing
    Outerwear
    Underwear, nightwear
    Hosiery and footwear
    Hats, gloves, accessories
    Care, repair, cleaning, storing
    Jewelry and watches
  C. Housing
    Rent
    Repairs paid by family
    Lodging at school or while traveling
    Vacation home
  D. Household operation
    Fuel, light, refrigeration, water, telephone
    Laundry sent out
    Paid household help, baby sitter
    Cleaning supplies
    Stationery, postage, telegrams

TABLE 3-1. (Continued)

  Moving, express, freight
  Garbage and trash disposal
E. Furniture and equipment
  Furniture
  Kitchen, cleaning, laundry equipment
  Floor coverings
  Household textiles
  China, silver, etc.
  Repairs
F. Automobile
  Gas, oil, anti-freeze
  Repairs, replacements, service
  Garage, parking, tolls
  Licenses, fees
  Fines, damages personally paid to others
  Accessories, association dues
G. Other transportation
  Local bus, trolley, taxi
  Train, bus, plane
  Purchase and upkeep of motorcycle, boat, etc.
H. Medical care (not covered by insurance)
  Physician, surgeon, dentist, etc.
  Clinic or hospital care
  Nursing care
  Medicines, drugs
  Medical appliances, supplies
I. Personal business
  Bank service charges
  Safety deposit box rental
  Legal expenses
  Losses (other than business)
  Funeral, cemetery
J. Recreation
  Paid admissions
  Play and sports equipment, supplies, fees, licenses
  Radio, TV, phonograph, piano, musical instruments, purchase and repairs
  Sheet music, phonograph records
  Cameras, films, supplies
  Pets, purchase and care
  Entertaining in and out of home
  Dues to social clubs
K. Education
  Books and supplies
  Tuition, special lessons
L. Reading
  Newspapers, magazines, books
  Book rentals, library fees
M. Personal care
  Haircuts, shampoos, waves
  Shaves, facials, manicures
  Toilet articles and preparations, such as soaps, toothpaste, lipstick, brushes, personal hygiene
N. Tobacco
  Cigarettes, cigars, tobacco
  Smokers' supplies
O. Alcoholic beverages
IV. Contributions (not in I and II)
  A. Religious organizations
  B. Relatives, friends
  C. Charity, health, cultural, educational organizations
V. Investments (not in I and II)
  A. Cash forms
  B. Private or corporate business
  C. Real estate

best when family members participate in establishing the family's financial goals and plans for attaining them and in operating the budget. At the same time, the budget provides appropriate independence for each member. This generally includes personal spending money for individuals. Responsibility for daily operation of part of the budget is placed on a specific person—for example, the wife may manage the food budget and the husband the auto budget. A budget, however, is not a cure-all for every one of the family's problems, financial or otherwise; and unforeseen events may cause the best laid plans to go awry.

While it is not necessary that a budget be written or detailed, there are certain advantages in a written budget: it forces the family to think through its financial situation for the next period in order to be reasonably specific in estimates. It provides an explicit plan that can be checked against general financial goals. Furthermore, a written plan may lessen later misunderstanding by family members.

Although a record of actual expenditures is not necessary for a good budget, some advantages of a record might be noted. It permits comparison of current expenditures with the budget to improve control of expenditures. A record of the past year's expenditures gives a better basis for analyzing them and preparing an improved budget for the next period. Such a record may also be useful for income-tax purposes in claiming exemptions and deductions.

Control of expenditures may be improved also through the use of checking accounts, charge accounts, and a variety of other means, such as setting up separate envelopes for different types of expenditures.

Steps in Construction

1. The first step in constructing the budget is to estimate income for the next period, probably a year, from all sources and all earners. For some families this is a known amount, but for others it is difficult to estimate. It may be constant or fluctuating from month to month. Expected income includes earnings from current work (net earnings from a business), investments, and other sources—any type that can be depended on. It is wise to list expected amounts week by week or month by month through the year when receipts or expenditures are irregular.

2. The second step is to list deductions from income that are required of a worker and citizen. These include involuntary taxes, job expenses, and premiums for insurance required by the job. (See

Table 3–1.) They are unavoidable expenses so that the sums are not available for family planning. Subtracting them from gross income gives the net income figure for each period.

    3. The third step is to list the family's contractual obligations for the next period. These include other taxes, debt repayment, and other insurances. Subtracting them from the net income figure gives the remaining income, period by period.

    4. The fourth step is to plan the use of the remaining, unobligated income in each period. What part shall be set aside for food, clothing, housing, household operation, furniture and equipment, auto, other transportation, medical care, and other categories? What part shall be used for gifts and contributions and what part for the savings program? The budget should include all items important to the family, which may be facilitated by referring to the Check List of Budget Items. The family may, however, place the items in whatever categories seem reasonable to it.

    If the first draft of the budget provides an insufficient amount for regular expenditures, revision is in order. The family might reduce expenditures in some categories without undue violence to actual needs. Many "necessities" are not nearly so necessary as one thinks; some are less desirable than the time used to attain them. A new dress or suit may seem necessary to the teenager, but how does it compare with the need for accumulating funds toward his education or with the parents' needs for leisure time? Everything costs what the family foregoes to acquire it; sometimes, lasting and important satisfactions are exchanged for ephemeral ones.

    If it is undesirable to reduce expenditures, other readjustments must be made. Perhaps income can be increased by an extra job for the earner or other members. Perhaps voluntary contributions to relatives or investments in corporate stocks must be decreased. It might be necessary to re-evaluate and rewrite some of the contractual obligations, such as decreasing monthly payments on the house. Other avenues are open to the family. It might draw on its past accumulation of savings; or it may make some of the future purchases on time payments, thus leveling out expenditures over a longer period of time. This is the purpose of the budget: to see the income and expenditure pattern as a whole for the next period and make necessary adjustments ahead of time.

    Table 3–2 presents a simplified example of the steps in constructing a budget for the hypothetical Adams family consisting of a husband and wife in their thirties and two school children. They are a healthy group, living in a northern city. Their furniture, equipment,

TABLE 3–2. Adams Family Budget for Next Year

[In dollars]

ITEM	JAN.	FEB.	MAR.	APR.	MAY	JN.	JY.	AUG.	SEP.	OCT.	NOV.	DEC.	TOTAL
1. GROSS INCOME: Husband's wages	600	600	600	500	500	400	400	300	400	500	600	600	6000
2. REQUIRED DEDUCTIONS, TOTAL	88	88	88	65	65	42	42	19	42	65	70	70	744
3. Federal income tax	70	70	70	50	50	30	30	10	30	50	70	70	600
4. Social Security tax	18	18	18	15	15	12	12	9	12	15	..	..	144
5. NET INCOME (Line 1 minus Line 2)	512	512	512	435	435	358	358	281	358	435	530	530	5256
6. CONTRACTUAL OBLIGATIONS, TOTAL	90	90	140	150	140	90	90	90	140	150	140	90	1400
7. Home loan (principal, interest, taxes, insurance)	90	90	90	90	90	90	90	90	90	90	90	90	1080
8. Life insurance	..	..	50	..	..	..	..	..	50	..	..	..	100
9. Health insurance	..	..	..	60	..	..	..	..	..	60	..	..	120
10. Automobile insurance	..	..	..	..	50	..	..	..	..	..	50	..	100
11. REMAINING INCOME (L.5 minus L. 6)	422	422	372	285	295	268	268	191	218	285	390	440	3856

TABLE 3–2. Adams Family Budget for Next Year

[In dollars]

ITEM	JAN.	FEB.	MAR.	APR.	MAY	JN.	JY.	AUG.	SEP.	OCT.	NOV.	DEC.	TOTAL
12. EXPENSES, TOTAL	286	262	367	266	232	244	241	364	253	262	248	375	3400
13. Food	125	100	100	125	100	100	125	100	100	125	100	100	1300
14. Clothing	10	10	100	10	20	10	10	100	10	10	10	100	400
15. Housing (repairs)	:	:	25	:	:	25	:	:	10	:	:	25	100
16. Household operation	50	50	40	35	20	20	20	20	25	35	40	50	400
17. Equipment and furnishings	10	10	10	8	7	7	7	7	7	7	10	10	100
18. Automobile	40	40	40	40	40	40	40	60	40	40	40	40	500
19. Other transportation	9	8	9	9	9	8	8	4	9	9	9	9	100
20. Medical care	10	10	10	10	7	7	6	7	6	7	10	9	100
21. Personal business	4	4	5	4	4	4	4	4	4	7	4	10	50
22. Recreation	10	8	10	9	9	9	9	50	9	9	9	9	150
23. Education	4	10	4	4	4	2	:	:	10	4	4	4	50
24. Reading	5	4	5	4	4	4	4	4	4	4	4	4	50
25. Personal care	9	8	9	8	8	8	8	8	9	8	8	9	100
26. CONTRIBUTIONS, TOTAL	12	11	25	12	10	11	11	6	10	12	12	24	156
27. Religious organizations	9	8	9	9	8	9	9	4	8	9	9	9	100
28. Relatives, friends	1	1	1	1	1	1	1	1	1	1	1	15	26
29. Charity organizations	2	2	15	2	1	1	1	1	1	2	2	:	30
30. INVESTMENTS: Cash forms	124	149	−20	7	53	13	16	−179	−45	11	130	41	300

and auto are paid for and usable, though growing older. The family is striving to buy its home and has about $1,000 in United States bonds.

The budget for an actual family might be considerably more complicated, including additional items of income, required deductions, contractual obligations, expenses, contributions, and investments. The Adams family's income, about the national median, is irregular enough to require planning to maintain evenly the family's level of living. As a result, insurance premiums are avoided during the summer months when income is lowest; temporary savings are accumulated during the months of higher income or lower expenses and drawn on at other times. All of the budget amounts are arbitrary ones and might not be advisable for all families, because of differences in values and goals.

Interrelationships of Items · The family needs to consider certain interrelationships among budget items. Each use of income costs the family what it gives up: by spending, it foregoes that much saving and sharing. By emphasizing ownership of up-to-date automobiles, it may forego the possibility of home ownership. By purchasing more durable goods, it gives up that much in nondurables; elaborate household equipment may eliminate higher education for the children or the broadening experience of travel.

Economizing in one area of the budget may increase costs in another. Perhaps these cancel out. Shopping to save on the food bill may increase transportation costs or, if carried too far, medical costs. A family that moves outside the city to save housing expense may find that it has higher costs for transportation and utilities.

Expanding expenditure in one area may necessitate increased expenditures in other areas. For instance, enlarged recreational activities may require more clothing and transportation costs. Moving to a high-income neighborhood may bring a felt need for more expensive furnishings, clothing, and recreation.

Furthermore, certain objectives can be achieved by a variety of means. Warmth can be achieved by the type of housing, heating system, clothing, or even by the food consumed. Warm clothing is more important in Europe than in the United States, whereas the heating system is emphasized in this country. The family's laundry can be done by a hired worker or by a durable piece of equipment in the home. Families of moderately good income in other lands are likely to hire services whereas ours purchase equipment.

ATTITUDES TOWARD MONEY

The discussion of the budgeting process cannot be concluded without considering attitudes toward money, since they are important to successful operation of the budget. Money is sought and used to buy wanted goods and services in the present and future, for one's family or for others. But, as Edith Neisser points out, money may give additional satisfactions directly: a feeling of independence, security, prestige, power, or virtue (money being the reward for hard work, thrift, and a good life).[8]

The husband's drive for a high income and the desire of the wife and children to be earners may be partly a search for these psychological satisfactions. Individuals with a low drive for money or for earning may have low desire for goods and services or a low desire for these other satisfactions from the acquisition of money; or their needs for goods and services and for psychological satisfactions may be met by other means.

In their use of money, some people are miserly, some extremely generous or extravagant, and some dictatorial. In their individual ways they may be seeking feelings of security, prestige, power, or virtue which they are not finding in personal and business relationhips. The careless person may be saying that money is not important or that he does not care much about life or the earner's life.

Money is not a useful tool for discipline of children. Cash rewards for virtue may give the child the idea that everything has a price; the greater the virtue, the greater the necessary monetary reward. Fines for punishment may lead him to believe that he can buy his way out of anything.

It is sometimes necessary to explain to the child that the family cannot afford something he wants, such as a week at a summer camp, even though the family would like him to have it. He needs to learn that most families have limited resources. But insufficient funds should not be an excuse when the truth is that the parents would not allow him to have the money for that purpose, such as the purchase of a car, even if they could well afford it. Affording it is not the only criterion for making decisions. At the same time, parents and others should avoid using gifts of money to children as easy substitutes for love or to salve a guilty conscience.

The wife and children may obtain money for personal use by

[8] Edith G. Neisser, *The Many Faces of Money* (New York: Human Relations Aids, 1958).

receiving an allowance, earning, asking as needed, using charge accounts, or receiving gifts. An allowance provides a feeling of independence and a dependable source of income so that the individual can learn to manage money. He learns that the amount is limited, choices must be made carefully, and savings must be accumulated for larger items and unexpected needs. The allowance might cover an increasing proportion of personal needs as the child grows, including most of them in the late high-school years. The child's allowance should not be considered payment for assuming his share of family responsibilities. Home chores can themselves be a worthwhile experience for him.

Earning at least part of his money is good training for the child in understanding the value of money. He might be paid for tasks that ordinarily would be done by a hired worker around the home or family business, he may find a part-time job, or do odd jobs. Asking for money as needed retains control of choice in the hand of the parent (or husband, in case of the wife), so that the individual does not receive training in the management of funds. However, he or she may become skillful in the management of parent or husband; some individuals prefer this method since they obtain more by it. Using family or personal charge accounts involves special problems where the young or irresponsible are concerned.

What restrictions should be placed on the child's use of his income or accumulated funds? It is desirable that the child be told which general types of items are to be covered by it. Perhaps small food items and toys at first, with movies and similar expenses added later, and progressing on to a large proportion of clothing items and other personal expenditures. Many times parents think the child's money is used wastefully. But he needs experience; even adults sometimes use money unwisely. Parents should teach the importance of fundamental values to their children. As they revise and improve their own hierarchy of values so that choices will be most satisfying in the long run, they should explain the revisions to the children if they are old enough to comprehend.

A useful way of helping children understand the problems of family financial management is to let them share increasingly interesting and important financial transactions as they grow older and more discreet. A junior-high child can learn about prices and values in foods by shopping for them. Planning menus is a further step in learning. Children may make deposits and withdrawals from their own bank accounts or they may assist their parents in this or in paying family bills. Eventually they may need to understand family

resources and goals, at least in general terms, to insure their cooperation and train them for adulthood.[9]

With today's family depending primarily on money income
for support, it is essential that the wife, as well as the husband and
children, learn to handle money wisely. The wife must play an
effective role in regular expenditures and be able to take over management of family finances in case of a temporary emergency or
widowhood.

QUESTIONS

1. What is the importance to the family of the general budgeting process?
2. How does the family's general financial plan differ from its
budget?
3. Explain Hoyt's classification of interests. Give examples. How
may these concepts be used to maximize satisfactions?
4. What is the significance of the family's use of time?
5. What are several specific financial goals of the family's budget?
6. Why may the choice of current goals differ from one family
to another?
7. What are the characteristics of a good budget for a family?
Can the same budget be used by many families?
8. What is your considered opinion on the necessity for the
budget being written and detailed and for a record of expenditures being
kept?
9. How would you explain the specific process of constructing the
budget?
10. How are attitudes toward money important to the family?
11. Should the wife and children, as well as the husband, learn
to handle money? What methods do you see as useful in giving them
training?

SUGGESTIONS FOR FURTHER READING

Household Finance Corporation. *Money Management: Children's Spend-
    ing.* Chicago, latest edition.
————. *Money Management for Young Moderns.* Chicago, latest
    edition.

[9] See Frances L. Ilg and Louise Bates Ames, The Gesell Institute of Child Development, *What You Should Tell Your Child About Money* (Washington, D.C.: Savings and Loan Foundation, 1965); and Sidonie M. Gruenberg and H. Krech, *Pennies in
Their Pockets: Helping Children Manage Money* (Chicago: Science Research Associates,
1955).

————. *Money Management: Your Budget.* Chicago, latest edition.

U. S. Department of Agriculture. *A Guide to Budgeting for the Family.* Home and Garden Bulletin No. 108. Washington, D.C.: Superintendent of Documents, latest edition.

————. *A Guide to Budgeting for the Young Couple.* Home and Garden Bulletin No. 98. Washington, D.C.: Superintendent of Documents, latest edition.

————. *Helping Families Manage Their Finances.* Home Economics Research Report No. 21. Washington, D.C.: Superintendent of Documents, latest edition.

"Age cannot wither her, nor custom stale
Her infinite variety."
—ANTONY AND CLEOPATRA

Prices

of /4

Consumer Goods

- SHORT-RUN CHANGES
- CYCLICAL CHANGES
- SECULAR CHANGES

The prices of consumer goods determine how much it costs a family to maintain a given level of living. Because of increased prices, it took $1.13 in 1966 to purchase approximately the same bundle of goods that $1.00 bought in 1957–59. Constant real income therefore requires that the family's money income rise or fall in proportion to changes in the price level, in the short and long run.

A price index is a useful indicator of relative changes in prices from one period to another. The Consumer Price Index of the U. S. Bureau of Labor Statistics measures monthly and annual changes in the prices of goods and services purchased by urban wage earners and clerical workers, with the years 1957–59 as a base.[1] For this purpose, the Bureau determines the items, their characteristics, and quantities commonly purchased by such families, then prices them monthly. The "fixed market basket" of goods and services includes about 400 items ranging from a haircut to a new house. If, for example, the bundle of goods and services cost $5,000 during the years 1957–59 and cost $5,650 in 1966, the index for 1966 would be 113.

Since the CPI is constructed for specific types of families,

---

[1] Sometimes called loosely "the cost of living index." See U. S. Bureau of Labor Statistics, *Monthly Labor Review* for data and further explanation of the Consumer Price Index.

others with low or high incomes, on farms, or in areas with unusual price conditions might find that changes in the index do not reflect changes in the costs of items they regularly buy. Furthermore, families who use unusual amounts of certain items may find that their costs have changed differently than the CPI shows. For instance, a family that uses especially large amounts of medical care may find that its costs have risen more, whereas a family that purchases relatively large amounts of clothing may find that its costs have risen less.

Changes in prices of consumer goods occur with variations in demand and in supply and cost conditions. Price changes are sometimes as frequent as hourly in big retail outlets, but sometimes very infrequent; sometimes small and sometimes large. The rate of change is often unequal for different commodities. All types of price changes —short-run, cyclical, and secular—are important to consumers.

SHORT-RUN CHANGES

Short-run changes in prices of consumer goods are sometimes sporadic, but sometimes they show a marked seasonal pattern, with certain months consistently higher or lower than others. Some fresh foods that are available only part of the year, such as strawberries and watermelons, have highest prices when the items reach the market at the beginning of their selling season. Prices of many foods fall to their seasonal lows at the end of their major harvest season. Seasonal highs for some nonfood items are related to the start of fall, the Christmas season, winter needs, summer needs, or production plans of manufacturers. Some items have seasonal lows of which the family can take advantage by increasing use or accumulating stocks as far as practical.

The importance of seasonality of prices is shown by special analyses by the Bureau of Labor Statistics.[2] Since actual price changes are a combination of secular trend, cyclical movements, seasonal variation, and irregular changes, other changes were abstracted statistically to isolate the effects of seasonal factors.

If no other factors affected prices, the seasonal factors would result in great differences in prices of many food items through the year. For example, prices of apples would vary from about 80 percent of the year's average in November to 130 percent of the year's average

[2] U. S. Bureau of Labor Statistics, *Seasonal Factors, Consumer Price Index: Selected Series*, Bulletin No. 1366, 1963; "The Method of Seasonal Adjustment for Consumer Price Index Series," 1966, and supplements; and "Seasonal Behavior of Components in the CPI," *Monthly Labor Review*, May 1967, pp. 14–20.

Figure 4–1. Seasonal Factors in Selected Consumer Prices

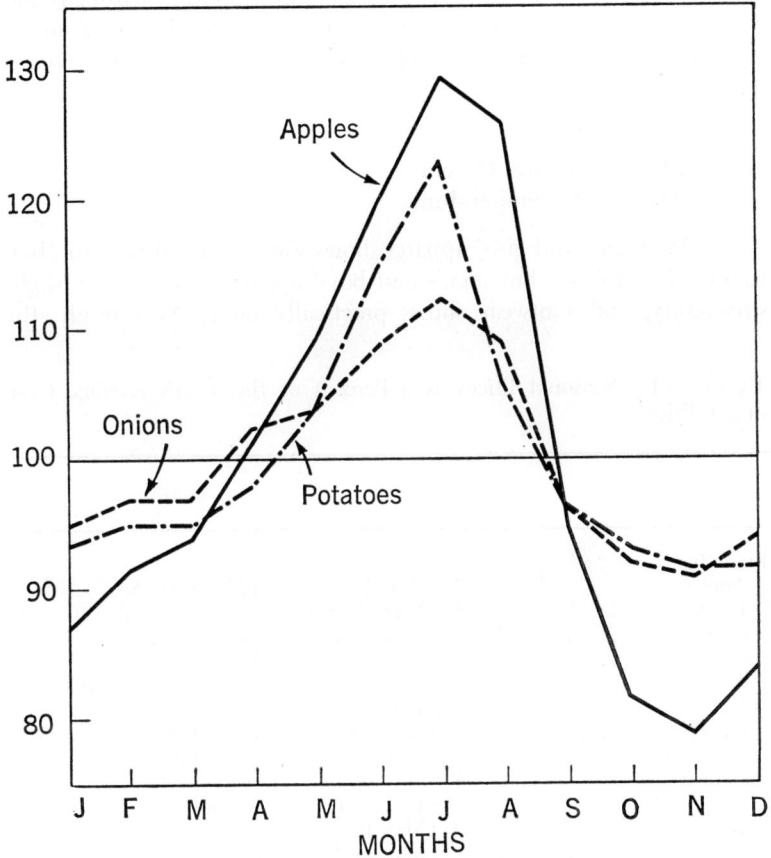

% of 1965
AVERAGE PRICES

source: U. S. Bureau of Labor Statistics.

in July, just before the major harvest season. Figure 4–1 shows the similarity of seasonal patterns for potatoes and onions. In the actual price data, these patterns are blurred by inflationary conditions. Advancing inflation through the year enlarges the midyear rise in prices and diminishes the drop after the harvest season. Worsening depression through the year would have opposite effects.

Other foods with important seasonal patterns are listed in the data shown in Table 4–1. Most of these are fresh fruits and vegetables. But eggs also showed sizable seasonal patterns and pork showed some. While these foods had notable seasonal changes, many foods had moderate changes and some, such as cereal and bakery products and American cheese, had practically none. As a result of the difference in degree of seasonality and the different months of troughs and peaks for different foods, the seasonal factor for total foods is much less. The average seasonal factors for grouped months were as follows:

101.0 in July
100.2 in August–October
99.8 in November–June

Women's and girls' apparel shows some seasonal pattern (bottom of Table 4–1), but men's and boys' apparel shows a very slight seasonality, and footwear shows practically none. As a result, the

TABLE 4–1. Seasonal Prices as a Percent of the Year's Average Consumer Prices*

ITEMS	LOWS	PEAKS
Fresh foods:		
Apples	83 in Oct.–Jan.	125 in June–Aug.
Potatoes	94 in Sept.–March	119 in June–July
Onions	95 in Sept.–March	110 in June–Aug.
Cabbage	88 in Aug.–Dec.	112 in Jan.–June
Tomatoes	72 in Aug.–Oct.	115 in Jan. and March–May
Lettuce	91 in July–Aug.	108 in Feb. and Nov.
Celery	95 in Aug.–Dec.	111 in July
Carrots	95 in March–May	105 in June–Aug.
Oranges	94 in Jan.–March	107 in Sept.–Nov.
Grapefruit	88 in Dec.–April	116 in July–Oct.
Eggs	90 in May–July	110 in Sept.–Oct.
Pork	97 in March–May	105 in Aug. Sept.
Other items:		
Women's and girls' apparel	99 in Jan.–Feb.	101 in Sept.–Dec.
New cars	98 in Sept.	102 in Nov.
Used cars	97 in Feb.	101 in June–Nov.
Major categories:		
Food	100 in Aug.–June	101 in July
Apparel and upkeep	100 in Dec.–Sept.	101 in Oct.–Nov.
Transportation	..	..

* Average seasonal factors for grouped months. 1965 factors for fresh foods. Seasonal factors used for adjusting components of the Consumer Price Index during 1966, for other items and major categories.
SOURCE: U. S. Bureau of Labor Statistics.

seasonal factors for total apparel and upkeep are small. The average seasonal factors for grouped months were as follows:

100.6 in October–November
99.6 in January–March
99.9 in April–June
99.6 in July–August
100.2 in September

Seasonal factors in prices of cars are of particular importance because of the large outlay involved. For new cars, prices are seasonally low in September and peak in November with the introduction of new models. Used cars vary from a low in February, when dealers have big stocks of trade-ins, to a peak in June–November. Since other costs of private transportation and of public transportation showed less seasonal patterns, the seasonal factors for total transportation were quite small. The average seasonal factors for grouped months were as follows:

100.4 in October–January
99.7 in February–April
100.0 in May–September

The seasonality of consumer prices may be summarized rather briefly. While there are important seasonal patterns for certain individual items in the family budget, only three major categories—food, apparel and upkeep, and transportation—showed seasonal patterns. The other major categories were characterized by very little seasonal variation and a relatively high degree of irregularity. Furthermore, the patterns of seasonal variation were so small and differed so greatly among the components of the all-items index that the movements offset one another. Thus, no seasonal pattern was shown for the all-items index of the CPI.

CYCLICAL CHANGES

Prices of consumer goods and services also respond, though imperfectly, to changes in general business conditions. Separate indexes for food, apparel and upkeep, rent, and medical care show that price changes may be quite unequal for different categories (Figure 4–2). For instance, in 1966 apparel and upkeep averaged 10 percent above its 1957–59 base, and medical care averaged 28 percent above its base in the same years.

Cyclical changes in the all-items index are of particular importance to families. Consumer prices for all items burgeoned during the prosperity period of World War I, then fell sharply in the brief postwar depression (Figure 4-3). They were at a high level during the prosperity of the later 1920's and fell importantly in the depression of the early 1930's. After the slow revival of the later 1930's, they rose rapidly during the prosperity periods of World War II and postwar years.

FIGURE 4–2. Consumer Price Index for Selected Categories

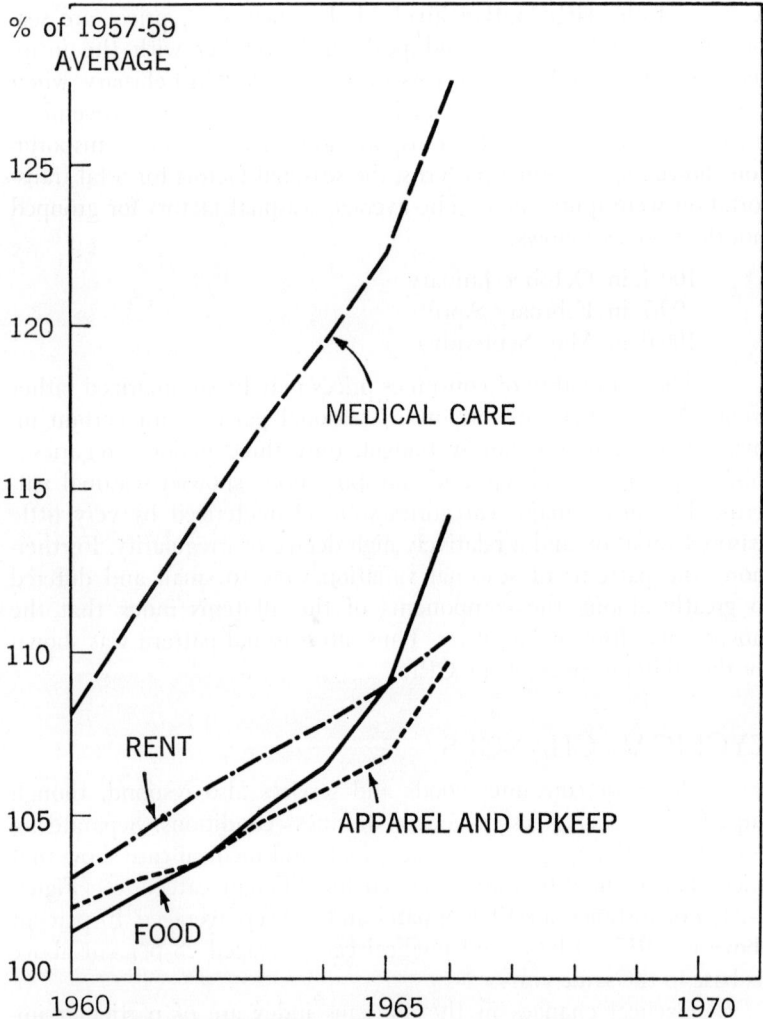

SOURCE: U. S. Bureau of Labor Statistics

Several periods of rapid price change at 5 percent or more over the previous year have occurred in this century:

YEARS	INDEXES
1915 – 1920 – 1922	... 35 – 70 – 58
1930 – 1933	... 58 – 45
1940 – 1943	... 49 – 60
1945 – 1948	... 63 – 84
1950 – 1951	... 84 – 90

FIGURE 4–3.   Consumer Price Index for All Items

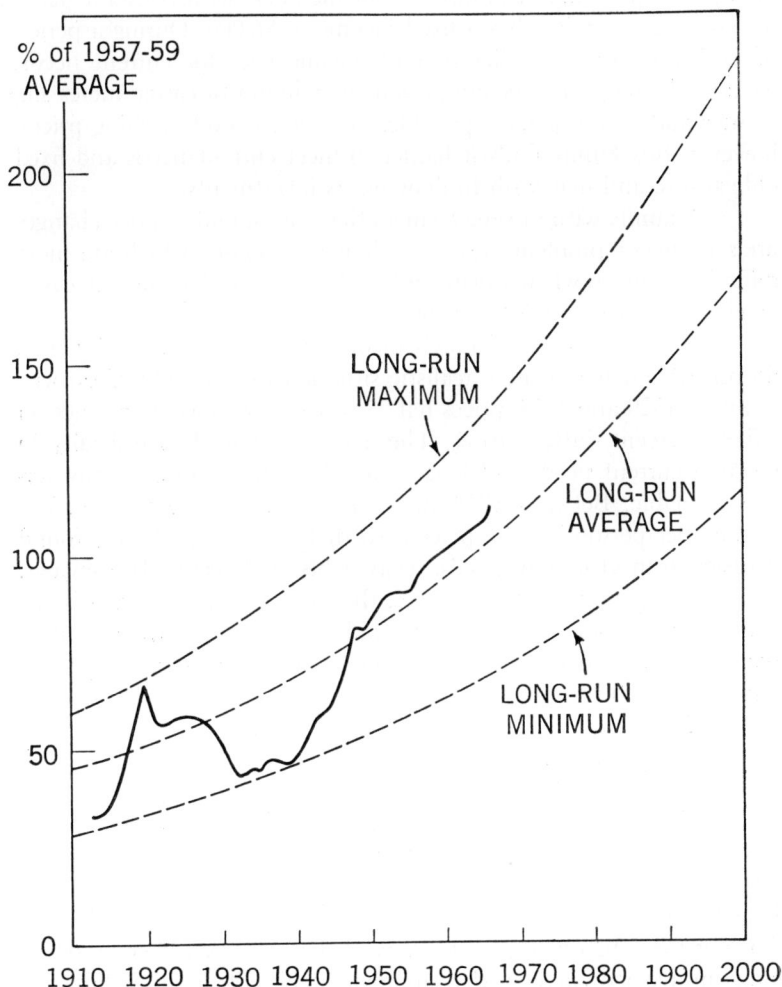

SOURCES: U. S. Bureau of Labor Statistics; long-run estimates by the author.

From 1915 to 1920 prices rose 97 percent, an average of 19 percent a year; and between 1920 and 1922 they fell 16 percent. From 1930 to 1933 they fell 23 percent. The three most recent periods of rapid price change have been upward with a 24 percent increase from 1940 to 1943, a 34 percent increase from 1945 to 1948, and an 8 percent increase from 1950 to 1951. Most of the periods of rapid change in this century were related to war periods.

Periods of rapid price change affect the family's ability to supply current needs, meet contractual obligations, and accumulate savings. Suppose that a family of four members with constant needs for goods and services has a fixed income of $6,000. During a period of falling prices, a smaller part of income goes for current needs. Meeting home payments and insurance premiums is easier; increasing savings and investments is possible. During a period of rising prices, however, this family finds it harder to meet current needs and fixed obligations, and may wish to draw on its investments.

A family with income changes that correspond to price changes finds its major problem area in its long-term debts, which are more difficult to meet when prices and dollar income decline but easier when both prices and dollar income rise.

Suppose that the family's income changes more rapidly than do prices, which is a more realistic situation for the bulk of earners. Between 1929 and 1933, prices fell 25 percent, but income per person fell 47 percent (after taxes). The average family had difficulty in meeting current needs and long-term debts, and it drew on any savings available. Between 1939 and 1944, prices rose 27 percent, but income per person rose 97 percent so that the average family found it easier to meet current needs, repay debts, and accumulate savings.

In a period of falling prices, the most fortunate family is the one whose income changes less rapidly than prices; whereas in a period of rising prices, the most fortunate has income increasing more rapidly than prices.

SECULAR CHANGES

Changes in consumer prices through the century need to be taken into account by the family as it makes long-range plans. The secular trend of consumer prices has been generally upward since 1894–95. Estimates of long-run prices are made in Figure 4–3 by drawing the long-run minimum curve below all low indices and the long-run average curve so that approximately half of the indices are below and half are above, then extending both curves for the remainder of the century. Sporadic as well as seasonal and cyclical fluctuations in prices are expected to vary above the long-run minimum and around the long-run average.

Estimates for the remainder of the century are based partly on the actual indices of the first part of the century and partly on prognostications of future government expenditures, fiscal and monetary policies, and other pressures. It is expected that high expenditures for defense will continue and that Congress will be unable to legislate sufficient taxes to meet them. Therefore, part of the costs will be met by borrowing from individuals and business, private banks, and finally and most inflationary, from the Federal Reserve Banks. It is expected that operations of the Federal Reserve System will attempt primarily to facilitate borrowing by the U. S. Treasury and prevent the onslaught of a depression rather than contain inflation. Other inflationary pressures in the economy, such as those of business and labor and the extension of credit, are taken into account. The inflationary projections are predicated on the continuance of our socio-political-economic system.

Continuous, moderate inflation has many pleasant results. It provides a fillip to business—a little extra money to encourage high-level production, compensate for errors, and cover higher wages. Earners obtain increased incomes through greater employment and higher pay rates. Borrowers (government, business, and individuals) find it easier to repay loans. Government obtains increased taxes without raising tax rates. Investors in variable-price items receive windfall profits.

The disadvantages of moderate inflation are more insidious. An increase of 1.5 percent compounded annually doubles the price level in 47 years, triples it in 74 years, and quadruples it in 93 years. A growth rate of 1.5 percent annually results in the following estimates of long-run price indices (1957–59 = 100):

YEAR	LONG-RUN ESTIMATES			ACTUAL
	MINIMUM	AVERAGE	MAXIMUM	PRICE INDEX
1910	31	46	60	..
1920	36	53	70	70
1930	42	62	81	58
1940	48	71	94	49
1950	56	83	109	84
1960	65	96	127	103
1970	75	112	147	..
1980	88	129	171	..
1990	102	150	198	..
2000	118	174	230	..

Each family needs to think carefully about these inflationary prognostications in making its plans. If long-run inflation continues, present college students can expect continuously higher price levels through their life cycles. In 10 years when they might want to buy a home, the general long-run price level might be 16 percent higher. In 20 years when their children are ready for college, prices might be 35 percent higher. By the time they are ready to retire, prices might have doubled.

Currently earned income tends to keep pace with long-run inflation. So long as the average family is earning an income, it has a reasonable chance of meeting increased costs of current goods and services without excessive hardship. Its greatest difficulty comes in meeting expenses which require saving in advance; but it may be able to obtain credit for these outlays. However, retired earners find the value of pensions and annuities continuously whittled away by inflation.

Suppose that a couple figures that an income equivalent to $300 a month in 1965 will be sufficient for them in their old age. If the prices of consumer goods increase according to the average projection, they will need about $350 a month in 1980 and $480 by the year 2000. If the productivity of the country continues to grow so that goods and services per person increase by 1.75 percent a year, they will need about $460 a month in 1980 and $870 in the year 2000 in order to maintain a status in society equal to that of $300 today. If they arrive at retirement with $300 a month, their feeling of poverty will be due partly to inflation and partly to the increasing real incomes of current earners.

Assuming the average long-run projections, a dollar placed in a safe deposit box now would buy at retirement in the year 2000 only what 60¢ buys today. A dollar invested today at 1½ percent compounded annually would buy at retirement about what a dollar buys today. It is only those dollars invested at higher rates that would have a net increase in real value. An earning rate, including capital gains, of about 3 percent compounded annually would about compensate for long-run inflation and participate in long-run increases in real income. The same principle applies to savings accumulated toward short-run goals. However, these estimates do not take into account cyclical changes in prices and productivity.

Consideration of changes in prices of consumer goods in the short run and long run help the family to be more knowledgeable about them and to consider more carefully its attitude toward their desirability and inevitability. At the same time, it should aid the family in considering its expenditures, savings, and investment programs as well as its income expectations through its life cycle.

QUESTIONS

1. What is the importance to the family of the changing prices of consumer goods? How do changes affect its financial resources?

2. What is the meaning of a price index? How do you use the price indices to calculate the percentage change in prices between two years (1915 to 1920, say?)

3. In general terms, how is the Consumer Price Index constructed?

4. For what group is the CPI constructed? What is the significance of this to other families?

5. Describe seasonal variations in prices of food, apparel, and transportation. What about seasonal variations in the all-items index?

6. What were some periods of important cyclical changes in consumer prices?

7. How did cyclical changes in prices affect families generally?

8. What is the meaning of secular changes in prices?

9. In general terms, what is the long-run prognostication presented for consumer prices and why? Do you agree? What would be the effects on families?

10. We have used constant dollars or 1957–59 dollars in discussing changes in incomes or expenditures or families. How has the CPI been used to deflate current dollars and obtain figures in terms of constant dollars? Why has it been done?

SUGGESTIONS FOR FURTHER READING

U. S. Bureau of Labor Statistics. *Monthly Labor Review,* latest issues.
————. *The Consumer Price Index,* latest monthly reports.

Consumer Credit / 5

- WIDESPREAD USE
- CONSIDERING THE USE OF CREDIT
- TYPES OF CONSUMER CREDIT
- METHODS OF REPAYING DEBT
- CALCULATING CHARGES FOR CREDIT
- LAWS ON CONSUMER CREDIT

Through the use of consumer credit, the family pledges future income to increase its financial resources for current support. It is thereby able to have more goods and services today than if it had to pay cash. For this privilege of forward buying, the family must pay a price.

Consumer credit is used by the family or individual for consumption purposes that do not increase the family's income directly, and seldom result in enough savings to repay the debt. Consumer credit thus differs fundamentally from producer credit, which is obtained for business purposes with the expectation that its use will provide earnings for repayment. The use of consumer credit therefore involves a different set of decisions.

WIDESPREAD USE

Short- and intermediate-term consumer credit, usually payable within three years, has grown tremendously from the small amount used at the turn of the century to about $90 billion today. Three-quarters of total consumer credit is instalment credit, to be repaid over a period of time, and one-quarter is noninstalment credit, as the following figures show: [1]

TYPE OF CONSUMER CREDIT	PERCENT OF CONSUMER CREDIT
Total consumer credit	100
Instalment credit, total	78
Automobile paper	33
Other consumer goods paper	20
Home repair and modernization loans*	4
Personal loans	21
Noninstalment credit, total	22
Single-payment loans	8
Charge accounts	8
Service credit	6

* Holdings of financial institutions. Holdings of retail outlets are included in "other consumer goods paper."

The most important use for consumer credit is in the purchase of automobiles: automobile paper comprises a third of all credit outstanding. In fact, seven-tenths of consumer credit is directly related to the purchase of goods and services, whereas only three-tenths is in the form of cash loans—two-tenths in instalment loans and one-tenth in single payment loans. Credit is used to some extent in a large proportion of the purchases of autos, furniture, and equipment, as well as clothing and other department store and mail order items.

As would be expected, the use of credit is widespread among consumers. The Board of Governors of the Federal Reserve System found that some personal debt was owed by more than half of all consumer units (families or individuals living apart from their families).[2] "Personal debt" included all short- and intermediate-term consumer credit other than 30-day charge accounts. About two out of five debtors owed less than $500, two owed $500–$1,999, and one owed more.

About a third of those with personal debt could presumably have chosen to pay cash. The percentage of debtors with liquid assets (checking accounts, savings accounts, and U. S. savings bonds) that were about equal to or greater than their personal debt increased with

[1] Board of Governors of the Federal Reserve System, *Federal Reserve Bulletin* (data at end of 1965).

[2] D. S. Pro'ector and G. S. Weiss, *Survey of Financial Characteristics of Consumers* (Washington, D.C.: Board of Governors of the Federal Reserve System, 1966), pp. 15–17, 45–50, 108–109, and 126–135. (Data as of end of 1962.) All quoted data on personal debt of consumer units is from this source.

income level as follows: 20 percent at incomes of 0–$2,999, 31 percent at $3,000–$4,999, 36 percent at $5,000–$7,499, 44 percent at $7,500–$9,999, and 56 percent at incomes of $10,000 and over.

Personal debt was much more frequent among younger age groups than among older. Eighty percent of consumer units with a head under 35 years old had personal debts, 72 percent of those 35–44, and 63 percent of those 45–54, contrasted with 38 percent of those 55–64 and 20 percent of those 65 and over.

Most likely to have some personal debt were consumer units headed by a person under 35 years old, with income of $7,500–$9,999 (total income of unit, before taxes). Ninety percent of these units had some personal debt. More than 80 percent of the young consumers with incomes of $3,000–$4,999 and $5,000–$7,499 had personal debts. These include the groups that are setting up homes and rearing children. They have enough income to get credit, but not enough to make exclusive use of 30-day charge accounts.

The following figures for consumer units with heads under 35 years old show the larger personal debts of those debtors with larger incomes:

1962 INCOME (HEAD UNDER 35)	ALL UNITS	ZERO DEBT	$1–$499	$500–$1,999	$2,000 AND OVER
0–$2,999	100	34	42	21	3
$3,000–$4,999	100	18	27	41	13
$5,000–$7,499	100	16	25	43	17
$7,500–$9,999	100	10	16	52	24
$10,000–$14,999 ...	100	30	12	35	23

PERCENTAGE DISTRIBUTION BY AMOUNT OF PERSONAL DEBT

Among young consumers with incomes of $7,500–$9,999, instalment debt on automobiles was the most common type of personal debt. Among young consumers with lower and higher incomes, other types of instalment debt were most common. The percentages with various types of personal debt were as follows:

1962 INCOME (HEAD UNDER 35)	INSTALMENT DEBT ON AUTO	OTHER INSTALMENT DEBT	NON-INSTALMENT DEBT	DEBT ON LIFE INSURANCE
0–$2,999	24	46	31	..
$3,000–$4,999	38	67	37	..
$5,000–$7,499	44	66	53	5
$7,500–$9,999	68	60	42	3
$10,000–$14,999 ..	47	55	35	4

PERCENT WITH GIVEN TYPE OF PERSONAL DEBT

While stimulation of the economy by extension of consumer credit on easy terms is needed in depressed periods, it may help to overheat the economy in prosperity periods. But lenders and retailers see credit extension as less risky in prosperity periods than in depression. As a result, the amount of credit outstanding fell a quarter, in dollars of constant purchasing power, from 1929 to 1933. The extension of new credit did not equal repayments and repossessions. Reduced credit as well as reduced incomes restricted consumer purchases. By 1965, on the other hand, extension of new credit had resulted in seven times as much outstanding as in 1929, in dollars of constant purchasing power. This allowed consumers to do more and more forward buying. Rises in credit extension in prosperity periods and decreases in depression thus serve to accentuate the swings in purchases and, therefore, in employment and income.

Since short- or intermediate-term consumer credit is readily available, particularly in prosperous periods, families need to plan thoughtfully the use of credit, shop carefully for credit services among various sources, and understand the laws on consumer credit, the methods of repaying debt, and ways of calculating credit charges.

CONSIDERING THE USE OF CREDIT

Lenders are eager to make loans since they are their stock-in-trade, and many retailers are happy to sell on credit terms. A merchant who sells on credit believes that it increases his volume of total sales or of items for which it is available, and that credit enhances the store loyalty of his customers. Also, he may make a profit on the credit service. Retailers compete in prosperity periods in lowering the down payment and lengthening the repayment period to encourage purchases. As a result, the consumer is beset by offers of easy credit that are hard to resist.

To the family, the use of consumer credit may mean the enjoyment of goods and services earlier than if it had to save ahead of time or, in some instances, obtaining items for which it would never save enough. A loan may be used to meet emergency expenses or to consolidate old indebtedness with the objective of clearing up debts. During a period of rising prices or anticipated shortages, use of credit allows the family to buy an item at a lower price and repay the debt with cheaper dollars. Certain additional advantages might be mentioned, such as convenience, a record of expenses, and, perhaps, ease in returning goods or obtaining repairs.

In spite of the possible advantages, the family needs to consider carefully whether it should use credit and to what extent. Some people feel insecure when they are in debt, while others accept debt as normal. Credit may be easy to get, but it is not always easy to repay. Will the use of additional credit mean undesirable curtailment of daily living expenses, difficulty in meeting other contractual obligations, or problems in case of emergency expenses? The family needs to total its expenses for the period of the credit contract to see that there is a margin for the additional obligations.

What effect will the use of credit have on the family's use of its income? Will it be tempted to overspend and thus be forced to forego permanent savings? The family has an obligation to provide for its own future and to withstand sales pressure that is not to its long-run advantage. Lenders and merchants are not especially generous to the unemployed or the destitute elderly who failed to save during their earning years. Will the use of credit encourage the family to spend for more important items or for less important ones, from the family's point of view? Perhaps a freezer or new car is more important than a vacation trip or education for the children. But the family needs to consider the alternatives carefully.

Will the use of credit reduce undesirably the family's flexibility in coping with future changes in expenses and income? Will the family's income remain at its present level or better until the debt is cancelled? A decrease in income for any reason, such as unemployment or sickness, compounds difficulties in meeting fixed obligations in addition to current living expenses. The family's optimism about the future is not always justified. Many families found that debts contracted in the late 1920's were difficult to repay out of the money earned in the early 1930's. Consumer credit, which amounted to 7 percent of disposable personal income after personal taxes in 1929, now amounts to 17 percent of income. This means that consumers now have a much higher amount of inflexibility built into their budgets.

Since credit costs money, the family also needs to decide whether this service is more valuable than other goods or services that might be purchased with the money. For instance, if the family purchases a $2,500 car with a $500 down payment and 36 monthly payments of $63.30 each, it pays $279 extra—enough to buy a new automatic washer. If, on the other hand, it makes a $1,500 down payment and makes 18 monthly payments of $59.55, it pays $72 extra. Thus, the family saves interest charges by borrowing less and by repaying the debt quickly.

The family may think ahead about credit costs by studying Table 5–1 which shows the equal monthly payments necessary to pay off a debt of $1,000 as well as the total interest payments made, under different loan terms. The table can be used for a debt of any size: $400 costs 0.4 times as much, whereas $2,500 costs 2.5 times as much. The importance of a shorter loan in reducing total interest costs is emphasized by looking at any column. For instance, a $1,000 loan at 6 percent costs $18 for interest when repaid in 6 monthly instalments, $48 in 18 months, but $95 in 36 months. The third way of cutting interest charges is by obtaining credit at the lowest possible interest rate. While $1,000 for 36 months costs $95 at 6 percent a year, it costs $649 at 36 percent a year (3 percent a month). Thus we note that shopping for credit as carefully as one shops for the car or other item can be highly profitable.

Comparison of the rate that the family has to pay for credit (perhaps 8–36 percent) with what it can earn on its savings in a bank or other investment (perhaps 4–10 percent) gives some perspective on the interest rate. If a family can discipline itself to replace regularly the amount in its savings account, it may withdraw the money for the car and forego an interest rate of perhaps 4 percent while saving the 12 percent that might be charged by an auto finance company.

TABLE 5–1. Equal Monthly Payments to Amortize a Debt of $1,000 in a Stated Number of Months

| ITEM | NOMINAL ANNUAL RATE OF INTEREST | | | |
	6%	12%	24%	36%
Monthly payment on principal and interest on loan for:				
6 months	$169.60	$172.55	$178.53	$184.60
12 months	86.07	88.85	94.56	100.46
18 months	58.23	60.98	66.70	72.71
24 months	44.32	47.07	52.87	59.05
30 months	35.98	38.75	44.65	51.02
36 months	30.42	33.21	39.23	45.80
Approximate total interest on loan for:				
6 months	$ 18	$ 35	$ 71	$108
12 months	33	66	135	206
18 months	48	98	201	309
24 months	64	130	269	417
30 months	79	162	340	531
36 months	95	196	412	649

TYPES OF CONSUMER CREDIT

The consumer may obtain credit directly from the retailer of goods and services on a charge account or instalment purchase or he may obtain a cash loan from a financial institution such as a commercial bank or consumer finance company. The family should familiarize itself with the important characteristics of the various types available before seeking credit.

The Creditor's Costs · Charges are made for consumer credit because of the costs to the retailer or lender. Dissimilar rates are charged for several reasons. General office expenses for facilities, equipment, and bookkeeping are less in some cases because of greater efficiency, a subsidy from other parts of the firm's operations in the form of free services and facilities, and the larger size of the loan which costs little more to process than does a small one.

Risk costs, such as expenditures for credit investigation, collection, repossession, reselling, and bad debts differ from one situation to another. Risk is lower on loans made to those individuals having established character, adequate capacity for repayment as shown by expected income contrasted with necessary expenditures, and capital investments. Differences in risk also are related to the type of loan made. Risk is less for a loan for durable goods than for emergency needs, for one involving the pledge of valuable collateral, and for one with a short repayment period.

The cost of money to the lender may differ, depending on what he must pay for his funds and what he gives up by lending the money rather than investing it in other directions. If a retailer borrows money at 4 percent, he must be reimbursed on any credit extended, either from credit charges or increased sales. If he could earn a net of 5 percent by investing the funds in additional inventory or by giving credit to someone else, he wants a 5 percent net return on credit extension.

Differences in charges for credit may exist also because of imperfect competition among firms because of a limited number of independent lenders, variation in service and ways of stating charges, and the ignorance and carelessness of consumer borrowers.

Charge Account Purchases · Charge accounts can be opened at many retailers, such as department stores, food stores, furniture and appliance dealers, and mail order houses, simply by filling out an application form and submitting to a credit investigation. The charge account permits purchases to be charged during the month; the bill is presented after the end of the month with the understanding that it will be paid in full, usually within ten days. This is also the nature of the credit given by doctors, dentists, and lawyers for their services, as well as by public utilities.

In general, no special fee is charged for the regular charge account service. Increased sales and profits due to the accounts may compensate for the costs of credit to the retailer; or those costs may be included in prices of the merchandise so that all purchasers at the store help to meet them. In some cases, the family may obtain a discount for cash. Otherwise, comparison of prices of similar merchandise at other retailers not offering credit (but offering similar services) will help the family ascertain the actual cost of the credit.

Variants of the open-charge account include the "option" account, which levies a charge such as $1 a month for each $50 balance outstanding after the 10-day waiting period. "Revolving credit" is extended by many stores to a limit set for a particular customer, frequently with a service charge of 1.5 percent a month on any unpaid balance. "Credit cards" have been extended for use at various outlets of a chain of gas stations for many years, but more recently they have been extended for use at a wide range of stores, restaurants, and hotels, sometimes abroad as well as in the states. The issuer of a multi-service plan generally reimburses the retailer directly, charges the retailer a percentage on credit card purchases, and charges the consumer a small annual membership fee.

Instalment Purchases · Auto dealers, department stores, furniture stores, mail order houses, and other retailers of durable as well as nondurable consumer goods frequently provide instalment credit for the purchase. The debt is usually discharged by equal payments for several weeks or months, extending up to a period of three years. The retailer, needing his funds for other purposes, frequently sells the instalment paper to a bank or a sales finance company, or in some cases the auto dealer may be acting as an agent of the sales finance company or bank.

The true charge for the credit from a reputable retailer is likely to be about 12–15 percent a year, but may range upward to an extremely high amount. The ways of stating charges include "no charge," a flat dollar charge, a percentage charge, or a combination of dollar and percentage charges. The charges may include a variety of items such as a stated interest charge, service charge, credit investigation fee, legal fee, charges for life insurance or disability insurance for the borrower, and insurance on the item itself. The stated interest rate is likely to be charged on the original loan, but may be charged on the declining balance or, in some cases, the original price of the item. The cost of credit to the family is the difference between the total of all costs it has to pay and the true cash price of the item—at that store or at another.

Instalment purchases are generally made under a conditional sale agreement, a chattel mortgage, or bailment lease. In each case, the goods may be repossessed if the payments are not met when due. Under the chattel mortgage, the consumer may have a deficiency judgment to pay if the resulting sale price does not cover the debt outstanding, or he may receive some payment for his equity. Under the bailment lease, the payments made by the consumer are considered rent; consequently there is no excess to pay or receive. Under the conditional sale agreement, either of the foregoing methods may be used, depending on law and the agreement.

Clauses which appear in some agreements provide protection for the seller, but may be injurious to the buyer:

A *wage assignment* clause gives the dealer the right, in case of default, to collect part of the buyer's pay directly from his employer until the debt is discharged. The portion may be large or small, depending on the contract, conscience, and the state law.

An *open-end* contract gives the seller repossession rights on a number of items purchased over a period of years until the debt on the last one has been completely discharged.

A *balloon* contract "balloons" at the end when the final payment is very large in contrast with the previous regular payments. This frequently means that the purchase has to be refinanced for a much longer period of time, thus enlarging total finance charges.

An *acceleration* clause provides that in case of default in a payment, all other payments become immediately due, which may result in a quick repossession of the goods.

Bank Loans · A loan from the personal loan department of a commercial bank may be obtained by preferred risks for the purchase of autos or furniture or for other uses. The loan may be secured by the pledge of collateral, such as an auto or negotiable securities, or it may be obtained on a promissory note. Banks prefer to make large loans and their credit investigations are fairly rigorous.

The bank loan is usually discounted in advance and payable in equal monthly instalments, though some are single-payment loans. Sometimes an additional service or investigation fee is levied. The true interest rate may approximate 9 percent a year on a new car loan, 12 percent a year on a home modernization loan, and 14–15 percent a year on an unsecured personal loan of $200–$2,000. Bank interest rates are likely to be lower than those of other lenders, primarily because of the bank's selection of risks and size of loans. Anyone with a good credit rating should see about a loan at his bank before obtaining credit from a more expensive source.

The family may also borrow on its savings account or against its shares in a savings and loan association, generally at a 6 percent rate, since no risk is involved to the lender. Using its savings directly may be cheaper, however, unless a short loan will avoid the loss of interest over a longer period.

Life Insurance Loans · A family needing money may borrow on the loan value of its life insurance policy at a rate of 5–6 percent a year, assuming that the policy has a loan value stated in the contract. Again, there is no risk involved to the lender. However, the insurance company has to make the charge because of bookkeeping costs and because it would otherwise be investing the money in another way.

Generally there is no pressure to repay the loan. This may be an advantage or disadvantage, depending on the family's circumstances and self-discipline. If the loan has not finally been repaid at the time that the policy comes due or is surrendered, the loan plus accumulated interest will be subtracted from the face value or cash surrender value, as the case may be.

Credit Union Loans · Credit unions are organized as cooperative societies by a firm's employees or their union, as well as by other groups, in order to cut the cost of consumer credit for members and to put small savings to work. Each member pays a small membership fee and purchases at least one share in the cooperative.

Loans are made to members at rates, including all special fees, that generally cannot exceed 12 percent a year and are sometimes less. The rate can be low, even though very small loans as well as larger ones are made, because of the low risk on these loans and low costs of doing business as a consequence of the contribution of services and facilities by members or sponsoring organizations.

The rate may approximate a true interest rate of 6 percent a year on a loan that is secured by a pledge of shares in the credit union, 9 percent a year on a new car loan, and 12 percent a year on a signature loan of up to $2,000. The loan is usually repaid in equal monthly instalments.

Consumer Finance Company Loans · Numerous consumer finance companies have been established under state small loan laws. They are also known as personal finance or small loan companies. They make loans for all sorts of consumer needs, but the bulk is used to repay old debts or meet emergency needs rather than to purchase durable consumer goods. The loans are generally repaid in equal monthly instalments. Security is given in some cases, though it may have more psychological than financial value.

Their rates average about 2.5 percent a month on the declining balance, with no additional fees, but vary from 1 percent to 3.5 percent depending on the size of the loan, the state law, and the firm's policy with regard to selection of credit risks. Loans vary from $10 to a maximum of about $600 or sometimes higher, as set by law. While the rate seems high in comparison with that of the lenders previously discussed, the risks are high because of weakly secured loans and the type of borrower. Costs of doing business are high on account of the small size of loans and the lack of any subsidy in their operations.[3]

Other Lenders · A family in financial need may take jewelry or other valuable items to a *pawnbroker* to obtain a loan on the item. The item may be redeemed by payment of the loan and interest, usually about 3 percent a month, but varying considerably. If the item is not redeemed within a specified time, the pawnbroker sells it. In some states, any profit on the item goes to the pawner (borrower). Pawning an item has a particular advantage to the family since it faces no demands for repayment of the loan or payment of interest—until it wishes to retrieve the item.

Remedial loan societies, present in some communities, have been established by public-spirited persons to aid those in distress. The rates are usually about 1 percent a month on the outstanding balance of a loan on pledged collateral.

---

[3] For further discussion of various types of consumer credit, see Wallace P. Mors, *Consumer Credit Facts for You* (Cleveland: Western Reserve University, 1959); and T. Smith and R. W. Johnson, *Operating Characteristics of Consumer Credit Institutions* (Washington, D.C.: Board of Governors of the Federal Reserve System, 1957).

Loan sharks operate outside the law, may charge extremely high rates, use unscrupulous methods of collection, and make loans to people who don't understand them or to poor risks.

Debt consolidators or pro-raters or managers should be noted at this point although they are not lenders. They have been expanding operations in recent years in those states where they are not banned. These people appeal especially to families heavily burdened by instalment debts who are being dunned by their creditors. They offer to consolidate all of the family's debts so that the family has only one payment to make—a weekly or other regular payment to the consolidator. The company then pays itself a fee and sends the remainder of the money to the family's creditors, generally pro-rating the payments on the basis of the amount owed the various creditors.

The debt consolidator's fee for its service may be 10–12 percent of the gross debt, or $120 on a total debt of $1,000. Some companies deduct their total fee from the first payments made by the family, and thereafter start pro-rating payments to the creditors. Creditors may receive payments so slowly that they continue dunning the family. If the family makes only the first scheduled payments to the consolidator, then withdraws from the plan, the family may find that very little payment has been made to its creditors.

METHODS OF REPAYING DEBT

A debt may be repaid by a single payment of interest and principal or by several payments. A loan of $1,000 for one year at 12 percent true annual interest (that is, on the declining balance) might be repaid with a single payment of $1,120 at the end of the year or by twelve equal monthly payments of $88.85.[4] At the end of each month, the interest charge is figured at 1 percent of the outstanding principal as of the beginning of the month. This is the first deduction from the total monthly payment, the remainder of which is applied to reduce the principal debt. Careful study of the amortization schedule in Table 5–2 will be fully repaid in the years ahead when equal monthly payments are made on instalment purchases, personal loans, and home mortgages. The table shows that, while the monthly payment is constant at $88.85 and the interest *rate* remains constant, the *amount* of interest declines month by month, and the amount used to reduce the principal increases regularly.

[4] For simplicity, the difference in effective annual rate of interest due to compounding is ignored in this discussion. To the consumer, the difference is not very significant.

With monthly amortization of the loan, the total interest was only $66.20 in contrast with $120 on the single-payment loan. Yet both loans were made at a 12 percent true annual rate of interest; in each case the family paid interest on the money it actually had to use. With the single-payment method, the family had the use of the total $1,000 for the whole year. With the monthly payment method, it had use of $1,000 for the first month, $921 the second month, and so on, down to $88 the twelfth month, for an average of $551.54. The amount of interest divided by the average outstanding principal would in each case equal 12 percent. Which method one chooses for repaying debt depends on his needs and willingness and ability to repay.

TABLE 5–2. Amortization Schedule for a Loan of $1,000 at 12% Annual Interest, Repaid by Twelve Monthly Instalments of $88.85

MONTH	OUTSTANDING PRINCIPAL OF LOAN AT BEGINNING OF MONTH	INTEREST DUE AT END OF MONTH	TOTAL PAYMENT AT END OF MONTH	REDUCTION OF PRINCIPAL AT END OF MONTH
1	$1,000.00	$10.00	$ 88.85	$ 78.85
2	921.15	9.21	88.85	79.64
3	841.51	8.42	88.85	80.43
4	761.08	7.61	88.85	81.24
5	679.84	6.80	88.85	82.05
6	597.79	5.98	88.85	82.87
7	514.92	5.15	88.85	83.70
8	431.22	4.31	88.85	84.54
9	346.68	3.47	88.85	85.38
10	261.30	2.62	88.85	86.23
11	175.07	1.75	88.85	87.10
12	87.97	.88	88.85	87.97
Totals	$6,618.53	$66.20	$1,066.20	$1,000.00

A contract allowing some flexibility in payments may have a great advantage. Although the family agrees to make twelve monthly payments of $88.85, at times it might be able to make an advance payment on the debt and at other times it might find it difficult to meet the regular monthly payment. As a simple illustration, assume that the family has some extra funds at the end of the first month, so pays the second month's principal payment of $79.64. A prepayment penalty of 1 percent amounts to 80¢, but $9.21 in interest is saved. The next month the interest charge is based on a debt of $841.51. On the other hand, perhaps the family cannot meet the payment at the end of the twelfth month. It pays the interest of 88¢ and makes the final payment of $88.85 at the end of the next month. The principles shown by these examples apply also in home loans where the amount involved is generally much larger.

The debt of $1,000 at 12 percent true interest rate, payable in a year, might also be discharged by several other payment methods, though they are not frequently used today. These include equal monthly payments on the principal ($83.33 in this case) plus the appropriate addition for interest (ranging from $10 the first month down to 83¢ the last month). Thus, total interest would be $65 and the average outstanding principal would be $541.66. Another method is for interest to be paid regularly (at $10 a month in this case) and the principal to be repaid at the end.

CALCULATING CHARGES FOR CREDIT

It is important that the family calculate the total credit charges and the true rate of interest for each loan to determine whether the credit is worthwhile and to compare credit charges on various loans.

The true rate of interest is the rate per period that is charged on the money which the family actually has to use, that is, the declining unpaid balance. On a cash loan, the unpaid balance is the cash received as reduced by succeeding payments on the principal. On a credit purchase, the unpaid balance equals the true cash price of the merchandise less the downpayment and any trade-in allowance, reduced further by any later payments on the principal. The true cash price may be learned from the retailer involved or from another offering similar services, with the exception of credit.

All other charges are, to the family, costs for credit. These may include specifically stated interest charges as well as service charges, credit investigation fees, and legal fees. They also include the cost of any required insurance which the family would not otherwise purchase: life and disability insurance on the borrower to insure repayment of the loan, or insurance against destruction of the collateral by fire, theft, or other means. The charge for credit also includes any increase in the price of the merchandise over its true cash price.

Methods of Stating Charges · The family's problems in calculating charges for credit are compounded by the variety of ways in which such charges are stated. The statement may be "no charge for credit", or there may be a stated dollar finance charge or finance rate or a combination of them. In each case, the real charge for credit is the difference between the true cash price and the total amount actually paid, including downpayment, trade-in allowance, and all other payments. The approximate true annual rate of interest is equal to the total credit charge divided by the average outstanding principal for a twelve-month loan. If the loan is for a longer or shorter period, divide this quotient by the actual number of months, then multiply the result by 12.

"No finance charge" might be made on the purchase of $1,500 worth of furniture with $400 down and a $1,100 note. But if a cash discount of $100 might have been obtained or if the furniture could have been purchased for $1,400 cash at a similar store, the actual credit extended was $1,000 at a cost of $100. If the loan was repaid in a lump sum at the end of a year, the true annual interest rate was 10 per cent $\left(\dfrac{100}{1,000}\right)$. If it was repaid in twelve equal monthly instalments, the principal would be reducing each month so that the average outstanding principal would approximate $500 and the true annual rate of interest would be about 20 percent $\left(\dfrac{100}{500}\right)$. If the credit was extended for ten months instead of a year, the true rate was 1 percent a month (equal to 12 percent a year) if the loan was repaid in a single sum at the end, but approximately 2 percent a month (24 percent a year) if the loan was repaid in 10 equal instalments.

A flat finance charge of $50 might be made for $1,000 of credit for one year. Repayment at the end of the year would mean a true rate of 5 percent. But repayment in 12 equal monthly instalments would mean an average outstanding principal of about $500, so that the true annual rate would approximate 10 percent.

When the credit charge is stated as a finance rate, it is usually stated in one of three ways. It may be stated as an *add-on rate*, which is frequently used in instalment sales of furniture and equipment and automobiles. For instance, on an original loan of $1,000 for one year, 12 percent is added, so that the total note is written for $1,120. If it is repaid in twelve equal monthly instalments, the true interest rate approximates 24 percent. (See Table 5–3.) If the 12 percent rate had, by chance, been added onto the original purchase price of $1,250 (neglecting the $200 downpayment and $50 trade-in allowance), the true interest rate would approximate 26 percent.

The *discount method* or "interest in advance" is used particularly on bank loans. For instance, a $1,000 note is signed for one year with 12 percent discounted. The borrower, therefore, receives $880 in cash. If the loan is repaid in a single payment at the end of the year, the true interest rate is 14 percent. If the borrower makes 12 equal monthly payments, the monthly reduction in the principal raises the approximate true interest rate to 27 percent.

Interest on the *declining balance* is the method of stating charges used by personal loan companies and credit unions, as well as by home mortgage lenders. A $1,000 loan for one year at 12 percent would be repaid by 12 monthly payments of $88.85, for a true rate of 12 percent, as shown by the amortization schedule in the foregoing section.

A comparison of the various methods indicates that a stated finance charge of 12 percent a year amounts to a true annual interest rate approximating 12 percent to 27 percent, depending on the base on which the charge is made and whether the loan is discharged by

TABLE 5–3. Comparison of Estimated True Interest Rate on a "$1,000 Loan" With a Stated 12 Percent Finance Charge for One Year, Under Different Methods of Calculating Charges and Repaying the Loan

ITEM	LOAN OR CREDIT ACTUALLY RECEIVED	MONTHLY INSTAL-MENT	TOTAL FINANCE CHARGE	AVERAGE UNPAID DEBT [*]	TRUE ANNUAL INTEREST RATE [*]
Add-on method:					
To original loan of $1,000—					
Single payment at end ...	$1,000	...	$120	$1,000	12%
12 monthly instalments ..	1,000	$93.33	120	500	24%
To cash price of $1,250—					
Single payment at end ...	1,000	...	130	1,000	13%
12 monthly instalments ..	1,000	94.17	130	500	26%
Discount method:					
Single payment at end	880	...	120	880	14%
12 monthly instalments	880	83.33	120	440	27%
Declining balance method:					
Single payment at end	1,000	...	120	1,000	12%
12 monthly instalments	1,000	88.85	66	552	12%

[*] Approximate.

a single payment or equal monthly payments. The consumer tends to ignore the difference in rate for $1,000 actually borrowed because the monthly instalment by the add-on method is only $4.48 more than under the declining balance method. However, the year's difference of $54 would pay for an automatic record player and is sufficient to double the true interest rate.

Calculating True Interest Rate · Previously in this discussion, a rough method of approximating the true annual interest rate has been employed for simplicity, although mathematical formulae using the actuarial, direct ratio, or constant ratio method are available for exact or nearly-exact calculation of the true interest rate. However, when it is readily available, the table provided by the Household Finance Corporation for calculating true interest rates on loans and instalment purchases payable in equal instalments is generally the most useful to families with limited skill in computation (Table 5–4). The method of calculation is as follows:

(1) **Find the Financing Cost in Dollars and Cents.**
In the case of a *loan*, total all payments to be made and subtract the amount of cash obtained from the lender. The difference is the *Financing Cost.*
In the case of an *instalment purchase*, total all payments including the down payment, and subtract the price at which you could buy for cash. The difference is the *Financing Cost.*

(2) **Determine the Total Amount to be Paid in Instalments.**
Total all instalment payments. Do not include the down payment.

(3) **Figure the Cost Ratio.**
Divide the *Financing Cost* by the *Total Amount Paid in Instalments.*

(4) **Use the Table to Find the True Interest Rate.**
When the *Cost Ratio* comes out exactly in hundredths (such as .080 or .110), locate the column headed with this figure. Follow down this column to the line for the number of payments in the contract. The figure at the intersection is the *true interest rate per instalment period* (week, month, or other).
When the *Cost Ratio* does not come out exactly in hundredths, an approximate answer can be obtained by rounding off to the nearest hundredth (second decimal place), and then using the table as explained above. For greater accuracy, see the note in the last column.

(5) **Annual Interest Rates.**
When the contracts to be compared have different instalment intervals, the true interest rates must be converted to apply to the same interval. Annual rates are commonly used for this purpose.
To convert to an *annual interest rate*, multiply the *true rate per instalment period* by the *number of instalment periods in a year* (12, if months; 52, if weeks, etc.). This method ignores compounding, which is consistent with the general practice of converting annual rates to monthly or other fractional year rates by taking a simple arithmetic fraction of the annual rate.

NOTE — *In case the Cost Ratio does not come out exactly in hundredths,* the *true interest rate* may be determined more accurately by interpolation.
For example, if the *Cost Ratio* is .0741 for 12 monthly instalments, the *true rate* is equal to the rate for .07, plus .41 times the difference between the rates for .07 and .08, as follows:
(1) Rate for .08 *Cost Ratio* (from Table) 1.31%
(2) Rate for .07 *Cost Ratio* (from Table) 1.13%

Difference 18%
(3) .41 × .18% = .07%
(4) 1.13% + .07% = 1.20% (*the true interest rate per month*)

TABLE 5–4. True Interest Rates Corresponding to Various Cost Ratios and Numbers of Instalments (The figures in the body of this table are true interest rates in percent, per instalment period)

Number of Equal Instalment Payments	COST RATIO													
	.02	.03	.04	.05	.06	.07	.08	.09	.10	.11	.12	.13	.14	.15
1	2.04	3.09	4.17	5.26	6.38	7.53	8.70	9.89	11.11	12.36	13.64	14.94	16.28	17.65
2	1.36	2.06	2.76	3.49	4.23	4.98	5.74	6.52	7.32	8.13	8.96	9.81	10.67	11.55
3	1.02	1.54	2.07	2.61	3.16	3.72	4.29	4.87	5.46	6.06	6.67	7.30	7.94	8.59
4	0.81	1.23	1.65	2.08	2.52	2.97	3.42	3.88	4.35	4.83	5.32	5.81	6.32	6.83
5	0.68	1.02	1.38	1.73	2.10	2.47	2.85	3.23	3.62	4.01	4.42	4.83	5.25	5.67
6	0.58	0.88	1.18	1.49	1.80	2.11	2.44	2.76	3.10	3.43	3.78	4.13	4.49	4.85
7	0.51	0.77	1.03	1.30	1.57	1.85	2.13	2.42	2.71	3.00	3.30	3.61	3.92	4.24
8	0.45	0.68	0.92	1.15	1.40	1.64	1.89	2.14	2.40	2.66	2.93	3.20	3.48	3.76
9	0.41	0.61	0.82	1.04	1.26	1.48	1.70	1.93	2.16	2.40	2.64	2.88	3.13	3.38
10	0.37	0.56	0.75	0.94	1.14	1.34	1.55	1.75	1.96	2.18	2.39	2.62	2.84	3.07
11	0.34	0.51	0.69	0.86	1.05	1.23	1.42	1.61	1.80	1.99	2.19	2.40	2.60	2.81
12	0.31	0.47	0.63	0.80	0.97	1.13	1.31	1.48	1.66	1.84	2.02	2.21	2.40	2.59
13	0.29	0.44	0.59	0.74	0.90	1.05	1.21	1.38	1.54	1.71	1.88	2.05	2.23	2.41
14	0.27	0.41	0.55	0.69	0.84	0.98	1.13	1.28	1.44	1.59	1.75	1.91	2.08	2.25
15	0.25	0.38	0.51	0.65	0.78	0.92	1.06	1.20	1.35	1.49	1.64	1.79	1.95	2.10
16	0.24	0.36	0.48	0.61	0.74	0.87	1.00	1.13	1.27	1.41	1.55	1.69	1.83	1.98
17	0.23	0.34	0.46	0.58	0.70	0.82	0.94	1.07	1.20	1.33	1.46	1.59	1.73	1.87
18	0.21	0.32	0.43	0.55	0.66	0.78	0.89	1.01	1.13	1.26	1.38	1.51	1.64	1.77
19	0.20	0.31	0.41	0.52	0.63	0.74	0.85	0.96	1.08	1.19	1.31	1.43	1.56	1.68
20	0.19	0.29	0.39	0.49	0.60	0.70	0.81	0.92	1.03	1.14	1.25	1.36	1.48	1.60
21	0.18	0.28	0.37	0.47	0.57	0.67	0.77	0.87	0.98	1.08	1.19	1.30	1.41	1.53
22	0.18	0.27	0.36	0.45	0.54	0.64	0.74	0.84	0.94	1.04	1.14	1.25	1.35	1.46
23	0.17	0.26	0.34	0.43	0.52	0.61	0.71	0.80	0.90	0.99	1.09	1.19	1.30	1.40
24	0.16	0.25	0.33	0.41	0.50	0.59	0.68	0.77	0.86	0.95	1.05	1.15	1.24	1.34
26	0.15	0.23	0.30	0.38	0.46	0.55	0.63	0.71	0.80	0.88	0.97	1.06	1.15	1.24
30	0.13	0.20	0.27	0.33	0.40	0.47	0.55	0.62	0.69	0.77	0.85	0.92	1.00	1.08
36	0.11	0.17	0.22	0.28	0.34	0.40	0.46	0.52	0.58	0.64	0.71	0.77	0.84	0.91
42	0.09	0.14	0.19	0.24	0.29	0.34	0.39	0.45	0.50	0.55	0.61	0.66	0.72	0.78
48	0.08	0.13	0.17	0.21	0.26	0.30	0.35	0.39	0.44	0.49	0.53	0.58	0.63	0.68
52	0.08	0.12	0.16	0.20	0.24	0.28	0.32	0.36	0.41	0.45	0.49	0.54	0.59	0.63
54	0.07	0.11	0.15	0.19	0.23	0.27	0.31	0.35	0.39	0.43	0.48	0.52	0.56	0.61
60	0.07	0.10	0.14	0.17	0.21	0.24	0.28	0.31	0.35	0.39	0.43	0.47	0.51	0.55

TABLE 5–4. True Interest Rates Corresponding to Various Cost Ratios and Numbers of Instalments (The figures in the body of this table are true interest rates in percent, per instalment period) (cont.)

Number of Equal Instalment Payments	COST RATIO												
	.16	.17	.18	.19	.20	.21	.22	.23	.24	.25	.30	.35	.40
1	19.05	20.48											
2	12.45	13.38	14.32	15.28	16.26	17.26	18.29	19.34	20.42				
3	9.25	9.93	10.62	11.32	12.04	12.78	13.53	14.30	15.09	15.89	20.20		
4	7.36	7.89	8.44	9.00	9.56	10.14	10.74	11.34	11.96	12.59	15.97	19.77	24.10
5	6.11	6.55	7.00	7.46	7.93	8.41	8.90	9.40	9.91	10.42	13.20	16.32	19.86
6	5.22	5.60	5.98	6.37	6.77	7.18	7.60	8.02	8.45	8.90	11.25	13.89	16.89
7	4.56	4.89	5.22	5.56	5.91	6.27	6.63	7.00	7.38	7.76	9.81	12.10	14.69
8	4.05	4.34	4.63	4.94	5.24	5.56	5.88	6.21	6.54	6.88	8.69	10.71	12.99
9	3.64	3.90	4.16	4.44	4.71	4.99	5.28	5.57	5.87	6.18	7.80	9.61	11.65
10	3.30	3.54	3.78	4.03	4.28	4.53	4.79	5.06	5.33	5.61	7.08	8.71	10.56
11	3.02	3.24	3.46	3.69	3.92	4.15	4.39	4.63	4.88	5.13	6.47	7.97	9.66
12	2.79	2.99	3.19	3.40	3.61	3.83	4.05	4.27	4.50	4.73	5.96	7.34	8.89
13	2.59	2.77	2.96	3.16	3.35	3.55	3.75	3.96	4.17	4.39	5.53	6.81	8.24
14	2.42	2.59	2.76	2.94	3.13	3.31	3.50	3.69	3.89	4.09	5.16	6.35	7.68
15	2.26	2.43	2.59	2.76	2.93	3.10	3.28	3.46	3.64	3.83	4.83	5.94	7.19
16	2.13	2.28	2.44	2.59	2.75	2.92	3.08	3.25	3.43	3.60	4.54	5.59	6.76
17	2.01	2.15	2.30	2.45	2.60	2.75	2.91	3.07	3.24	3.40	4.29	5.27	6.38
18	1.90	2.04	2.18	2.32	2.46	2.61	2.76	2.91	3.06	3.22	4.06	4.99	6.03
19	1.81	1.94	2.07	2.20	2.34	2.48	2.62	2.76	2.91	3.06	3.85	4.74	5.73
20	1.72	1.84	1.97	2.10	2.23	2.36	2.49	2.63	2.77	2.91	3.67	4.51	5.45
21	1.64	1.76	1.88	2.00	2.12	2.25	2.38	2.51	2.64	2.78	3.50	4.30	5.20
22	1.57	1.68	1.80	1.91	2.03	2.15	2.27	2.40	2.53	2.66	3.34	4.11	4.97
23	1.50	1.61	1.72	1.83	1.95	2.06	2.18	2.30	2.42	2.54	3.20	3.94	4.76
24	1.44	1.55	1.65	1.76	1.87	1.98	2.09	2.21	2.32	2.44	3.07	3.78	4.57
26	1.34	1.43	1.53	1.63	1.73	1.83	1.94	2.04	2.15	2.26	2.85	3.49	4.22
30	1.16	1.25	1.33	1.42	1.50	1.59	1.68	1.78	1.87	1.97	2.48	3.04	3.67
36	0.97	1.04	1.11	1.19	1.26	1.33	1.41	1.49	1.57	1.65	2.07	2.54	3.07
42	0.84	0.90	0.96	1.02	1.08	1.15	1.21	1.28	1.35	1.42	1.78	2.19	2.64
48	0.74	0.79	0.84	0.90	0.95	1.01	1.06	1.12	1.18	1.24	1.56	1.92	2.31
52	0.68	0.73	0.78	0.83	0.88	0.93	0.98	1.04	1.09	1.15	1.44	1.77	2.14
54	0.66	0.70	0.75	0.80	0.85	0.90	0.95	1.00	1.05	1.11	1.39	1.71	2.06
60	0.59	0.63	0.68	0.72	0.76	0.81	0.85	0.90	0.95	1.00	1.25	1.54	1.86

SOURCE: The above reprinted with permission of Household Finance Corporation from their 1957 publication, "Consumer Credit Cost Calculator."

Let us take several examples to illustrate use of the method. Mr. Jones purchased a watch for $105, at $5 down and $10 a week for 10 weeks. But a $5 discount could have been obtained for cash.

(1) Financing cost was $5 (total payments of $105 less $100 cash price).

(2) Total amount paid in instalments was $100 ($10 for 10 weeks).

(3) Cost ratio was 0.05 $\left(\dfrac{5}{100}\right)$.

(4) True interest rate was 0.94 percent a week, or 49 percent a year.

Miss Bailey signed a $500 note at her bank at a discount rate of 8 percent, the note to be repaid in 12 monthly instalments of $41.67.

(1) Financing cost was $40.

(2) Total amount paid in instalments was $500.

(3) Cost ratio was 0.08.

(4) True interest rate was 1.31 percent a month, or 16 percent a year.

Alternative Method · A simplified method of finding the approximate true annual interest rate, developed by C. M. Jaeger, is as follows: [5]

(1) Ascertain the total credit charge.

(2) Multiply the credit charge by the appropriate factor below for the number of monthly or weekly instalments:

MONTHLY PAYMENTS		WEEKLY PAYMENTS	
NUMBER OF PAYMENTS	FACTOR	NUMBER OF PAYMENTS	FACTOR
6	343	12	800
9	240	16	612
12	185	20	495
15	150	24	416
18	126	28	359
21	109	32	315
24	96	36	281
30	77	40	254
36	65	44	231
42	56	48	212
48	49	52	196
54	44	78	132
60	39	104	99

[5] Emma G. Holmes and Carol M. Jaeger, "A Simplified Method of Finding the Annual Interest Rate on Installment Credit," *Family Economics Review*, U. S. Department of Agriculture, September 1966, pp. 15–17.

(3) Divide the result by the cash loan or the credit received. For example, Mrs. Wulff bought a refrigerator priced at $310 cash with a downpayment of $10 and agreed to pay $14.50 a month for 24 months. Thus the credit charge was $48 (14.50 times 24, minus 300). The factor for 24 monthly payments is 96. The credit received is $300. The calculation, then, is as follows:

$$\frac{\text{Credit charge times factor}}{\text{Credit received}} = \frac{48\ (96)}{300} = \frac{4,608}{300} = 15.36\%$$

LAWS ON CONSUMER CREDIT

Two major types of regulation of consumer credit are used. The first requires lenders to disclose pertinent facts about the credit contract on the assumption that consumers can then judge for themselves and compare costs. As we have seen, however, consumers have difficulty in making comparisons because of the great variety in amount and length of credit extended and ways of stating charges.

The second type of regulation sets maximum limits on the amount of the loan and the charges that may be made. The effect of legal limits on credit charges is to set limits on the type of loan that the legal lender can make in terms of its risk and ordinary costs. If the limit is set "too low" in relation to what the consumer borrower is willing to pay, the more risky or costly loan cannot be obtained from a legal lender, and the family is driven to illegal lenders.

Protection of the consumer's interests, without harming reputable dealers and lenders, requires a written contract including the following features: a precise statement of the amount of credit extended; the use of one all-inclusive charge for credit rather than a variety of fees and charges; the rate stated in a uniform way on all contracts, for instance, on the declining balance; the exact amount and number of instalments; any delinquency or refinancing charges that may be made and their timing; provision for savings by early repayment; and provision of a fair method of settlement in the case of repossession and resale of pledged collateral. (See Table 5–5.)

TABLE 5–5. A Good Credit Contract

Service stated
   Amount of credit advanced
     Money received *or*
     Cash price less the downpayment and trade-in allowance.
   Length of loan.

Cost stated
Repayment schedule with exact amount due each period.
Charge for credit including any additional fees
In dollars *and*
In true annual rate.

Results of default stated
Delinquency charges.
Collateral pledged (chattel mortgage, wage assignment, etc.).
Notice to be given before repossession of chattels.
Any repossession charges.
Possibility of a deficiency judgment.
Any rebate if excess over debt received at sale of chattels.

Results of early repayment stated
Any interest saved by early repayment or a large principal payment.
Any special fee charged.

Form of contract
Written contract covering above items.
No blank spaces.
With licensed lender or reputable dealer.
Consumer reads before signing.

Laws on Retail Purchases · About sixteen states have some type of law regulating instalment sales, but in half of these the law applies only to auto purchases. For instance, the Maryland Motor Vehicle Sales Finance Act permits a maximum charge on the "principal balance owed" of 9 percent a year on new cars, 12 percent a year on models up to two years old, and 15 percent a year on models over two years old. The "principal balance owed" is defined as the cash price less down payment, plus delivery costs, installation charges, insurance costs, and official fees. The Pennsylvania Motor Vehicle Sales Finance Act allows a maximum interest charge on the "principal amount financed" (defined as the total of the unpaid cash price plus insurance premium) of 6 percent a year on new cars, 9 percent a year on models up to two years old, and 12 percent a year on models over two years old. The auto finance laws of other states are roughly similar.

The trade practice rules of the Federal Trade Commission dealing with instalment sales of automobiles require written disclosure of the cash price, trade-in allowance and down payment, insurance costs and coverage, official fees, total unpaid balance to be financed, finance charge, and the amount and number of instalments to be paid.[6] Attempts have been made to require disclosure of terms on other instalment purchases.

[6] Federal Trade Commission, *Trade Practice Rules Relating to the Instalment Sale and Financing of Motor Vehicles*, 1951.

Some states have laws that apply to all types of instalment purchases. Ohio permits a base finance charge of 50¢ for each $50 per month plus a base service charge of 50¢ for each of the first four $50 units of unpaid balance and 25¢ per month for each of the next four $50 units. The family needs to learn all aspects of its state laws dealing with credit purchases of merchandise.

Small Loan Laws · Thirty-nine states have small loan laws that are classified as operative and three have no laws.[7] For example, the Maryland law states that a licensed lender may lend up to $300 at a maximum rate of 3 percent a month on the unpaid balance. Interest is not payable in advance or compounded. No additional charges are valid. The loan may be repaid prior to its maturity with interest on the payment to that date. Loans up to a face amount of $1,500 are covered under a related law which permits a 6 percent discount charge plus fees on a specific schedule up to $30 on a face amount of $1,500.

The more complicated Pennsylvania law provides that a licensed lender may lend an individual $600 or less at a maximum rate per month of 3 percent on the unpaid principal of not over $150, 2 percent on the unpaid principal of $150 to $300, and 1 percent on the unpaid principal over $300. The loan cannot be made for more than 24 months and interest on the unpaid balance after 24 months shall be payable at no more than 6 percent a year. The interest is not payable in advance or compounded. Extra fees are prohibited. Loans up to $2,000 may be made at a maximum rate of 6 percent plus stated fees.

Suppose that a family borrowed $600 and the maximum rates were charged under the Pennsylvania type of law. At the end of the first month, during which the family had use of the full $600, the interest charge would total $10.50, calculated as follows:

3 percent on first $150 = $4.50
2 percent of next $150 = 3.00
1 percent of next $300 = 3.00

When the loan has been reduced to $200, the interest charge for the month would total $5.50.

    [7] Wallace P. Mors, *Small Loan Laws* (Cleveland: Western Reserve University, 1958), pp. 7–10.

Other Loan Laws · Nearly all states have usury laws with maximum loan rates to consumers at 6 percent to 12 percent a year. Maryland's usury law sets a maximum rate of 6 percent and only under special laws can higher rates be charged. Banks generally interpret usury rates as discount rates. Merchants consider that usury laws do not apply to credit selling.

Credit unions are usually prohibited from charging more than 1 percent a month on the declining balance under federal or state law, as in Maryland.

Home repair and modernization loans under Title I of the National Housing Act have a maximum loan amount of $3,500 and a maximum term of 60 months. The lender is allowed to charge a discount of not more than $5 per $100 per year on the first $2,500 of the loan and $4 per $100 per year on the amount above $2,500. The maximum true interest rate thus approximates 9–10 percent.

QUESTIONS

1. How does the use of consumer credit affect the family's current financial resources?
2. Contrast consumer credit with producer credit.
3. How important is the use of consumer credit today? How does its use vary among families?
4. How does credit extension and repayment differ in prosperous and depressed periods? Why? What may be the effect on the individual family? How does the extension of credit serve the economy?
5. What advantages does consumer credit have for lenders and merchants?
6. What advantages does consumer credit have for consumers?
7. What does the family need to consider in deciding whether to use credit and how much?
8. Explain each of the two basic aspects of buying credit service: the service to be received and its costs.
9. How can the family cut its costs for credit?
10. Why are charges made for the use of consumer credit? Why do charges vary from one loan to another?
11. Discuss the various types of consumer credit as to type of loans, type of borrower, usual true interest rate, method of stating charges, anv special contracts and clauses.
12. Describe an amortization schedule showing interest payments on the declining balance.
13. What are various methods of stating the charge for credit?
14. How can the rate of charge be approximated?

15. What is the meaning of "true interest rate"?

16. Why is it important to calculate the true interest rate on various types of credit?

17. Verify the rough approximations to the true interest rate for each example given in the text. Then use the table to calculate the true annual rate of interest for each.

18. What are the important types of laws on consumer credit?

19. What requirements (legal or voluntary) are necessary for the protection of consumers?

20. Obtain the latest information on consumer credit laws in your state and evaluate them from the family's point of view. Are any attempts currently being made to revise these laws?

21. Obtain materials on loan schedules from your local lending institutions and calculate the charges in dollars and in true annual rate of interest.

22. Obtain an example of a finance charge for instalment credit on the purchase of an auto, furniture, or similar item. Calculate the charges.

SUGGESTIONS FOR FURTHER READING

Board of Governors of the Federal Reserve System. *Federal Reserve Bulletin,* latest issues.

————. *Survey of Financial Characteristics of Consumers,* report of latest Survey.

Botts, Ralph R. *Farmers' Handbook of Financial Calculations and Physical Measurements.* U. S. Dept. of Agriculture, Agric. Handbook No. 230. Washington, D.C.: Superintendent of Documents, 1964.

U. S. Department of Agriculture. *What Young Farm Families Should Know About Credit.* Farmers' Bulletin No. 2135. Washington, D.C.: Superintendent of Documents, latest edition.

Income Taxes / 6

- INCOME TAXES AND
  GOVERNMENT FINANCE
- NATURE OF INCOME TAXES
- MAJOR REGULATIONS

The subject of income taxes is a painful one to many people since these taxes frequently constitute a sizable sum that directly affects the family budget. If a sufficient amount of taxes will not be automatically withheld by the employer during the year, money must be accumulated for additional payments at the end of each quarter and at tax filing time or other means found for paying the extra taxes. The number of ads for tax loans in early spring indicates that lenders expect many families to be looking for other means. Sales taxes and many other taxes are automatically included as we buy goods and services, so that we have less opportunity to get far in debt on those taxes.

Since income after taxes is decidedly smaller than before taxes for many families, the family bases its plans for personal uses of income on the net amount after taxes. When we look at data on family incomes, we want to know whether income taxes have been deducted. When we are considering jobs, we may compare not only the employment conditions and gross pay, but also the net return after taxes. This is particularly true when it is a second job for the earner or a paid job for the wife, as we noted earlier.

An understanding of our income tax system aids the family in filling out the tax forms or providing the necessary data for a specialist to do the chore. Prior knowledge of various provisions indicates subjects on which we should keep records and cancelled checks in order to cut our taxes and justify our statements. Young people today need to start with a considerable amount of information on income taxes that older generations accumulated gradually as these taxes came to have an increasingly important effect on family budgets.

INCOME TAXES AND GOVERNMENT FINANCE

Most families have to pay income taxes and will probably continue to do so throughout their lives since the federal government is largely dependent upon this tax for its funds. About five-tenths of the government's net budget receipts (excluding trust fund receipts) comes from individual income taxes. Another three-tenths comes from corporation income taxes; and the remaining two-tenths is provided by excise taxes, estate and gift taxes, customs, and miscellaneous items. (See Figure 6–1.) The data for recent fiscal years, ending June 30 of the year, are as follows: [1]

	BILLIONS OF DOLLARS		
	1966	1967*	1968*
Net budget receipts	105	117	127
Individual income taxes	55	62	73
Corporation income taxes	30	34	34
Excise taxes	9	9	9
Estate and gift taxes	3	3	3
Customs	2	2	2
Miscellaneous receipts (less interfund transactions)	5	6	6

* Estimated.

Individual income taxes were not always an important source of federal revenue. In colonial times, customs duties were the major source and continued to be most important as late as 1913. Even in 1940, individual income taxes provided only a fifth of federal funds. At the peak of the war period, these taxes came to provide more than two-fifths. From 1957 on, they provided half or more of federal funds.

We might look briefly at the government's budget to see why it needs to spend so much money—about $500 for each person in the country, exclusive of trust fund expenditures. The first and biggest slice of more than half goes for national defense. Add the expenditures for interest on the public debt, most of which was created by national defense programs of the past, and for veterans benefits and

[1] Treasury Department and Bureau of the Budget.

FIGURE 6–1. Federal Administrative Budget Receipts and Expenditures

SOURCES OF
INCOME DOLLAR

USES OF
EXPENDITURE DOLLAR

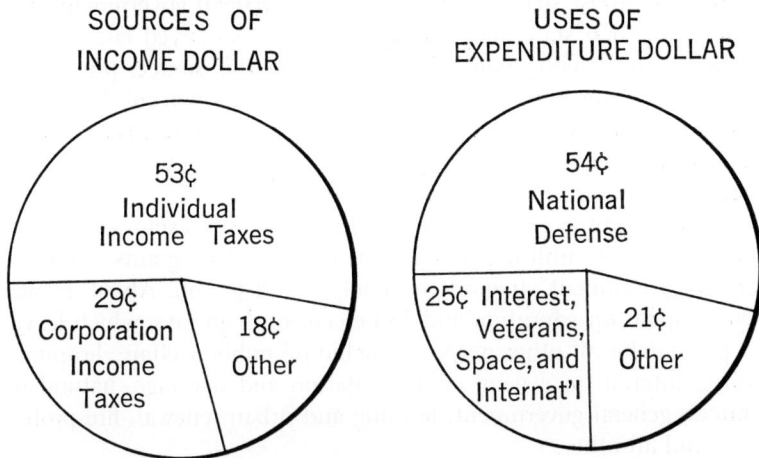

SOURCES: Treasury Department and Bureau of the Budget, fiscal year 1966.

services, and the total becomes seven-tenths. If the costs of space research and technology and of international affairs and finance are included, the proportion rises to eight-tenths related to defense—past, present, and future. Not many of us have the courage or knowledge to suggest cuts in these items.

This leaves a grand total of two-tenths for expenditures on health, labor, and welfare; agriculture and agricultural resources; natural resources; commerce and transportation; education; general government; and housing and community development—in declining order. These also are proper purposes and some may need expansion. In total, we probably cannot expect much decrease in federal expenditures in the foreseeable future. This is not to condone wasteful use of money in any part of the government budget, any more than in the family budget.

Federal expenditures for recent fiscal years may be summarized as follows:

| | BILLIONS OF DOLLARS | | |
	1966	1967*	1968*
Budget expenditures	107	127	135
National defense	58	70	75
Interest, veterans benefits and services, space research and technology, and international affairs and finance ..	27	30	30
All other	22	26	29

* Estimated.

The sources of revenue and types of expenditures of states and localities contrast sharply with those of the federal government. Tax revenue of total state and local governments is derived largely from property taxes, with about 45 percent from this source, plus about 33 percent from sales and gross receipts taxes, 8 percent from individual income taxes, and 14 percent from all other taxes. Half of such tax revenue accrues to state governments and half to local governments (counties, municipalities, and townships).

Expenditures of state and local governments, exclusive of those for trust funds, utilities, and liquor stores and of grants from the federal government, amount to about $300 a person. About 42 percent is spent on education and 13 percent on highways, which leaves 45 percent for all other purposes, including public welfare, hospitals, police, interest on general debt, sanitation and sewerage, natural resources, general government, housing and urban renewal, fire protection, and all other.[2]

NATURE OF INCOME TAXES

As we have noted, some states also employ individual income taxes. State tax rates are much lower than federal (often a constant percentage or slightly rising), and some have regulations that correspond to federal regulations. Study of the income tax of one's own state and its relation to the federal tax is necessary for every taxpayer. For general usefulness, the present discussion is limited to the federal income tax.

Although individual income taxes were first collected in 1863 under legislation that expired in 1871, few families had sufficient incomes to be affected. The income tax was revived by 1913, but again affected few people because of the low level of family income and the relatively high exemptions provided by the law—$2,000 net income for a married couple as late as 1940. With the advent of World War II, however, exemptions were cut drastically and money incomes rose so that most single adults and families became liable for payments. Currently, more than 60 million returns are filed each year. At the same time, tax rates increased precipitously. For example, a married couple with two dependents and a net income of $5,000 had small income tax liability until 1941 when it increased to $271. It rose to $755 in 1944 and 1945, then dropped to $520 in the period 1954–60 and $286 in 1966.

---

[2] U. S. Bureau of the Census, *Governmental Finances in 1964–65.*

While the federal income tax is used primarily to finance the government, particularly at times of heavy defense expenditures, it is also used for other purposes. One is to curb inflation by skimming off some of the excess buying power of consumers at a time when industrial capacity and manpower are already fully utilized. At the same time, the taxes are supposed to encourage economic growth and to be efficient to collect.

Another purpose of the income tax is to redistribute income. This is done by taking an increased proportion of increased income, which means that the tax places the greatest liability on those presumed to be most able to pay. The income tax is therefore classified as a *graduated tax* or progressive tax. For example, a couple taking standard deductions currently pays a tax of almost $500 on earnings of about $5,000, or almost $16,000 on earnings of $50,000. Because of the presumed differences in their financial condition, a single person pays more and a larger family pays less at each income level, as the following comparison shows:

INCOME, 1966	SINGLE PERSON	COUPLE	COUPLE WITH 3 CHILDREN
$4,999	$ 667	$ 497	$ 181
$7,000	1,064	829	501
$10,000	1,742	1,342	1,000
$50,000	21,630	15,960	15,060

MAJOR REGULATIONS

It is necessary that each family and single adult understand the income tax law in regard to filing a tax return, reporting income, claiming exemptions and deductions, and calculating the tax. The following discussion provides basic information for those with limited experience in filing tax returns. For detailed information on current income tax regulations, see the following official publications:

Internal Revenue Service, *Federal Income Tax Forms*, latest edition, Washington, D.C.: U. S. Treasury Department. Includes tax returns and instructions which are mailed to taxpayers and are available free at your local post office, bank, and Internal Revenue Service office.

Internal Revenue Service, *Your Federal Income Tax*, latest edition, Washington, D.C.: Superintendent of Documents. Provides detailed instructions for preparing tax returns. Currently costs 50¢ a copy.

For additional assistance, see:

> Your local representative of the IRS.
> An independent tax expert, particularly if you have unusually complicated problems.
> The latest edition of *Your Income Tax* by the J. K. Lasser Tax Institute.

Filing a Tax Return · A tax return must be filed by April 15, that is, mailed to the District Director of Internal Revenue, in order to determine whether additional payments or refunds are due. Any additional payment must be included with the return. Penalties are enforced for failure to file a return on time and for underpayment of taxes.

A return must be filed by every citizen or resident of the United States who had, in the previous year, a gross income of $600 or more or, for those 65 years old or over, of $1,200 or more. Anyone with a lower income from which income taxes had been withheld should file a return in order to obtain a refund of the tax.

In recent years, a standard tax form which anyone is eligible to use has been supplemented by a simple, brief form which may be used when income does not exceed a specified amount and when certain other conditions are met. The individual needs to study the specific rules and determine which form is advisable in his own situation.

A married couple has a choice of filing a *joint return* or *separate returns*. The "split-income" feature which the law provides on a joint return often results in a lower total tax than would the sum of separate returns. The advantage is obvious when the husband is the sole earner but is less so when the husband and wife earn about the same amount. Assume, for simplicity, that a husband and wife had a total income of $4,999, no additional exemptions, and used the current tax table. A joint return would mean a tax of $497. If each received $2,499.50, their tax on two separate returns would total $498. But if the husband received $4,999 and the wife received nothing, their tax would be $553 if they filed separate returns.

A joint return may be filed by a couple married by the end of the tax year or by a widowed person whose spouse has died during the year. A joint return must include all income, exemptions, and deductions of both spouses; and each assumes full legal responsibility for the entire tax. A separate return includes only the income received and allowable deductions paid by that spouse out of his or her income. If one spouse itemizes deductions, the other must also; and each spouse claims personal exemptions for himself, if each has some income.

In order that the taxpayer be current in payment of his income tax, he must file a *Declaration of Estimated Income Tax* for the current calendar year and make quarterly payments during the current year, under certain conditions. These are when his total expected tax exceeds his withholding tax by $40 or more and when expected income exceeds $10,000 for a married couple entitled to file a joint return and for other household heads, or $5,000 for other persons.

Reporting Income · All income, except that specifically excluded by law, must be reported on the tax return. The taxpayer benefits by studying the detailed rules for reporting each income item each year that he receives a given type of income. Following are examples of income that must be reported:

> Wages, salaries, bonuses, commissions, fees, tips, gratuities.
> Dividends.
> Interest on tax refunds, bank deposits, bonds, notes, U. S. Savings bonds.
> Profits from business or profession or partnership.
> Profits from sales or exchanges of real estate, securities, or other property.
> Industrial, civil service, and other pensions, annuities, endowments.
> Rents and royalties from property, patents, copyrights.
> Your share of estate or trust income.
> Employer supplemental unemployment benefits.
> Alimony, separate maintenance or support payments.
> Prizes and awards.

The types of income that should not be included on the tax return include the following:

> Disability retirement payments and other benefits paid by the Veterans Administration.
> Dividends on veterans' insurance.
> Life insurance proceeds upon death.
> Workmen's compensation, insurance, damages, etc., for injury or sickness.
> Interest on state and municipal bonds.
> Federal Social Security benefits.
> Railroad Retirement Act benefits.
> Gifts, inheritances, bequests.

Claiming Exemptions · Each legal exemption on the income tax return reduces taxable income by $600 at present. How much it reduces the tax liability depends on the rate at which an individual's income is taxed. For instance, a married couple would save about 19 percent of $600, or $114, on each exemption if it had a joint income of about $4,000–$8,000 after deductions; or $192 at an income of about $20,000–$24,000; or up to $420 at an income over $200,000.

All family exemptions are included on a joint return or separated on separate returns. The exemptions are as follows:

> For the *taxpayer* personally (maximum of three exemptions)—
> One (the minimum)
> One additional, if he was blind
> One additional, if he was 65 years old or over
> For the *wife* of taxpayer (maximum of three exemptions)—
> One, personal
> One additional, if she was blind
> One additional, if she was 65 or over
> One for *each child* of the taxpayer (own child, stepchild, or adopted child) if the child—
> (1) Received less than $600 income, AND
> (This limitation does not apply if the child was under 19 or was a student. Under these circumstances, if the child had a taxable income, he would file a return and claim his exemption also.)
> (2) Received more than half of his support from the tax-taxpayer, AND
> (3) Did not file a joint return with his spouse, AND
> (4) Was a citizen or resident of the United States or a resident of Canada, Mexico, the Republic of Panama, or the Canal Zone.
> One for *each additional person* who had the taxpayer's home as his principal place of abode and was a member of his household for the entire tax year, if that person met the same income, support, tax filing, and residence requirements stated above.
> One for *each person related* in stated ways to the taxpayer or his wife (on a joint return) if that person met the income, support, tax filing, and residence requirements as previously stated even though he does not live in the taxpayer's home. The person might be related as child, parent, grandparent, brother, sister, grandchild, or in certain other specified ways.

A full $600 exemption can be claimed for each dependent who was born or died during the tax year, if the tests for claiming an exemption for him were met during the part of the year that he was alive. If the taxpayer's spouse died during the year, the number of his exemptions is determined as of the date of his death. If more than one taxpayer contributed to the support of a person, the contributors may sign a Multiple Support Declaration designating one person to claim the exemption.

The taxpayer's contribution to the support of a dependent includes the expense incurred for food, shelter, clothing, medical and dental care, education, and like items, the fair market value for shelter provided, as well as cash contributions. The dependent's support from other sources includes his money receipts (including nontaxable items), the value of additional items purchased from his own funds, and the value of other goods and services received without money payment. Scholarships received by a student may be omitted from the calculation of his support from other sources.

Claiming Deductions · Each legal deduction reduces taxable income by that amount. How much it reduces the tax depends on the individual's tax rate. The taxpayer has the option of taking the "standard deduction," presently defined as 10 percent of income or based on the number of exemptions but in no case to exceed $1,000, or of itemizing his deductions. In general, if legal deductions exceed the standard deduction, it is worthwhile to itemize them. A record, and cancelled checks kept during the year, aid in making the decision and in supporting claims. Detailed rules on claiming deductions should be studied annually to refresh the memory and to note any changes. The major types of legal deductions, subject to specific limitations, are as follows:

> Medical and dental expenses (not compensated by hospital, health, or accident insurance) for—
> Physicians, dentists, nurses, and other professional practitioners
> Drugs or medicines
> Hospitals
> Transportation necessary to get medical care
> Eyeglasses, artificial teeth, medical or surgical appliances, braces, etc.
> X-ray examinations or treatment
> Premiums on hospital or medical insurance

Contributions to nonprofit organizations such as—
Religious
Charitable
Educational
Scientific
Literary
Organizations for the prevention of cruelty to children and
animals
Veterans' organizations
Fraternal organizations, if used for charitable, religious, etc.,
purposes
Governmental agencies which will use the gifts for public
purposes
Interest paid on personal debts, such as—
Bank loans
Your personal note to an individual
Home mortgages
Instalment purchases of personal property (automobile, tele-
vision)
Life insurance loan, if you pay the interest in cash
Delinquent taxes
State and local taxes such as—
Real estate taxes
General sales taxes
Gasoline taxes
Income taxes
Personal property taxes
Other deductions for—
Expenses for the care of children and other dependents if
such care enables the taxpayer to be gainfully employed
Casualty losses and thefts not otherwise compensated
Expenses for education to maintain or improve skills re-
quired in your employment
Employee business expenses (not otherwise listed) for safety
equipment, tools, supplies, dues to unions or professional
societies, business entertainment, and fees to employment
agencies
Periodic payments of alimony or separate maintenance under a court decree

Calculating the Tax · The individual pays taxes on his net taxable
income after subtracting allowable adjustments to income, exemptions, and personal deductions. The application of the principle

differs according to the method of calculation. Those using a tax table for persons with incomes under $5,000 find the tax amount in the table for a person with given income (before personal deductions) and with a stated number of exemptions. The tax amounts in the table take into consideration the standard deduction. Persons with other than the standard deduction use the tax rate schedules for calculating taxes on their taxable income after first subtracting exemptions and deductions.

In any case, the tax rate depends on the taxpayer's *tax filing status* which is one of the following:

Single taxpayer
Married taxpayer, filing a separate return
Married taxpayers, filing a joint return
Widow or widower, under certain conditions
Unmarried or legally separated taxpayer who qualifies as head of household

An unmarried taxpayer qualifies as *head of a household* when he furnishes over half the cost of maintaining in his home a household occupied during the entire year by any related person (other than his unmarried child) for whom he is entitled to an exemption, or for his unmarried child or grandchild even though such child is not a dependent. The home the taxpayer maintains for his father and mother need not be the taxpayer's residence. An unmarried taxpayer with a taxable income of $8,000 after exemptions and deductions would presently pay a tax of $1,500 if he were head of a household, or $1,630 if he were not.

After the total tax has been calculated by using the appropriate tax table or tax schedule, the taxpayer subtracts the amounts of quarterly payments made during the tax year on estimated tax payments and the amount of federal income taxes that were withheld currently from his earnings by his employer. The *withholding tax* was instituted during World War II as a part of the enlarged federal income tax program. Its purposes are to keep earners reasonably up-to-date in their tax payments, to curb inflation, and to provide funds regularly and easily to the Federal Treasury.

The complexities of the federal individual income tax law were noted by Mortimer J. Caplin at the time of his retirement as Commissioner of Internal Revenue in 1964.[3] Caplin suggested that de-

---

[3] F. C. Porter, "Retiring Tax Chief Would Drop Deductions and Reduce Rates," *The Washington Post*, June 1, 1964. See also *The Wall Street Journal*, L. Silberman, "Filing-Time Furor: Pressure Is Increasing for Moves to Simplify Income Tax Regulations," April 14, 1965; and "Tax-Simplifying Moves Pick Up Steam In and Out of Congress," April 21, 1965.

ductions and exclusions be removed from the law, thus providing a broader tax base and making it possible to reduce rates. Study of the detailed instructions for filing tax returns and experience with the changing regulations indicate reasons for this suggestion. Special deductions provided for one group of "disadvantaged" persons have set forces in motion to provide special deductions for another group. So the list of deductions and exclusions grows competitively. Furthermore, it is clear that the deductions, the capital gains provisions, the income splitting provision for married couples, and many of the special exclusions are much more important to those with very high incomes than to other taxpayers.

QUESTIONS

1. What is the effect of income taxes on the family's financial resources? In what other ways is the tax important to the individual?
2. What are the major sources of federal revenue? What are the major types of federal expenditures?
3. How do the types of federal revenue and expenditure contrast with those of state and local governments?
4. What is meant by a graduated income tax? Give examples.
5. What changes in income tax law during World War II made knowledge of it important to most families?
6. Who must file a tax return? Why? Where? When?
7. Explain the use of each of the tax forms.
8. What is the advantage of a joint return?
9. What is the declaration of estimated tax?
10. What is the withholding tax?
11. Explain the requirements for claiming legal exemptions for the taxpayer, his wife, children, others in the household, and relatives outside the household.
12. What are some important types of nontaxable income?
13. What are important types of taxable income?
14. What important types of deductions may be claimed by the family?
15. How does a family decide whether to list deductions or take the standard deduction?
16. If some people understate their incomes or overstate their deductions on their returns, what effect does it have on other people?
17. Explain in general terms how to fill out a tax form and how to calculate the tax.
18. Obtain copies of current individual income tax forms and of instructions.
    (a) Fill out the brief form for Joseph A. and Helen B.

Adams who have three children and a wage income of
$4,971. Calculate their total tax.

(b) Fill out a form for the Browns, also with three children,
and a total income of $50,000 from personal services
and no other income. Calculate their total tax, taking
standard deductions.

19. Study the detailed instructions for filing tax returns to determine special provisions for important types of taxable income and special limitations on various deductions.

SUGGESTIONS FOR FURTHER READING

Internal Revenue Service. *Federal Income Tax Forms.* Washington,
D.C.: U. S. Treasury Department, latest edition.
————. *Your Federal Income Tax.* Washington, D.C.: Superintendent
of Documents, latest edition.
J. K. Lasser Tax Institute. *Your Income Tax.* Latest edition.
Peckman, Joseph A. *Federal Tax Policy.* Washington, D.C.: Brookings
Institution, 1966.

Part Two

Your

Expenditures

Family Expenditure Patterns / 7

- CONSUMER SPENDING
- ADEQUATE AMERICAN BUDGET
- EQUIVALENT INCOMES

As we know, families spend their incomes for a great variety of goods and services—large and small. Before proceeding to the discussion of the individual family's budget for specific categories, we want to see what importance the nation's consumers give to each type of outlay and the variation from one group of families to another. The individual may find general help in making his financial plans also by study of the estimates of the composition and cost of an adequate American budget and of the scale of equivalent incomes for families of different size and composition to maintain the same level of living.

CONSUMER SPENDING

Studies of consumer expenditures show national aggregates as well as family averages. Though the data are obtained in different ways for different purposes, both types are useful here.

National Aggregates · The Department of Commerce estimates of national aggregates, compiled largely from reports of business, provide a broad general view since they include expenditure data for all consumers—families and others, with urban, rural nonfarm, and farm residence. Annual estimates present current information and permit long-run comparisons. The latest data show that out of $548 billion of gross personal income of families and individuals, a seventh went for personal tax and nontax payments and personal contributions to social security, leaving consumers $469 billion to use as they saw fit.[1] They spent 95 percent and saved the rest.

The current division of income is not the one always made in the past. Personal outlays took 95 percent of disposable personal income in 1929, but were 102 percent of it in 1933 when consumers drew on savings in an attempt to maintain their level of living in spite of a drastic drop in income. At the peak of the war effort in 1944 when incomes had risen greatly, only 75 percent of income went for personal outlays because of the shortage of durable goods and the campaign to stimulate saving. But that situation was short-lived and, in recent years, outlays have normalized at the new high level of income, so that consumers find it possible regularly to spend about 95 percent.

Data on consumption categories in Table 7–1 indicate the wide range and, at the same time, the great importance of food, which absorbed 18 percent of personal income. Shelter took 14 percent; and utilities, household operation, and house furnishings and equipment totalled 13 percent. Twelve percent went for transportation and 9 percent for clothing, 6 percent for medical care, 5 percent for recreation, and 5 percent for personal business. The smallest categories were, in declining order, alcoholic beverages, tobacco, personal care, religious and welfare activities, private education and research, reading, and foreign travel and other.

Today about 60 percent of disposable income (in contrast with 67 percent in 1929) goes for "necessities," defined as food, the housing total, clothing, and medical care. At the same time that the consumption level has risen for these necessities, a larger part of income has been freed for "discretionary" spending and saving. The use of discrimination in these choices is therefore a subject of concern to individuals and society.

Average Outlays of Families · A different approach to the question of how families spend their money is made by collecting information on income, expenditures, and savings directly from families. For our purposes these surveys have some major advantages over national

---

[1] U. S. Department of Commerce, *Survey of Current Business*, July 1966 and August 1965.

TABLE 7–1. Use of Aggregate Personal Income

ITEM	BILLIONS OF DOLLARS 1965	PERCENT OF DISPOSABLE INCOME 1965
Gross personal income	548.3	..
Personal contributions for social insurance	13.2	..
Personal tax and nontax payments	66.0	..
Disposable personal income	469.1	100.0
Personal saving	25.7	5.5
Personal outlays	443.4	94.5
Interest paid by consumers	11.3	2.4
Personal transfer payments to foreigners	.6	.1
Personal consumption expenditures	431.5	92.0
Food	85.4	18.2
Housing, total	125.0	26.7
Shelter	63.2	13.5
Utilities	17.9	3.8
Household operations	18.8	4.0
Housefurnishings, equipment	25.3	5.4
Transportation	57.8	12.3
Automobile	54.1	11.5
Public	3.8	.8
Clothing, accessories, upkeep	43.4	9.3
Medical care	28.1	6.0
Recreation	21.4	4.6
Personal care	7.5	1.6
Tobacco	8.4	1.8
Alcoholic beverages	12.9	2.8
Private education and research	5.6	1.2
Reading	4.9	1.0
Personal business	22.1	4.7
Religious and welfare activities	5.6	1.2
Foreign travel and other	3.2	.7

NOTE: Detail may not add to totals because of rounding.
SOURCE: U. S. Department of Commerce, *Survey of Current Business*, July 1966.

aggregates: They show average family situations, and data are in dollar amounts that are comprehensible to us. In addition, the data may be analyzed to show the relationship to variables such as family size, income, and residence.

The Survey of Consumer Expenditures 1960–1961, by the U. S. Bureau of Labor Statistics and the U. S. Department of Agriculture, provides the latest data from a large-scale comprehensive study, the most recent in a series of comparable surveys, including those for 1935–36, 1941–42, and 1950 (urban only). About 4,500 urban families and single consumers were interviewed for 1960, and a total of about 9,200 for 1961—4,900 urban, 2,300 rural nonfarm, and 2,000 farm. In order to compare families by residence, the 1961 data are used here. These data collected in the spring of 1962 with final tabulations published in 1966 are the best indicators currently available of spending patterns of various types of families. Data for the early 1970's may be available a few years thereafter.

The data for all families and single consumers in Table 7–2 show average income of about $6,540 with personal taxes of $700, gifts and contributions of $280, personal insurance premiums of $300, and savings of $230. Total expenditures for current consumption average $5,040, with the amounts varying from $1,230 for food and $1,460 for the housing total, down to $760 for transportation, $520 for clothing, and $340 for medical care, and on down to smaller amounts for recreation, personal care, tobacco, alcoholic beverages, education, reading, and miscellaneous items. The percentages spent for various categories are similar to those in the estimates of national aggregates although the latter are more recent and the categories used for data obtained from business necessarily differ somewhat from those used for data obtained from families.

Almost every category of expenditures was highest for urban families of two or more persons, somewhat lower for rural nonfarm, and lowest for farm. Similar differences are shown for single consumers. These differences are due partly to the higher incomes of urban families, partly to where they live, and partly to their smaller amounts of free goods and services, particularly home-produced food. While urban families spent 59 percent more than farm for current consumption, their total of goods and services including free items was 39 percent higher. Urban food, purchased plus free, was only 7 percent higher.

The particular effect of one variable can be seen most clearly by holding constant the other important variables. This type of analysis shows that, when other conditions are equal, large families generally spend larger total amounts for current consumption than do small families, and city families spend larger amounts than do rural nonfarm or farm. (See Table 7–3.) Although high-income families spend larger amounts for current consumption than do low-income families of the same size and urbanization, the high-income families spend a lower proportion of income. These results clearly indicate the pressures toward expenditure of available income that are created by large families, urban living, and low income.

TABLE 7–2. Expenditures and Savings of Families and Single Consumers, by Residence

ITEM	ALL FAMILIES AND SINGLE CONSUMERS		FAMILIES			URBAN SINGLE CONSUMERS
	AVERAGE	PERCENT	URBAN	RURAL NONFARM	FARM	
Family size	3.2	..	3.5	3.8	4.0	1.0
Proximate money income[1]	$6,540	..	$7,770	$5,860	$5,030	$3,430
Personal taxes[2]	700	..	880	510	320	420
Income after taxes	5,840	100.0	6,890	5,350	4,710	3,010
Expenditures for current consumption .	5,040	86.3	5,960	4,660	3,740	2,590
Food	1,230	21.1	1,450	1,170	900	610
Housing, total ...	1,460	25.0	1,730	1,270	950	940
Shelter	660	11.3	800	490	320	550
Utilities	250	4.3	270	290	240	120
Household operations ...	290	5.0	350	240	160	180
House furnishings and equipment	260	4.5	310	260	230	90
Transportation ...	760	13.0	880	810	640	300
Clothing	520	8.9	630	450	450	220
Medical care	340	5.8	400	320	320	170
Recreation	200	3.4	240	180	130	90
Personal care	150	2.6	170	130	110	70
Tobacco	90	1.5	100	90	70	40
Alcoholic beverages	80	1.4	90	50	30	50
Education	50	.9	70	40	40	10
Reading	40	.7	50	40	30	30
Miscellaneous ..	110	1.9	130	100	80	60
Gifts and contributions	280	4.8	310	220	220	260
Personal insurance premiums	300	5.1	370	270	210	120
Net savings	230	3.9	250	210	540	50
Value of free items .	190	..	210	200	140	110
Value of home produced food ...	40	..	10	70	460	..

NOTE: Detail may not add to totals because of rounding.
[1] Income adjusted for simplicity by the present writer by the addition to money income of "other money receipts" and subtraction of "account balancing difference."
[2] Includes income taxes, poll taxes, and personal property taxes.
SOURCE: U. S. Bureau of Labor Statistics and U. S. Department of Agriculture, *Survey of Consumer Expenditures 1961*. These data collected in the spring of 1962 from 9,200 families with final tabulations published in 1966 are the best indicators currently available of spending patterns of various types of families. Data for the early 1970's may be available a few years thereafter.

We can make some generalizations from these and other data: (A) Family expenditures are determined by three major types of factors

(1) Family resources, their amounts and kinds.
(2) The market situation, including goods and services available and their prices.

TABLE 7–3. Expenditures for Current Consumption, by Family Size, Residence, and Income (Average not shown for cells of less than 30 families)

RESIDENCE AND MONEY INCOME AFTER TAXES	1	NUMBER OF PERSONS IN FAMILY 2	3	4	5	6 OR MORE
Urban:						
Under $1,000	$1,060	..	..	..	..	..
$1,000–$1,999	1,520	$2,070	..	..	..	..
$2,000–$2,999	2,340	2,650	$2,910	..	..	..
$3,000–$3,999	3,090	3,590	3,740	$4,220	..	..
$4,000–$4,999	3,690	4,260	4,610	4,740	$4,950	$4,760
$5,000–$5,999	4,300	4,790	5,470	5,660	5,760	5,450
$6,000–$7,499	5,140	5,770	6,250	6,420	6,360	6,500
$7,500–$9,999	..	7,000	7,610	7,670	7,620	8,160
$10,000–$14,999	..	8,590	9,640	10,230	10,040	9,660
$15,000 and over	..	15,510	..	..	..	..
Rural nonfarm:						
Under $1,000	940	1,060	..	..	..	..
$1,000–$1,999	1,540	1,730	1,980	..	..	..
$2,000–$2,999	2,320	2,610	2,850	..	..	2,860
$3,000–$3,999	..	3,220	3,450	3,790	..	4,110
$4,000–$4,999	..	3,960	4,600	4,650	4,540	4,740
$5,000–$5,999	..	4,730	5,010	5,310	5,540	5,370
$6,000–$7,499	..	5,180	6,160	6,020	6,350	6,120
$7,500–$9,999	..	6,450	6,610	7,540	7,610	7,750
Farm:						
Under $1,000	980	1,810	..	..	..	..
$1,000–$1,999	1,220	1,900	2,220	2,360	..	2,100
$2,000–$2,999	..	2,310	2,720	3,130	..	2,670
$3,000–$3,999	..	2,750	3,460	3,680	..	3,720
$4,000–$4,999	..	3,080	3,990	3,960	..	4,300
$5,000–$5,999	..	3,790	4,320	4,490	4,600	4,740
$6,000–$7,499	..	4,690	4,450	5,380	5,160	5,540
$7,500–$9,999	..	..	..	5,540	..	6,520

SOURCE: U. S. Bureau of Labor Statistics and U. S. Department of Agriculture, *Survey of Consumer Expenditures 1961*. These data collected in the spring of 1962 from 9,200 families with final tabulations published in 1966 are the best indicators currently available of spending patterns of various types of families. Data for the early 1970's may be available a few years thereafter.

(3) Needs and preferences of families as affected by family size and composition, stage of the life cycle, residence, and other conditions.

(B) Consumer expenditures in dollars are not always regularly related to current money income. This occurs because—

(1) Some groups can spend more than their income by using savings or credit. For example, in periods of high employment, many familes with the lowest incomes have savings on which to draw or have good prospects which enable them to obtain credit. Elderly persons draw on savings, whereas expanding families use credit extensively.

(2) Some groups can limit expenditures on certain items because they have free goods and services. For example, farm families, particularly those with large families and moderate incomes, may have a considerable amount of home-produced food which cuts food expense. Older families have an accumulation of durable goods which cuts spending on these items.

(C) Consumer expenditure in dollars does not always represent the consumption level, that is, the value of goods and services consumed. Low expenditures may be counterbalanced by sizable amounts of free goods and services. High expenditures may include large purchases of consumer durables, only part of whose services are used in the purchase year.

(D) While consumer expenditures vary greatly from year to year for some families, due to variations in income or replacement of consumer durables, the consumption level, that is, the value of goods and services consumed in a year, changes much more slowly.

(E) It also appears that the more nearly equal the distribution of income in a society, the more closely income and expenditure are related to the stage of the family life cycle.

ADEQUATE AMERICAN BUDGET

In 1945 Congress directed the Bureau of Labor Statistics "to find out what it costs a worker's family to live in the large cities of the United States" [2]—a large order. Thereafter, a technical advisory committee assisted in developing basic standards and methods by which the Bureau constructed a list of items and quantities in a budget for a city worker's family, then priced them in large cities in

[2] U. S. Bureau of Labor Statistics, *Workers' Budgets in the United States: City Families and Single Persons, 1946 and 1947,* Bulletin No. 927, 1948.

1946–47. Later, a similar method was used for developing and pricing a budget for a retired couple. Because of great increases in levels and standards of living of American families since the war, the Bureau revised and repriced the budgets in 1959 to reflect standards prevailing in the 1950's.[3] Currently, new budgets are being published, reflecting the standards prevailing in the 1960's.

The budgets were designed to estimate the amount needed to "satisfy prevailing standards of what is necessary for health, efficiency, the nurture of children, and for participation in community activities." Thus, the budgets are above a "minimum level." The budgets *do not* show how an "average family" spends its money or how it should. But they provide a point of departure for a family's consideration of its own budget.

The goods and services included in the original budgets and in the revisions were based on recognized scientific standards, as far as possible and selections of specific items meeting the standards were based on actual choices of families as shown by consumption data. The recommendations for nutritional adequacy of the National Research Council and the housing standards developed by the American Public Health Association and the U. S. Public Housing Administration were adopted and translated into a list of foods and description of housing by reference to actual practices of families. For clothing and other goods and services, allowances were established to meet prevailing standards of what is necessary for health, efficiency, and participation in social and community activities, with adjustments to take account of geographical differences.

City Worker's Family Budget · The city worker's budget was developed for a family of four, including the employed husband, 38 years old; the wife, a full-time homemaker doing all the cooking, cleaning, and laundry for the family without paid assistance; a boy, 13 years old, in high school; and a girl, 8, in grade school. The husband has no additional dependents.[4]

The allowance for food at home in the new budget is based on the moderate-cost food plan of the U. S. Department of Agriculture for a family of this composition.

The clothing items allow for variations in practices of families

---

[3] H. H. Lamale and M. S. Stotz, "The Interim City Worker's Family Budget," *Monthly Labor Review*, 1960, pp. 785–808; and M. S. Stotz. "The BLS Interim Budget for a Retired Couple," *Monthly Labor Review*, 1960, pp. 1141–1157.

[4] U.S. Bureau of Labor Statistics, *City Worker's Family Budget for a Moderate Living Standard, Autumn 1966*, Bulletin No. 1570–1, 1967.

in different climates, and are based on a special analysis of the Survey of Consumer Expenditures 1960–61.

The family rents or owns and lives alone in a separate house or apartment of 5 (5 or 6 for owners) rooms (including the kitchen) and a bathroom. It is located within reasonable commuting distance of places of employment and shopping, schools, and churches. The dwelling has hot and cold running water, ordinary safeguards against unsafe or unsanitary conditions, electric lighting, and heating equipment and fuel sufficient to maintain an average room temperature of 70° in the winter months in the specific locality. The dwelling has the usual housefurnishings and equipment, such as a gas or electric range, mechanical refrigerator, and a washer. Allowances are made for some purchases each year in order to maintain inventories. Supplies of cleaning materials are provided.

Local transportation is provided for usual purposes; and a used automobile is assumed for most families, particularly in small cities and the suburbs. Allowances are also made for medical care, recreation and reading, personal care, tobacco, gifts and contributions, and other items. Details of all items are presented in the Bureau's report.

The budget cost estimates for various categories in the U. S. urban average are shown in Table 7–4. In addition, regional estimates are available for nonmetropolitan areas (2,500 to 50,000 population), and separate budget estimates for 39 metropolitan areas, including Boston, New York-Northeastern New Jersey, Philadelphia, Chicago, Cleveland, Detroit, Kansas City, Minneapolis-St. Paul, Atlanta, Baltimore, Dallas, Washington, D. C., Denver, Seattle, Los Angeles-Long Beach, and Honolulu.

Budget for a Retired Couple · The budget for a retired couple was prepared for a husband and wife, 65 years or over, who live alone in a city, are self-supporting, in reasonably good health, and able to take care of themselves. The wife does all of the cooking and most of the cleaning and laundry.

The food allowance in the new budget is based on the moderate-cost food plan of the U. S. Department of Agriculture for an elderly couple. Clothing items vary from city to city. Details of allowances for these items and for transportation, medical care, recreation, and other items are available in the published report.[5] The couple is assumed to live alone in either a 5 or 6-room owned dwelling or a two- or three-room rented dwelling unit (including kitchen)

5 U. S. Bureau of Labor Statistics, *Retired Couple's Budget for Moderate Living Standard*, Autumn 1966, Bulletin No. 1570–4, 1967.

TABLE 7–4. Annual Cost of City Worker's Family Budget[1] by Major Components, Urban United States, Autumn 1966

ITEM	ANNUAL COST
Food	$2,143
Food at home	1,824
Food away from home	319
Housing: Total	2,214
Renter families	1,736
Homeowner families	2,374
Shelter: Total[2]	1,733
Rental costs[3]	1,255
Homeowner costs[4]	1,893
Housefurnishings	265
Household operations	216
Transportation: Total[5]	815
Automobile owners	860
Nonowners of automobiles	151
Clothing	756
Husband	174
Wife	187
Boy	168
Girl	154
Clothing materials and services	72
Personal care	214
Medical care: Total	468
Insurance[6]	219
Physician's visits	89
Other medical care	284
Other family consumption	719
Reading	65
Recreation	306
Education	55
Tobacco	134
Alcoholic beverages	72
Miscellaneous expenses	87
Cost of family consumption; Total[7]	7,329
Renter families	6,850
Homeowner families	7,488
Other costs	413
Gifts and contributions	253
Life insurance	160
Occupational expenses	80
Social security and disability payments	289
Personal taxes: Total[7]	1,080
Renter families	961
Homeowner families	1,119
Cost of budget: Total[7]	9,191
Renter families	8,594
Homeowner families	9,390

[1] The family consists of an employed husband, aged 38, a wife not employed full-time outside the home, an 8-year-old girl, and a 13-year-old boy.

[2] The average costs of shelter were weighted by the following proportions: 25 percent for families living in rented dwellings, 75 percent for families living in owned homes.

[3] Average contract rent plus the cost of required amounts of heating fuel, gas, electricity, water, specified equipment, and insurance on household contents.

[4] Interest and principal payments plus taxes, insurance on house and contents, water, refuse disposal, heating fuel, gas, electricity, specified equipment, and home repair and maintenance costs.

[5] The average costs of automobile owners and nonowners were weighted by the following proportions of families: Boston, Chicago, New York, and Philadelphia, 80 percent for automobile owners, 20 percent for nonowners; 8 other metropolitan areas with 1.4 million of population or more in 1960, 95 percent for auto owners and 5 percent for nonowners (Baltimore, Cleveland, Detroit, Los Angeles, Pittsburgh, San Francisco, St. Louis, and Washington, D.C.); all other areas, 100 percent for auto owners.

[6] The average costs of hospitalization and surgical insurance (as a part of total medical care) were weighted by the following proportions: 30 percent for families paying full cost of insurance; 26 percent for families paying half cost; 44 percent for families covered by noncontributory insurance plans (paid for by employer).

[7] The total represents the weighted average costs of renter families (25 percent) and owner families (75 percent).

SOURCE: U. S. Bureau of Labor Statistics, *City Worker's Family Budget for a Moderate Living Standard*, Autumn 1966, Bulletin No. 1570–1, 1967.

with a private bathroom, hot and cold running water, electric lighting, and installed heating. It is located in a neighborhood with outdoor space and is close to public transportation. Owned homes are presumed to be mortgage-free for the retired couple. The dwelling has the usual housefurnishings and equipment, including a gas or electric range, mechanical refrigerator, and small electric appliances. Provision is made for some replacements and for some laundry and household help.

As with the City Worker's Budget, budget cost estimates are given for the U. S. urban average, with regional estimates for nonmetropolitan areas and separate budget estimates for 39 metropolitan areas.

Budgets for a Lower and a Higher Standard · The Bureau of Labor Statistics is deriving budgets for living standards both lower and higher than the "modest" standard of the traditional City Worker's Family Budget and the Retired Couple's Budget. Cost estimates for the lower and higher standards for the same geographical areas covered by the revised modest CWFB and RCB, based on spring 1967 prices, are expected to be released by early 1968. Estimates of the spring 1967 costs of the revised modest standard CWFB and RCB are to be released at the same time. In the future, the BLS expects to publish annually the budget estimates, based on spring pricing, for the two types of families at three standards of living. (Still in the early planning stage is the proposed Single Working Woman's Budget.)

The *lower standard* budget for each family type might be considered "minimum-adequate," according to the BLS. A family living at the level of the "minimum" budget over a decade could hardly be considered to have maintained an adequate standard of living in terms of the generally prevailing standard of the majority of American families. The budget is expected to approximate the standards frequently considered appropriate as goals for assistance and income-maintenance programs.

The *higher standard* budget will describe the standard associated with the level and manner of living which has been achieved by a majority of American families, according to the BLS. The budget will approximate the so-called "American standard of living" and will be more appropriate than the "modest-but-adequate" budgets for use in determining the ability of self-supporting families to pay for fee services, eligibility for scholarships, and in general economic analysis.

EQUIVALENT INCOMES

Since a cost estimate for various types of families is frequently needed, the BLS developed a scale of equivalent incomes or budget costs for city families of different size and composition. The scale was derived from 1950 data and a revised scale was derived from data obtained in the Survey of Consumer Expenditures (1960–61).[6] The scale was based on the assumption, validated by analysis of studies of consumption patterns, that groups of families spending the same proportion of income on food attain equal levels of living. For this purpose, income was defined as income after taxes and occupational expenses.

This is the most extensive scale ever developed since it shows relative costs of maintaining a given level of living for families of a great variety in size, composition, and age of members (Table 7–5). The base for the scale is the cost for a four-person family, including a husband 35–54 years old, his wife, and two children, the older 6 to 15 years of age.

Such a scale is useful in the analysis of survey data on family income and expenditure and in the plans for public assistance programs. The scale may also be used by the individual family for estimating the budget needs of another family, the changes in cost of

---

[6] U. S. Bureau of Labor Statistics, *Revised Equivalence Scale: For Costs by Family Type*, Bulletin No. 1570–2, 1968.

TABLE 7–5. Scale of Equivalent Incomes* or Budget Costs for City Families of Different Size, Age, and Composition
[4-person family—husband, age 35–54, wife, 2 children, older 6–15 = 100]

SIZE AND TYPE OF FAMILY	AGE OF HEAD			
	UNDER 35	35–54	55–64	65 OR OVER
One person	35	36	32	28
Two persons:				
Husband and wife	49	60	59	51
One parent and child	40	57	60	58
Three persons:				
Husband, wife, child under 6	62	69	..	..
Husband, wife, child 6–15	62	82	88	81
Husband, wife, child 16–17	..	83	88	..
Husband, wife, child 18 or over	..	82	85	77
One parent, 2 children	67	76	82	75
Four persons:				
Husband, wife, 2 children (oldest under 6)	72	80	..	..
Husband, wife, 2 children (oldest 6–15)	77	100	105	95
Husband, wife, 2 children (oldest 16–17)	..	113	125	..
Husband, wife, 2 children (oldest 18 or over)	..	96	110	89
One parent, 3 children	88	96	..	..
Five persons:				
Husband, wife, 3 children (oldest under 6)	87	97	..	..
Husband, wife, 3 children (oldest 6–15)	96	116	120	..
Husband, wife, 3 children (oldest 16–17)	..	128	138	..
Husband, wife, 3 children (oldest 18 or over)	..	119	124	..
One parent, 4 children	108	117	..	..
Six persons or more:				
Husband, wife, 4 children (oldest under 6)	101	..	..	..
Husband, wife, 4 children (oldest 6–15)	110	132	140	..
Husband, wife, 4 children (oldest 16–17)	..	146	..	..
Husband, wife, 4 children (oldest 18 or over)	..	149	..	..
One parent, 5 children	125	137	..	..

* The scale values shown in this table are the percentages of the spendable income of the base family required to provide the same level of living for urban families of different size, age, and composition.
SOURCE: U. S. Bureau of Labor Statistics, *Revised Equivalence Scale: For Estimating Equivalent Incomes or Budget Costs by Family Type*, Bulletin No. 1570–2, 1967.

a given level of living through the life cycle, and the cost of rearing a child.

Costs for Other Families · It is sometimes useful to estimate what another family needs to live at a certain level. For instance, the parental family may be considering the supplementation of the income of a daughter or young couple; or a mature family may be considering the need for aiding an elderly parent. The supplementation needed (excluding unusual costs of medical care) may be estimated as the difference between the approximate cost of a given level of living and the income actually received. The costs for young and elderly families equal to levels of $5,000, $7,000, and $9,000 for the standard family of four would be estimated as follows:

FAMILY MEMBERS AND AGES	INCOME EQUIVALENT TO STATED AMOUNT FOR FAMILY OF FOUR		
	$5,000	$7,000	$9,000
Man, 47, wife, children, 15, 9	$5,000	$7,000	$9,000
Daughter, 22	1,750	2,450	3,150
Son, 23, daughter-in-law, 20	2,450	3,430	4,410
Grandmother, 70	1,400	1,960	2,520

Thus, if a young couple were having a hard time getting started in business and could clear only $200 a month, the parents might decide to supplement the earnings so that the couple could live in a city at a level equivalent to $7,000 for a family of four.

Another kind of problem is posed by a city group of brothers and sisters with different incomes and types of families who are faced with the necessity of helping their elderly parents to the extent of at least $2,000 annually. A rough but objective judgment of their relative abilities may be made by use of the scale through setting a given level of living (such as $7,000) as a base, as follows:

FAMILY MEMBERS AND AGES	EQUIVA-LENT INCOME	ACTUAL NET INCOME	EXCESS AVAIL-ABLE	PRO-RATA CONTRI-BUTION
Man, 47, wife, children, 15, 9 .	$ 7,000	$ 9,000	$ 2,000	$ 400
Woman, 35	2,520	4,020	1,500	300
Man, 40, wife, child, 18	5,740	8,240	2,500	500
Woman, 43, one child	3,990	4,990	1,000	200
Man, 45, wife, children, 18, 16, 14, 12	10,430	13,430	3,000	600
Totals	$29,680	$39,680	$10,000	$2,000

While family income ranged decidedly and the number of members from one to six it appears that all families can probably maintain a level equal to that of $7,000 for a family of four and make some contribution to the retired parents.

Costs Through Family Cycle · Costs of maintaining a given level of living through the life cycle may be estimated by use of the scale of equivalent incomes. While two cannot live as cheaply as one, they can live more cheaply than two can live separately. The young man's expenses increase about half at marriage and roughly a quarter for each of the first three children. When the three children are in their teens, expenses are at a maximum, about three times the cost for the man alone. Thereafter costs decline as the children marry and the couple ages.

To illustrate the changing cost in dollars through the life cycle, we might consider a level equal to $7,000 for a city family of four and compare with costs at a $10,000 level, as follows:

FAMILY MEMBERS AND AGES	INCOME EQUIVALENT TO STATED AMOUNT FOR FAMILY OF FOUR	
	$7,000	$10,000
Man 21	$2,450	$ 3,500
Man 23, wife 21	3,430	4,900
Man 32, wife 30, children 8, 5, baby ..	6,720	9,600
Man 41, wife 39, children 17, 14, 9 ...	8,960	12,800
Man 54, wife 52	4,200	6,000
Widow 65	1,960	2,800

The index of costs during the family life cycle with three children would be approximately as follows (costs for parents and two schoolage children = 100):

HUSBAND'S AGE	NUMBER OF PERSONS	INDEX OF COSTS
21	1	35
23	2	49
24	3	62
27	4	72
30	4	77
32	5	96
35	5	116
40	5	128
42	5	119
46	4	96
49	3	83
50	3	82
54	2	60
55	2	59
65	2	51
66	1	28

The income figures given at the various stages of the family life cycle are in terms of dollars of constant value. Inflationary conditions would change the figures in terms of then-current dollars.

While this illustration was built on the latest data on the average timing of the family cycle in the United States, a family might prefer to make cost estimates for its own anticipated life cycle. Perhaps, also, a family considers it appropriate to select another level of living. A level equal to $14,000 for the standard family of four would require 2 times as much at each stage as for the $7,000 level.

Cost of Raising a Child · The scale may also be used to estimate the cost of raising a child. The cost is related to several factors, including the size and composition of the family in which the child is reared, the family's definition of its job, and the family's level of living.

A child in a one-child family costs more than does a child with brothers and sisters, even at the same level of living. Expenses for toys, clothing, books, and the like, quickly outgrown, help to explain the differences, since they can be handed down in the multi-child family. In general, also, the cost is related to which child it is: The first child adds more to expenses than does the second; the third adds more than the first, probably because of added housing needs; and the fourth child adds decidedly less.

The composition of the family in other respects also affects the cost of raising a child. A child raised by one parent costs more than does a child with two parents in the home, whereas a child in a home with a number of adult relatives probably costs less. What we are seeing again is the advantage of a large-sized consumption unit over a small-sized one—a lower cost per person for a given level of living.

The cost of raising a child is also affected by the family's definition of its job. Does it mean to age 18 or through high school; or is the family standard lower? On the other hand, does it require support to age 22, with or without additional training financed by the parents?

It obviously costs much more to raise a child when family income is $10,000 than $7,000. Therefore, the cost of raising a child is estimated as a multiple of the annual budget. Use of the scale indicates that it costs roughly three times annual family expenditures to raise a child to age 18, and four times annual family expenditures to raise a child to age 22, excluding costs for higher education. But the multiplier differs considerably with the number of children raised.

Such estimates are further complicated by changes in family living conditions during its life cycle. Rising prices of consumer goods would enlarge the dollar cost of raising a child as a multiple of today's budget. Advances or declines in the family's level of living may drastically affect the estimate. If the family's level of living is much higher when the child is in the expensive teens, his total cost to age 18 will be a larger multiple of the young family's present budget.

QUESTIONS

1. How may the family use data on average consumer spending?
2. Differentiate between national aggregates and surveys of family expenditures. What are the special advantages of each?
3. What do the two types of studies show with regard to major categories?
4. How does total spending on current consumption differ among families?
5. Describe the method of construction of the "adequate American budget." Describe the level of living provided and the costs.
6. What is the meaning of the "scale of equivalent income"? How is it derived?
7. For what purposes may the scale be used?
8. Using the scale, compare the economic level of the following families:

A young man living alone and earning $5,000 after taxes.
A young mother and child with an income of $3,000 after taxes.
A middle-aged couple with two school age children and an income of $8,000.
A retired couple with an income of $4,000.

9. What types of situations might invalidate the above comparison?
10. How do costs of a given level of living vary during the family life cycle? What is the importance to you today?
11. What important assumptions are made in estimating the cost of raising a child? How would you estimate your parents' cost for raising you?

SUGGESTIONS FOR FURTHER READING

U. S. Bureau of Labor Statistics. *City Worker's Family Budget*, latest data for a moderate living standard and for a lower and a higher standard.

————. *Monthly Labor Review,* latest issues.

————. *Retired Couple's Budget,* latest data for a moderate living standard and for a lower and a higher standard.

————. *Scale of Equivalent Income for City Families,* latest revision.

————. *Surveys of Consumer Expenditures,* latest surveys.

U. S. Department of Agriculture. *Surveys of Consumer Expenditures,* latest surveys.

U. S. Department of Commerce. *Survey of Current Business,* latest issues.

The Food Budget / 8

- ESTIMATING BUDGET AMOUNT
- PLANNING PURCHASES
- BUYING FOOD
- HOME PRODUCTION AND CARE IN USE

The food budget deserves first consideration since it is by far the most important category in the family budget, taking 18 percent of disposable income. The proportion spent on food and food services has declined through the years as incomes have risen. At the same time, the quantity of food and food services per person has increased decidedly. When it is desirable, many families can decrease their food costs without foregoing good diets.

ESTIMATING BUDGET AMOUNT

To estimate the amount to budget for food in the next period, the experienced person or family may start with the record of expenditures and items purchased last week, studying them for possible changes to improve the quality of the diet or cut costs. Inexperienced persons may use, as a starting place, the data on average food expenditures of families of different size, residence, and income, given in Table 8–1. These data show the sizable yearly amounts spent on food and the variation from one group of families to another. Larger amounts are generally spent on food by large families, city families, and high-income families, other conditions being equal. However, the proportion of income spent on food is lower for high-income families since they do not expand food expenditures in direct proportion to

TABLE 8–1. Food Expenditures, by Family Size, Residence, and Income (Average not shown for cells of less than 30 families)

RESIDENCE AND MONEY INCOME AFTER TAXES	NUMBER OF PERSONS IN FAMILY					
	1	2	3	4	5	6 OR MORE
Urban:						
Under $1,000	$ 290	..	..	..	..	..
$1,000–$1,999	450	$ 620	..	..	..	..
$2,000–$2,999	620	760	$ 800	..	..	..
$3,000–$3,999	710	890	1,020	$1,120	..	..
$4,000–$4,999	810	990	1,210	1,320	$1,480	$1,420
$5,000–$5,999	760	1,130	1,320	1,420	1,490	1,710
$6,000–$7,499	1,050	1,240	1,420	1,590	1,750	1,890
$7,500–$9,999	..	1,430	1,840	1,840	2,090	2,150
$10,000–$14,999	..	1,730	2,020	2,220	2,320	2,610
$15,000 and over	..	2,490	..	..	..	..
Rural nonfarm:						
Under $1,000	290	370	..	..	..	..
$1,000–$1,999	450	520	690	..	..	..
$2,000–$2,999	540	690	790	..	..	1,050
$3,000–$3,999	..	800	960	1,090	..	1,460
$4,000–$4,999	..	950	1,080	1,170	1,340	1,510
$5,000–$5,999	..	960	1,160	1,390	1,400	1,700
$6,000–$7,499	..	1,060	1,340	1,440	1,660	1,700
$7,500–$9,999	..	1,440	1,390	1,580	1,880	1,940
Farm:						
Under $1,000	320	480	..	..	..	..
$1,000–$1,999	360	480	570	670	..	720
$2,000–$2,999	..	570	740	800	..	840
$3,000–$3,999	..	680	740	800	..	1,040
$4,000–$4,999	..	640	880	980	..	1,200
$5,000–$5,999	..	760	980	1,150	1,020	1,260
$6,000–$7,499	..	790	1,000	1,180	1,270	1,560
$7,500–$9,999	..	..	..	1,140	..	1,690

SOURCE: U. S. Bureau of Labor Statistics and U. S. Department of Agriculture, *Survey of Consumer Expenditures 1961.* These data collected in the spring of 1962 from 9,200 families with final tabulations published in 1966 are the best indicators currently available of annual spending patterns of various types of families. Data for the early 1970's may be available a few years thereafter.

increased income. In other words, food is a necessity with inelastic demand.

A preliminary report from the nationwide Food Consumption Survey of 1965–66 also showed increases in food expense with income level, due partly, however, to increased average size of households

(Table 8–2). At each of the major income levels, $3,000 to $9,999, average food expense per person in one week in the spring of 1965 was highest for urban households and lowest for farm, as follows:

HOUSEHOLD INCOME	URBAN	RURAL NONFARM	FARM
$3,000–$4,999	$ 8.80	$ 7.80	$ 6.10
$5,000–$6,999	10.60	9.00	7.10
$7,000–$9,999	12.00	10.70	8.20

TABLE 8–2. Weekly Food Expense and Money Value, by Residence and Income (All housekeeping households, one week in April, May, or June 1965)

RESIDENCE AND 1964 MONEY INCOME AFTER TAXES [1]	HOUSEHOLD SIZE [2]	FOOD EXPENSE [3]	MONEY VALUE OF ALL FOOD [4]
Urban:			
Under $3,000	2.3	$17.20	$18.40
$3,000–$4,999	3.2	28.00	28.80
$5,000–$6,999	3.4	36.30	37.20
$7,000–$9,999	3.5	42.40	43.20
$10,000 and over	3.6	54.20	55.20
Rural nonfarm:			
Under $3,000	2.8	16.10	19.70
$3,000–$4,999	3.7	28.80	32.30
$5,000–$6,999	3.9	35.10	37.70
$7,000–$9,999	3.8	40.80	42.80
$10,000 and over	3.8	48.60	50.80
Farm:			
Under $3,000	3.8	17.40	27.80
$3,000–$4,999	4.0	24.50	35.20
$5,000–$6,999	4.2	29.70	40.20
$7,000–$9,999	4.0	32.40	42.60
$10,000 and over	4.4	36.60	47.90

[1] Median family income before taxes was 5% higher in 1965 than in 1964 (*Current Population Reports*, Series P-60, No. 51).
[2] Total number of meals served from home food supplies divided by 21.
[3] Includes alcoholic beverages, averaging about a dollar or less.
[4] In addition to food expense, includes money value of home produced food which averaged 30¢ for urban households, $1.90 for rural nonfarm, and $9.80 for farm, plus the money value of food federally donated and received as gift and pay, averaging less than $1 for each residence group.
SOURCE: Consumer and Food Economics Research Division, U. S. Department of Agriculture, *Money Value of Food Used by Households in the United States, Spring 1965*, Preliminary Report on Food Consumption Survey 1965–66, CFE–300, 1966.

However, money value of all food, including home produced and free food, per person was about the same for various residence groups at a given income level, as follows:

HOUSEHOLD INCOME	URBAN	RURAL NONFARM	FARM
$3,000–$4,999	$ 9.00	$ 8.70	$ 8.80
$5,000–$6,999	10.80	9.70	9.70
$7,000–$9,999	12.20	11.20	10.80

Data for families of different sizes will be published in a few years, as will data for the entire year based on surveys in the four seasons. About 7,500 housekeeping households of one or more members were interviewed during spring 1965, and 2,500 households in each of the following three seasons, for a total of about 15,000 households.

Some of these families ate several meals at restaurants, but many ate most meals at home. While restaurant meals are generally more expensive than similar food prepared at home, the restaurant price includes costs of equipment, space, and labor for preparing and serving food. A single person or a family that regularly eats many meals at restaurants may find it cheaper to eat all meals out than to provide facilities at home. However, many prefer the convenience and pleasure of home facilities. A family that already has the equipment and space narrows its consideration to the cost of food items brought into the home. Since the majority of families eat most of their meals at home, the ensuing discussion of food budgets will center on their problems.

Cost of a Week's Food · Estimates of the costs of a week's food at home by research home economists at the U. S. Department of Agriculture provide another approach to planning the food allowance (Table 8–3). The costs are for individuals by sex-age group for three food plans—low-cost, moderate-cost, and liberal—all nutritionally adequate. The family is assumed to buy all foods at the store, prepare all meals at home or take packed lunches, and to follow average food consumption practices. These estimates are made quarterly, with regional estimates once a year.

The weekly costs for individuals, which vary by sex and age, may be used to estimate the cost for a family by totalling costs for individuals. Adjustments may be needed since costs assume average height, weight, activity, and physiological condition for each sex-age group. The costs given are for individuals in 4-person families. For families of other size, the following adjustments are suggested:

    1 person—add 20 percent
    2 persons—add 10 percent
    3 persons—add 5 percent
    5 persons—subtract 5 percent
    6 or more persons—subtract 10 percent

TABLE 8–3.   Cost of One Week's Food at Home[1] Estimated for Food Plans at Three Cost Levels, June 1966, U. S. Average

SEX-AGE GROUPS [2]	LOW-COST PLAN	MODERATE-COST PLAN	LIBERAL PLAN
Children, under 1 year	$3.10	$ 4.00	$ 4.30
1–3 years	3.90	5.10	5.90
3–6 years	4.60	6.20	7.10
6–9 years	5.60	7.40	8.80
Girls, 9–12 years	6.40	8.50	9.60
12–15 years	7.00	9.40	10.90
15–20 years	7.30	9.60	10.90
Boys, 9–12 years	6.50	8.70	10.00
12–15 years	7.40	10.30	11.70
15–20 years	8.80	11.70	13.40
Women, 20–35 years	6.70	8.80	10.10
35–55 years	6.50	8.50	9.80
55–75 years	5.50	7.40	8.40
75 years and over	5.00	6.60	7.70
Pregnant	7.90	10.30	11.60
Nursing	9.10	11.80	13.10
Men, 20–35 years	7.60	10.10	11.90
35–55 years	7.00	9.40	10.90
55–75 years	6.40	8.60	9.80
75 years and over	5.90	8.30	9.50

[1] The costs given are for individuals in 4-person families. For individuals in other size families, the following adjustments are suggested: 1-person—add 20 percent; 2-person—add 10 percent; 3-person—add 5 percent; 5-person—subtract 5 percent; 6-or-more-person—subtract 10 percent.

These estimates were computed from quantities in food plans published in *Family Economics Review*, October, 1964. The costs of the food plans were first estimated by using the average price per pound of each food group paid by nonfarm survey families at three selected income levels in 1955. These prices were adjusted to current levels by use of *Retail Food Prices by Cities* released periodically by the U. S. Bureau of Labor Statistics.

[2] Age groups include the persons of the first age listed up to but not including those of the second age listed.

SOURCE: Consumer and Food Economics Research Division, Agricultural Research Service, U. S. Department of Agriculture.

Thus a young woman cooking alone may plan about $8.00 a week ($6.70 plus 20 percent) for a low-cost food plan, and a young man may plan $9.10. The young couple can eat somewhat more cheaply together than when they cooked separately. Food costs increase as the children are born and as they advance in age to the top costs when the children are in their teens. Thereafter food costs decline as the children leave home. Estimates at different stages of the family life cycle are as follows:

FAMILY MEMBERS	WEEKLY COST, LOW-COST PLAN
Man 22, wife 20	$15.70
Man 28, wife 26, children 4, 2, and baby	24.60
Man 43, wife 41, boy 19, girl 17, boy 15	36.50
Man 49, wife 47	14.90
Woman 65	6.60

Regional estimates for December 1965, for the cost of one week's food at home for a family of four (man and woman 20–34 years old, child 6–8 years, and boy 9–11 years) were as follows for the different food plans:

REGION	LOW-COST PLAN	MODERATE-COST PLAN	LIBERAL PLAN
U. S. average	$26	$34	$40
Northeast	29	37	42
North Central	28	34	40
South	23	30	36
West	28	35	41

A family that has eaten a liberal diet during the early years of marriage may move to a moderate-cost plan and even to a low-cost plan as the children advance in age, if there has been no accompanying increase in income. Choice of the cost level will depend not only on income related to family size and composition, but also on family values and goals, standards and tastes. Finicky appetites or demand for expensive cuts of meat and out-of-season foods raise expenses, whereas willingness to eat plentiful and inexpensive foods lowers them. Costs of the diet may also be increased by certain national and religious customs as well as by frequent entertainment and restaurant meals. Local prices may be high or low. Of course, free food received as pay, gifts, or charity reduces food costs. Expenses for food are also affected by skill in management of the food budget.

PLANNING PURCHASES

Good management of the food budget improves the quality of the diet, cuts costs, and increases convenience. Attainment of these objectives may be limited by one's knowledge, skill, and interests, as well as by the availability of funds, time and energy, and necessary equipment and space.

The first step in management of the food budget is to plan ahead for the purchase and use of foods. This requires provision for a nutritionally adequate diet. But foods are selected for reasons other than nutrition and health; in fact, a relatively small proportion of the usual expenditure for food is required to supply physiological needs. A pleasing taste and a variety in taste, color, and texture are wanted. Economy, convenience, and status value are important in food selection. Many foods are selected because of sheer habit, however the habit may have been established in the first place.

An Adequate Diet · The primary goal of a good food plan is a nutritionally adequate diet—vitamin pills and medical and dental bills are expensive substitutes. Knowledge of physiological needs is far greater for food nutrients than for any other item in the family budget, with the possible exception of certain types of medical care. Research on the nutritional needs of the body has made great strides in the past fifty years, and has established that an adequate diet is necessary for growth, repair and maintenance of body processes, energy, and a feeling of well-being.

In spite of nutrition research, educational programs, and higher incomes, many households have inadequate diets. Since the increase in average food expense from 1955 to 1965 appeared to be due primarily to increased food prices, inadequacy may be almost as prevalent now as earlier, unless consumption of milk products and fruits and vegetables is higher, which is questionable. Until analyses of dietary levels in 1965 are available, we should heed the warning signals provided by the earlier survey which showed that inadequacy was much more prevalent for calcium and ascorbic acid than for other nutrients, though still important for others.[1] With increases in income, there was an irregular downward movement in the percentage of households having inadequate amounts of the nutrients, but even the high income group was not meeting the requirements in all re-

---

[1] U. S. Department of Agriculture, *Household Food Consumption Survey 1955.* Analyses of dietary levels of households in 1965 will be available in 1968.

spects. The percentage of households of two or more persons that used less than recommended amounts of eight nutrients was as follows:

NUTRIENT	ALL HOUSE-HOLDS, 1955	INCOME CLASS	
		UNDER $2,000	$10,000 AND OVER
Protein	8	18	1
Calcium	29	39	17
Iron	9	15	6
Vitamin A value ..	16	32	5
Thiamine	17	18	14
Riboflavin	19	31	12
Niacin	7	15	2
Ascorbic acid	25	45	8

Food must regularly supply needed amounts of proteins, minerals, vitamins, fats, and carbohydrates. This can be done by including these foods daily: [2]

Milk group: Some milk. Cheese and ice cream can replace part of the milk.

Children, 3 to 4 cups. Teenagers, 4 or more cups.

Adults, 2 or more cups. Pregnant women, 4 or more cups.

Nursing mothers, 6 or more cups.

Meat group: 2 or more servings.

Meats, poultry, fish, eggs, dry beans, peas, nuts.

Vegetable-fruit group: 4 or more servings, including—

A dark-green or deep-yellow vegetable important for vitamin A (at least every other day).

A citrus fruit or other fruit or vegetable important for vitamin C (daily).

Other fruits and vegetables including potatoes.

Bread-cereals group: 4 or more servings.

Bread or cereals—whole grain, enriched, restored.

Table 8–4 lists the items included in the various food groups.

Low-Cost Sources of Nutrients · In addition to planning for a nutritionally adequate diet, the family may plan to use low-cost sources of nutrients. This may be done by emphasizing the low-cost food

---

[2] U. S. Department of Agriculture, *Essentials of an Adequate Diet,* Home Economics Research Report No. 3, 1957, p. 1.

TABLE 8–4. Items Included in Eleven Food Groups

GROUP NAME	FOODS INCLUDED
Milk, cheese, ice cream	Milk—whole, skim, buttermilk, dry, evaporated, condensed. Cheese; cream; ice cream.
Meat, poultry, fish, including bacon and salt pork	Beef, veal, lamb, pork. Variety meats such as liver, heart, tongue. Luncheon meats, bacon, salt pork; also mixtures that are mostly meat. Poultry. Fish and shellfish.
Eggs	Eggs, including those used in cooking.
Dry beans, peas, nuts	Dry beans of all kinds, dry peas, lentils. Soybeans and soya products. Peanuts, peanut butter, and tree nuts. Soups that are mostly legumes.
Flour, cereals, baked goods	Flour and meal. Cereals, including ready-to-eat cereals. Rice, hominy, noodles, macaroni, spaghetti. Bread, cake, other baked goods. Mixtures that are mostly grains.
Potatoes	Potatoes, fresh and processed.
Dark-green and deep-yellow vegetables	Broccoli, chard, collards, kale, spinach, other dark greens, green peppers. Carrots, pumpkin, yellow winter squash, sweet potatoes.
Citrus fruit, tomatoes	Grapefruit, lemons, limes, oranges, tangerines. Tomatoes.
Other vegetables and fruits	Asparagus, beets, brussels sprouts, cabbage, cauliflower, celery, corn, cucumbers, green lima beans, snap beans, lettuce, okra, onions, peas, rutabagas, sauerkraut, summer squash, turnips. Apples, bananas, berries, cherries, dates, figs, grapes, melons, peaches, pears, plums, prunes, raisins, rhubarb. All vegetables and fruits not included in other groups.
Fats and oils	Butter, margarine, mayonnaise, salad dressing, salad and cooking oils, drippings, fat, lard, and other shortening, suet.
Sugars, sweets	Sugar (beet and cane), granulated, powdered, brown; maple sugar. Molasses, sirup, honey, candy. Jams, jellies, preserves. Powdered and prepared desserts.

SOURCE: U. S. Department of Agriculture, 1962.

groups—dry beans, peas, and nuts; flour, cereals, and baked goods; and potatoes—from among the eleven food groups. Also, one may use low-cost foods within groups, which generally include the following items:

Nonfat dry milk solids
Pork liver, hamburger, chicken, beef liver
Dry beans, cooked at home
Oatmeal, whole-grain or enriched bread
Fresh potatoes
Orange juice, cabbage, kale, spinach, carrots, sweet potatoes
Margarine and lard
Granulated sugar

On the other hand, certain foods chosen for flavor and variety are likely to be high cost sources of nutrients. Those wanting to control their food budgets need to watch the quantities of the following items placed in the grocery basket:

Ice cream, fancy cheeses
Rib lamb chops, porterhouse or sirloin steak, loin pork chops
Nuts
Fancy baked goods, snack foods
Potato chips
Fresh fruits and vegetables, out of season, such as tomatoes, asparagus, melons
Pickles, catsup and chili sauce, olives
Butter, salad dressings
Candy, jellies and jams, prepared desserts
Coffee, tea, soft drinks

USDA Food Plans at Three Cost Levels · The Department of Agriculture has prepared a low-cost, a moderate-cost, and a liberal food plan, each giving the suggested weekly quantity of food in the 11 food groups for 20 sex-age groups. (See Tables 8–5, 8–6, and 8–7.) These food plans are based on the nutrients needed by a healthy individual of average height, weight, and activity as specified in the Recommended Dietary Allowances of the National Research Council, 1963. Since the nutrients are in terms of calories, protein, minerals, and vitamins, the home economists used data on the composition of various foods in terms of nutrients and data on family food habits in the United States as shown by the 1955 Household Food Consumption Survey and made allowances for food losses in preparation to convert these nutrients into terms of foods commonly bought at stores.

The quantity for a family may be calculated by adding together the requirements for individual members for each food group. Then the actual grocery order may be constructed by referring to Table 8–4 for the foods within each food group. This is a time-saving way of planning purchases and insuring that necessities are conveniently available. For a family consisting of a husband and wife 33 years old, a boy 11, and a girl 8, the weekly quantities are as follows:

FOOD GROUPS		LOW-COST PLAN	MODERATE-COST PLAN
Milk, milk products	quarts	16.50	17.50
Meat, poultry, fish	pounds	11.50	17.25
Eggs	number	25.00	29.00
Dry beans, peas, nuts	pounds	1.38	.88
Flour, cereals, baked goods	pounds	12.50	11.50
Citrus fruits, tomatoes	pounds	7.50	9.00
Dark-green, deep-yellow vegetables	pounds	3.50	3.50
Potatoes	pounds	10.00	8.50
Other vegetables, fruits	pounds	19.75	22.50
Fats, oils	pounds	2.12	2.75
Sugars, sweets	pounds	3.00	3.88

The low-cost plan includes larger quantities of three food groups—dry beans, peas and nuts; grain products; and potatoes. The more generous amounts of milk, eggs, meat, fruits and vegetables in the other two plans provide more varied menus. The more expensive plans also provide for more expensive choices within the food groups than does the low-cost plan. The family may select a plan that most nearly meets its needs, then vary it according to the activity, height, and weight as well as tastes of family members, taking into account differences in costs in the community or through time.

A family can meet its nutritional needs on a less expensive diet than the USDA low-cost plan provides by further emphasizing the three low-cost food groups—potatoes; dry beans and peas; and flour and cereals—and by selecting the lower cost items within each of the eleven food groups. This is done in the USDA's economy food plan, designed for temporary use, which costs about a quarter less than the low-cost plan. In fact, one may go further. For example, the nutrient allowances recommended for a young woman would be supplied by a day's diet composed of a pound loaf of whole wheat bread,

TABLE 8-5. Low-Cost Family Food Plan

WEEKLY QUANTITIES OF FOOD[2] FOR EACH MEMBER OF FAMILY

SEX-AGE GROUP[1]	MILK, CHEESE, ICE CREAM[3] (Qt.)	MEAT, POULTRY, FISH[4] (Lb.)	(Oz.)	EGGS (No.)	DRY BEANS, PEAS, NUTS (Lb.)	(Oz.)	FLOUR, CEREALS, BAKED GOODS[5] (Lb.)	(Oz.)	CITRUS FRUIT, TOMATOES (Lb.)	(Oz.)	DARK-GREEN AND DEEP-YELLOW VEGETABLES (Lb.)	(Oz.)	POTATOES (Lb.)	(Oz.)	OTHER VEGETABLES AND FRUITS (Lb.)	(Oz.)	FATS, OILS (Lb.)	(Oz.)	SUGARS, SWEETS (Lb.)	(Oz.)
Children:																				
7 months to 1 year	+	1	+	5	0	0	1	0	1	8	0	+	0	8	1	0	0	1	0	2
1 to 3 years	+	1	12	5	0	1	1	8	1	8	0	+	0	12	2	+	0	+	0	4
3 to 6 years	+	2	0	5	0	2	2	0	1	12	0	+	1	+	3	+	0	6	0	6
6 to 9 years	+	2	4	6	0	+	2	12	2	0	0	8	2	+	4	+	0	8	0	10
Girls:																				
9 to 12 years	5½	2	8	7	0	6	2	8	2	+	0	12	2	+	5	0	0	8	0	10
12 to 15 years	7	2	8	7	0	6	2	12	2	+	1	0	2	8	5	0	0	8	0	12
15 to 20 years	7	2	12	7	0	6	2	8	2	+	1	+	2	+	4	12	0	6	0	10
Boys:																				
9 to 12 years	5½	2	8	6	0	6	3	0	2	0	0	12	2	8	5	0	0	8	0	12
12 to 15 years	7	3	8	6	0	6	4	+	2	0	0	12	3	+	5	+	0	12	0	12
15 to 20 years	7	3	8	6	0	6	4	12	2	0	0	12	4	+	5	8	0	14	0	14
Women:																				
20 to 35 years	3½	3	+	7	0	6	2	8	1	12	1	8	2	0	5	0	0	6	0	10
35 to 55 years	3½	3	+	7	0	6	2	+	1	12	1	8	1	8	4	8	0	4	0	0
55 to 75 years	3½	2	8	5	0	4	2	0	2	0	1	0	1	+	3	12	0	4	0	6
75 years and over	3½	2	+	5	0	+	1	8	2	0	1	0	1	+	5	0	0	4	0	+
Pregnant[6]	5½	3	12	7	0	6	2	12	3	+	2	0	1	8	5	8	0	6	0	6
Lactating[6]	8	3	12	7	0	6	3	12	3	+	1	8	3	+	5	8	0	10	0	10
Men:																				
20 to 35 years	3½	3	8	6	0	6	3	+	1	12	0	12	3	+	5	8	0	12	1	0
35 to 55 years	3½	3	+	6	0	6	3	12	1	12	0	12	3	0	5	0	0	10	0	12
55 to 75 years	3½	3	0	6	0	+	2	12	1	12	0	12	2	+	4	8	0	10	0	10
75 years and over	3½	2	12	6	0	+	2	8	1	8	0	12	2	0	4	+	0	8	0	8

[1] Age groups include the persons of the first age listed up to but not including those of the second age listed.
[2] Food as purchased or brought into the kitchen from garden or farm.
[3] Fluid whole milk, or its calcium equivalent in cheese, evaporated milk, dry milk, or ice cream.
[4] Bacon and salt pork should not exceed ⅓ pound for each 5 pounds of meat group.
[5] Weight in terms of flour and cereal. Count 1½ pounds bread as 1 pound flour.
[6] Three additional quarts of milk are suggested for pregnant and lactating teenagers.
SOURCE: U. S. Department of Agriculture, 1964.

TABLE 8-6. Moderate-Cost Family Food Plan

WEEKLY QUANTITIES OF FOOD [2] FOR EACH MEMBER OF FAMILY

SEX-AGE GROUP [1]	MILK, CHEESE, ICE CREAM [3]	MEAT, POULTRY, FISH [4]		EGGS	DRY BEANS, PEAS, NUTS		FLOUR, CEREALS, BAKED GOODS [5]		CITRUS FRUIT, TOMATOES		DARK-GREEN AND DEEP-YELLOW VEGETABLES		POTATOES		OTHER VEGETABLES AND FRUITS		FATS, OILS		SUGARS, SWEETS	
	Qt.	Lb.	Oz.	No.	Lb.	Oz.	Lb.	Oz.	Lb.	Oz.	Lb.	Oz.	Lb.	Oz.	Lb.	Oz.	Lb.	Oz.	Lb.	Oz.
Children:																				
7 months to 1 year	5	1	8	6	0	0	0	14	1	8	0	4	0	8	1	8	0	1	0	2
1 to 3 years	5	2	4	6	0	1	1	4	1	8	0	4	0	12	2	12	0	4	0	4
3 to 6 years	5	2	12	6	0	1	1	12	2	0	0	4	1	0	4	0	0	6	0	8
6 to 9 years	5	3	4	7	0	2	2	8	2	4	0	8	1	12	4	12	0	10	0	14
Girls:																				
9 to 12 years	5½	4	4	7	0	4	2	8	2	8	0	12	2	0	5	8	0	8	0	12
12 to 15 years	7	4	8	7	0	4	2	8	2	8	1	0	2	4	5	12	0	12	0	14
15 to 20 years	7	4	8	7	0	4	2	4	2	8	1	4	2	0	5	8	0	8	0	12
Boys:																				
9 to 12 years	5½	4	4	7	0	4	2	12	2	4	0	12	2	4	5	8	0	10	0	14
12 to 15 years	7	4	12	7	0	4	4	0	2	4	1	12	3	0	6	0	0	14	1	0
15 to 20 years	7	5	8	7	0	6	4	8	2	8	1	12	4	0	6	8	1	2	1	2
Women:																				
20 to 35 years	3½	4	12	8	0	4	2	4	2	4	1	8	1	8	5	12	0	8	0	14
35 to 55 years	3½	4	12	8	0	4	2	4	2	4	1	8	1	4	5	0	0	6	0	8
55 to 75 years	3½	4	4	6	0	2	1	8	2	4	0	12	1	4	4	4	0	4	0	8
75 years and over	3½	3	8	6	0	2	1	4	2	4	0	12	1	0	3	12	0	6	0	8
Pregnant [6]	5½	5	8	8	0	4	2	12	3	4	2	0	1	8	5	12	0	12	0	8
Lactating [6]	8	5	8	8	0	4	3	12	3	8	1	8	2	12	6	4	0	12	0	12
Men:																				
20 to 35 years	3½	5	0	7	0	4	4	0	2	4	0	12	3	0	6	8	1	0	1	4
35 to 55 years	3½	4	12	7	0	4	3	8	2	4	0	12	2	8	5	12	0	14	1	0
55 to 75 years	3½	4	8	7	0	2	2	8	2	4	0	12	2	4	5	8	0	12	0	14
75 years and over	3½	4	8	7	0	2	2	4	2	4	0	12	2	0	5	4	0	8	0	12

[1] Age groups include the persons of the first age listed up to but not including those of the second age listed.
[2] Food as purchased or brought into the kitchen from garden or farm.
[3] Fluid whole milk, or its calcium equivalent in cheese, evaporated milk, dry milk, or ice cream.
[4] Bacon and salt pork should not exceed ⅓ pound for each 5 pounds of meat group.
[5] Weight in terms of flour and cereal. Count 1½ pounds bread as 1 pound flour.
[6] Three additional quarts of milk are suggested for pregnant and lactating teenagers.
SOURCE: U. S. Department of Agriculture, 1964.

TABLE 8–7. Liberal Family Food Plan

WEEKLY QUANTITIES OF FOOD [2] FOR EACH MEMBER OF FAMILY

SEX-AGE GROUP [1]	MILK, CHEESE, ICE CREAM [3]	MEAT, POULTRY, FISH [4]		EGGS	DRY BEANS, PEAS, NUTS		FLOUR, CEREALS, BAKED GOODS [5]		CITRUS FRUIT, TOMATOES		DARK-GREEN AND DEEP-YELLOW VEGETABLES		POTATOES		OTHER VEGETABLES AND FRUITS		FATS, OILS		SUGARS, SWEETS	
	Qt.	*Lb.*	*Oz.*	*No.*	*Lb.*	*Oz.*	*Lb.*	*Oz.*	*Lb.*	*Oz.*	*Lb.*	*Oz.*	*Lb.*	*Oz.*	*Lb.*	*Oz.*	*Lb.*	*Oz.*	*Lb.*	*Oz.*
Children:																				
7 months to 1 year	5	1	8	7	0	0	0	14	1	12	0	+	0	8	1	8	0	1	0	2
1 to 3 years	5	2	12	7	0	1	1	+	1	12	0	+	0	12	2	12	0	+	0	+
3 to 6 years	5	3	+	7	0	1	1	8	2	4	0	8	0	12	4	8	0	8	0	10
6 to 9 years	5½	4	+	7	0	2	2	+	2	12	0	8	1	8	5	4	0	10	1	0
Girls:																				
9 to 12 years	5½	4	12	7	0	+	2	+	3	0	0	12	1	12	6	0	0	10	0	14
12 to 15 years	7	5	12	7	0	2	2	+	3	0	1	0	2	0	6	0	0	12	1	2
15 to 20 years	7	5	8	7	0	2	2	0	3	0	1	+	1	12	5	12	0	10	0	14
Boys:																				
9 to 12 years	5½	5	0	8	0	+	2	12	2	12	0	12	2	+	6	8	0	10	1	0
12 to 15 years	7	5	8	8	0	+	3	12	3	0	0	12	3	0	6	8	0	14	1	+
15 to 20 years	7	6	4	6	0	6	+	+	3	+	0	12	+	+	7	+	1	+	0	2
Women:																				
20 to 35 years	4+	5	8	8	0	+	2	0	3	0	1	8	1	+	6	+	0	8	1	2
35 to 55 years	4+	5	8	8	0	+	1	12	3	0	1	8	1	0	4	8	0	6	0	12
55 to 75 years	4+	4	12	6	0	1	1	+	3	0	0	12	1	0	+	8	0	6	0	12
75 years and over	4+	4	4	6	0	1	1	0	3	0	0	12	0	12	6	0	0	+	0	10
Pregnant [6]	5½	6	0	8	0	4	2	8	+	0	2	0	1	+	6	+	0	6	0	12
Lactating [6]	8	6	0	8	0	4	3	12	+	0	1	8	2	8	6	+	0	14	0	+
Men:																				
20 to 35 years	4+	6	0	7	0	4	3	12	3	0	0	12	2	12	7	12	1	0	1	8
35 to 55 years	4+	5	8	7	0	+	3	+	3	0	0	12	2	+	6	8	0	14	1	4
55 to 75 years	4+	5	0	7	0	2	2	8	3	0	0	12	2	0	6	0	0	10	0	2
75 years and over	4+	5	0	7	0	2	2	+	2	12	0	12	1	12	5	12	0	8	0	14

[1] Age groups include the persons of the first age listed up to but not including those of the second age listed.
[2] Food as purchased or brought into the kitchen from garden or farm.
[3] Fluid whole milk, or its calcium equivalent in cheese, evaporated milk, dry milk, or ice cream.
[4] Bacon and salt pork should not exceed ½ pound for each 5 pounds of meat group.
[5] Weight in terms of flour and cereal. Count 1½ pounds bread as 1 pound flour.
[6] Three additional quarts of milk are suggested for pregnant and lactating teenagers.
SOURCE: U. S. Department of Agriculture, 1964.

an eighth of a pound of margarine, a quart of skim milk reconstituted from nonfat dry milk, a cup of cooked dry beans, and a cup of cooked kale. These items may be purchased for about 49¢ on today's market, almost half the cost of the low-cost plan. While this diet is simple, it is nutritionally adequate, which is more than can be said for the diets of many of the world's people.

BUYING FOOD

The second step in management of the food budget is to buy skillfully in order to obtain the best quality of foods, cut costs, or increase convenience. Certain shopping practices are generally helpful. Shop with a list of needed items that shows details of type and size and is organized into food groups or areas of the store. Keep a running list during the week and make a late check on newspaper ads in order to complete the list and take advantage of specials. Make few shopping trips during the week, and plan them for times when the stores are well-stocked and least crowded. At the store, take time to select carefully; avoid impulse buying of items that are not needed. Shop alone if that improves management of the food money.

Safety in Foods · The primary goal of good buying is to obtain a safe food supply. Many safeguards have been established to protect consumers; however, it is possible to circumvent them through ignorance or determination. Foods are particularly prone to health dangers because of disease in the animal or the human handler, insecticides or other additives used, spoilage, infestation by insects and rodents, and unsanitary conditions.

Tuberculosis, undulant fever, typhoid fever, enteritis, scarlet fever, septic sore throat, infantile diarrhea, and diphtheria may be transmitted to man through milk and milk products that have not been produced, processed, and distributed under carefully controlled sanitary conditions from disease-free animals or from milk and milk products that have not properly been pasteurized.

Meat animals and poultry may carry various diseases such as tuberculosis, undulant fever, trichinosis, and psittacosis which make their meat unfit for human consumption. Or meats and poultry and their products may be handled in an unsanitary way. The U. S. Department of Agriculture has the responsibility for inspecting all meats and poultry and their products that are shipped in interstate commerce to determine that they are fit for human consumption. This involves inspecting animals before and after slaughter and checking that they are handled under sanitary conditions. The carcasses are then stamped "U.S. INSP'D & P'S'D." State and local laws frequently seek to extend similar types of inspection to meats that are produced and sold locally.

The Federal Food and Drug Administration is charged with preventing the sale in interstate commerce of contaminated foods (those that have been produced, processed, or held under unsanitary conditions; those that have been contaminated by filfth, insects, or rodents; those containing harmful residues of insecticides, coloring, other food additives, or chemicals that have migrated from the packaging into the foods). State and local laws sometimes seek to extend similar types of inspection to foods produced and sold locally. In addition, state agencies may inspect the health of food handlers in retail food stores and restaurants and the sanitary conditions and practices of the establishments, as well as seek to prevent the sale of foods that may have been contaminated in floods or by the water and chemicals used in extinguishing fires.

In spite of the efforts of food producers, processors, and distributors to provide a safe food supply and the efforts of federal, state, and local agencies to enforce laws, the family must be alert to insure a safe food supply for itself. Millions of people are involved in providing the food supply—some are ignorant, some negligent, and accidents occur. In addition, federal, state, or local agencies may labor under inadequate laws, ineffective penalties, insufficient funds, ineptitude, or carelessness.

Quality in Foods · The second goal of food buying is to obtain good quality foods at their peak of nutritive value and taste. This requires ability to judge quality in foods and to use knowledgeably the aids available. While detailed study of the means of identifying quality in foods is not possible within the scope of the present work, certain general principles can be pointed out.

A number of foods are graded by the U. S. Department of Agriculture, by the state, or by producers or packers. Federal grade standards and specifications are available for more than 100 foods. Use of these grades is voluntary in general, except with regard to substandard grades of certain items sold in interstate commerce which must be marked "Below Standard in Quality." It is incumbent on the food buyer to know the grade terms and their meanings for the different foods purchased.

These grades are based on the palatability characteristics of the foods—flavor, tenderness, color, size, shape, odor, appearance, maturity, freedom from defects—and are a guide to the appropriate use and method of preparation. Different grades of a food are equally safe for human consumption and are about equal in nutritive value. The grades are generally stated as A, B, C or in numbers or in terms.

Some of the common federal grades for food are as follows:

FRESH FRUITS AND VEGETABLES:
U. S. Grade A
U. S. Grade B
Offgrade

MEATS:
USDA Prime
USDA Choice
USDA Good
USDA Standard
USDA Commercial
USDA Utility

PROCESSED FRUITS AND VEGETABLES:
U. S. Grade A or U. S. Fancy
U. S. Grade B or U. S Choice
   or Extra Standard
U S. Grade C or U. S. Standard
Substandard

POULTRY:
USDA Grade A
USDA Grade B
USDA Grade C

SHELL EGGS:
U. S. Grade AA
U. S. Grade A
U. S. Grade B
U. S Grade C

BUTTER:
U. S. Grade AA or U. S. 93 score
U. S. Grade A   or U. S. 92 score
U. S. Grade B   or U. S. 90 score
U. S. Grade C   or U. S. 89 score

Many foods do not appear in retail stores with standard grade letters or terms attached although many of them have been graded at an earlier stage in the marketing process to simplify orders. For these the buyer needs to learn through study and experience to judge quality by inspection. Descriptive terms used on labels of many foods are helpful in identifying the wanted item—Rome Beauty apples, Idaho potatoes, early June peas, homogenized milk. Brands may be helpful in identifying the quality wanted and the retailer also may be helpful. Comparison of fresh items such as oranges, apples, spinach sometimes indicates that higher quality is possible by selecting items from bulk displays than by purchasing prepackaged items.

Economy and Convenience in Food Buying · The first step in economizing on the food budget is to obtain accurate *weights and prices*.

Canned foods sold in interstate commerce that are below the standard for fill of the container must be marked "Below Standard in Fill," and such cans are frequently sold at reduced prices. Items that have been packaged before they reach the retailer have the weight marked on the package. The accuracy of weights and prices of items weighed by the retailer depends upon accurate scales, accuracy in weighing, and pricing policies.

A Wisconsin study of store-packaged meats, poultry, and potatoes indicated that an important proportion of the packages were short-weight—44 percent of the fresh and smoked meat packages, 48 percent of the poultry, and 37 percent of the potatoes.[3] Of the packages of fresh meats, 44 percent were underweight, 44 percent correct, and 12 percent overweight. Apparently an important cause of inaccuracy was failure to make allowance for the weight of the wrapping material. For instance, if no allowance is made for the weight of a half-ounce package, calves liver at $1.39 a pound would mean a rate of $1.44 a pound when one pound is ordered or $1.60 a pound when four orders are placed for four ounces each.

Purchasing *seasonal specials* is a good way of saving money. Fresh foods bought at the height of the harvest season are not only lower in price but also most succulent. Taking advantage of seasonal specials requires flexibility in meal plans and knowledge of the seasonality of prices. For instance, oranges and grapefruit have their seasonal lows in the early part of the year, tomatoes in late summer and early fall, and apples in late fall and early winter. Pork is lowest in spring, and eggs are lowest in late spring and early summer. Current information on seasonal specials is carried by the news media.

Purchasing foods at *special sales* may afford sizable savings. These may be week-end specials, loss leaders, or other promotional sales. Meats, fresh produce, and canned foods (as well as soaps and other nonfood items) are often offered at such sales. The amount of savings is determined by regular prices, quality of the sale products, and whether the family can use the sale items in a reasonable time without waste. Available money and storage limit the family's ability to take advantage of sales opportunities. The food buyer needs to beware of special sales and store displays that encourage impulse buying of unneeded items that might jeopardize a tight food budget.

Another method of saving in food buying is to purchase the *quality necessary* for the purpose, but not to buy a higher quality

[3] C. L. Jackson, "Supervision of Food Package Weights in Wisconsin," 3 pp., processed, 1959.

than needed. For instance, Grade A canned tomatoes are generally whole, perfect in looks and even in ripeness, whereas Grade C tomatoes are somewhat mashed and imperfect. If the tomatoes are to be used for sauce or soup, Grade C may be as useful as A. If the store's brand sells at 20¢ a pound for Grade A, 15¢ for B, and 11¢ for C, a sizable saving is made by using the lowest grade that meets the need. The fully-ripe flavor of certain Grade C foods, such as canned tomatoes or peaches, is preferred by some people. In fact, Substandard Grade might be used when it is available.

Tasty and nutritious meat can be provided by using good or a lower grade of beef or by using cheaper cuts of meat with proper cooking. If the various cuts of meat should sell at a dollar a pound, the cost per pound of raw lean meat would vary from $1 for flank steak, choice grade, to about $2 for brisket of beef, and up to $3.45 for hind shank of beef (Table 8–8). Of course, this would be a most unusual situation. Recently at a local market, chuck roast was on special sale at 38¢ a pound, while some other popular cuts were selling at $1.19–$1.39. Comparing the costs by multiplying the retail price by the amount in the table (e.g., for chuck roast, 0.38 times 1.57) shows that net costs of raw lean meat ranged from 60¢ a pound for chuck roast to $2.59 for rib lamb chops, as follows:

MEAT	RETAIL PRICE PER POUND	FACTOR FROM TABLE	COST PER POUND OF RAW LEAN MEAT
Chuck roast, 5th rib, choice	$0.38	1.57	$0.60
Loin pork chops	1.19	1.50	1.78
Rib lamb chops, choice	1.29	2.01	2.59
Sirloin steak, wedge bone, choice	1.29	1.46	1.88
Porterhouse steak, choice	1.39	1.65	2.29

The choice of brands may provide savings so long as the one chosen is acceptable to the family. On a recent day the local supermarket had several brands of catsup in 12- and 14-ounce bottles which varied from 16¢ to 26¢ per 14 ounces. Canned pear halves varied from 24¢ to 35¢ for a 1-pound can. All-purpose flour in 5-pound bags varied from 45¢ to 65¢. Instant coffee in 5- or 6-ounce containers varied from 89¢ to $1.50 per 6 ounces. The important question is whether there are differences that the family can discern in taste tests where brand names are covered. In some cases, several distributors purchase identical foods from the same processor and have these foods labeled with their own brands. Will these brands reach the

TABLE 8–8.   Cost per Pound of Raw Lean Meat When the Various Cuts Sell at Retail at a Dollar a Pound (Bone-in)

KIND AND CUT OF MEAT	COST PER POUND	KIND AND CUT OF MEAT	COST PER POUND
Beef, choice grade:		Pork, fresh:	
Blade rib—6th	$1.54	Boston butt	$1.19
Brisket	1.96	Picnic	1.63
Chuck rib—5th	1.57	Ham	1.60
Chuck rib—3rd and 4th	1.49	Loin, roasts and chops	1.50
Chuck rib—1st and 2nd	1.35	Spareribs	1.69
Club steaks	1.72		
Flank steaks	1.00	Lamb, choice grade:	
Hind shank	3.45	Leg	1.51
Porterhouse steaks	1.65	Loin chops	1.88
Ribs—11th and 12th	1.95	Rib chops	2.01
Ribs—7th and 8th	1.70	Shoulder	1.69
Round, heel	1.18		
Round steak	1.21		
Rump, knuckle out	1.70		
Short plate	1.87		
Shoulder arm roast	1.45		
Sirloin, double bone	1.63		
Sirloin, round and wedge bone	1.46		
T-bone steaks	1.71		

SOURCE: L. Page, "The Cost of Lean in Selected Cuts of Meat," *Family Economics Review*, June 1959, p. 2, adapted from *Meat for the Table* by Sleeter Bull, New York, 1951, 240 pp.

consumer at the same price? On the other hand, does the brand name always insure a constant quality of product?

Savings may be made by taking advantage of *quantity* purchasing. This means watching to see what size of package or number of units gives the lowest price per pound or quart. For instance, a local supermarket had one brand of nonfat dry milk with the price per quart of reconstituted milk ranging from 9.0¢ for the 3-quart package to 6.5¢ for the 20-quart package. One brand of tea equalled $2.43 a pound for a box containing 16 bags, but $2.20 a pound for a box with 100 bags. Elbow macaroni varied from 25¢ a pound in an 8-ounce box to 19.5¢ a pound in a 2-pound box. Sometime ago, a brand of cereal was 29¢ for a 6½-ounce box or 33¢ for eight individual packages totalling 5 ounces—71¢ versus $1.06 a pound. Another brand of cereal was 37¢ for 10 individual packages of a variety of cereals totalling 11¼ ounces. Similar amounts of the cereals purchased in regular sized boxes would have cost 24¢. Of course, the individual packages may protect freshness and provide variety which the family prefers.

Purchasing multiple units may also provide savings because of the usual pricing policies of stores. Sometimes these savings are small in cents but large in percentage. For instance when catsup was offered at 2/31¢, one cent could be saved by purchasing two at a time, a saving of 3 percent. Evaporated whole milk at 8/81¢ meant an 8 percent saving. And a canned soft drink at 6/49¢ allowed a 9 percent saving. Of course, not every family has the money, storage space, or need for such large quantities.

Savings may also be made by purchasing foods in simpler types of *packaging*. Sometimes savings are quite high. Using the same brand and same size of container, as nearly as possible, the following illustrations show the price per pound in the simpler and more complex packages and the savings by purchasing in the simpler package:

ITEM	PRICE PER POUND	SAVING
Brand A salt:		
Box, 1 lb. 10 oz. for 12¢	$0.074	94%
6 tiny individual salt shakers,		
2.4 oz. for 19¢	1.267	
Brand B flour:		
Bag, 2 lb. for 33¢	.165	29%
Shaker, 13 oz. for 19¢	.234	
Brand C tea:		
Loose, 8 oz. box for 87¢	1.740	16%
100 tea bags, 8 oz. box for $1.04 ...	2.080	
Brand D crackers:		
Jumble pack, 1 lb. box for 41¢	.410	12%
3 wax packets, 10 oz. box for 29¢ ..	.464	

The family may, of course, consider the convenience to be worth the extra cost.

Savings may be made by selecting foods of less desired *characteristics*. Artificial or natural color of eggs, oranges, apples may affect the prices at which they sell without affecting their food value or flavor. Frequently the small sizes of eggs, oranges, dried prunes, olives, and similar items sell at lower prices per edible pound than do the larger sizes. For instance, when eggs of the same quality or grade are compared, eggs of different sizes are an equally good buy at the following prices per dozen: [4]

4 U. S. Department of Agriculture, *How to Buy Eggs by USDA Grades and Weight Classes*, Leaflet No. 442, 1966.

EXTRA LARGE EGGS		LARGE EGGS		MEDIUM EGGS		SMALL EGGS
59¢	=	51¢	=	45¢	=	38¢
69¢	=	60¢	=	53¢	=	44¢
79¢	=	69¢	=	61¢	=	51¢
89¢	=	77¢	=	68¢	=	57¢

In other words, to be as good a buy as large eggs, medium eggs should be priced ⅛ less and small eggs should be priced ¼ less than large. If the price spread is greater than this, buy the smaller eggs to get more for the money.

One *store* may offer foods at lower prices than do other stores. These differences may be temporary or long-run; they may be on certain items only or on a large proportion of items. Shopping from store to store aids in comparing prices for separate items or for the total grocery order. Lower prices are made possible by greater efficiency due to higher turnover or the type of organization as well as by lower profit margin, less expensive location, or lack of "extra services." If the less expensive location is also a less convenient one, the additional time and money costs of patronizing the store need to be considered.

Foregoing *services* of delivery, credit, telephone orders, and sales people is generally an important way of saving perhaps 10 percent or more on the food bill. However, it requires a greater amount of time and energy and may involve increased costs for transportation and baby-sitters. Therefore, it is necessary to determine whether savings on the food budget are made at the cost of increased expenditures in other areas.

It is clear that the family has to answer the convenience-economy question in its own situation, and its answer may be different at various stages of the life cycle. A convenient store is conveniently located, has a wide variety of items, is well arranged, and offers special services. Sometimes the family has to forego convenience in order to economize, when it is a more important goal. But sometimes the savings made by foregoing convenience are absorbed by increased costs necessitated in other parts of the budget.

Premiums and Trading Stamps · Are premiums and trading stamps actually free? Or are prices raised to cover their costs? Are these premiums worth any extra amount they cost? In each instance the buyer needs to check prices to determine the value to the family. Early stamp-giving stores may increase their volume by a fifth or more, sufficient to cover the cost of stamps, so that they do not need to raise prices. But the situation has advanced beyond that stage. Some large chains have moved in recent years to eliminate trading stamps and cut prices.

The effect on prices of giving trading stamps was recently studied at one retail chain food store, in which prices were compared before and after trading stamps were introduced.[5] Prices of 185 items, a representative sample of the dry grocery items in the store, were taken three months before and eight months after the store added stamps. At the end of the period, prices had risen 3.5 percent, on the average, after adjustment for the general rise in dry grocery prices. When the redemption value of the stamps was subtracted, the average price rise was 2.02 percent. Trading stamps cost the retailer about 2 percent of his gross sales. According to this study, the cost was passed on to the consumer.

HOME PRODUCTION AND CARE IN USE

Home production of foods by the family for its own use may provide better quality products, savings, or greater convenience; or it may be simply a pleasant and satisfying activity. Although quality of home-produced products is sometimes better than those commercially produced, quality is sometimes inferior according to the judgment of the family or specialists. The savings, after payment for all purchased items and use of equipment, may or may not be greater per hour than could be saved or earned by other uses of time. Families living a distance from retailers of wanted foods sometimes find home production more convenient than frequent shopping.

Home production of foods includes the actual production of foods at home, as well as preservation and preparation for the table. While home gardens and orchards and home-provided milk, eggs, poultry, and meats are important types of home production for some families, housekeeping households used an average of only $2 a week of home-produced foods in the spring of 1965.[6] Home production accounted for only 1 percent of the money value of food used at home by urban families, 7 percent in rural nonfarm areas, and nearly a third for farm families. While the current figures may be lower, it is worth noting that in 1955, 40 percent of all housekeeping households produced some food for home use, but only 21 percent of the

[5] J. D. Bromley and W. H. Wallace, "The Effect of Trading Stamps on Retail Food Prices," Contribution No. 1091, Rhode Island Agricultural Experiment Station, 1965.

[6] U. S. Department of Agriculture, *Money Value of Food Used by Households in the United States, Spring 1965*, Food Consumption Survey, 1965–66, Preliminary Report, 1966.

urban contrasted with 60 percent of the rural nonfarm and 98 percent of the farm did so.[7]

Home Preservation · Although many families preserve foods at home, it is not a universal practice and average quantities are not large in comparison with approximately 1,400 pounds of food consumed annually per person.[8] Housekeeping households canned an average of 42 quarts of foods and froze an average of 66 pounds in 1954. Home canned foods averaged only 16 quarts for urban households, 62 quarts for rural nonfarm, and 138 quarts for farm. While 44 percent of all households canned some foods, only 29 percent of urban in contrast with 63 percent of rural nonfarm and 87 percent of farm did. Home-frozen foods averaged only 21 pounds for urban households and 60 pounds for rural nonfarm, but 333 pounds for farm households. Only 19 percent of all households engaged in home freezing, including 9 percent of urban, 23 percent of rural nonfarm, and 62 percent of farm.

Savings by home preservation are affected importantly by the prices paid for the food. If the food is purchased on local markets, the saving may not be great. The saving is also affected by the cost of necessary equipment, which is small for canning equipment used frequently, but is sizable when certain expensive equipment is used.

A recent study estimated costs of a $250, 16-cubic-foot freezer having a 480-pound capacity under three conditions—with no turnover of frozen food and with turnovers of 50 percent, and 150 percent (Table 8–9). Annual freezer costs varied from $63 when all food was purchased already frozen up to $96 when 1200 pounds of food were packaged and frozen at home. However, freezer costs per pound of food declined decidedly as turnover increased to 1200 pounds at which point the cost was 5¢ a pound for food purchased already frozen and 8¢ a pound for food packaged and frozen at home. The cost of the food itself was not included in these figures. The costs included depreciation based on 15 years' expected life, annual repairs estimated at 2 percent of purchase price, return on investment foregone at 3¾ percent a year, electricity at 2½¢ per kilowatt-hour for maintaining 0° F. and freezing food, and packaging at 2½¢ a pound.

Whether a family's food budget will be reduced or increased by use of a home freezer depends on whether food is homegrown or purchased, the kinds and quantities of foods frozen, and how the

[7] U. S. Department of Agriculture, *Household Food Consumption Survey of 1955.*
[8] U. S. Department of Agriculture, *Supplement for 1964 to U. S. Food Consumption . . . Sources of Data and Trends, 1909–63*, Supplement to Statistical Bulletin No. 364, 1965.

TABLE 8–9. Costs of Operating a Home Freezer (Estimates for 16 cubic-foot freezer with 480-pound capacity, priced at $250)

EXPENDITURE ITEM	USE DURING YEAR		
	480 LB. OF FOOD	720 LB. OF FOOD	1200 LB. OF FOOD
Types of annual costs:			
Fixed costs, total	$63.17	$63.17	$63.17
Net depreciation	16.67	16.67	16.67
Repairs	5.00	5.00	5.00
Interest foregone	9.38	9.38	9.38
Electricity for maintaining 0° F. ..	32.12	32.12	32.12
Variable costs for foods packaged and frozen at home, total	13.20	19.80	33.00
Electricity for freezing food	1.20	1.80	3.00
Packaging	12.00	18.00	30.00
Total annual freezer cost:			
Food purchased already frozen	$63.17	$63.17	$63.17
Food packaged and frozen at home	76.37	82.97	96.17
Freezer cost per pound of food:			
Food purchased already frozen	.13	.09	.05
Food packaged and frozen at home ..	.16	.12	.08

SOURCE: U. S. Department of Agriculture, *Home Freezers, Their Selection and Use*, Home and Garden Bulletin No. 48, 1964, 22 pp.

freezer is used. If the home freezer saves the cost of frequent trips to the grocery or the locker plant, this saving may be considered. At any rate, it is clear that a freezer may be a great convenience and may provide the family with better quality foods and more varied meals throughout the year. Economy and convenience were largely the reasons given for acquiring a home freezer by about 500 families in the Ft. Wayne, Indiana area in 1964–65.[9] Economy was listed more often by farm than urban families, probably because of preservation of home-produced items.

Home Preparation · While urban families do little home production or home preservation of food, they, as well as rural families, commonly prepare foods at home for the table. Today's markets offer many choices in the amount of built-in services that may be purchased with foods. While bakery bread is almost universally used, other products are purchased in a variety of forms. A chicken dinner, for instance, may be prepared from raw ingredients; from canned

[9] U. S. Department of Agriculture, *Homefreezer Management Survey*, preliminary report.

chicken, frozen peas, and dehydrated mashed potatoes; or it may be purchased ready to heat and serve.

In general, convenience foods cost more money although they save time. A recent study, however, found that some convenience foods were cheaper than the home-prepared item using fresh foods. Largest savings on the average food bill were provided by use of instant coffee, frozen orange concentrate, canned peas, canned cherries, and frozen peas.[10]

The family needs to compare convenience foods and home-prepared foods in its own situation on the basis of quality, money cost, and time saving. Is the palatability of the convenience food acceptable to the family? Some people find one or more of the money-saving convenience foods unacceptable, except in emergencies. On the other hand, is the commercially prepared food better than the homemaker can dependably produce or, perhaps, than the family appreciates? This could be true of certain of the finer baked goods or of a frozen lobster newburg or spinach soufflé. Such items may be reserved for special occasions when the homemaker wants an assured product without hazarding expensive raw materials and considerable time.

At times of household emergencies such as the sickness or absence of the homemaker or the arrival of unexpected guests, the money cost of the commercially-prepared food might properly be compared with the cost of comparable restaurant meals. But generally the cost of the convenience food is compared with the cost of preparing a similar item at home from raw ingredients. This means the same proportion of fruit in a cherry pie, the same proportion of beef in beef stew, of chicken in chicken chow mein, of eggs in potato salad, of fruit in fruited gelatin. The comparison should not be made on the basis of a standard home recipe if it includes more meat or other expensive ingredients than does the convenience food. One study reported that commercially prepared foods that cost twice as much or more than home-prepared included frozen beef patties in gravy, canned chicken meat, most of the frozen dinners, and frozen pizza.[11]

A fair comparison is based also on the cost of the same size of serving of home-prepared food as of the commercially prepared.

[10] H. H. Harp and D. F. Dunham, *Comparative Costs to Consumers of Convenience Foods and Home-Prepared Foods,* U. S. Department of Agriculture, Marketing Research Report No. 609, 1963, pp. 7–9.
[11] G. Gilpin, et al, *Meat, Fish, Poultry, and Cheese: Home Preparation Time, Yield, and Composition of Various Market Forms,* U. S. Department of Agriculture, Home Economics Research Report No. 30, 1965, p. 1.

When a homemade pie from canned fruit is the same size as a commercially-prepared pie of the same quality, the cost comparison can be fairly straightforward for the average sized family. But when only one or two servings are wanted for a small household and freezer storage is limited, a 25¢ individual pie is cheaper than a 35¢ full-size pie made at home, with much of it to be thrown away or eaten unwillingly or unwisely.

Since time saving is the important advantage of convenience foods, an estimate of it needs to be made. This involves the difference in time to produce the same quality of product from raw materials. A complete dinner that is prepared from raw materials in 50 minutes of active time for 50¢ less than an individual frozen dinner means a saving of 1¢ a minute or 60¢ an hour by home preparation. But if the homemaker could prepare the same dinner for her family of five with very little extra time, her saving is five times as great, or $3 an hour.

Time comparisons are generally based on active working time and ignore cooking time, waiting time, and defrosting time. For the person who is bound at home by other duties, this makes little difference. But for the employed homemaker or one who is frequently out of the house, the waiting time may be an important factor. But waiting time is not exclusive to home-prepared food. In fact, a frozen meat loaf dinner may take longer to reheat in the oven than it takes to prepare hamburgers and vegetables on the top of the range.

In other words, decision on the use of convenience foods depends on the individual family's standards for palatability and variety in foods, the quantity needed, and its resources of money and time. The sizable family with a homemaker at home may use convenience foods for emergencies or special treats. A couple or a single person wanting variety and having limited storage space for frozen foods may find that convenience foods save money as well as time, or that the money saving per hour is small. Persons with limited cooking facilities or skills may find convenience foods cheaper than the alternative of restaurant meals.

For an example of methodology, let us look at an earlier pilot study that compared the time and money cost of individual ingredients and a commercial mix for preparing four baked products— yellow cake, baking powder biscuits, pie crust, and chocolate chip cookies. The quality of the commercial product was duplicated as nearly as possible, and the amount prepared was the same in both instances. Savings ranged from 3.7¢ for pie crust to 13.4¢ for the cookies (Table 8–10). But since the pie crust took 4 extra minutes and the cookies took 14 extra, the savings per hour of work were almost equal at 56¢ and 57¢. In other words, large savings alone did not make a higher hourly saving if they required correspondingly greater time.

Care in Production and Use · But good management of the food budget goes beyond saving money. It also requires that the methods for insuring safety in purchased foods be applied at home. Home-produced foods must be free from insecticides and disease-bearing organisms. Foods must be preserved, prepared, stored, and served in appropriate ways to prevent the growth of such organisms and to protect foods from contamination by insecticides, insects, rodents, and filth. A sanitary place, equipment, food handler, and methods are essential. To provide foods on the table that are most nutritious and appetizing while minimizing cost requires proper storage for each food, avoidance of waste in cleaning foods, proper cooking methods, avoidance of plate waste, and use of leftovers.

TABLE 8–10. Average Money and Time Cost in Preparing Four Baked Products from Individual and Premixed Ingredients (Dawson, Minnesota, 1955–56)

ITEM	MONEY COST (CENTS)	TIME COST (MINUTES)	SAVINGS PER HOUR (CENTS)
Yellow cake (1.6 lb.):			
Commercial mix	40.7	18	..
Individual ingredients	33.4	27	..
Difference between two methods ...	7.3	9	49
Chocolate chip cookies (1.0 lb.):			
Commercial mix	44.1	13	..
Individual ingredients	30.7	27	..
Difference between two methods ...	13.4	14	57
Baking powder biscuits (0.7 lb.):			
Commercial mix	12.8	13	..
Individual ingredients	8.6	18	..
Difference between two methods ...	4.2	5	50
Pie crust (0.3 lb.):			
Commercial mix	8.5	13	..
Individual ingredients	4.8	17	..
Difference between two methods ...	3.7	4	56

SOURCE: E. Asp, I. Noble, and F. Clark, "Pilot Study of Money and Time Spent in Preparing Baked Products from Individual and Premixed Ingredients," *Journal of Home Economics*, November 1957, pp. 717–719. Reprinted with permission of the American Home Economics Association.

QUESTIONS

1. How important is food in the average family budget? How does it differ among families?
2. An "inelastic demand" for food means what kind of response to income changes?
3. What classes of expenditures are part of the total cost of eating at home? Is it always cheaper to eat at home?
4. What is the latest estimated weekly cost of the low-cost food plan for a young couple? For a young couple with two school-age children?
5. What assumptions are made in estimating costs of the three food plans?
6. What are the major objectives of good management of the food budget? What are the four major steps in management?
7. What are the requirements for an adequate diet? Does high food expenditure guarantee adequacy?
8. What are important low-cost sources of nutrients?
9. How do the food plans at three cost levels differ from one another?
10. What specific shopping practices generally improve management of the food budget?
11. Discuss various safeguards established to insure safety of the food supply.
12. What aids are available for determining quality in foods?
13. How easy is it to save both time and money in food buying?
14. Describe important methods for economizing in the purchase of foods.
15. Home production of foods includes what three stages? How important is each stage in the United States? Why?
16. How can the family judge the advisability of using convenience foods?
17. What are some examples of good care of foods in the home?
18. Select a family and a cost level for food. Estimate the weekly cost of the plan. Calculate needed weekly quantities for each of the eleven food groups. Decide on what specific foods to buy for the family to meet the requirements of the plan. Plan menus. Price a week's grocery order at the store.

SUGGESTIONS FOR FURTHER READING

Household Finance Corporation. *Money Management: Your Food Dollar*. Chicago, latest edition.

——————. *Money Management: Your Shopping Dollar*. Chicago, latest edition.

U. S. Department of Agriculture, Washington, D.C. Single copy of latest edition of following publications free from the Department as long as free supply lasts.

Cost of Food at Home Estimated for Food Plans at Three Cost Levels, U.S. Average.

Family Fare . . . Food Management and Recipes. G–1.

Family Food Budgeting . . . for Good Meals and Good Nutrition. G–94.

Food for Families with School Children. G–13.

Food for the Family with Young Children. G–5.

Food for the Young Couple. G–85.

Food Guide for Older Folks. G–17.

A Fruit and Vegetable Buying Guide for Consumers. G–21.

Home Freezers, Their Selection and Use. G–48.

How to Buy Eggs by USDA Grades and Weight Classes. Leaflet No. 442.

How to Buy Poultry by USDA Grades. Marketing Bulletin 1.

Money-Saving Main Dishes. G–43.

Nutrition . . . Up to Date, Up to You. GS–1.

Shopper's Guide to U. S. Grades for Food. G–58.

"The fashion wears out more apparel than the man."
—Much ado about nothing

The Clothing Budget / 9

- ESTIMATING BUDGET AMOUNT
- PLANNING PURCHASES
- BUYING CLOTHING
- HOME PRODUCTION AND CARE
  IN USE

We still think of food, clothing, and shelter in that order, so we will consider the clothing budget next, although the declining proportion spent on clothing has put it in fourth place for more than a decade. Clothing, accessories, and upkeep now take 9 percent of disposable income—half as much as food and roughly seven-tenths as much as shelter or transportation.

While incomes have been rising, the quantity of clothing purchased per person has increased little in contrast with other important categories in the budget. This lessened emphasis on clothing is related to the trend to casual clothing, the decline in use of clothing for prestige, the greater durability of some modern fibers, the change in the composition of the population which now includes a higher proportion of preschool children and elderly people, and the increasing competition of other types of expenditures—autos, TV, freezers, houses, vacations, and travel.

ESTIMATING BUDGET AMOUNT

In estimating the amount for clothing in the next period, the experienced person or family may draw on records of expenditures and items purchased in the past year to give a broad estimate. But a longer period of records is helpful for items replaced infrequently. Inexperienced persons or those without records may use, as a starting place, the data on average clothing expenditures of families of different size, residence, and income, given in Table 9–1.

The average amount spent on clothing varies decidedly from one group of families to another. Large families generally spend more on clothing than do small families, other conditions being equal, and city families usually spend more than do rural nonfarm families. At

TABLE 9–1. Clothing Expenditures, by Family Size, Residence, and Income (Average not shown for cells of less than 30 families)

RESIDENCE AND MONEY INCOME AFTER TAXES	NUMBER OF PERSONS IN FAMILY					
	1	2	3	4	5	6 OR MORE
Urban:						
Under $1,000	$ 40	..	..	..	..	..
$1,000–$1,999	90	$ 100	..	..	..	..
$2,000–$2,999	230	170	$ 230	..	..	..
$3,000–$3,999	290	280	340	$ 460	..	..
$4,000–$4,999	390	340	460	450	$ 550	$ 540
$5,000–$5,999	410	400	530	590	550	620
$6,000–$7,499	450	560	660	700	720	790
$7,500–$9,999	..	670	830	890	940	1,050
$10,000–$14,999	..	880	1,120	1,310	1,300	1,230
$15,000 and over	..	1,800	..	..	..	..
Rural nonfarm:						
Under $1,000	50	60	..	..	..	..
$1,000–$1,999	80	80	180	..	..	..
$2,000–$2,999	160	150	260	..	..	300
$3,000–$3,999	..	200	270	300	..	460
$4,000–$4,999	..	270	370	400	410	510
$5,000–$5,999	..	360	440	540	490	590
$6,000–$7,499	..	450	710	630	700	730
$7,500–$9,999	..	580	620	820	950	960
Farm:						
Under $1,000	80	140	..	..	..	..
$1,000–$1,999	70	160	240	310	..	350
$2,000–$2,999	..	180	310	340	..	430
$3,000–$3,999	..	240	400	440	..	570
$4,000–$4,999	..	250	400	460	..	530
$5,000–$5,999	..	310	450	540	590	730
$6,000–$7,499	..	430	510	700	690	820
$7,500–$9,999	..	..	..	760	..	920

SOURCE: U. S. Bureau of Labor Statistics and U. S. Department of Agriculture, *Survey of Consumer Expenditures 1961.* These data collected in the spring of 1962 from 9,200 families with final tabulations published in 1966 are the best indicators currently available of annual spending patterns of various types of families. Data for the early 1970's may be available a few years thereafter.

the upper income levels, city families are likely to spend more than similar-sized farm families, among whom high income is more frequently a temporary phenomenon to which they adjust expenditures only moderately. But at the lower income levels, city families tend to spend less than similar farm families among whom temporarily low income is more common. While high-income families generally spend more money on clothing than do low-income families of the same size and residence, the proportion does not vary with income in a clear way.

Some assistance in estimating amounts to budget for different family members may be obtained from the detailed analyses of various surveys. In general, expenditures increase with age of children to a peak in the late teens and early twenties, before marriage. Among adults, expenditures decline as they advance in age. The elderly spend about as much as children 6–11 years old and about half as much as a man 30–39 years old.

The estimated scale of clothing expenditures for different sex-age groups in nonfarm families with moderate incomes, given in Table 9–2, may be used to compare costs for different families. For example, relative costs at different stages of the family life cycle might be estimated as follows (expense for a male 30–39 years old = 100):

FAMILY MEMBERS	FAMILY SCALE
Man 22, wife 20	215
Man 28, wife 26, children 4, 2, and baby	310
Man 43, wife 41, boy 19, girl 17, boy 15	525
Man 49, wife 47	220
Woman 65	55

If a family of four budgets $750 for clothing, a tentative division among family members might be somewhat as follows:

FAMILY MEMBERS	SCALE	BUDGET
Man 38	100	$200
Wife 36	145	290
Boy 13	80	160
Girl 8	50	100
Total	375	750

PLANNING PURCHASES

Good management of the clothing budget improves the quality of the wardrobe, reduces costs, and increases convenience through ease of care and ready availability of items for use. These objectives

TABLE 9–2. Estimated Scale of Clothing Expenditures for Sex-Age Groups in Nonfarm Families with Moderate Incomes (Expense for male 30–39 years old = 100)

AGE	SCALE FOR MALES	SCALE FOR FEMALES
Under 2	20	20
2–5	35	40
6–11	50	50
12–15	80	85
16–17	105	110
18–29:		
Unmarried	115	165
Married	85	130
30–39	100	145
40–49	105	115
50–59	65	100
60 and over	50	55

are incompletely attained because of the limitations of skills and interests, money, time and energy, and equipment and space.

Clothing provides protection from the weather and from infection and injury. Substitute garments make personal hygiene simpler. Garments should be comfortable for the wearer, a problem particularly during periods of rapid growth. In addition, we want our clothing to be appropriate for the occasion, for one's occupation and position, and for the age-sex-size group. Clothing similar to that of their peer group is especially important to adolescents. Some choices of clothing emphasize high fashion, prestige, beauty, modesty, originality, the enhancement of individual attractiveness, economy, or convenience.

The first step in managing the clothing budget is to plan the purchases necessary to replenish the wardrobe. The items may be listed in *various categories* on the basis of use as outdoor wraps, outer garments, underwear and nightwear, hosiery, hats, footwear, other clothing, clothing materials, and clothing upkeep. For a large part of the nation, appropriate garments are needed for both indoor and outdoor wear when the weather is quite hot, quite cold, and very wet. Those who live in areas with limited change in weather or who stay indoors during inclement weather can manage with less varied wardrobes.

A careful *try-on inventory* of the wardrobe of each family

member perhaps twice a year will help to determine what that member has in comparison with his needs for the coming season. What items can be worn as they are? Which ones need minor changes? Which need major changes? Proceed to make these changes. Which items are no longer usable? Move them to other members of the family or dispose of them. Now is the time to determine what supplements are needed for the wardrobe. Any supplements should be planned carefully so that they fit well into the wardrobe.

To save money, it may be necessary to *cut down* on the person's ideas of his needs. Furthermore, there are definite advantages in limiting the quantity of items in the wardrobe at a given time. The garments available will have harder wear before they are outgrown or out of style. A smaller wardrobe minimizes remodelling, care, and storage problems. The advantages of a limited wardrobe are especially obvious for children who outgrow a large inventory of garments and shoes before many items show wear.

In general, it is desirable to *maintain the wardrobe* by making some replacements each year rather than allow the wardrobe to fall to a low level, then struggle to rebuild it. Thus one always has some new garments. Also, regular replacement evens out the expenditures year by year. Of course, there are times when wholesale replacement or accumulation is necessary—after periods of reduced income, after a change in occupation or other activities, a change of climate, or an extreme change in fashions or the size of the person.

A record of last year's clothing purchases is a help in planning for yearly recurring items, but a *long-term plan* is needed for items infrequently replaced, so that these items may be "staggered" through the years and among family members. Even those items replaced frequently, such as hosiery, underwear, and shoes, may need to be staggered through the year or money must be accumulated regularly for them, especially when several family members are involved.

Savings may be made and the quality of the wardrobe improved by using *hand-me-downs* or exchange plans for children and other family members. Acceptance depends on sensible attitudes in the family and the community. Children's clothing may be usable longer when it includes *growth features* such as extra length of sleeves, depth of hems, elastic waist bands, and mix and match separates. However, faded fabric destroys the advantage of some of these growth features, and garments may be discarded for other reasons before the growth feature is needed.

Multiple-use garments have many advantages. Some garments

can be worn for school, work, shopping, church, and some recreational activities with small changes. Some garments are readily demoted so that they have multiple uses through time—from church and other dress occasions at first on down to home activities or rough sports. Other garments, such as formal evening clothes, have one type of use only.

Avoiding extremes in style and fit of garments will help to insure longer use for them. Relatively expensive items that are expected to be the backbone of the wardrobe over a period of time might best be in classic styles, whereas high style may be enjoyed in small items and accessories, items that wear out fast, and items that will not be wanted for long-time use. This might include party garments.

The use of a *basic color scheme* can improve the wardrobe and lower cost. Though a monochromatic color scheme is the easy way, it is not necessary. Variety can be achieved with a wardrobe built around black or brown or blue by selecting colorful accessories or some large items in different colors that blend with accessories in basic colors.

BUYING CLOTHING

The second major step in management of the clothing budget is to buy wisely according to plan. This involves knowing what is wanted, shopping around for it, and avoiding impulse items that do not fit into the plan. Study the labels on fabrics and garments; try on garments critically, perhaps with the assistance of an outspoken friend; wear or take to the store the items that are to be complemented by the new purchase. Shop when the stores are not crowded and when there is time for care.

Safety in Clothing · A major safety problem in clothing and fabrics is flammability. A wise buyer will be constantly alert for this hazard. The Flammable Fabrics Act of 1953 sets legal limits to flammability characteristics of fabrics in wearing apparel in order to prevent sale in interstate commerce of those that exhibit rapid and intense burning, such as the torch sweaters. The flammability of fabrics used in clothing as well as in curtains, drapes, upholstery, carpets, and bedding needs to be considered particularly when the items are used by invalids, children, the elderly, or by careless persons.

A different type of hazard in fabrics results from the allergies of some persons to certain fibers of animal origin such as wool, fur, and feathers, to fabrics that shed lint, and to the dust that is collected by some fabrics. The variety of fibers and fabrics available today makes it possible to minimize hazardous fabrics in the immediate environment of persons with such allergic reactions, once the cause has been identified.

Cleanliness and the destruction of bacteria carried in fabrics are necessary for personal hygiene and the prevention of growth of disease organisms. Sanitation requires fabrics that can withstand frequent cleansing. This means laundering with detergents and appropriate kinds and amounts of disinfectants, depending on the heat of the water. For some garments, it means dry cleaning followed, most importantly, by steam pressing.[1]

All garments should be fitted properly for comfort and the avoidance of irritation. Especially hosiery and shoes must be well fitted and the style wisely chosen to avoid irreparable damage to the foot. While proper fit, style, and state of repair of the shoe are particularly important for the child, his foot is so pliant and grows so fast at certain times, and his understanding of food needs is so slight that considerable effort may be required to protect his foot from being permanently misshapen. Shoes need to be inspected carefully not only at purchase but also periodically during wear, perhaps monthly when the child is growing rapidly. Specialists disapprove of handing down shoes on the basis that a shoe that has conformed to the foot of one person has a harmful effect on the foot of a later user.

Quality in Clothing · Judging the qualities of garments is a major job at the time of purchase. Research studies indicate that the qualities most wanted in garments are good style, color, fit, durability, comfort, performance in use, and ease of care. Identification of these qualities on the market is the special problem of the consumer-buyer who has to depend primarily on inspection and informative labels.

Knowledge of the *fibers* from which a fabric is constructed aids in judging its probable comfort, durability, performance, and care, as well as the appropriateness of its price. Since there are over a million possible combinations of fibers in fabrics and since identification by inspection is impossible with today's advanced technology, the informative label is especially important.

---

[1] Ethel McNeil, "What About Bacteria in Cold Water Laundering?", *Agricultural Research*, U. S. Department of Agriculture, 14(7):12–13, 1966; and Robert R. Banville and Ethel McNeil, "The Microbiology of Dry Cleaning," *Applied Microbiology*, 14 (1):1–7, 1966.

The Wool Products Labeling Act of 1939 requires that any product containing wool (excluding floor coverings and upholsteries) and sold in interstate commerce must be labeled to show the percentage by weight of wool, reprocessed wool, reused wool, and each fiber other than wool if it amounts to 5 percent or more of the weight.

The Fur Products Labeling Act of 1951 requires that any article of wearing apparel made in whole or in part of fur and sold in interstate commerce must bear a label stating the true English name of the animal that produced the fur and, when such is the case, that it is used fur, that the fur has been bleached or dyed, and that the fur product is composed in substantial part of paws, tails, bellies, or waste fur. Thus, rabbit, muskrat, squirrel, or wolf must be so labeled rather than hopefully masquerading as beaver, chinchilla, ermine, mink, or sable.

The Textile Fiber Products Identification Act of 1958 requires that fiber content be given on the labels of all wearing apparel, yard goods, draperies, furnishings, rugs, and bedding sold in interstate commerce. The label shows the percentage by weight in decreasing order of all fibers, by generic name, that constitute 5 percent or more of the total. A recent amendment permits the mention of fibers that constitute less than 5 percent if they have a functional significance. The generic (general or family) names of textile fibers that must be used in labeling are as follows:

NATURAL FIBERS	MANMADE FIBERS—NONCELLULOSIC
Cotton	Acrylic
Wool	Glass
Linen	Lastrile
Silk	Metallic
	Modacrylic
MANMADE FIBERS—CELLULOSIC	Nylon
	Nytril
Acetate	Olefin
Triacetate	Polyester
Rayon	Rubber
	Saran
	Spandex
	Vinal
	Vinyon

Additional generic names for new manufactured fibers may be added when necessary by the Federal Trade Commission. These generic names may be accompanied by registered trade marks. The characteristics, uses, and care of these fibers differ considerably. The summary of the characteristics of the major fibers used for clothing in Table 9–3 may be used by the consumer-buyer in selecting the most desirable fibers for various purposes.

TABLE 9–3. Summary of Characteristics of Major Fibers Used in Clothing

CATEGORY AND GENERIC NAME	FIBER CHARACTERISTICS IN BRIEF
Natural fibers:	
Cotton	Absorbent, strong, durable. Stands frequent, hard laundering. Special finishes available to impart wash-wear and wrinkle resistant properties, produce durable creases, retard flame, and control mildew and shrinkage.
Wool	Highly absorbent, durable, resilient, warm. Special finishes available to control moths and shrinkage and produce durable creases.
Flax (linen)	Highly absorbent, strong, extremely durable. Stands frequent, hard laundering. Special finishes available to control mildew, wrinkles, and shrinkage.
Silk	Highly absorbent, strong, resilient. Generates static electricity.
Manmade fibers— cellulosic:	
Acetate	Moderately absorbent, resilient. Sensitive to acetone and iron heat. Dries quickly. Resists shrinkage. Durable pleating by heat-setting.
Triacetate	Low absorbency, resilient. Less sensitive to acetone and iron heat than acetate. Special finishes available to control static. Durable pleating by heat-setting.
Rayon	Some highly absorbent. Some newer types are stronger and more durable. Special finishes available to control shrinkage, wrinkles.
Selected manmade fibers— noncellulosic:	Properties common to all fibers below: Nonabsorbent, strong, resilient. Easy to wash and quick drying. Durable pleating by heat-setting. Resist moths, mildew, shrinkage, nonoily stains. Oils and perspiration hard to remove. Sensitive to heat in ironing. Accumulate static electricity in dry, cold weather.
Acrylic	Durable. High bulking power. Warm without weight. Some pill.
Modacrylic	High bulking power. Warm. Somewhat sensitive to acetone.
Nylon	Very strong, lightweight. Tends to gray and yellow. Some pill.
Olefin	Some very strong. Lightweight.
Polyester	Excellent wash-and-wear. Some pill.

Qualities of the fabric are affected not only by the fiber used, but also by the type of *yarn* and the *weave* or construction. The yarn created from the fibers may be fine or large, smooth or uneven, tightly or loosely twisted—each giving a special feature to the fabric. The fabric may be constructed by weaving, knitting, bonding, or felting. Yarns of fairly even size, closely woven together, produce the most durable fabric. Knitted fabrics are more likely than woven ones to stretch or shrink.

Special *finishes* affect the qualities of the fabric. Some finishes make fabrics resistant to wrinkles, soil, flame, moths, or mildew; some make them repellent to water or wind. Some of these finishes may eventually be removed from the fabric by repeated cleansing. Some finishes affect durability, stain removal, and the feasibility of alterations, even on a new garment. Trade practice rules of the Federal Trade Commission prohibit the use of terms such as "preshrunk" on woven cotton yard goods unless the statement includes the amount of residual shrinkage, if any.

The fit of a garment can be judged most accurately if its *size* is stated in terms of standard sizes and if it has a shrinkproof finish. The Commercial Standard for the sizing of women's patterns and apparel was declared in 1958 by the U. S. Department of Commerce. A large number of organizations have voluntarily accepted this standard.

Labels are most helpful when they contain information about the fiber, fabric construction, special finishes, and size of the garment. It is also desirable to know that the fabric is *colorfast* and that the colors harmonize with colors of other fabrics or clothing items available on the market. Information as to the *care required* is also especially important for today's consumer. Permanent labels sewn into the garment should be most helpful. Care required may range from "dry clean only" to "wash gently by hand in luke-warm suds" to "machine wash in hot water and tumble dry."

Careful inspection is helpful in determining the *workmanship* of a garment which affects its appearance, fit, and durability. A garment with good workmanship is cut on the grain, matching the pattern of the fabric, with flat and wide seams and generous hems. It is sewn with small stitches, has reinforcements at points of strain, has neat closures, and trims that are securely attached. Any lining, padding, interfacing, and trim are durable for use and cleaning. Some imperfections such as large stitches, poor buttonholes, and poor trim can be improved at home.

Economy in Buying Clothing · For many people, economy is an important goal in buying clothing and textiles. Various methods help us to economize. Textile products such as sheets and towels are generally labeled as to *measurements*. In purchases of yard goods, the measuring devices and methods as well as *pricing policies* must be accurate in order to insure getting the money's worth. The buyer needs to think of an item offered at $2.89 or $2.98 as a $3 item rather than as a $2 one.

In some clothing and textile items, savings can be made by purchasing *multiple units* at one time. Some common examples are hosiery and underwear, sheets and towels. Not only may the price per unit be lower for the large purchase, but also the total wear life may be greater. For instance, six pairs of identical hosiery generally wear much longer than six varied pairs that eventually degenerate into unmatched singles. When the family uses matching sets of bath-towels, handtowels, and washcloths, purchases of the less durable items may be gauged in terms of the wear life of the most durable item. One bathtowel, three handtowels, and six washcloths may be a more practical set than one unit of each item.

Economy may be effected by purchasing the *quality necessary* for the use, but not excessive quality. A garment that is to have hard wear (such as a coat, suit, or street or work shoes) needs to be durable, whereas an item that is to be worn little (such as a Halloween costume or formal party garment) may be low on durability. In each case it is probable that the cost per hour of use will be minimized, assuming that a higher price is paid for the durable item than for the nondurable.

However, durability of clothing and textile items does not always increase proportionately to increases in price. While the lowest-priced shirts, blouses, suits, shoes, sheets, and towels may not be very durable because of the sleaziness of the fabric or short-cuts in workmanship, the highest-priced garments may not be as durable as moderate-priced ones. High-priced garments may incorporate fine and unique fabric that is not as durable as a less luxurious type. Much of the reason for the high price may be the originality of the style.

Appropriate durability for children's clothing requires special consideration. Most clothing for children needs to be durable enough to withstand rough use and frequent laundering, but not so durable as to last far beyond the time when the garment fits the child's size and needs. Furthermore, the frequency of losses and of bad tears and stains means that a highly durable or fine garment may be used no longer than a simpler one.

Sometimes savings can be made by comparing *brands*. The same brand name does not guarantee the same fiber, fabric, and other characteristics at one time or from time to time. Nor does a different brand guarantee differences in characteristics. Garments with a given combination of qualities may be produced by many manufacturers. Furthermore, shirts or hosiery or sheets made by one manufacturer on his regular production line may be sold under a nationally advertised prestige brand as far as possible; additional production may be sold under store brands, particularly those of stores belonging to a chain. Informative labels help to identify objectively the similarities and differences. Of course, to some people a prestige brand is a satisfaction in itself. One man expressed his attitude by buying a prestige brand hat, since people were most likely to see its label, but selecting a little known brand of shoes.

Savings may be made on clothing and textiles by purchasing them at *special sales* if the items are needed and will be used. Sometimes special sales are advertised and savings indicated where no real reductions exist. At times the sale items have been specially purchased for the sale and are not the store's regular merchandise. They may be irregulars or seconds and may or may not be worth the sale price. Seasonal sales are held for certain items, such as the January white sales and the August fur sales. Frequently prices are 10–20 percent lower, stocks are wider, and merchandise is better quality at these sales since they are special promotional sales attempting to even out sales through the year. Other special promotional sales, such as the annual sale or manager's sale, may offer regular stock at a saving of 10 percent or more.

Clearance sales are frequently useful times to purchase clothing items since the store may cut prices drastically—by a third, a half, or more. The store may want to clear out this season's merchandise before the next season's shipments arrive or to clear items that are being discontinued or going out of style. The selection is likely to be limited in size, color, and style. These sales are generally before the end of the current wearing season, so that a winter coat or suit bought in January may still be worn two or three months. However, the item may be shopworn and require special cleaning or repairs before use. And the buyer has the problem of storing it until the next season. Also, the buyer takes the risk of whether the person for whom it is purchased will be able and happy to wear the garment by next winter. Will the size be right, the style usable, the color suitable for next year's wardrobe; and will the garment meet the individual's clothing needs at that time as related to activities and climate?

Clothing items are sold by many types of *stores*—department stores, specialty stores, mail order houses, discount stores, and variety stores. The store may be small or large, chain or independent. Prices may differ from one to another on a given item because of differences in sales volume, efficiency of operation, profit margin, or expense of the location. Since a cheaper location usually means a lower turnover, the cost per item may not be less. A retailer with a prestige name and his label in the garment may be able to charge more for it than could a mail order house.

At times it is possible to save money on clothing by foregoing *special services* such as credit and delivery. Discount stores and specialty stores may not provide credit and delivery services. Mail order houses may set special charges for credit and delivery. However, these services are so widespread today among large department stores that it may be difficult to save by foregoing the services. Probably these stores differ more today in the luxury of their appointments, the sophistication of displays, and the kind of help from sales persons, so that savings may more readily be made by foregoing some of these services. When one does not need to inspect or try on several items before making a selection, savings may be found by checking the catalogs of mail-order houses.

HOME PRODUCTION AND CARE IN USE

Savings may be made or quality and convenience may be improved by home production. Limitations on home production are imposed, however, by one's skill, interest, time to use in acquiring skill and in doing the work, and the equipment and space available.

Home production of clothing takes a variety of forms. It may involve simply quick *repairs* to prevent further disrepair. It may mean small *alterations* on new garments or old such as changing trim, hems, seams, or improving the workmanship of new ready-made garments by refinishing seams and buttonholes. It may extend to *home care* of garments—day-by-day and out-of-season care. This includes proper laundering, stain removal, pressing, and careful storage of out-of-season garments where they will be protected from insects, heat, light, and moisture.

Remodelling or restyling of garments is another type of home production, but this may require even more skill in planning and performance than does the construction of a new garment. For example, the fabric, scale of design, color, and bulkiness, as well as the pattern style that can be used on the old fabric—all must be appropriate for the person who will wear the remodelled garment. These matters are especially serious in remodelling adult garments for children.

Although the total savings from successful remodelling are sometimes sizable, they may be small per hour of work. Furthermore, the garment may be a dismal failure. The fabric may not last long after the remodelling has been completed. Since the money costs of a remodelled garment sometimes include a new pattern, special cleaning or dyeing, some new fabric, new trims, buttons, and notions, one should consider whether it is wiser to invest in one new garment than to remodel several for the same wardrobe.

Making New Garments · The creation of new garments at home is probably the type of home production most commonly thought of in the clothing area. But homemade clothing is probably less widespread and important in the total picture today than earlier when surveys showed that some homemade items had been acquired during the year by 11 percent of husbands, 25 percent of boys 2–15 years old, 40 percent of wives, and 60 percent of girls 2–15. For the wives, homemade items comprised a sixth or more (up to a quarter) of the acquisitions of aprons and smocks, housedresses, separate skirts, and dresses for street or dress, in declining order. For girls, homemade items comprised a sixth or more (up to a quarter) of the acquisitions of playsuits and like items, all dresses, separate skirts, and pajamas, in declining order.[2]

Just how much does home sewing pay? Some years ago a series of studies was made by the Department of Agriculture in which cotton housedresses, daytime dresses, and children's dresses similar in style and construction to garments purchased ready-made were constructed in a laboratory, under conditions roughly comparable to those in homes. These studies are particularly useful to us for their development of methodology that can be applied in the home situation.

Five examples of each type of garment in a common price range were purchased on the market. Then fabrics, findings, and commercial patterns that matched them as well as possible were selected for use in the laboratory. Matching commercial patterns for

[2] Margaret L. Brew, Roxanne R. O'Leary, and Lucille C. Dean, *Family Clothing Inventories and Purchases . . . With an Analysis to Show Factors Affecting Consumption,* U. S. Department of Agriculture, Agriculture Information Bulletin No. 148 (Washington, D.C.: Superintendent of Documents, 1956).

the housedresses could not be purchased, so the patterns available were used. Also, duplicates of the housedresses were purchased and ripped apart for patterns to see if costs would differ if matching patterns could have been found. (This work was not included in counting the time to make the dress, but an estimated cost of a pattern was counted as a cost.)

The time for making each garment was recorded, excluding interruptions. A record was made of money costs for fabric, findings (trimmings, belts, buttons, thread, zippers), pattern, and power. The cost of equipment was not counted. The laboratory worker was a skilled seamstress who constructed the garments according to the pattern with no alterations.

The results indicated that sizable savings could be made. Savings were highest on near-duplicates of the daytime dresses that were purchased ready-made at an average price of $10.15: $4.91 was saved on a size 14, amounting to $1.72 an hour (Table 9–4). Savings were slightly less on a size 20 which required somewhat more fabric and time. Savings averaged $2.16 on the child's dress that cost $4.39 ready-made—a saving of $1.11 an hour.

Savings were smallest on housedresses. The housedresses made from commercial patterns cost more to make than did copies of the ready-made ones because of more yardage and the need for zippers

TABLE 9–4. Average Money and Time Cost for Five Models of Each Homemade Garment

TYPE OF GARMENT	COST, READY-TO-WEAR	COST, HOME-MADE	MONEY SAVINGS	TIME COST (HOURS)	SAVINGS PER HOUR
Cotton daytime dress (size 14)	$10.15	$5.24	$4.91	2.86	$1.72
Cotton daytime dress (size 20)	10.15	5.56	4.59	2.94	1.56
Child's dress, cotton (size 8) .	4.39	2.23	2.16	1.94	1.11
Housedress (size 14):					
Copy of ready-to-wear	3.45	2.32	1.13	1.46	.77
Made from commercial pattern	(3.45)	2.84	.61	2.02	.30
Housedress (size 20):					
Copy of ready-to-wear	3.45	2.36	1.09	1.54	.70
Made from commercial pattern	(3.45)	3.03	.42	2.16	.19

SOURCE: Margaret L. Brew, Carol M. Jaeger, and Margaret Smith, *Exploratory Studies of Measuring Money Savings and Time Costs of Homemade Clothing*, U. S. Department of Agriculture, ARS 62–8, 1958.

not found on the ready-made. Those made from commercial patterns also took more time because of set-in sleeves and more gores in the skirt. As a result, savings of 77¢ an hour were made on the size 14 housedresses that were copies of the ready-made dresses, but 30¢ an hour on the housedresses made from commercial patterns. Whether a homemaker would be able to lay out the pattern, cut, and construct a garment as rapidly as did the laboratory workers is another matter (even excluding interruptions).

Materials to make the daytime dress or child's dress cost about half of the price of the ready-made garment, whereas materials to make the housedress cost two-thirds of the price of the ready-made, thus leaving little possible savings through home sewing. The homemaker, buying materials on the retail market, has to compete with the manufacturer who may be able to purchase the materials in huge lots at a quarter as much and, furthermore, can take advantage of mass production methods to save time.

A student reported that she had constructed 17 garments for her college wardrobe at a saving of $92, and that similar items would have cost $184 at the store. Since it took her 157 hours to construct the garments, she saved 58¢ an hour.[3] A graduate student who was a high-school teacher of clothing made a cotton shirtwaist blouse, duplicating as nearly as possible the fabric, findings, pattern and construction of a ready-made blouse priced at $3.29. She made a saving of $1.62 and it took her 164 minutes longer to shop for her materials and construct the blouse than if she had bought it ready-made, so that she saved 59¢ an hour. By the time she had completed her blouse, the ready-made blouse was on sale for $2.89, so that she finally saved $1.22, or 45¢ an hour.

It appears from the various studies that home sewing pays highest per hour for higher-priced garments in which the fabric and findings are a small proportion of the cost; for individuals with high skill and speed in planning and performance; for those who are hard to fit in ready-made garments that require expensive alterations; for those who want an unusual style; for those who complete the garment quickly so that it can be worn early; and for those who already own all necessary equipment. It probably pays well also for those who have low standards for their own personal creations. Whether savings are finally made on the clothing budget depends on whether the savings are absorbed by making more garments.

[3] L. Gramlow, "Does Home Sewing Pay?" *Forecast for Home Economists*, January 1955, p. 25.

The individual needs to figure her own time and money costs in making the garments that are useful to her family with the equipment she has. Also she needs to count the costs of any additional equipment. If a sewing machine costs $200 and she saves about $1 an hour by making a variety of garments, she will need to work 200 hours (or make approximately 40 cotton daytime dresses) before it is paid for. Of course, there is no income tax on any savings made through household production. Savings per hour need to be calculated in order to compare with other uses of time—other means of saving, other means of earning, and other uses of time for recreational, community, or cultural purposes. Of course, an individual may sew for sheer enjoyment of a hobby, even if it costs money. Golfing, gardening, and bowling all cost money.

Care in use of garments also helps the clothing budget. This includes using appropriate garments for an activity, protecting clothing with rainwear, alternating use of garments, and hanging, airing, brushing, and steaming them. But wear them—don't save them for the indefinite future. Garments are a poor long-time investment; they fade, become outdated and outgrown.

QUESTIONS

1. How important are clothing expenditures to consumers? What has been happening to these expenditures over the long run? Why?

2. How do average clothing expenditures of families differ with their size, residence, and income? How may such figures be used by the individual family?

3. How do clothing expenses generally vary from one sex-age group to another? Based on the scale, how would clothing expense vary during the family life cycle under normal conditions?

4. What are the purposes of good management of the clothing budget?

5. What methods help to plan wisely the purchases of clothing?

6. Describe the Flammable Fabrics Act.

7. Describe the Wool Products Labeling Act; the Fur Products Labeling Act; and the Textile Fiber Products Identification Act.

8. Explain the difference in characteristics of some natural fibers, some manmade fibers that are cellulosic, and some manmade fibers that are noncellulosic.

9. What additional factors affect the quality of clothing?

10. What buying methods may be used to save money on clothing? Evaluate each.

11. What are several different levels of home production of clothing?

12. What special problems are involved in remodelling?

13. Which types of garments seem to be most commonly made at home?

14. What methods are used in studying the savings through home sewing?

15. What have laboratory studies shown about savings from making certain garments?

16. In what situations does home sewing probably pay best?

17. What is the importance of care in use of garments to the clothing budget?

SUGGESTIONS FOR FURTHER READING

American Home Economics Association. *Textile Handbook.* Washington, D.C., latest edition.

Erwin, Mabel D. and Kinchen, Lila A. *Clothing for Moderns.* New York: Macmillan, 1964.

FMC Corporation, American Viscose Division. *Fiber Facts.* Philadelphia, latest edition.

Household Finance Corporation. *Money Management: Your Clothing Dollar.* Chicago, latest edition.

Tate, Mildred and Glisson, Oris. *Family Clothing.* New York: Wiley, 1961.

U. S. Department of Agriculture, *Consumers All: The Yearbook of Agriculture 1965.* Washington, D.C.: Superintendent of Documents, 1965, pp. 339–390.

U. S. Department of Agriculture, Washington, D.C. Single copy of latest edition of following publications free from the Department as long as free supply lasts.

Buying Women's Coats and Suits. G–31.
Leather Shoes—Selection and Care. FB–1523.
Men's Suits, How to Judge Quality. G–54.
Sanitation in Home Laundering. G–97.

"This castle hath a pleasant seat; the air
Nimbly and sweetly recommends itself
unto our gentle senses."
—MACBETH

The Shelter Budget / 10

- ESTIMATING BUDGET AMOUNT
- SELECTING A DWELLING
- COMPARING OWNERSHIP AND
  RENTAL
- THE HOUSE AS AN INVESTMENT
- OBTAINING A MORTGAGE
- AMORTIZING THE MORTGAGE

The shelter budget is of great importance because of its relation to family living conditions as well as the large outlay of funds
it involves (amounting to 14 percent of disposable income). The
proportion for shelter has been running about the same through the
sixties as it was in 1929. However, the amount of shelter services per
person has more than doubled, largely due to the strong postwar
trend for couples and unmarried persons to maintain private dwelling
units rather than to live in the households of large family groups.

ESTIMATING BUDGET AMOUNT

Experienced families may draw on their records of shelter costs
in previous years to estimate budget amounts for the next period,
while taking into account changed conditions and any need for improvements in quality or economy. A beginning family or one con-
templating a change in its shelter arrangements may find helpful the
data on average shelter expenditures of families of different size,
residence, and income, given in Table 10–1. The large amount for
shelter is shown clearly by these figures.

But expenditures differ from one group of families to another. Highest amounts are generally spent by urban families, with less by rural nonfarm, and least by farm families, other conditions being equal. No regular difference is shown between the expenditures of large families and small families. Although high-income families spend more on housing than do others, the proportion decreases with income.

Since most people live in housing units with cooking facilities, the present discussion is largely in terms of their needs and considerations. Approximately seven-tenths of these housing units are single-family houses, and the others are in structures with multiple units. Such single-family houses comprise six-tenths of the units inside standard metropolitan statistical areas (SMSA's), but almost nine-tenths outside these areas.[1] While single-family units are common in the country as a whole and in the suburbs, they are, of course, scarce in the center of metropolises where land values are exceedingly high. We are most aware of recent construction activity, particularly of apartments, but this adds a small proportion to the immense housing inventory of the country. On the other hand, when we seek a change of housing, we look at units that are currently vacant and available for occupancy, and find that less than half of them are single-family houses, because most vacant units are rental units.[2]

Family Plans · To determine how much it can and should pay for shelter each month, the family first takes into account its expected income. Then it considers:

> Its necessary expenses and debts for all items other than shelter.
> Its need for insurances and savings.
> Its shelter needs and the cost of meeting them.

Once the family has tentatively decided on its monthly budget for shelter, it can look for rental housing within its budget. This may result in reconsideration of the budgeted amount. But the family's decisions are even more complicated if it wishes to purchase a house. Its monthly budget for shelter is a starting point. Then the family must determine:

---

[1] U. S. *Census of Housing: 1960.* A housing unit generally includes private cooking facilities or, at least, direct access from the outside or through a common hall.

[2] U. S. Bureau of Census, *Current Housing Reports,* Series H–111, No. 47, 1967 (data for last quarter of 1966).

What portion of the monthly budget must go for regular expenses of the house, such as taxes, repairs, and insurance.

What size of loan can be financed by the remaining amount of the monthly budget. For instance, $100 a month available for principal and interest will finance a 30-year loan of $17,000 at 6 percent interest.

TABLE 10–1. Shelter Expenditures, by Family Size, Residence, and Income (Average not shown for cells of less than 30 families)

RESIDENCE AND MONEY INCOME AFTER TAXES	NUMBER OF PERSONS IN FAMILY					
	1	2	3	4	5	6 OR MORE
Urban:						
Under $1,000	$ 300	..	..	..	..	..
$1,000–$1,999	400	$ 360	..	..	..	..
$2,000–$2,999	500	470	$ 480	..	..	..
$3,000–$3,999	600	530	520	$ 560	..	..
$4,000–$4,999	660	630	640	630	$ 600	$ 710
$5,000–$5,999	890	730	750	760	760	680
$6,000–$7,499	1,060	760	810	870	890	830
$7,500–$9,999	..	1,000	960	960	910	960
$10,000–$14,999	..	1,080	1,180	1,250	1,200	1,100
$15,000 and over	..	1,830	..	..	..	..
Rural nonfarm:						
Under $1,000	140	130	..	..	..	..
$1,000–$1,999	210	190	130	..	..	..
$2,000–$2,999	320	290	280	..	..	180
$3,000–$3,999	..	320	380	370	..	280
$4,000–$4,999	..	400	470	440	420	400
$5,000–$5,999	..	550	610	540	620	520
$6,000–$7,499	..	630	650	650	670	540
$7,500–$9,999	..	810	790	860	810	720
Farm:						
Under $1,000	130	200	..	..	..	..
$1,000–$1,999	130	170	180	230	..	120
$2,000–$2,999	..	210	200	290	..	160
$3,000–$3,999	..	300	260	280	..	230
$4,000–$4,999	..	310	350	360	..	320
$5,000–$5,999	..	380	440	380	400	280
$6,000–$7,499	..	440	480	440	470	470
$7,500–$9,999	..	..	..	510	..	470

SOURCE: U. S. Bureau of Labor Statistics and U. S. Department of Agriculture, *Survey of Consumer Expenditures 1961*. These data collected in the spring of 1962 from 9,200 families with final tabulations published in 1966 are the best indicators currently available of annual spending patterns of various types of families. Data for the early 1970's may be available a few years thereafter.

The price the family can pay for a house is determined also by the amount available for a down payment. A large down payment means that the family can pay for a more expensive house than if the down payment is small. To calculate its down payment, the family first sets aside necessary amounts for

>   Closing costs
>   Prepayment of share of year's taxes
>   Any service charge to obtain mortgage
>   Any immediate repairs or improvement of the house
>   Any prepayment of property insurance
>   Moving costs
>   Any furniture or equipment required immediately
>   Emergencies

In summary, there is no simple answer to the question of the price the family can pay for a house. Each family has to make the decision on the basis of its own particular circumstances. And its circumstances sometimes change. Some families agree to pay more than they find they are able to afford through the years and have to make readjustments. Others pay less than they could afford, preferring to spend their money in other ways or to invest it.

Special Cost Considerations · The climate and price level in the community affect what the family has to pay to satisfy its needs. The population is moving to metropolitan areas where housing is more expensive. Only 6 percent now live on farms whereas 65 percent live in 212 standard metropolitan statistical areas—less than half in the central cities of 50,000 or more, and more than half in the areas surrounding them. In fact, almost four-tenths of the total population live in the 29 SMSA's with population of one million or more. The population growth of the 1960's has been most extreme in the suburbs of central cities and in the West, whereas the population on farms has declined.[3]

The location of the dwelling may affect importantly certain other expenses of the family. Transportation costs are frequently much higher for those outside the central city. A suburban or rural family may find that two cars are necessary for the same mobility as that provided the city family by cheap public transportation. Food

3 U. S. Bureau of the Census, *Current Population Reports*, Series P–27, No. 37, 1967 (1966 data); P–20, No. 163, 1967 (1966 data); and P–25, No. 347, 1966 (1965 data).

and other costs are higher for those who are remote from a good shopping center. In some neighborhoods, the family feels that it has to spend more for clothing, entertainment, and furnishings in order to equal the level of its neighbors.

Seeking a community with low taxes is not always economical in the long run since the taxes are used to support schools and the services of local government. Low taxes in suburban developments often prove temporary as the communities grow and services become necessary.

Good housing construction and facilities minimize expenses for repairs, for property insurance, and for heating, cooling, water supply, hot water, and disposal of household wastes. Families who move into rural areas frequently find that their costs for water and sewage disposal are higher than in urban areas.

Comparing costs of different dwellings is sometimes complicated. For instance, the rental rate may include simply the shelter cost or it may include certain utilities, furnishings, and services. The purchase price may be for the unfurnished dwelling, or it may include some furnishings or equipment. Streets, sidewalks, and sewers may be provided or it may be necessary to add them later.

Careful selection of a dwelling to avoid frequent moves helps to minimize the attendant costs. The obvious cost is that for the van, but there is also loss due to breakage and other damage to property. The new dwelling may require considerable cleaning or redecoration and remodelling. Curtains and carpets owned by the family may not be usable, and some furniture may not be suitable in the new home. Furthermore, there may be a period when rent or other monthly costs must be paid on both dwellings. Moving from one owned home to another multiplies the special costs for purchase and sale. Consideration should be given also to the strain and effort involved in moves that could have been avoided by better planning.

SELECTING A DWELLING

Good housing provides protection from excessive cold or heat in a safe, healthful, and efficient place for carrying on homemaking and personal activities. It is convenient to places of employment and other interests. It provides privacy for the family and the individual and yet allows for companionship and community activities. An attractive home and environment give aesthetic satisfaction and may have prestige value.

Housing needs differ from one family to another. A family that places high value on housing will be willing to forego other satisfactions, whereas another family may place more emphasis on food or education. The physical condition of some family members may necessitate wider doorways or a downstairs bedroom and bath. Large families that engage in many activities and much entertainment at home need more space and facilities for them.

The stage of the family life cycle also makes great difference in housing needs. In choosing a home, the family should consider the future course of its life cycle and the adaptability of the dwelling. A minimum level at each stage of the family life cycle might be as follows: [4]

The beginning family needs two or three rooms to include living room space, bedroom space, and a kitchen, with a bathroom and closet space.

The expanding family needs a living room, a larger kitchen with eating space, a bathroom, laundry, more storage space, and play space for the children indoors and outdoors; also, more bedrooms—one for the parents and one for each two children of the same sex or each child of opposite sex.

The launching family needs at least as much space as the expanding family and preferably more—a recreation room, study, or dining room, private traffic ways in the house, and more storage space.

The middle-age family could again use an apartment or small house with a living room, kitchen, bedroom, and bath. Entertainment, particularly of its children, may cause the family to want more rooms.

The old-age family has similar minimum needs for a living room, kitchen, bedroom, and bath. An extra bedroom may be needed in case of illness in the home. A one-floor arrangement and the limited responsibility of apartment living may become more desirable as age advances.

Housing Standards · Census data for 1960 showed that, among occupied housing units, 87 percent had one room or more per person, indicating that serious crowding was relatively infrequent. And 75 percent had full modern plumbing facilities, including hot running water and private toilet and bath, in a structure that was in sound

[4] Adapted with modifications from Tessie Agan, "Housing and the Family Life Cycle," *Journal of Home Economics*, May 1950, pp. 351–354.

TABLE 10–2.   Check List for Selection of a Dwelling Unit

Neighborhood

Has available:
  Water supply
  Sewage disposal
  Removal of garbage
  Removal of trash
  Electricity
  Fuel supplies
  Telephone
  Fire protection
  Police protection
  Sidewalks
  Streets
  Street lighting
  Pleasant planting and
    landscape design
  Suitable and effective
    zoning ordinance

Free from:
  Surface floods
  Accident hazards
  Noise and vibration
  Odors, smoke, dust
  Disease hazards
  Moral hazards

Access to center of:
  Employment
  Education
  Shopping
  Health services
  Outdoor recreation
  Religious, social, and
    cultural activities

The Lot

Outdoor space
No flooding of site
Landscaping
Attractive views
Parking facilities
Suitable and effective
  building code

Construction of Dwelling

Safe from accident
  hazards
Safe from fire hazards
Noise protection
Heating (75° at 3 feet
  from floor and
  vertical differential
  not exceeding 10°)
Lighting—natural and
  artificial
Ventilation
Hot and cold running
  water
Toilet facilities
Sewage disposal
Garbage disposal
Attractive dwelling
Good foundation
Structure in good
  condition
Sufficient electric
  current and outlets
Suitable building code

Housing Space
Indoor space, minimum:

Persons	Square feet
1	400
2	750
3	1,000
4	1,150
5	1,400
6	1,550

Housing Space
(continued)

FHA minima for
  3-bedroom house:

Room	Square feet
Living room	170
Dining room	95
Living-dining	210
Kitchen	70
Kitchen-dining	110
3 bedrooms	280

One closet per bedroom,
  2' x 3'
One closet near living
  room, 2' x 3'
Linen closet near bedroom

Pleasant and convenient
  arrangement of space

Space for all activities:
  Homemaking—
    Food preparation,
      preservation
    Laundering
    Sewing
    Care of infants or
      sick
    Cleaning
  Personal—
    Eating
    Recreation,
      self-improvement
    Entertainment
    Sleeping, dressing
    Personal cleanliness,
      sanitation
  Other—
    Storage
    Heating equipment
    Hot water heater
    Circulation between
      areas of dwelling
    Entrance, egress

SOURCES: Committee on the Hygiene of Housing, American Public Health Association, *Standards for Healthful Housing: Planning the Neighborhood*, 1948, 90 pp.; *Planning the Home for Occupancy*, 1950, 56 pp.; and *Construction and Equipment of the Home*, 1951, 77 pp. Federal Housing Administration minimum standards for houses on which they insure loans.

condition. In 1950, 85 percent had a kitchen sink and 94 percent had electric lighting, both of which are probably nearly universal today.

While national data provide perspective on the general situation of families, the individual may want more direct help in selecting his own housing. For that purpose the family may benefit by studying the check list for selection of a dwelling unit given in Table 10–2. The list includes desirable characteristics of the neighborhood, the lot, construction of the dwelling, and space in the dwelling, and is worth careful study and consideration on each point. It may be adapted in selecting an apartment or house to buy, build, or rent in an urban or rural community.

Type of Dwelling Unit · The family or individual has to choose between rooms, an apartment, and a house. Each has certain advantages, and only the individual or family can determine which are most weighty.

A furnished room or two is frequently preferred by the single person who wishes to do little cooking or entertaining at home. This may be a young earner, an elderly person, someone who moves frequently or is seldom at home. The total costs for housing, utilities, furnishings, equipment, and meals may be lower for a single person in a room than in an apartment or house.

An apartment generally entails no personal responsibility for care of the sidewalk, furnace, repairs, and like items, which may be a decided advantage over a house to an elderly couple or a person who is frequently out of town. The costs of certain services, such as janitorial and heating, are shared with others in the building and are generally cheaper than when privately provided. In some metropolitan areas such as New York and Chicago, many apartments are more conveniently located than are most private dwellings.

A house generally gives the family more freedom and privacy, both indoors and outdoors, since it usually provides some outside space. The family has the pleasure of working outdoors and of imposing its own personal standards. It may be able to save by performing some of the chores for itself.

An older home or apartment usually provides more space in a substantially constructed dwelling. A new place has more modern facilities and arrangement of space and requires fewer repairs during the first years. Choice of a ready-built apartment or house means that the family can see what it is getting and know the exact price, exclusive of repairs.

Selection of an apartment before construction is complete may allow the family to choose the color scheme or equipment. Building its own home allows the family to choose the lot and house plan to suit itself, presumably. But compromises are frequently required because of building costs which are estimated at roughly $14 per square foot for 1600 square feet, and lower costs for larger houses. Of course, the type of structure, its facilities, and local conditions determine actual costs.

COMPARING OWNERSHIP AND RENTAL

Renting an apartment or house generally has several advantages over buying. For one thing, no down payment is required. As a result, rental is a preliminary step to purchase in many cases. Rental may give the family a chance to accumulate money toward home ownership or for another type of investment that the family considers more desirable. At the same time the family can study the community and learn the characteristics of desirable housing. The renter has the further advantage of limited financial responsibility—usually the amount of the monthly rent—which makes it easier to budget expenses. Gross rent, including an estimate for utilities and fuel, averaged $75 for dwelling units within standard metropolitan statistical areas and $58 for nonfarm units outside these areas in 1960. Only a third in SMSA's were in one dwelling unit structures. Recent data for rental units that are vacant and available for occupancy show median rents of $75 inside SMSA's and $46 outside SMSA's, with rentals for three-tenths of vacancies including amounts for all utilities.[5] Undoubtedly rental rates are greater in the center of metropolises.

Although none of the foregoing factors influence them, many families continue to rent. Their reason is the greater mobility that renting affords. Moves can be made more quickly and with less financial loss. Because of the special costs of buying and selling, it may be cheaper to rent at a relatively high rate than to buy if one will remain in the house less than three years. Mobility is desired because of the expectation of changes in income and family needs. But it is important primarily because of changes in place of employment. Mobility is especially useful to the young couple as it seeks occupational advancement. The earner may be handicapped if he refuses to move.

[5] U. S. Bureau of Census, *Current Housing Reports*, Series H–111, No. 43, 1966 (data for 1965).

Some large employers estimate that they transfer certain types of executives to other locations about every three years compared with every five years a decade ago. In a 12-month period, 1 out of 5 persons change residence. Two-thirds of the movers do not cross county lines. Of the other third, half move in the same state and half move to a different state. Young adults in their 20's move much more frequently than do other age groups.[6]

The owner, on the other hand, has several advantages over the renter. He has independence with regard to decisions on redecoration and improvements; and he may be able to save considerably by doing the work himself. A home owner may feel that he is more deeply a part of the community and therefore take greater part in community affairs.

The property owner has special income tax advantages in counting as deductions the property taxes and interest on the mortgage. This may save money on his taxes, depending on the amount of his other legal deductions. The home owner also avoids paying taxes on the interest or dividends he would otherwise receive on other types of investment of his funds.

The most important financial advantage for many owners is that home ownership, requiring regular savings, constitutes an investment which is a hedge against inflation. Purchase establishes the basic level of housing costs over the long run since these costs change slowly. Thus the owner has lower costs than the renter in a future inflationary period. Furthermore, the owner may be able to sell the house later at a gain.

Home ownership has been increasing in popularity since the war, perhaps due to choice, but perhaps because of a dearth of appropriate rental units for families with children. Owned homes totalled 64 percent of all occupied housing units at the end of 1966—a decided increase from 55 percent in 1950 and 44 percent in 1940. The median value of owner-occupied one-dwelling unit structures in 1960 was $13,500 inside SMSA's and $8,600 in other nonfarm areas. Within SMSA's where two-thirds of the population lives, 45 percent of the structures were valued at $10,000–$17,500. Half of the remainder were valued lower, and half, higher. Median asking price for the nation's vacant units was approximately $13,000 in both 1965 and 1960.

While the majority of owner-occupied units are single-family homes, 2 percent in central cities are in structures with 5 or more

[6] U. S. Bureau of the Census, *Current Population Reports*, P–20, No. 156, 1966 (1966 data).

units that may be classified as apartments. In a cooperative apartment, each owner meets a proportionate share of the annual interest, taxes, and other expenses of the cooperative. He may be called upon to pay extra amounts if one of the buyers is unable to pay his share. The smaller the cooperative's mortgage, the larger a new owner's initial investment, other conditions being equal. The members control the choice of future owners.

In a condominium apartment, the owner has individual title to the apartment he occupies and common ownership of the land, hallways, and such joint property. He obtains his own mortgage with terms suited to his individual situation. The interest and property taxes clearly count as deductions on his income tax statement. He is free to sell his unit as advantageously as possible.

Costs of Ownership · The renter usually has a single monthly bill to pay for his shelter. This covers a wide variety of costs which the owner has to meet piecemeal—some regularly under contract and some sporadically. In discussing ownership costs, let us consider the cost of the shelter itself and abstract it from all costs for utilities, furnishings and equipment, and household operation.

At the beginning, the family must make a down payment and pay the closing costs. The *down payment* may be small or large depending on what the family has available and the mortgage terms it is able to negotiate, but is generally a minimum of 3 percent to 25 percent of the appraised value. The purposes of the down payment are to protect the lender in case the property falls in value and to encourage the borrower to complete payments on the mortgage.

The *closing costs* include a variety of items necessary to protect the buyer such as appraisal fees, survey fees, legal fees for examination of the contract, mortgage, and deed, title search and title guarantee, tax on property transfer, notary fees, and recording fees for the deed and mortgage. Closing costs may amount to about 2 percent of the purchase price. If a mortgage is obtained, there may be a mortgage commission or service charge and credit investigation fees. The maximum charge is 1 percent for the processing of an FHA or VA loan.

Assuming that a mortgage is obtained, there will be monthly or annual *principal* and *interest* payments until the debt is discharged. The interest rate approximates 6 percent. If an FHA-insured mortgage is obtained, there will be a *mortgage insurance fee* to pay, at the rate of 0.5 percent a year on the mortgage outstanding. The mortgage contract may require that monthly payments also be made toward taxes on the property and insurance against hazards to the property. This is termed a PITI contract.

Property taxes are usually due annually or semiannually and average perhaps 2 percent of the value of the property. At the time of purchase, the buyer may be required to pay the remainder of the year's taxes in advance.

Special assessments are made for streets, sewers, and like items until their cost has been amortized. Property without these facilities is likely to be cheaper at the time of purchase, but, as the community grows, they will probably be added. Sewers, for instance, may cost $8 a front foot. Generally these improvements may be paid for in cash or instalments at interest, perhaps 6 percent. Local law frequently requires that all debts on assessments be paid by the seller at the time of sale.

Property insurance includes insurance against damage due to fire and lightning, and sometimes coverage is extended to wind, water, vandalism, and other hazards. The annual premium depends on the amount and kind of coverage as well as the construction of the house and the incidence and severity of the hazard in the community, but may average about 0.2 percent of the house value. Savings may be made by purchasing insurance three or five years in advance. It is wise to keep the property insured to the full amount of its replacement value, although a lending institution may require an amount equal only to the mortgage.

Certain related types of insurance which are purchased by both owners and renters might be considered at this time. These include insurance on household contents against theft, fire, and other types of damage. A record of household contents is useful in making claims under such a policy. Comprehensive personal liability insurance protects the family against liability for damages, to the extent of the policy, due to the injury to people or their property that occurs on the family's property. It also covers damage caused anywhere by the family members, except through operation of an auto. The "homeowner's" policy, including all of the foregoing types of insurance, is highly popular and may cost little more than the fire and extended coverage policy.

An additional cost to the home owner is that for *repairs and replacements* which include everything from a minor repair or redecoration to replacement of a roof. These needs are somewhat unpredictable for the next month, but are reasonably predictable over the long run, at perhaps 1.5–2 percent a year of the value of the property. The expanding family with high expenses and the elderly family with reduced income may postpone repairs for a number of years. Eventually that family or the next owner finds that considerable repairs and replacements must be made. A modest house that has had minimum repairs for seven years since it was built may cost 7–10 percent of its current value to restore it to good condition, whereas one that has had minimum repairs for fifteen years since it was built may require 20–25 percent since it may by then require a new roof or furnace, modernization of the kitchen, new shrubs, and other sizable replacements. Higher costs would be required in situations of harder use than ordinary. As one contractor said about estimating costs of repairing a house: "Estimate the best you can, then double it, then add 25 percent for things you can't see."

The home owner may also make major *improvements* such as the addition of an extra room or garage. But he should be cautious in estimating how much these increase the sale value of the property. Overimprovement of an old house does not generally pay well financially, though the family may get much pleasure from it.

In addition to the foregoing explicit, out-of-pocket expenses, the home owner has certain implicit costs. One is the *family labor* for repair or improvement of the property, in addition to the direct money costs of such items. This assumes, of course, that some earnings or savings could have been made by other uses of family labor.

Another implicit cost is the *interest foregone* on the money invested in the property, that is, the return that could have been earned by investing the money in another type of equally hazardous venture. At least one should count about 4 percent on the down payment, initial repairs and improvements, and closing costs since that amount could have been earned on Government bonds. If the family uses $15,000 in cash to buy a house and could have obtained a 10 percent return otherwise, it foregoes $1,500 annually. For this reason, some businessmen prefer to invest in their own business.

Finally, the implicit cost of *depreciation* needs to be considered. This is essentially a function of use and time. A house depreciates because of physical wear and tear from use and the elements and because of obsolescence of the house style and facilities. A well-constructed house in an undated architectural style, with modern facilities, and constantly in good repair suffers least depreciation. However, use and time take their toll, though slowly in the normal situation, which may make it difficult for the family to see in its own home.

Depreciation may be calculated on the original value of the

house or on the declining value. A 2 percent annual depreciation on the original value shows a smaller fall in value in the early years than does 3 percent on the declining value, but equal at the end of the thirtieth year, and more in the later years (Table 10–3). The declining balance method, while more complicated, is generally preferred by accountants because of the greater depreciation of physical assets in their early years and because the property never declines to zero value, though it approaches it.

In summarizing the various cost items, the down payment, principal payments, improvements, and special assessments constitute the family's investments. The expense items include the closing costs,

TABLE 10–3. Depreciated Value of House During 50 Years (Percent of original value)

	DEPRECIATED VALUE AT ANNUAL DEPRECIATION OF—			DEPRECIATED VALUE AT ANNUAL DEPRECIATION OF—	
AGE OF HOUSE	2 PERCENT OF ORIGINAL VALUE	3 PERCENT OF DECLINING VALUE	AGE OF HOUSE	2 PERCENT OF ORIGINAL VALUE	3 PERCENT OF DECLINING VALUE
NEW	100.0	100.0	26	48.0	45.3
1	98.0	97.0	27	46.0	43.9
2	96.0	94.1	28	44.0	42.6
3	94.0	91.3	29	42.0	41.3
4	92.0	88.5	30	40.0	40.1
5	90.0	85.9	31	38.0	38.9
6	88.0	83.3	32	36.0	37.7
7	86.0	80.8	33	34.0	36.6
8	84.0	78.3	34	32.0	35.5
9	82.0	76.0	35	30.0	34.4
10	80.0	73.7	36	28.0	33.4
11	78.0	71.5	37	26.0	32.4
12	76.0	69.4	38	24.0	31.4
13	74.0	67.3	39	22.0	30.5
14	72.0	65.3	40	20.0	29.6
15	70.0	63.3	41	18.0	28.7
16	68.0	61.4	42	16.0	27.8
17	66.0	59.6	43	14.0	27.0
18	64.0	57.8	44	12.0	26.2
19	62.0	56.0	45	10.0	25.4
20	60.0	54.4	46	8.0	24.7
21	58.0	52.7	47	6.0	24.0
22	56.0	51.2	48	4.0	23.3
23	54.0	49.6	49	2.0	22.6
24	52.0	48.1	50	0	21.9
25	50.0	46.7			

mortgage fee, interest payments, FHA-mortgage insurance fee, property taxes, any interest on the special assessments, property insurance, repairs and replacements, and the implicit costs of family labor, interest foregone, and depreciation.

At the time of sale, the owner is likely to have several types of special costs:

The real estate agent's commission at approximately 6 percent of the final sale price.

A mortgage discount or premium if an FHA or VA mortgage is obtained by the buyer.

Some closing costs in some places or situations.

Repairs and improvements to make the property salable. Whether the seller will regain the money put into such repairs is a question since the buyer may have a different opinion of their desirability.

Penalty charge of perhaps 1 percent of the owner's outstanding mortgage for its early repayment.

The seller is also required to pay all outstanding debts on the property. These may include:

Prepayment of his share of the year's property taxes.

Prepayment of the unpaid principal on the mortgage.

Debts for special assessments, property repairs, and improvements.

Water and utility bills to date of sale.

THE HOUSE AS AN INVESTMENT

The Federal Housing Administration's figures for new homes they financed in 1965 indicated an average price of $16,825, including $3,442 for the lot. The mortgage averaged $15,929 for a term of 31.7 years. The costs were as follows:

Total beginning costs	$1,272
Down payment	896
Closing costs	376
Monthly costs	125.79
Principal, interest, taxes, FHA-insurance, and hazard insurance	117.10
Repairs (estimated)	8.69

If such a house rents unfurnished for $1,682.50 a year, the buyer's monthly costs are somewhat lower than the monthly rent of $140.21. But the buyer had beginning costs on which he could have earned $51 at 4 percent a year. On net, the buyer's annual costs are about $122 lower.

Some buyers in special situations look on their ownership costs as the equivalent of rent, with no expectation of keeping the property for a long period or of selling it for a reasonable price if the military installation or atomic or space research or other facility is closed. If the buyer has no additional financial responsibility on the mortgage contract, his costs for living in his own home for seven years, the average duration of FHA mortgages, would average about $145 a month, $5 higher than the renter's costs, but would average about $183 a month if he lives in the house only two years. The cost would be as follows:

COSTS	7 YEARS	2 YEARS
Total costs	$12,195	$4,393
Beginning costs	1,272	1,272
Interest foregone	357	102
Monthly costs	10,566	3,019

It is obvious that the owner's total costs over the long run depend importantly on two major items—the original price he pays for the property and the price for which he can eventually sell the property. Thus, the changing price of property constitutes a significant source of profit or loss for the homeowner.

Changing Sale Prices · Sale prices of houses may change slowly or rapidly, by large or small amounts. Declines in sale prices in the last depression have been estimated at 60 percent. Losses were extreme in one-industry towns that were boom towns in the twenties and "ghost towns" in the thirties, but more moderate in communities with less fluctuation in business. When employment declined, many families had difficulty in meeting their mortgage payments and could sell the property for too little to cover the outstanding mortgage. Many lost their homes and any equity they had built.

On the other hand, the owner may gain decidedly in the long run if inflation advances. Inflation at a rate of 3 percent compounded annually just about compensates for physical depreciation and ordinary obsolescence of the house, at 3 percent of the declining value, so that its price remains about constant. More violent cyclical or long-run inflation or increase in construction cost results in generally rising sale prices and rentals even though the property is getting older, so that the owner has windfall profits. With inflation or growing population, the value of the lot may increase greatly, no matter what happens to the value of the house.

Rising house values are supported by mortgage money that is readily available at acceptable interest rates. On the other hand, a tight money market and high interest rates may mean that property prices have to be reduced in order to make a sale. Some sellers found this situation in the tight money market of 1966. While $100 a month that the buyer has available for principal and interest will finance a 30-year loan of $17,000 at 6 percent interest, it will finance a 20-year loan of only $12,000 at 8 percent interest.

In addition to inflation, other conditions help maintain a house's value, thus increasing the owner's gain. An obvious one is minimum physical depreciation and obsolescence of the property. A wide market with many potential buyers or renters is another. A growing community makes an important contribution in this direction, as opposed to the situation in a declining community. A neighborhood that has increased in popularity or has an unusual feature, such as a nearby park which becomes more precious with the passing years, may bring great gains.

A generally acceptable style of the house, rather than a highly individualistic and unconventional one; a size that can be used by families of various sizes, including perhaps three bedrooms or expansion possibilities; the availability of generally wanted facilities such as streets and schools which the family cannot independently provide for itself—all of these increase the potential market.

The price range of the house is also important since there are many more people interested in a moderate-priced house than in a high-priced one. As a seller remarked about his unusual and interesting house in a high price range: "Those who like it can't afford it, and those who can afford it figure they might as well build to suit themselves." A moderate-priced house for the neighborhood is in a stronger position than a high-priced one since the neighborhood is important in establishing property value. This involves a good relationship between the value of house and lot, with the house worth approximately five times as much as the lot.

Whatever the cause of a rise in value of property, the rate of return on investment is enlarged by a small down payment and monthly costs no more than rent. Suppose a person has $10,000 to invest and can buy a small house for cash or an apartment building for $100,000 with a 10 percent down payment. If all property values increase 20 percent by the time he sells the property, he gains $2,000 on the small house or $20,000 on the apartment.

In the postwar inflation, many young couples have used this principle advantageously. Starting with a minimum downpayment on a small house and reselling later at higher prices, they have been able to move into successively larger houses. However, the situation is quite different if property values fall, so that a person with a thin equity may lose all. If rents and property values fall 10 percent and sale is necessary, the owner of the small house loses $1,000, but the owner of the apartment loses $10,000, his entire investment.

As in the case of any other investment, the home owner may "eat up" his investment. He may sell the property or borrow on it to obtain money for current living expenses. Or he may draw on his investment in a less obvious way by postponing all but the most necessary repairs. Many elderly people on reduced incomes do this as they "let the house fall down around them."

Clearly, the major financial gain from home ownership comes in inflationary periods. The owner has a "hedge against inflation." In general, property values rise as much or more than the general price level for consumer goods. On the other hand, investment in low-priced rental property may pay quite high rates of current return, particularly in risk situations.

A *Fair Market Price* · At the time of purchase or sale, objective appraisal of the property helps the family determine what is a fair market price for the time. The professional appraiser uses three methods, then integrates the results. The basic method is to estimate the price of the property in relation to the final sale price of similar properties in the same area or a comparable one. This can be done by checking sale prices or the amount of real estate transfer taxes at the county recorder's office.

A second method is to compute the capital value of the net income from the property. The gross income is represented by the rent that could be obtained, and the net income results after deductions for taxes, insurance, repairs, and depreciation. While the appraiser works with costs in a particular situation, when costs approximate 60 percent of income and buyers are willing to accept a 4 percent return, the process of determination is as follows:

	MONTHLY RENT	
ITEM	$150	$200
Gross annual income	$ 1,800	$ 2,400
Net annual income (40% of gross income)	720	960
Capital value at 4% net return	18,000	24,000

Thus the property is priced at 10 times its annual rent. Investors in rental property, demanding a high return, might pay less than 5 times the annual rent for units renting at low rates to persons who cannot afford homeownership. On the other hand, a family demanding an unusually nice home may have to pay a price that is 13 or more times the annual rent it could possibly get since few people will pay over $200 a month.

While estimated costs differ from one house to another, the acceptable net rate of return depends on current returns available from alternate investments of equal risk and on the expectation of inflation in value of the property. When the current return on alternatives is low and the expectation of inflation is high, buyers are willing to accept a low current net return. Buyers of homes for themselves and of rental property may have quite different alternatives.

The third method that the appraiser uses is more complicated. He calculates the cost of reproducing the house under present building costs, then allows for depreciation, and adds the value of the land. While the appraiser deals with a specific house in its own community, rough estimates can be based on national figures. The Boeckh index of the cost of constructing given types of dwellings is helpful in a general estimate of the cost of reproduction. The average depreciated value of property of different ages can be estimated from the data in Table 10–3. The average price of the land can be estimated by use of the indexes of prices of finished land.

The Boeckh index shows great changes in construction cost through the years (Table 10–4). For instance, a house that cost $1,990 to construct in 1915 cost about $11,520 to build in 1965, in the average situation. But there were many rises and falls in the intervening years. The peak of 1920 was not reached again for a couple of decades. The cost in 1950 was double the pre-war figure for 1939, and the cost in 1965 was triple the pre-war figure. The average increase over the previous year has varied decidedly from one period to another as follows:

1916–20	+17.5 percent
1921–39	− 0.7 percent
1940–51	+ 7.6 percent
1952–65	+ 2.1 percent

In fact, war and postwar inflation in housing has been so great that it has compensated for many errors. The more modest advance

TABLE 10–4. Boeckh Index of Construction Cost of Residences (1957–59 = 100)

YEAR	INDEX	PERCENT CHANGE FROM PREVIOUS YEAR	YEAR	INDEX	PERCENT CHANGE FROM PREVIOUS YEAR
1915	19.9	. . .	1940	37.6	3.3
1916	21.2	6.5	1941	40.7	8.0
1917	24.8	17.0	1942	43.0	5.7
1918	29.5	19.0	1943	44.9	4.4
1919	34.3	16.3	1944	48.8	8.7
			1945	52.3	7.2
1920	44.2	28.9	1946	57.4	9.8
1921	35.5	−19.7	1947	69.5	21.1
1922	32.7	− 7.9	1948	78.2	12.5
1923	36.6	12.0	1949	76.1	− 2.7
1924	36.1	− 1.4	1950	80.3	5.5
1925	35.7	− 1.1	1951	86.5	7.7
1926	36.1	1.1	1952	88.8	2.7
1927	35.6	− 1.4	1953	90.4	1.8
1928	35.7	0.3	1954	89.7	− 0.8
1929	37.3	4.5	1955	92.4	3.0
			1956	96.5	4.4
1930	36.3	− 2.7	1957	98.3	1.9
1931	33.5	− 7.7	1958	99.2	0.9
1932	28.3	−15.5	1959	102.5	3.3
1933	28.4	0.4	1960	104.2	1.7
1934	30.8	8.5	1961	104.5	0.3
1935	30.0	− 2.6	1962	106.3	1.7
1936	31.1	3.7	1963	108.5	2.1
1937	34.8	11.9	1964	111.6	2.9
1938	35.8	2.9	1965	115.2	3.2
1939	36.5	2.0	1966	120.1	4.3

SOURCE: Table reprinted with permission of E. H. Boeckh and Associates, Inc.

in construction costs since 1952 has caused some specialists to say that "houses were forced to take their own depreciation," that is, costs of construction were no longer rising enough to compensate for usual depreciation. Of course, individual communities differed considerably from these averages. In some rapidly growing metropolitan areas, predictions were made of 10 percent increases for 1966 and further increases of 4–8 percent by 1967.

Table 10–5 shows the great changes that have occurred in the last 30 years in the average price of land sites under single-family houses approved for FHA mortgage insurance. The average price in 1950 was a fifth higher than the pre-war price in 1939, but the 1965 price was triple the pre-war price. While these annual figures are based on a small proportion of all existing housing and the land sites differed through the years, the figures give a rough approximation of changing values.

Now we may use the data in these three tables to estimate the value of property in the average situation. Supposing a new house was purchased in 1950 for $8,000, including the lot worth $1,000. The price of the house in 1965 would be estimated as follows:

> Price of house in 1950 multiplied by change in construction cost (i.e., construction cost index in 1965 divided by index in 1950) multiplied by depreciated value of house 15 years old.

$$7,000 \left(\frac{115.2}{80.3} \right) .633 = 6,357$$

The lot price in 1965 would be estimated as follows:

> Lot price in 1950 multiplied by change in prices of lots (i.e., index in 1965 divided by index in 1950).

$$1,000 \left(\frac{147.1}{52.6} \right) = 2,797$$

The total 1965 price for the house and lot in the average situation would therefore be estimated as 6,357 plus 2,797 or $9,154.

If $1,000 worth of salable improvements was added in 1955 when they finished the attic and again in 1960 when they added a garage, their present value would be calculated as follows:

$$\text{1955 improvement.} \quad 1,000 \left(\frac{115.2}{92.4} \right) .737 = 919$$

$$\text{1960 improvement.} \quad 1,000 \left(\frac{115.2}{104.2} \right) .859 = 950$$

The total price for the property including improvements would then be estimated roughly at $11,023 in 1965.

TABLE 10–5. Average Market Price of Land Sites Under Existing Single-Family Houses Appraised for FHA Mortgage Insurance

YEAR	PRICE*	INDEX (1957–59 = 100)	PERCENT CHANGE FROM PREVIOUS YEAR
1938	$1,010	46.2	. . .
1939	956	43.7	−5.3
1940	948	43.4	− .8
1941	981	44.9	3.5
1942	935	42.8	−4.7
1943	956	43.7	2.2
1944	924	42.2	3.3
1945	857	39.2	−7.3
1946	833	38.1	−2.8
1947	915	41.8	9.8
1948	970	44.4	6.0
1949	1,098	50.2	13.2
1950	1,150	52.6	4.7
1951	1,222	55.9	6.3
1952	1,296	59.3	6.1
1953	1,461	66.8	12.7
1954	1,591	72.8	8.9
1955	1,707	78.1	7.3
1956	1,931	88.3	13.1
1957	2,041	93.3	5.7
1958	2,150	98.3	5.3
1959	2,369	108.3	10.2
1960	2,356	107.7	− .5
1961	2,513	114.9	6.7
1962	2,738	125.2	9.0
1963	2,874	131.4	5.0
1964	2,987	136.6	3.9
1965	3,218	147.1	7.7

* Prices of land sites under new houses were within about $200 of these prices except in 1940–42 when they were about $300 lower. Data for new houses were not available for 1943–45.

SOURCE: Federal Housing Administration.

Supposing, on the other hand, that a house was purchased for $6,000 in 1929, including a $1,000 lot. Its price in 1932, three years later, might be estimated in the average situation as follows, if lot prices fell two-thirds:

$$\text{House price.} \quad 5,000 \left(\frac{28.3}{37.3}\right).913 = 3,464$$

$$\text{Lot price.} \quad 1,000 \ (.333) = 333$$

The total price in 1932 might therefore be estimated at $3,797.

It should be recognized, however, that the cost of building a house differs a great deal from city to city. The sale price of the same new home—a 1,300 square foot brick rambler on a concrete slab—varied in 1966 from about $11,500 in Phoenix to $22,000 in Washington, D.C., excluding the lot price, among the eighteen cities for which reports were compiled by the National Association of Real Estate Editors. Prices in the cities surveyed were as follows:[7]

$12,000–$14,000 Phoenix, Fort Worth, Houston.

$15,000–$18,000 Oklahoma City, San Diego, Columbus (Ohio), Newark, Hartford, Hollywood (Fla.), Detroit, Seattle.

$20,000–$22,000 Grand Rapids, Cleveland, Pittsburgh, Boston, Lafayette (Ind.), Cedar Rapids (Iowa), and Washington, D.C.

Now that we have looked at the various methods of determining a fair market price for a house, a final word should be said. Paying a fair market price for the house does not insure (1) That the family can afford the house and (2) That the house is in good condition, meets family needs, or is a good investment.

OBTAINING A MORTGAGE

Mortgage debt has climbed even faster than has income since 1930. Mortgage debt on one- to four-family nonfarm dwellings now approximates $225 billion, about 45 percent of annual disposable personal income.[8] This contrasts with the beginning of 1930 when such debt was only $19 billion and equalled about 25 percent of income.

More than half of all owner-occupied nonfarm dwellings are mortgaged.[9] Few families are able to pay the full price in cash when they purchase a home, and almost no families are able to purchase their first home for cash. Therefore, they seek a loan to cover the remainder of the purchase price in addition to their down payment. A mortgage is a lien or claim on property which is pledged as security for the payment of a debt. A loan secured by a mortgage may be obtained from various lenders such as savings and loan associations and building and loan associations, mutual savings banks, commercial banks, life insurance companies, or private lenders.

---

[7] J. B. Willmann, "Price of Building Basic Home Compared in 18 U. S. Cities," *The Washington Post*, October 8, 1966.

[8] Federal Home Loan Bank Board, Federal Housing Administration, and Veterans Administration, data for beginning of 1967.

[9] *U. S. Census of Housing: 1960.*

The mortgage may be a conventional one, FHA-insured, or VA-guaranteed. In recent years more than three-fifths of the mortgage debt outstanding on one- to four-family nonfarm dwellings has been on conventional mortgages, one-fifth on FHA-insured mortgages, and less than a fifth on VA-guaranteed mortgages. Of the annual increase in mortgage debt outstanding, about three-quarters is now on conventional loans and most of the remainder is on FHA-insured.

Conventional Mortgage · A conventional mortgage is obtained directly from the lender without the assistance of the special federal programs. The mortgage terms depend on the federal and state laws under which the institution operates, competitive conditions, and alternative opportunities, as well as individual circumstances and judgment.

The common rate of interest on these loans ranges around 6 percent a year. The minimum down payment ranges from 10 percent to 25 percent. The maximum length, depending on the lender and the type of loan, is likely to be 20 or 25 years, but sometimes 30. It pays the individual borrower to shop around for the best terms available. A buyer able to make a 50 percent down payment on a new home and to assume a 10-year mortgage may at times get a rate as low as 5 percent by serious shopping.

Conventional first mortgages extended on new homes in August 1966 averaged about $20,200 with mortgage fees at 0.8 percent and interest at 6.2 percent. The loans, amounting to 74 percent of the price of the property, were extended for 25 years on the average.

The borrower may be required to pay for commercial mortgage insurance if the loan amounts to more than 70–80 percent of the appraised value of the property. Although commercial mortgage insurance generally insures only the top 20 percent of the loan, it cuts the lender's risk greatly. The charge may be 0.5 percent of the loan the first year, then 0.25 percent of the principal balance each succeeding year. The lender may be willing to forego the insurance in later years.

FHA-Insured Mortgage · The Federal Housing Administration will insure the mortgage which the family is seeking from a private lender approved by FHA on application of the borrower if the family's income and expenses, the condition of the property, and the mortgage terms meet their requirements.

An FHA-insured mortgage can generally extend no more than

30 years. The maximum interest charge is 6 percent a year on the declining principal, but these rates are changed from time to time. FHA regulations allow the buyer to pay an initial service charge, if the lender requires it, of no more than 1 percent of the mortgage amount in most situations. In addition, there is an FHA-insurance premium of 0.5 percent a year on the declining principal, to be paid by the borrower. In case of default by the borrower, the FHA uses the insurance fees to reimburse the lender for any losses. Because of this insurance, lending institutions may make FHA loans with smaller down payments and longer repayment periods than otherwise.

The minimum down payment required by FHA is as follows, although the lender may require more:

3 percent on the first $15,000 of appraised value;
10 percent on the next $5,000; and
25 percent on additional value.

The law also states $30,000 as the maximum loan amount that FHA can insure on a one-family dwelling.

Thus, on a house appraised at $15,000, a minimum down payment of $450 would be required by FHA. But on a house appraised at $35,000, a down payment of $5,000 is required to obtain the maximum insured loan. Therefore, a person buying a more expensive house may find that he can get better terms on a conventional mortgage than with FHA. There may be some special advantage in an FHA mortgage due to FHA appraisal of a standing house and supervision of construction on new houses. Furthermore, an FHA mortgage may contain an "open-end" provision allowing the addition of loans for improvements, alterations, and repairs up to the amount of the original mortgage (or over, in the case of the addition of rooms).

VA-Guaranteed Mortgage · For eligible veterans, the Veterans Administration will guarantee 60 percent of the mortgage amount up to a maximum of $7,500 guaranteed. The amount guaranteed declines as the mortgage declines. No charge is made on the buyer or the lender, except, in some cases, a fee of 0.5 percent of the loan amount. The lender will be reimbursed for any loss on the guaranteed part of the loan. Such loss then becomes a debt that the veteran or serviceman owes the Government. The loan cannot extend for more than 30 years at a maximum rate of 6 percent per year on the declining balance, though these rates are changed occasionally. VA does not require any downpayment, but the lender may.

Mortgage Discounts · The lender may charge a "mortgage discount," sometimes called points, premium, or bonus. Mortgage discounts vary from time to time and place to place with the availability of funds and alternative investments. The discount may amount to 1 percent of the mortgage or 8 percent or higher.

If the borrower seeks a loan of $10,000 at 5.25 percent and the lender demands a 6 percent return, an advance payment of $600 (6 percent discount or six points) to the lender means that his yield will be equivalent to 6 percent a year on the $9,400 actually lent, under the common assumption that the mortgage will be paid in full in 12 years. Or on a loan at 5.75 percent, an advance payment to the lender of $610 gives him an average yield of 6.58 percent a year on the $9,390 lent. Roughly speaking, each additional discount point raises the yield about 0.13 percentage points.

Conventional mortgages require no discounts so long as interest rates move freely. But when the free market rate would exceed the legal maximum or would meet borrower resistance, then a discount is likely to be charged. The borrower pays any discounts that are demanded on a conventional mortgage. That is, in the preceding example, he signs a mortgage for $10,000 and receives a loan of $9,390.

The FHA and VA maximum interest rates are generally below the rate that lenders are able to get on conventional mortgages. The argument has been that the lender has no risk on the insured or guaranteed part of the loan and should be able to lend more cheaply. But many lenders have felt that their risks on conventional loans and other investments such as corporate bonds have been minimum in recent years. So they have compensated for the interest rate difference by charging a mortgage discount.

Since FHA and VA prohibit the home buyer from paying a discount, the seller pays it. The seller then tries to pass this cost on to the buyer in an increased price for the house. The home buyer who pays the discount directly or by an increased price finds that the discount results in the "capitalization" of part of his credit charges.

Mortgage discounts complicate the picture in the transfer of property. If an owner wants to realize $14,500 on the sale of his home, he may be advised to ask $17,500 to allow for a $500 price-cut plus other expenses, under the assumption that the buyer will make a minimum down payment and obtain an FHA-insured mortgage for the remainder, presumably at 6 percent discount. If the house sells for $17,000 and the seller has an outstanding mortgage of $8,000, he will finally receive about $6,400 in cash. The seller's situation will be as follows:

Gross receipts $16,019
 Downpayment from buyer (FHA minimum) 650
 Mortgage loan less discount, presumed to be 6%
  ($16,350−$981) 15,369
Costs .... $ 9,600
 Selling costs 1,520
  Repairs and redecoration 500
  Real estate agent's fee at 6% of sale price 1,020
 Prepayment of mortgage 8,080
  Mortgage outstanding 8,000
  Fee for prepayment of mortgage at 1% 80

It might be noted that the seller would have gained an equal amount by selling his house directly "as is" for $14,500 cash or on a conventional loan. Thus, selling costs amounted to about 15 percent. In the tight money market of 1966, when discounts as high as 10–15 percent were sometimes quoted, total selling costs of 20 percent were not unusual.

The buyer paid $17,000 for a house with a down payment of $650 and an FHA-insured mortgage of $16,350. If this loan is repaid within the next 20 years, it will cost him about the same as the needed $15,369 at about 0.75 percentage points higher than the stated interest rate. In addition, he will pay the annual FHA insurance fee of 0.5 percent on the declining balance.

The lender holds an FHA-insured mortgage of $16,350 for which he has actually lent $15,369. Thus his net return on the $15,369 will be equivalent to 0.75 percent plus the stated rate.

Special Features and Loans · A *package provision* in the mortgage may be a benefit to the home buyer. Such a provision allows the buyer to include certain appliances or necessary remodelling as part of the original mortgage at the original rate of interest. This rate is likely to be lower than he could otherwise obtain. On the other hand, the borrower will be paying interest for 20 or 30 years on the extra amount. If he can manage to pay for the added items more quickly, he may save money even at a higher rate of interest. For instance, an $11,000 mortgage, including $1,000 for equipment, for 30 years at 6 percent would cost $1,160 more for interest over the whole period than would a $10,000 mortgage. If the equipment could be paid for in 12 monthly instalments at 12 percent true interest, the loan would cost only $66 in interest.

An *open-end feature* can be useful to the home buyer at a later time when he needs to improve the house or needs money for medical or school expenses. With such a feature, he can borrow additional money on the mortgage without the expense of obtaining a new mortgage.

Interest rates are much higher on some *home improvement loans* than on first mortgages. This is because the stated rate may be a discount rate based on the original loan. The discount rate may be 4 percent, 5 percent, or higher a year, equivalent to a true interest rate on the declining unpaid principal of about double the discount rate, since monthly payments are made on the principal.

The buyer of a private home with an FHA-insured mortgage must generally be prepared to pay the down payment and initial charges in cash or its equivalent. However, many people, especially those who buy houses financed partially by the seller, have *second mortgages*. Second mortgage rates may be stated as discount rates at 5 or 6 percent for a relatively short term—3–5 years. The rate amounts to about 10–12 percent true interest since monthly payments on the principal are made. Some lenders seek to charge more.

The buyer may seek a second mortgage when the purchase price of the house is greater than he can pay with a first mortgage and the amount he has available for a down payment. The lender who holds a second mortgage is in a risky position since he has only a second lien on the property. His claim is to any residual after the first mortgage has been discharged, which explains the higher interest rates. If the first mortgage is foreclosed, the holder of the second mortgage may have to pay off the first mortgage in order to prevent loss of his money. On the other hand, a property owner may be happy to give a second mortgage when it represents a higher price for the property than he could otherwise get. Thus, any amount received would be windfall profit.

AMORTIZING THE MORTGAGE

Before the mid thirties, most mortgages required annual interest payments, with the principal debt due after 3 or 5 years. If the family could not pay off the loan, it needed to have the loan renewed or to obtain a new loan, perhaps at a higher rate of interest. If it failed, the mortgage was foreclosed and the family lost the house. Today, most mortgages are amortized (paid off) by equal monthly payments on interest and principal through the term of the mortgage. Interest is regularly charged on the declining principal. Mortgages differ, however, in the interest rate, in the length of the loan, and in other provisions. The family should shop as carefully for a loan as for a house in order to obtain the best terms available.

Although the interest rate on a mortgage usually remains constant throughout the term of a mortgage, other methods may be used. Sometimes interest is charged on a *sliding scale*—for example, 6 percent for a number of payments, then 5.5 percent for a number of payments, and so on. Whether a sliding scale or a flat rate is preferable depends on the terms that can be arranged under each and the situation of the family. On the average, the interest rate charged in the early years is most important to the family since a large proportion of mortgages are cancelled within 12 years, frequently due to resale of the property.

A *rate-escalation clause*, sometimes included in mortgage contracts, allows the lender to increase the interest rate on an existing mortgage when conditions warrant. Rate escalation may result in an increased monthly payment or longer duration of the mortgage. Such a clause permits the lender to pass the risk of a fixed interest rate on to the borrower when current interest rates rise. An unwary home buyer may accept such a clause when he signs a standard agreement to assume an existing mortgage that was originally obtained by a builder or other borrower. Such clauses cannot be included in FHA-insured or VA-guaranteed mortgages.

Payment of Constant Interest Rate · Since the interest rate usually remains constant for the duration of the mortgage, our discussion will focus on this type of mortgage. Table 10–6 shows the monthly payment on principal and interest to amortize a $1,000 debt in 10 to 35 years at annual rates of interest varying from 5–8 percent. For example, a 30-year mortgage at 6 percent costs $6 per month per $1,000. A $10,000 mortgage costs $60 a month.

The figures in the table show how a lower interest rate decreases the monthly payment. A 10-year loan costs $11.62 at 7 percent, $11.11 at 6 percent, and $10.61 at 5 percent. In other words, a decrease in the interest rate by 1 percentage point cuts these monthly costs about 50¢ per $1,000 of debt, and cuts cost 60–70¢ on longer mortgages. The table also shows how the longer term lowers the monthly payment. A 6 percent loan costs $11.11 a month for 10 years, $6.45 for 25 years, or $5.71 for 35 years.

The lowering of monthly payments per $1,000 of loan is im-

TABLE 10–6. Equal Monthly Payments to Amortize a Debt of $1,000 in a Stated Number of Years

	NOMINAL ANNUAL RATE OF INTEREST			
ITEM	5%	6%	7%	8%
Monthly payment on principal and interest on loan for:				
10 years	$10.61	$11.10	$11.62	$12.14
20 years	6.60	7.17	7.76	8.37
25 years	5.85	6.45	7.07	7.72
30 years	5.37	6.00	6.66	7.34
35 years	5.05	5.71	6.39	7.11
Approximate total interest on loan for:				
10 years	$ 273	$ 333	$ 394	$ 457
20 years	584	721	862	1,009
25 years	755	935	1,121	1,316
30 years	933	1,160	1,398	1,642
35 years	1,121	1,398	1,684	1,986

portant to many borrowers since it enables them to buy a higher priced house. When a family has $100 a month available for principal and interest payments, it can carry a $19,000 mortgage at 5 percent or $17,000 at 6 percent over a 30-year period. But it can carry only $14,000 at 6 percent on a 20-year mortgage. Two hundred dollars a month will finance twice as large a mortgage in each instance.

The lower part of the table shows the approximate total interest payments over the full length of the mortgage, in addition to repayment of the $1,000 borrowed. For example, a 30-year mortgage at 6 percent costs about $1,160 in total interest plus the $1,000 principal. On the loans listed above, the total interest payments would be as follows:

MORTGAGE TERMS	TOTAL INTEREST	INTEREST AS PERCENT OF PRINCIPAL
$19,000, 5%, 30 years	$17,727	93
$17,000, 6%, 30 years	19,720	116
$14,000, 6%, 20 years	10,094	72

Thus, the total amount of interest is smaller—

> The lower the interest rate,
> The shorter the term, and, of course,
> The smaller the mortgage.

The family can minimize its mortgage and thereby cut total interest charges by purchasing a lower priced house or by making a larger down payment. Furthermore, a large down payment is an important feature of a low-risk mortgage and may result in a lower rate of interest. A low-risk mortgage extends for a short term. It is secured by a desirable property which is likely to maintain or increase in value or, at worst, decline little in a market reversal. In some situations, this means a fairly new house, attractive to the mass market. The buyer's prospects are good for meeting the payments. A reasonable interest rate on a low-risk mortgage runs about 1–1.5 percent above the rate paid on savings accounts in the area. The rate on a high-risk mortgage runs about 1.5–2 percent above the rate on savings accounts.

Arguments appear in favor of a large mortgage as making a house easier to sell. This may occur if interest rates go up. But it will not be an attraction to a buyer with a good credit rating if interest rates remain constant or decline. It is questionable whether the family would want to turn its mortgage over to a poor credit risk since the family will probably continue to have some financial responsibility. Furthermore, the bank holding a mortgage may refuse to approve the transfer. Thus the borrower who obtains a larger mortgage than necessary may find that he pays much more interest during his period of ownership without any special advantage at resale.

Since early payments on a mortgage are devoted largely to interest payments, the debt outstanding declines slowly during the early years if monthly payments are made exactly as scheduled. On a 6 percent loan for 30 years, 93 percent of the debt is outstanding after 5 years, 84 percent after 10 years, and 71 percent after 15 years, midway through the payments (Table 10–7). A smaller proportion of the debt is outstanding at the midway point of the mortgage contract when the interest rate is lower or the term is shorter.

Prepayment of Mortgage · The home buyer needs to make certain that the mortgage he signs contains a *prepayment clause* which allows for early repayment, in full or in part, in case he should later find such prepayment possible and advantageous. Without a prepayment clause, the debtor can be held to the terms of the agreement, with

TABLE 10–7. Percent of Debt Outstanding on Loan Amortized by Equal Monthly Payments as Scheduled

	PERCENT OF DEBT OUTSTANDING AFTER—					
TERMS OF LOAN	5 YEARS	10 YEARS	15 YEARS	20 YEARS	25 YEARS	30 YEARS
10-year loan:						
5% interest	56	0				
6% interest	57	0				
20-year loan:						
5% interest	84	62	35	0		
6% interest	85	64	37	0		
25-year loan:						
5% interest	89	74	55	31	0	
6% interest	90	76	58	33	0	
30-year loan:						
5% interest	92	81	68	50	28	0
6% interest	93	84	71	54	31	0

full monthly interest and principal payments to the end of the contract. With a prepayment clause, he can retire the mortgage by repaying the outstanding principal if he should sell the property or otherwise obtain the necessary money, perhaps by getting a new mortgage with better terms. Thus he can avoid the interest that would be due over the remainder of the contract. Whether the borrower should use other windfall money from increased earnings or gifts to reduce the principal on his mortgage depends on his alternatives. Where can he save or make the most money without greater risk?

While some mortgages can be paid off without a penalty, others include a penalty charge of 1 percent of the outstanding balance or 90 days' interest. Such a penalty helps repay the lender for his additional effort in reinvesting funds. Higher penalties of 2 percent of the balance or 180 days' interest are sometimes charged.

Some mortgage contracts, including FHA and VA mortgages, allow for extra monthly payments on the principal without penalty. Such extra payments shorten the mortgage and cut the interest charges greatly during the early years, even when a 1 percent penalty is charged. Obtain the loan schedule from the lender and make extra payments in the exact amounts on the schedule so that the schedule will not be changed. With a $10,000 mortgage at 6 percent for 30 years, the monthly payment on interest and principal is $60. The amortization schedule is as follows for the early months:

PAYMENT NUMBER	INTEREST PAYMENT	PRINCIPAL PAYMENT	BALANCE OF LOAN
1	$50.00	$10.00	$9,990.00
2	49.95	10.05	9,979.95
3	49.90	10.10	9,969.85
4	49.85	10.15	9,959.70
5	49.80	10.20	9,949.50
6	49.75	10.25	9,939.25
7	49.70	10.30	9,928.95
8	49.65	10.35	9,918.60

When the first payment is due, add to it the payment on principal shown for the second payment ($60.00 plus $10.05). Thus both payments have been made according to the original loan schedule, but the interest charge of $49.95 for the second month has been saved. Next month, the third payment is made instead of the second. Or suppose that the family has an extra $35 on hand when the fourth payment is due. It might add to the fourth payment the payment on principal shown for the fifth, sixth, and seventh periods ($60.00 plus $10.20 plus $10.25 plus $10.30 = $90.75), thus saving $149.25 on interest. Next month, the eighth payment is due. A 1 percent penalty on this last extra payment would amount to only 31¢.

Foreclosure · The mortgage may be foreclosed for failure to make regular monthly payments or to meet other conditions of the mortgage, such as keeping the property in repair. Foreclosures reached their all-time peak in 1933 and an all-time low in 1946, but have been generally increasing since then. Foreclosures on nonfarm one- to four-family houses have increased decidedly in recent years, amounting to about five per 1,000 mortgaged units in 1966. In the 1960's, the foreclosure rate has been highest on FHA mortgages, somewhat lower on VA, and lowest on conventional.[10]

When a mortgage is foreclosed, the family loses the house and may have some additional costs to pay. If the mortgage outstanding is $15,000 at the time of foreclosure and the property sells for $14,000, a "deficiency judgment" of $1,000 can be issued against the debtor in most states, if he "assumed" the mortgage when he purchased the house. Collecting on the deficiency judgment is another matter. If

[10] Federal Home Loan Bank Board.

the buyer's deed says that he received the property "subject to the mortgage," no deficiency judgment can be issued against him. But the earlier seller of a house with this type of deed is responsible for the debt if the buyer defaults.

Avoiding Foreclosure · Certain provisions in the mortgage contract may help avoid foreclosure of the mortgage. A *loan modification agreement* is a good safeguard for the buyer since it allows adjustments of the terms of the mortgage in case of serious change in the borrower's financial condition. At such a time the loan may be modified to permit lower monthly payments and a longer repayment period.

Forbearance provisions may help the home buyer avoid foreclosure during temporary emergencies. Forbearance plans may be worked out between the lender and borrower. Such a plan usually allows the borrower to pay only interest on the mortgage, or interest and a reduced amount of principal, until he can again meet the payments in full, presumably in about six months.

Under FHA regulations, lenders may extend forbearance for 18 months without FHA approval if the default is related to sickness, death, reduced income, or natural disaster. Lenders can recast the mortgage for the total unpaid amount including delinquent interest and extend the maturity date of the mortgage by the relief period. If foreclosure should finally result, in spite of the forbearance agreement, the FHA pays the lender any interest that was due and unpaid before the foreclosure.

QUESTIONS

1. Why is the housing budget of special importance to families?
2. How does the expenditure on housing vary from one family to another according to data?
3. How does the family go about determining the monthly amount to spend on housing?
4. What price house can the family buy? What conditions need to be given careful consideration?
5. What related costs need to be considered in determining the amount to pay for shelter?
6. Why do housing needs differ from one family to another?
7. How generally are certain important facilities found in U. S. homes?

8. Describe important characteristics of the neighborhood, the lot, construction of the house, and housing space to be used in selecting a dwelling.

9. Compare an apartment with a house, an older dwelling with a new one. Consider the advantages of planning your own dwelling.

10. Compare the advantages of ownership and rental. What is the special advantage of each?

11. What are the important costs of home ownership? Which items may be counted as investment?

12. What are the special costs of selling an owned home?

13. What are the conditions under which, in general, the home owner makes the greatest gain over the renter? When does the renter gain most?

14. How can the family judge whether home ownership is a good investment?

15. How is a fair market price determined? What is its significance to the family?

16. What has happened to the cost of constructing residences through the years? How do costs compare among communities?

17. How does a change in the cost of new construction affect prices of older houses?

18. What has happened to prices of land sites through the years? Why?

19. What is a mortgage? Where may a mortgage be obtained?

20. What are the characteristics of a conventional mortgage? An FHA-insured mortgage? A VA-guaranteed mortgage?

21. What are mortgage discounts?

22. Describe each: a package provision; an open-end feature; a home improvement loan; a second mortgage.

23. How are mortgages usually amortized today? Differentiate among a constant interest rate, a sliding scale, and rate escalation.

24. How can the monthly payment on the mortgage be lowered?

25. What kind of mortgage terms assist the family in buying a higher priced home than it could otherwise manage?

26. How can the family minimize the total interest charges that it will pay in buying a home?

27. In the ordinary situation of a 30-year loan at 6 percent interest, how much of the mortgage debt is outstanding after 5 years? After 10 years? After 15 years?

28. What is the importance of a prepayment clause?

29. Explain the simple method of making advance payments on the mortgage.

30. Why are mortgages foreclosed? What are possible results?

31. Explain each: a loan modification agreement; forbearance provisions.

SUGGESTIONS FOR FURTHER READING

Hanford, Lloyd D. *Investing in Real Estate*. Chicago: Institute of Real Estate Management, 1966.

Household Finance Corporation. *Money Management: Your Housing Dollar*. Chicago, latest edition.

Meltzer, Bernard C. "Real Estate Dialogues." Latest issues of syndicated column in newspapers.

Unger, Maurice A. *Real Estate, Principles and Practices*. Cincinnati: South-Western, 1964.

U. S. Bureau of the Census. *Current Population Reports*, latest reports.

—————. *U. S. Census of Housing*, latest reports.

U. S. Department of Agriculture. *Consumers All: The Yearbook of Agriculture 1965*. Washington, D.C.: Superintendent of Documents, 1965, pp. 1–80, 150–157, and 183–187.

U. S. Department of Housing and Urban Development. *Annual Report*, latest reports.

The
Automobile / 11
Budget

- ESTIMATING BUDGET AMOUNT
- COSTS OF AUTO OWNERSHIP
- ECONOMY IN PURCHASE AND OPERATION
- AUTOMOBILE INSURANCE

Transportation takes 12 percent of disposable income of today's consumers—almost as much as shelter and decidedly more than clothing. This contrasts with 1929 and most of the 1930's when the 9 percent for transportation was decidedly lower than for shelter or clothing, as well as food. After the restrictions of the war period, transportation quickly returned to its former position, then began to advance in importance. For the past thirteen years, transportation has been at approximately the 12 percent level.

The amount of transportation services per person is now about 2.5 times what it was in 1929. Higher incomes have permitted more families to own autos, better autos, and multiple autos, and to drive greater distances to places of employment and shopping from suburban areas where much of postwar population growth has occurred. Only 7 percent of our expenditure on transportation has been for public transportation of all types in recent years.

ESTIMATING BUDGET AMOUNT

The experienced family may base its transportation budget on its records for the previous year, after making certain that the records are complete, by taking into account changes in prices, needs, and family circumstances. The process is simpler for those using public transportation than for those operating autos. The family auto may require more repairs as it ages, and finally the budget has to provide for the purchase of a new car.

The large amount that families spend for transportation is indicated in Table 11–1. The higher the income, the larger the amount spent. But the highest percentage of income was generally spent for transportation by families in the middle income groups where some spent 15–16 percent. Transportation costs usually averaged $1,000 or more a year for any group having 90 percent or more auto ownership.

Additional data from this survey showed that rural nonfarm families more commonly owned autos than urban families, when they had equal incomes and numbers of persons, and their average transportation costs ran somewhat higher than for urban families. While farm families were most likely to own autos, other conditions being equal, their average transportation costs tended to be lower than for urban families since part of the auto cost was generally chargeable to the farm business.

The family needs to consider carefully the advantages of public transportation and of the private auto in its own situation. In this discussion, we are dealing with transportation for consumer purposes, including getting to and from work. Public and private transportation costs are high for many people in business such as salesmen, farmers, and executives. Such costs are reimbursed by the employer or are counted as occupational expenses, rather than family expenses, and are deducted from gross income. Business decisions on transportation are based on profit-making. Family decisions are based on quite different factors. It is true, however, that when auto ownership is required for business purposes, family use of the car usually involves modest additional cost.

For consumer purposes, the single rider generally finds public transportation cheaper than the private auto when all costs are considered. On the other hand, the auto may be cheaper when several members of a family ride together to work and shop, for recreation, vacations, and other activities. The person or family that takes occasional long trips by public transportation is in quite a different position than the household that makes many short trips. It is important that each family consider its own situation objectively. One does not need to have an auto simply because most people do. Sometimes there are more important goals from the individual's point of view. An acquaintance with moderate income has managed considerable foreign travel chiefly by foregoing auto ownership.

TABLE 11–1. Transportation Expenditures of Urban Families, by Family Size and Income [Average not shown for cells of less than 30 families]

ITEM AND MONEY INCOME AFTER TAXES	NUMBER OF PERSONS IN FAMILY					
	1	2	3	4	5	6 OR MORE
Transportation expense:						
Under $1,000	$ 40	..	..	..	..	..
$1,000–$1,999	50	$ 130	..	..	..	..
$2,000–$2,999	180	210	$ 310	..	..	..
$3,000–$3,999	330	530	460	$ 520	..	..
$4,000–$4,999	590	730	740	640	$ 640	$ 500
$5,000–$5,999	780	770	980	920	920	550
$6,000–$7,499	900	1,010	990	1,000	810	770
$7,500–$9,999	..	1,220	1,200	1,180	980	1,060
$10,000–$14,999	..	1,520	1,700	1,620	1,320	1,430
$15,000 and over	..	3,030	..	..	..	..
Transportation as a percent of income*:						
Under $1,000	5	..	..	..	..	..
$1,000–$1,999	3	8	..	..	..	..
$2,000–$2,999	7	8	11	..	..	..
$3,000–$3,999	9	14	13	14	..	..
$4,000–$4,999	13	15	15	12	13	10
$5,000–$5,999	15	14	16	15	16	9
$6,000–$7,499	13	15	14	14	11	11
$7,500–$9,999	..	14	13	13	11	12
$10,000–$14,999	..	13	14	13	11	12
$15,000 and over	..	12	..	..	..	..
Percent owning an auto at end of year:						
Under $1,000	11	..	..	..	..	..
$1,000–$1,999	7	25	..	..	..	..
$2,000–$2,999	26	48	46	..	..	..
$3,000–$3,999	47	69	77	74	..	..
$4,000–$4,999	54	77	83	87	81	77
$5,000–$5,999	65	85	93	88	93	82
$6,000–$7,499	76	90	91	94	92	88
$7,500–$9,999	..	94	93	93	90	96
$10,000–$14,999	..	92	97	97	97	97
$15,000 and over	..	93	..	..	..	..

* Income adjusted for simplicity by the present writer by the addition to money income of "other money receipts" and subtraction of "account balancing difference."

SOURCE: U. S. Bureau of Labor Statistics, *Survey of Consumer Expenditures 1961*. These data collected in the spring of 1962 from 4,900 families are the best indicators currently available of spending patterns of various types of families. Data for the early 1970's may be available a few years thereafter.

The private auto may be virtually a necessity for getting to employment or shopping areas when one lives in a distant suburb or in the open country. Sometimes a car is required to get to the commuter train. In a moderate-sized city where public transportation is available, an auto may be classified as a comfort rather than a necessity. The auto may be a faster, more convenient, or more comfortable means of transportation.

In some situations, auto ownership is a distinct luxury. Those living and working in the central part of a metropolis may find auto operation prohibitively expensive, unless their incomes are very high. For local transportation, an auto may be a decided impediment, though it may have prestige value. The big-city owner's chief use of the auto may be for weekend trips into the surrounding country.

Registrations are reported for 75 million automobiles including taxicabs, or 1 auto per 2.6 persons in the country—a fantastic ratio.[1] Private autos are used by two-thirds of workers to get to work, which explains the traffic congestion during rush hours.[2] More than three-fourths of all households own an auto. This includes the 53 percent that own one auto and 25 percent that own two or more.[3] Today's figure for three or more cars is probably higher than the 2 percent reported in 1960.[4]

It is obvious these days that most households in the suburbs of metropolitan areas have a car and that many have more than one. On the other hand, and fortunately for the movement of traffic, auto ownership is much less common in the central cities of metropolitan areas. For the country as a whole, auto ownership is almost universal among those with higher incomes. In fact, nine-tenths or more of the families and single consumers with incomes of $5,000 and over own autos, as the following data show:[5]

MONEY INCOME AFTER TAXES	PERCENT OWNING AUTOS
Total	76
Under $1,000	27
$1,000–$1,999	31
$2,000–$2,999	53
$3,000–$3,999	73

[1] U. S. Department of Commerce, Bureau of Public Roads, *Highway Statistics*, annual report for 1965.

[2] U. S. Bureau of Census, *1960 Census of Population*.

[3] U. S. Bureau of Census, *Current Population Reports*, Series P–65, No. 15, 1966 (1965 data).

[4] U. S. Bureau of Census, *1960 Census of Housing*.

[5] U. S. Bureau of Labor Statistics and U. S. Department of Agriculture, *Survey of Consumer Expenditures*, 1960–61.

$4,000–$4,999 82
$5,000–$5,999 89
$6,000–$7,499 92
$7,500–$9,999 94
$10,000–$14,999 97
$15,000 and over 97

COSTS OF AUTO OWNERSHIP

Facing the costliness of operating an auto is difficult for Americans. Yet for many it is the real budget buster—not clothing, not housing, not even food, though we like to blame our difficulties on them. Somehow we feel protective toward the auto and hide its costs, most importantly from ourselves. A young couple keeping a careful record may find that it spends about equal amounts on food, apartment rent and utilities, and its auto.

Auto costs differ considerably from one family to another. A family with a heavy car with full accessories, perfectly maintained, and traded in every other year has much higher costs than a family that is willing to drive an older and simpler car. A car costs more in places that are a great distance from an auto assembly plant. A credit purchase is more expensive than a cash purchase. A family with more than one car has to budget for the fixed costs of each as well as the variable costs.

A family that drives its car a great deal because of the size of the family and its many activities or the location of the home has higher expenses than a family that drives little. Blustery winter weather requires snow tires, anti-freeze, and sometimes towing charges. Of course, Texans would mention the need for an air-conditioner. Garage, parking, and insurance are tremendously more expensive in a metropolis than in a small town: A garage may cost $50 a month and be necessary for protection from vandalism. Parking near work may cost $3 or more a day. Insurance may vary from $300 to $700 for a popular-priced car.

Keeping in mind all of the individual differences, we may look at the estimated cost of auto operation when a new car is purchased for $3,000 and driven 10,000 miles a year, which are current averages. The estimates are presented primarily to develop a method of estimating car costs over the long run. It assumes a cash purchase, for simplicity, and that the owner does not live in a metropolis or have daily parking expenses in such an area. The general estimates are provided to give the family a starting place for constructing its own estimates.

Costs are divided into fixed costs that change little regardless of how much driving is done during a year, and variable costs that vary directly with the mileage. Total costs include most of the following items:

FIXED COSTS	VARIABLE COSTS
Depreciation	Maintenance
Interest payments	Repairs
Sales tax	Tires and batteries
Insurance	Gas and oil
Garage	Toll roads
Licenses	Parking
Other taxes	Fines

However, both fixed and variable costs may vary from year to year. Certain fixed costs are determined at the time of purchase, but other fixed costs, such as those for insurance, garage, and licenses, may change from one year to the next. Furthermore, variable costs per mile may increase as the car ages.

Depreciation on a car is generally much greater during its first year or two than in later years, and is estimated variously for the popular-priced cars under normal conditions as:

30 percent to 40 percent the first year,
15 percent to 25 percent the second year,
10 percent to 15 percent the third year,
about 10 percent the fourth year,
about 8 percent the fifth year, and
about 6 percent the sixth year.

High mileage generally results in greater depreciation. Other abnormal conditions affect the resale value of the car. During the war some people made windfall profits by selling unneeded cars. On the other hand, when business is slow, the old car may not sell for as much as the family had expected. The actual depreciation is not known until the time of resale.

In the example of a new car purchased for $3,000 and driven 10,000 miles a year, the heavy depreciation changes for the first two years are primarily responsible for the total cost of $1,800 the first year and $1,300 the second year (Table 11–2). Thereafter, depreciation falls a great deal and insurance falls some. These decreases more than offset increases in variable costs so that total costs are about $1,100 in the third and fourth years and about $1,000 in the fifth and sixth years. This means that costs per mile approximate 18¢ the first

TABLE 11–2.   Estimated Cost of Automobile Operation When New Car Purchased for $3,000 Cash and Driven 10,000 Miles a Year

COST ITEMS	FIRST YEAR	SECOND YEAR	THIRD YEAR	TOTAL, 3 YEARS	FOURTH YEAR	FIFTH YEAR	SIXTH YEAR	TOTAL, 6 YEARS
Total costs	$1,805	$1,300	$1,095	$4,200	$1,070	$1,015	$960	$7,245
Fixed costs, total	1,380	850	620	2,850	570	490	410	4,320
Depreciation*	960	540	330	1,830	300	240	180	2,550
Sales tax	90	...	...	90	...	...	...	90
Insurance	200	180	160	540	140	120	100	900
Garage	120	120	120	360	120	120	120	720
License	10	10	10	30	10	10	10	60
Variable costs, total	425	450	475	1,350	500	525	550	2,925
Maintenance, repairs, tires, batteries	100	125	150	375	175	200	225	975
Gas and oil	275	275	275	825	275	275	275	1,650
Parking, tolls, fines	50	50	50	150	50	50	50	300
Average total cost per mile	0.180	0.130	0.110	0.140	0.107	0.102	0.096	0.121
Total cash expenses	3,845	760	765	5,370	770	775	780	7,695**
Car price and tax	3,090	...	...	3,090	...	...	...	3,090
Fixed costs (excluding depreciation)	330	310	290	930	270	250	230	1,680
Variable costs, total	425	450	475	1,350	500	525	550	2,925

* Depreciation estimated at 32% first year; 18% second year; 11% third; 10% fourth; 8% fifth; and 6% sixth.
** Figure differs from $7,245 for total costs by $450, the estimated value of car at end of 6 years.

year and 13¢ the second year, but fall to about 11¢ in the third and fourth years and to 10¢ in the fifth and sixth years.

A family that trades in its car every two years enjoys the prestige and convenience of a new model at an annual cost approximating $1,550. But a family that keeps its car six years might have an annual cost of more nearly $1,200. The lower part of the table showing annual cash expenses explains the reasoning of a family that clings to an aging car until it requires major repairs totalling some hundreds of dollars.

The costs of extra mileage may also be estimated from the figures in the table. The annual cost might vary from about $1,000 for a car driven 2,000 miles a year in the first three years of ownership up to about $2,800 for a car driven 30,000 miles a year for two years. At the same time, the cost per mile might fall from about 51¢ to 9¢. The method of estimate using figures from the table is as follows:

COST ITEMS	COSTS IN FIRST 3 YEARS AT ANNUAL MILEAGE OF—			COSTS IN FIRST 2 YEARS AT 30,000 MILES A YEAR
	2,000	10,000	20,000	
Total costs	$3,120	$4,200	$5,865	$5,515
Fixed costs	2,850	2,850	2,850	2,230
Variable costs	270	1,350	2,925	2,925
Extra depreciation * ...	..	..	90	360
Average cost per year	1,040	1,400	1,955	2,758
Average cost per mile	0.512	0.140	0.098	0.092

* Estimated at 0.5% for each 1,000 miles over 18,000 a year.

When a car ages to the point that it has practically no resale value, the costs may be estimated roughly as follows:

COST ITEMS	2,000 MILES A YEAR	10,000 MILES A YEAR
Total costs	$240	$760
Liability insurance	100	100
License	10	10
Gas and oil, 3¢ a mile	60	300
Maintenance, repairs, tires, batteries	60	300
Parking, tolls, fines	10	50
Average cost per mile	0.12	0.076

Leasing a Car · The family may also have private use of a car by renting it by the month, week, day, or hour, as needed. Rates are lower for a long-term lease, for a lease that omits extra conveniences, for a less expensive model of car, and in certain areas. The rental rate is stated as a flat charge per period with sometimes an additional charge per mile. The charge covers depreciation, regular expenses for maintenance, repairs, and licenses, and certain insurances—collision, fire, and theft. Public liability insurance is not included. The rate may or may not include the cost of gas and oil.

If the family can rent a car similar to our $3,000 model for $125 a month plus gas and oil on a 24-month lease, costs for the first three years or 60,000 miles might be compared as follows:

COST ITEMS	COSTS IN FIRST 3 YEARS AT ANNUAL MILEAGE OF—		COSTS IN FIRST 2 YEARS AT 30,000 MILES A YEAR
	10,000	20,000	
Total cost of owning	$4,688	$6,353	$5,832
Fixed, variable, and extra depreciation	4,200	5,865	5,515
Interest foregone *	488	488	317
Total cost of leasing	5,775	6,750	5,150
Long lease at $125 monthly ...	4,500	4,500	3,000
Liability insurance	300	300	200
Gas and oil	825	1,650	1,650
Parking, tolls, fines	150	300	300

* Interest on $3,090 at 5 percent compounded annually.

In this case about $700 might be saved by a long-term lease when the car is driven 30,000 miles a year. Leasing and owning may be equally expensive at about 25,000 miles a year. A student might wonder how car rental agencies can cover costs and make profits under such conditions. The answer lies in the lower prices that the agencies pay for fleets of cars, their lower maintenance costs, and their better resale prices for used cars than the individual owner can usually achieve.

Since many agencies provide rental cars that are new or almost new, the family that purchases a new model each year might base its comparison of ownership and rental on first year costs. Recently a new car (list price about $2,650) rented for $129 a month on a 6-month lease, with no additional rental charge up to 15,000 miles, with family purchases of gas and oil. At the same rate, the rent for the $3,000 car with which we have been working might approximate $146 a month. Here we find that the cost of leasing is about the same as the cost of owning a new car when it is driven 20,000 miles a year, but leasing may be cheaper at higher mileages. The comparison is as follows:

COST ITEMS	COST OF NEW CAR, FIRST YEAR, AT ANNUAL MILEAGE OF—		
	10,000	20,000	30,000
Total cost of owning	$1,959	$2,439	$3,064
Fixed, variable, and extra depreciation	1,805	2,285	2,910
Interest foregone	154	154	154
Total cost of leasing	2,177	2,502	2,827
6-month lease at $146 monthly ...	1,752	1,752	1,752
Liability insurance	100	100	100
Gas and oil	275	550	825
Parking, tolls, fines	50	100	150

The owner has a unique advantage: Once the car is paid for, he can nurse it along until it collapses. But there are special advantages in leasing. The family has no money tied up in the investment and avoids borrowing to pay for the car. A new car may be supplied frequently—perhaps at 10,000 miles. Furthermore, the family is encouraged to watch carefully its use of the car. A family needing two cars because the husband travels a great deal on business may find that it is better to buy the family car and to lease the car for business purposes since it accumulates mileage rapidly. Rental expenses are easier to separate for reimbursement by the employer or for income tax purposes.

A family that needs a car or a second car occasionally may also find that rental is cheaper, even at the relatively high short-term rates. For a standard-size car, rental may approximate $1.50 an hour, $10 a day, or $50 a week, plus 10¢ a mile, which includes the usual costs plus gas and oil. Week-day rates may be lower and week-end rates may be higher. The rate for a single month may be about $200 plus 5¢ a mile, plus gas and oil.

At a rental cost of $10 a day plus 10¢ a mile, the family can drive a rented car 2,600 miles a year for $559 in 26 days, $845 in 52 days, or $1,417 in 104 days. The costs are estimated as follows:

COST ITEMS	2,600 MILES A YEAR		
	26 DAYS	52 DAYS	104 DAYS
Total cost of rental	$559	$845	$1,417
Rental, $10 a day	260	520	1,040
Rental, 10¢ a mile	260	260	260
Liability insurance	26	52	104
Parking, tolls, fines	13	13	13

While these costs seem high for a relatively small amount of driving, they are probably lower than ownership of a new car. Rental costs may also be lower than ownership of a car that is less than 6 years old and is used less than once a week.

ECONOMY IN PURCHASE AND OPERATION

Several questions are constantly in the minds of car owners. When will we need a new car? How will we pay for it? How can we save on the price and operation? Most of these questions are shared by prospective owners. Let us look at each question separately.

When Will We Need a New Car? · Some families consider that they need a new car every year or two principally because of style changes. Other families like to get a new car frequently because of mechanical improvements or the greater dependability of a new car. These families are willing to assume the high annual depreciation charges connected with regular ownership of a late model car in order to obtain the special advantages. Unfortunately some find that their new cars have defects ranging from small leaks to inoperative brakes which may or may not be corrected perfectly, quickly, without inconvenience, and without additional expense.

Other families are principally interested in low-cost transportation, even if it is not completely dependable. They operate older cars that suffer little annual depreciation. Eventually a point is reached where a new car or a better used car is cheaper than maintaining an old car. Complete records of costs and a careful estimate of repairs that are necessary next year will help the family to decide when this point has been reached. Such costs can be fairly large before they approach the first year's depreciation of roughly $1,000 on an average new car or $500 on a year-old car.

Through the years various studies have indicated that many people consider an old car usable. For example, the Survey Research Center found that only a sixth of the cars owned were under 2 years old, but almost twice as many were 8 years old or over. The distribution by age was as follows: [6]

AGE OF CAR	PERCENT OF CARS
Less than 2 years old	16
2 and 3 years old	22
4 to 7 years old	33
8 years old and over	30

[6] Survey Research Center, University of Michigan, *Survey of Consumer Finances*, data for 1965.

At any rate, the family must be realistic about the future need for replacing the car. Service-life expectancy under one owner averages 6 years for a new auto and 4 years for a used auto. The older the principal driver, the longer the service-life expectancy. Cars with a woman driver have a longer service-life expectancy than those with a man driver. Cars manufactured in the United States have a longer service-life expectancy than those manufactured abroad, but perhaps foreign cars are more frequently driven by young men. The average service-life expectancy for a new car varies from about 5 years for younger men to about 8 years for elderly women.[7]

How Will We Pay for the Car? · Forty percent of new cars are purchased for cash, including the trade-in allowance, and 53 percent of used cars are purchased for cash, according to the Survey Research Center. This means that a large proportion are financed, generally on equal payments over a period of months.

The family needs to plan ahead to accumulate sufficient funds for a down payment or cash purchase of its first car or a replacement of its present car. Regular monthly savings is the best way for most families. After the present car is paid for, the family might place an amount equal to the monthly payment in an earmarked fund in order to accumulate a sizable cash fund by the next purchase date. If the present car was financed for 24–36 months, an equal monthly accumulation for an equal period thereafter may provide for the cash purchase of the next car.

Cash purchase results in sizable savings. A $3,000 car purchased with a $500 down payment and a $2,500 loan repaid in 36 equal monthly instalments at 0.75 percent interest a month—about the most lenient terms one could obtain—would cost about $362 for interest. Cash purchase of the car would free this sum for extra purchases of gas and oil or for the purchase of a washer and dryer.

The cost of credit is worth emphasizing at this point since a large proportion of all consumer credit is used for auto purchase. The family needs to plan carefully its use of credit and to shop widely and wisely for it. Total credit charges are lowered by a lower rate of interest, a shorter repayment period, and a smaller loan. The loan is minimized by a larger down payment or the purchase of a simpler car. Total interest on a $1,000 loan varies from about $26 for a 6-month loan at 0.75 percent a month up to $649 on a 36-month loan at 3

[7] Jean L. Pennock and Carol M. Jaeger, "Household Service Life of Durable Goods," *Journal of Home Economics*, January 1964, pp. 22–26 (1961 data).

percent a month. A $700 loan would cost seven-tenths as much, and a $3,400 loan would cost 3.4 times as much.

Total interest on a $1,000 loan repaid in equal monthly instalments approximates the following figures:

NUMBER OF EQUAL MONTHLY PAYMENTS	MONTHLY RATE OF INTEREST *					
	0.75%	1%	1.5%	2%	2.5%	3%
6	$ 26	$ 35	$ 53	$ 71	$ 89	$108
12	49	66	100	135	170	206
18	73	98	148	201	254	309
24	96	130	198	269	342	417
30	120	162	289	340	433	531
36	145	196	301	412	528	649

* True rate on declining unpaid balance.

Study of these figures emphasizes the value of saving ahead of time, repaying the loan quickly, and of shopping for the best credit terms.

Since credit is frequently easier to obtain for the purchase of a new car because of new car guarantees, some families feel forced or tempted to select one although they need other items more than they need a new car. Monthly payments may be lower than on a used car because of a lower interest rate and a longer repayment period. The required down payment may comprise a smaller part of the purchase price. The difference for the family budget is that the payments for the new car may continue for 36 months rather than the 12 months on the used car. The family finally invests a great deal more in the new car and pays much higher total interest charges because of the larger debt and the longer repayment period.

A cash or near-cash purchase places the individual in a stronger bargaining position. He can select a used or new car, a cheap or expensive car, one make or another, and from any dealer, as he prefers. He is a free agent. Furthermore, the buyer may be more careful in expenditure of his cash funds than in obligating himself to monthly payments. A mild-mannered woman remarked on what serious shopping she was doing for a new car since she had accumulated money for her first cash purchase, in contrast with her casual shopping in previous years when she signed for long term loans.

How Can We Save on Price and Operation? · Census reported recently that 19 percent of all households planned to purchase an auto within 12 months—more than half planning on a new auto.[8] These families have many decisions to make before the purchase is finally consummated. The decisions affect the family's safety, comfort, convenience, and pleasure, as well as the cost of purchase and operation. Changes in family needs and resources and in the autos available and their prices require reappraisal of the situation at each purchase.

Visits to auto showrooms and used car lots, study of informational materials and newspaper ads, discussions with friends and mechanics—all aid in the decision on the kind of car that best meets family needs and budget. The choices are many: a new or used car; a compact, intermediate, or full-size car; the make and model; special features; optional equipment; a foreign- or U. S.-manufactured car. The family wants to select the features necessary for its purposes, but does not want to pay for features not needed.

Savings may be made by purchasing a current model at dealers' clearance sales just before the new models arrive, thus avoiding part of the first year's high depreciation cost. Purchasing a used car permits the family to avoid the heavy depreciation charges of the first year or two. An average price of $920 was paid for the 11 million used cars purchased in 1964 in contrast with an average price of $3,140 for the 7 million new cars purchased, according to the Survey Research Center.

Some used cars in excellent condition were traded in simply because the original owner wanted a newer or different model or make. Some carry a dealer's guarantee. When a used car is in questionable condition, it may be desirable to have it checked by a local auto mechanic or by a diagnostic car care center that makes over a hundred tests. Safety requires good brakes, tires, directional signals, lights, seat belts, and a good overall condition of the car. A reputable dealer, his guarantees, and repair service are important to the car buyer who frequently has inadequate knowledge.

One should generally compare prices at several dealers before making a decision. The manufacturer's suggested retail price for a new car is not necessarily the sale price. Auto dealers do not work on the one-price system to which we are accustomed at the grocery and department stores. Comparative shopping may result in a discount of about 15 percent on a sticker price of $2,000–$3,000, 18 percent on a price of $3,000–$4,000, and 20 percent on a price of $4,000–$5,000. An acquaintance who set out to purchase a $5,100 car a couple of years ago finally paid $3,700 in cash with no trade-in. She and her husband

---

[8] U. S. Bureau of Census, *Current Population Reports*, Series P–65, No. 15, 1966 (July 1966 data).

had decided on the make, model, and accessories wanted, and she visited the showroom of every dealer in the area—about 14—who offered that make of car. She kept a list of each dealer's name, address, and price as she progressed. She admitted that it was a big job, taking considerable time and driving. But she saved $1,400—about 23 percent.

Bargaining is more complicated when one has an old car to trade in. He needs to ascertain the fair market price of his old car, then bargain on the difference between the new car price and the trade-in price. Checking your local credit union, your local mechanic, newspaper ads, friends, and various dealers will help to determine a fair price for the trade-in. Sometimes the family decides to sell its old car directly and to purchase without a trade-in. Or a family needing a second car may keep the old car for this purpose.

Maintenance and repair may be costly on a new auto as well as on an older auto. Keeping the car in perfect condition with frequent diagnosis of any possible weaknesses may lead to overmaintenance and repair and a large bill. The charge for diagnosis and for parts and service may be much higher on a high-priced car than on a low-priced or aged car. A mechanic who will differentiate between perfectionist repairs and necessary ones and who will make repairs in a simple and inexpensive way, by grinding a new hole and adding a bolt instead of replacing a part, is a great boon to the owner who is trying to economize.

The family can also play a part in cutting costs of auto operation. Some are able to perform services for themselves, including everything from washing to minor repairs. Others can perform few or none of these services. All can control their driving methods and speed for greater safety and economy. Control of car mileage can also play an important part in cutting expenses. Decreasing travel by 100 miles a week may decrease direct costs for gas and maintenance by $208 a year, plus savings on parking. Walking short distances, consolidating trips, and using public transportation can all be practiced to cut mileage.

AUTOMOBILE INSURANCE

It is imperative that the family plan for sufficient automobile insurance. Inadequate insurance may be the most expensive economy of a lifetime, resulting in loss of savings or judgments against future income. About 50,000 people are killed annually in motor-vehicle accidents and 4 million are injured—a total of 2 persons out of 100.[9] Almost half of all accidental deaths are due to motor-vehicle accidents, as are about a tenth of nonfatal injuries. There is also a tremendous amount of property damage resulting from auto accidents. During 40 to 60 years of driving, one is likely to be involved in several accidents. Liability for personal or property damage is therefore a real hazard as is the death or nonfatal injury of a family member or damage to the family auto.

High accident rates, high costs of medical care and auto repair, and high court awards mean that auto insurance rates cannot be low. But a good insurance policy may be the best bargain you will ever buy. Rates vary according to the kinds and amounts of coverage, the use made of the car, the car's value, the place of residence and local accident rate, and the driver's record. Those classified as safe drivers may pay a reduced premium. Those classed as high-risk pay a higher rate. Because of the wide variation in all of these factors, one person's insurance policy may cost less than a hundred dollars a year, whereas another person's policy may cost several hundred dollars.

An auto insurance policy includes several types of coverage. Each owner selects the types and amounts to suit his needs and resources. He separates the various hazards into three categories: those that occur frequently and result in modest loss; those that occur infrequently, but can result in a great loss; and those that are unlikely ever to occur. Protection against the first group of hazards is met properly by provisions in the family budget for emergency expenses. Protection against the second group of hazards is properly provided by insurance. The last group of hazards is likely to be ignored.

Coverages for public liability are the most necessary types. Coverage for *bodily injury liability* protects the family against judgments resulting from bodily injury or death of others up to the limit of the policy. While the law may require at least 15/30, that is a maximum of $15,000 for each person and a maximum of $30,000 for each accident, the family may consider a larger protection to be a greater bargain. Coverage of 100/300 may cost about $50 a year in situations where 15/30 costs about $40 a year. While costly accidents occur infrequently, which explains the relatively small increase in premium, the potential protection is great. Adequate public liability coverage is a necessary cost of operating a car these days.

Coverage for *property damage liability* protects the insured against loss through claims or judgments resulting from damage to

9 U. S. Dept. of Health, Education, and Welfare, Public Health Service, annual report, *Vital Statistics of the United States*, 1964.

the property of others. While the expense is not likely to exceed $5,000 in one accident, protection of $10,000 may be desirable and cost a relatively small additional amount. Such coverage may cost $20 to $30 a year in a suburban community.

In case of bodily injury or property damage over $100, most states now require proof of financial responsibility in the form of a minimum auto insurance policy or deposit of a sum of money. Otherwise they suspend the operator's licenses and car registrations until he has been judged not liable or has paid the damages up to a stated amount. Proof of financial responsibility before obtaining licenses is better protection for the public. In order to register a car in Maryland, one must have at least $15/30,000 of personal injury insurance and $5,000 of property damage insurance or pay a fee of $35 to the Unsatisfied Claims Fund. The fund protects insured motorists against damages caused by uninsured motorists.

In the auto insurance policy, coverage of bodily injury caused by *uninsured motorists* to a maximum of $10,000 each person or $20,000 each accident may cost as little as $2. *Medical payments* up to perhaps $500 for each person injured while riding in the insured's car may be added for a small charge, perhaps $5. *Comprehensive* coverage includes fire and theft and other types of damage to the auto, but not loss caused by collision or upset, and may cost a minimum of about $10 a year. *Towing and labor costs* coverage is also added on some policies.

Collision coverage pays for damage to the insured's auto in a collision or upset. The coverage may have a $50 or $100 deductible clause, meaning that the insured pays the first $50 or $100 cost for repairs in each accident. There may be a saving of $20 to $30 a year by selection of the $100 deductible. In the later years of ownership when the car's resale value has fallen, perhaps after the second year, the family needs to consider carefully whether to retain its collision insurance. What is the maximum to be received in case of total loss and what is the insurance premium for that protection?

QUESTIONS

1. How does transportation expense compare with clothing and shelter expense in importance?

2. What kind of household would find public transportation most economical?

3. Which households are most likely to own a car? More than one?

4. What might be the approximate annual cost for ownership and operation of a popular-priced car?

5. Differentiate between fixed and variable costs. How would you estimate your costs?

6. Why do auto expenditures differ greatly from one family to another?

7. Discuss the possibilities of leasing a car and compare it with buying.

8. How does the family decide when to trade in its old car?

9. Discuss plans for accumulating funds toward a bigger down payment on the family's next car. What are the advantages?

10. How can a family economize on auto price and operation?

11. Describe the various types of hazards covered by auto insurance. Consider the importance of each to the family.

SUGGESTIONS FOR FURTHER READING

American Automobile Association. *Your Driving Costs,* latest edition.

Automobile Manufacturers Association. *Auto Facts and Figures,* latest edition.

Consumers' Research. *Consumer Bulletin,* buying guide, latest issues.

Consumers Union. *Consumer Reports,* buying guide, latest issues.

Household Finance Corporation. *Money Management: Your Automobile Dollar.* Chicago, latest edition.

Insurance Information Institute. *Casualty Insurance Handbook.* New York, latest edition.

National Safety Council. *Accident Facts.* Chicago, latest edition.

U. S. Bureau of the Census. *Current Population Reports.* Series P–65, latest reports.

"For there was never yet philosopher
That could endure the toothache patiently."
—Much Ado About Nothing

The
Medical Care / 12
Budget

- ESTIMATING BUDGET AMOUNT
- COSTS OF DISABILITIES
- MANAGING MEDICAL CARE
  EXPENSES
- HEALTH INSURANCE

While medical care takes only 6 percent of disposable income of consumers, this part of the budget deserves special attention because of its importance to family welfare and its complexities. The present proportion for medical care, increasing at about 0.1 percentage points annually, contrasts with the 3.5 percent for medical care in 1929.

At the same time, the amount of medical care per person has about tripled since 1929. Higher incomes have permitted a greater use of medical care, and the public has been educated to recognize the value of this type of expenditure. More medical care has been required because of the larger proportion of elderly and the higher birth rates. Great advances in medical techniques and drugs have made more expensive treatments available and have served to extend the lives of many who would have died at an earlier age a few decades ago. This includes particularly the elderly and the newly born. Coverage by various types of health insurance has served to facilitate or encourage the use of medical care.

Medical care is to be thought of in the broadest terms as including physicians' services, nursing and hospital services, drugs and devices, and related items and services. As used here, medical expenditures include only those paid directly by families, thus excluding public health services and government support of hospitals and medical services, which comprise about a third of all national expenditures on health.[1] The present discussion is limited to medical care for the civilian, noninstitutional population. The need for medical care varies from the most dire to the most ethereal. It may be necessary for preservation of life, relief of pain, or promotion of health. In addition, it is used by some for cosmetic purposes and by others for inflation of the ego.

ESTIMATING BUDGET AMOUNT

Among the categories of expenditure, medical care is the most difficult to budget accurately. Food, clothing, and shelter needs exist for all people and are reasonably regular. Expenditures for automobiles and tobacco can be reduced if one has the will power. But an appendectomy may suddenly be required to save the life of one person, or it may be unnecessary for another. A family's past experience is insufficient basis for planning its medical care budget for the next period; it may have low costs for many years, then suddenly be hit by a tremendous bill. Furthermore, disability may mean reduced income for the family, if it strikes the earner, or costs of replacing the homemaker's services.

In other words, the family or individual need for medical care is to an important extent unpredictable and uncontrollable. Need varies greatly for a specific family from one period to another and among families at a given time. A study by the Health Information Foundation showed that 3 percent of the families studied had no medical expense in a year, whereas almost 5 percent paid $1,000 or more. The distribution of families is shown on the top of p. 233.[2] Of course, some families received free medical care and some received limited care.

While expenses for medical care vary tremendously from one family to another, it is worthwhile to look briefly at the figures on average expenses in Table 12-1. At a given income level, families tend to spend more with the first increases in family size, but to spend

---

[1] U. S. Department of Health, Education, and Welfare, Social Security Administration, *Research and Statistics Note No. 10–1965*, "National Expenditures for Health Care Purposes by Object of Expenditures and Source of Funds, 1960–1963."

[2] Health Insurance Institute, *Source Book of Health Insurance Data 1960*, pp. 55–56, data for May 1957–June 1958.

AMOUNT OF EXPENSE	PERCENT OF FAMILIES
All levels	100
No expense	3
$1–$99	31
$100–$299	34
$300–$499	15
$500–$999	12
$1,000 and over	5

less with later increases in size. Among families of a given size, expenses on medical care tend to increase irregularly with income, and vary irregularly as a proportion of income.

When we look at health expenses of individual persons, we see extreme variations. In a 12-month period, 5 percent had expenses of $500 or more (Table 12–2). The percentage was practically the same for the various income groups. Such high expense for health care generally indicates a calamitous disability rather than a high level of living. On the other hand, 18 percent of all persons had no health

TABLE 12–1. Medical Care Expenditures of Urban Families, by Family Size and Income [Average not shown for cells of less than 30 families]

MONEY INCOME AFTER TAXES	NUMBER OF PERSONS IN FAMILY					
	1	2	3	4	5	6 OR MORE
Under $1,000	$ 90	..	..	..	..	..
$1,000–$1,999	110	$ 220	..	..	..	..
$2,000–$2,999	190	310	$170	..	..	..
$3,000–$3,999	210	310	270	$440	..	..
$4,000–$4,999	210	320	340	280	$240	$280
$5,000–$5,999	310	350	370	350	350	310
$6,000–$7,499	200	440	430	420	400	360
$7,500–$9,999	..	500	520	470	480	500
$10,000–$14,999	..	540	590	560	690	560
$15,000 and over	..	1,010	..	..	..	..

SOURCE: U. S. Bureau of Labor Statistics, *Survey of Consumer Expenditures 1961.* These data collected in the spring of 1962 from 4,900 families are the best indicators currently available of spending patterns of various types of families. Data for the early 1970's may be available a few years thereafter.

TABLE 12–2.   Health Expenses Per Person *

ITEM	FAMILY INCOME				
	ALL INCOMES	UNDER $2,000	$2,000– $3,999	$4,000– $6,999	$7,000 AND OVER
Percent distribution of persons by health expenses:					
All persons	100	100	100	100	100
No expense	18	30	24	16	11
$1–$49	34	32	35	38	32
$50–$99	17	13	14	18	21
$100–$249	17	14	14	16	21
$250–$499	8	7	8	8	9
$500 and more	5	4	5	5	6
Average health expenses per person by age:					
All persons	$129	$112	$116	$119	$153
Under 15 years	59	29	43	60	80
15–44 years	131	97	108	132	156
45–64 years	191	154	169	189	221
65 years and over ..	208	162	213	210	308

* Civilian, noninstitutional population.
SOURCE: U. S. National Center for Health Statistics, *Vital and Health Statistics: Data from the National Health Survey,* Public Health Service Publication No. 1000, Series 10, No. 9, pp. 43 and 45 (1962 data).

expenses. Thirty percent of persons in families with incomes under $2,000 had no health expenses contrasted with only 11 percent in families with incomes of $7,000 and over. While needs differ, the important cause is undoubtedly the difference in money available.

Average health needs and expenses increase with the age of the individual. The estimated scale of health expenses presented in Table 12–3 may be helpful in comparing average health expenses at different stages of the life cycle for males and females. Expenses for those under 17 years old are about six-tenths of the amount for a man 25–44 years old. During the childbearing years, expenses for women are much higher than for men. Thereafter, expenses for both women and men increase, and the differences between them decrease.

COSTS OF DISABILITIES

While the individual's disabilities are unpredictable, those of large groups are reasonably predictable. The increasing disability as

TABLE 12–3. Estimated Scale of Health Expenses for Sex-Age Groups [Expense for male 25–44 years old = 100]

AGE	SCALE FOR MALES	SCALE FOR FEMALES
Under 6	60	55
6–16	60	60
17–24	75	145
25–44	100	160
45–64	165	185
65 and over	225	235

SOURCES: Author's estimates based on Public Health Service Publication No. 1000, Series 10, No. 27, p. 20, on average expense by sex-age groups, and No. 9, p. 45, on expense by age groups at upper income levels.

age advances is the outstanding conclusion from a study of the data on incidence in Table 12–4. For instance, in a year elderly men average about 36 days of restricted activity including 13 days of bed disability, compared with boys under 17 years old who average 11 days of restricted activity including 5 days of bed disability. After childhood, females have more disability days than do males.

Acute conditions are most frequent among children, but they are disabled by them no more days in a year than are the elderly by their relatively few acute conditions. Chronic conditions are least frequent among children and seldom limit their major activity. But the proportion of persons with chronic conditions increases with age, and the conditions become more disabling. Among men 45–64 years old, one or more chronic conditions were reported by 64 percent, including 16 percent who had to limit or forego their major activity. Chronic conditions were reported by 82 percent of elderly men, including 49 percent who had to limit or forego their major activity.

The proportion of persons in the major working years with one or more chronic conditions is higher in families with low income than in those with higher income. These chronic conditions may, then, be an important cause of low family income. The incidence of chronic conditions is as follows for persons 45–64 years old: [3]

[3] Public Health Service Publication No. 1000, Series 10, No. 9, p. 53 (data for July 1962–June 1963).

FAMILY INCOME	PERCENT OF PERSONS
Under $2,000	77
$2,000–$3,999	68
$4,000–$6,999	62
$7,000 and over	61

In general, the young have colds and other respiratory conditions, childhood diseases, and need immunization; young women require medical care at childbirth. The number of major types of acute conditions per 100 persons per year is as follows for different age groups: [4]

ACUTE CONDITIONS	UNDER 17	17–44		45 AND OVER
		MALES	FEMALES	
All acute conditions	303	154	207	142
Infective and parasitic diseases	52	14	19	11
Respiratory conditions	169	76	112	79
Injuries	37	40	20	22
All other acute conditions ..	45	24	56	30

During the important working years, acute conditions decline, but chronic conditions increase, especially in the later years. Thereafter, chronic conditions become increasingly important and severe.

Generally, if we survive accidents, we live to develop heart disease, cancer, or circulatory diseases from which we eventually perish (since "old age" is an unacceptable medical reason these days). These diseases of the later years can involve long and expensive care. Accidents are by far the major cause of death for those one to twenty-four years old. The death rate per 100,000 population in these age groups is as follows: [5]

CAUSES	1–4	5–14	15–24
All causes	100	44	106
All accidents	31	18	57

But the leading causes of death change with age, as follows:

CAUSES	25–44	45–64	65 AND OVER
All causes	230	1,171	6,242
All accidents	44	56	
Cancer and related	40	273	889
Diseases of heart	47	465	2,892
Cerebral hemorrhage and related ..		86	926

[4] Public Health Service Publication No. 1000, Series 10, No. 26, p. 19 (data for July 1964–June 1965).

[5] Public Health Service Publication No. 600, Revised 1965, pp. 14–15 (data for 1963).

TABLE 12–4. Incidence of Disabilities in a Year*

ITEM	MALES				FEMALES			
	UNDER 17	17–44	45–64	65 AND OVER	UNDER 17	17–44	45–64	65 AND OVER
All disabilities:								
Days of restricted activity, average per person	11	10	21	36	10	15	24	41
Bed disability days, average per person	5	4	6	13	5	6	8	15
Acute conditions:								
Days of restricted activity, average per person	9	6	6	9	9	9	9	12
Bed disability days, average per person	4	2	2	4	4	4	3	5
Number of conditions, average per person	3	2	1	1	3	2	2	1
Chronic conditions:								
Days of restricted activity, average per person	2	4	15	27	1	7	15	29
Bed disability days, average per person	1	1	4	10	1	2	5	10
Percent of persons with one or more chronic conditions	23	48	64	82	20	53	68	85
With limitation of activity**	2	8	20	53	2	8	20	45
But not in major activity	2	2	4	5	1	4	6	9
In amount or kind of major activity	1	5	11	27	1	4	12	27
Unable to carry on major activity	.	1	5	22	.	.	1	9

* Civilian, noninstitutional population, July 1964–June 1965.
** These data for persons under 45 years old apply to July 1961–June 1963; and for persons 45 years old and over, to July 1963–June 1965.
SOURCE: U. S. National Center for Health Statistics, *Vital and Health Statistics: Data from the National Health Survey,* Public Health Service Publication No. 1000, Series 10, No. 17, p. 12; No. 25, pp. 12, 17, 20; No. 26, pp. 19–21, 32–33; and No. 32, p. 46.

An idea of the approximate cost of some kinds of medical care helps the family in considering possible expenses. For instance, the average cost per patient day in the hospital was $42 in 1964 and the cost per patient stay averaging about eight days was $320.[6] Average total costs of some of the larger common disabilities ranged from about $100 to $600 according to a large study a few years ago. The costs for selected disabilities were as follows: [7]

DISABILITY	COST	DISABILITY	COST
Tonsillectomy	$128	Gastroenteritis	$143
Appendectomy	333	Cystitis	174
Thyroidectomy, subtotal ..	451	Fractures, upper limb	228
Normal deliveries	297	Fractures, lower limb	396
Caesarean section	633	Burns	456
Pneumonia	191	Poisonings	120
Kidney infections	195		

Some of the uncommon disabilities are also uncommonly expensive. Examples of the costs of specific medical cases reported a few years ago were as follows: [8]

DIAGNOSIS	COST	DIAGNOSIS	COST
Cancer of bladder	$2,148	Poliomyelitis	$2,192
Acute appendicitis with		Acute coronary	
peritonitis	889	thrombosis	3,673
Fractured hip	2,376	Acute gangrenous	
Extensive second- and		appendicitis	2,154
third-degree burns	3,551	Brain tumor	2,609
Brain tumor	1,951	Poliomyelitis	2,941
Leukemia	1,707	Acute coronary	
Nephritis	989	thrombosis	893

The price indexes for medical care have increased more than for other major categories in the family budget due to increased costs of the various types of care. According to the Consumer Price Index, hospital room rates are about six times as high as in 1935, and physicians' and dentists' fees are more than twice as high for similar services. Optometric examination and eyeglasses, and prescriptions

[6] American Hospital Association, and Health Insurance Association of America. Quoted in *Source Book of Health Insurance Data 1965*, Health Insurance Institute, p. 63.
[7] Office for Dependents' Medical Care, Department of Defense, *The Dependents' Medical Care Program First Annual Report*, June 1958. Average cost under Medicare plan for dependent spouses and children of members of the uniformed services, 1957.
[8] 84th Congress, Committee on Armed Services, *Report to Accompany HR 9429*, 1956.

and drugs are about 1.5 times as high as in 1935. The distribution of the medical care dollar in 1965, according to the Department of Commerce figures, was as follows:

Hospital services .... 30¢
Physicians' services .... 28¢
Medicines and appliances .... 21¢
Dentists .... 10¢
Net cost of health insurance............ 7¢
Other professional services .... 5¢

MANAGING MEDICAL CARE EXPENSES

While the focus here is on the direct costs for medical care, the family can help to minimize these costs by its support of public programs for the control of various hazards to life and health such as air pollution, auto accidents, communicable diseases, and impure foods and drugs.

Each family member can work directly to cut medical needs by the development of good health practices and by care to prevent accidents at home, on the street, and on the job. One may select employment and other activities without undue accident or disease rate, or at least be aware of the high rate when such exists. Regular medical check-ups and immunization along with early medical advice help to prevent the development of major disabilities.

In addition to efforts to minimize the need for medical care, the family must prepare ahead of time for the cost of any needs that develop. It may build savings in cash or other forms on which to draw in case of need. Such savings are generally most appropriate for the ordinary, predictable costs. Employment with sick leave policy, Workman's Compensation, and Social Security give some assistance when the earner is disabled, at least to the extent of some compensation for loss in income. Elderly persons have some protection against direct costs through the Medicare section of the Social Security program, discussed in Chapter 16. Because these methods may prove insufficient for the costs of more unusual types of medical care, many families also purchase health insurance of various types.

Optimism, ignorance, indifference, and inability cause many families to make insufficient financial preparation ahead of the time of need for medical care. In an emergency, they use current earnings by cutting other expenses or their savings program. They seek to enlarge current earnings by adding additional workers or a substitute worker if the earner is incapacitated. When these methods fail, they go into debt for medical care such as physicians' services, and borrow money to pay any hospital or other bills that must be paid in cash. At the extreme, the family may have to depend on free or partially free care from private or public charity.

Before a grave emergency arises, we need to develop considered attitudes toward extremes in medical care. It is a miracle that an artificial kidney or pacemaker for the heart can keep a person alive for several months. But let us inquire into this miracle from the point of view of the individual. How do we define being "alive"? How much does the patient suffer, and how long is the convalescence? What is the level of recovery, how long does it last, and how is the period of final degeneracy affected? What is the financial cost and the cost in labor and strain on family members? The following news item points up the problem:

DOCTOR SEES DYING DIFFICULT IN U. S.

Reuters

Perth, Australia, Aug. 18—A British medical authority to-day expressed a hope that when his time came to die it would be in Britain and not the United States.

"America has lots of expensive instruments that keep you alive when you should be dead," said Sir George Pickering, regius professor of medicine at Oxford University.

Sir George told reporters he agreed with Dr. Charles Mayo, head of the Mayo Clinic, who said recently that people should be allowed to die as well as live.—*The Washington Post*, August 19, 1965.

HEALTH INSURANCE

Because it is difficult to predict the need for large expenditures on medical care and to meet such expenses out of savings or current earnings, some amount of health insurance is purchased for more than eight-tenths of the civilian noninstitutional population (Table 12–5). The phrase "health insurance," a nice euphemism, covers a wide variety of policies that provide financial protection in case of a disabling illness or accident. These policies are purchased by the individual or family or by a group (usually the employees of a company) from insurance companies or nonprofit organizations; or such benefits are provided under independent plans provided by the employer or other organizations. The major types of health insurance policies will be considered in three categories of coverage—general medical expense, major medical expense, and loss of income.

TABLE 12-5. Persons With Health Insurance, by Type of Insurer [Millions of persons]

PROTECTION	TOTAL	INSURANCE COMPANIES			BLUE CROSS, BLUE SHIELD, AND MEDICAL SOCIETY PLANS	INDEPENDENT PLANS
		TOTAL [1]	GROUP POLICIES	INDIVIDUAL AND FAMILY POLICIES		
General medical expense:						
Hospital expense	151[1]	93	65	40	63	7
Surgical expense	141[1]	90	65	35	54	9
Regular medical expense	109[1]	55	47	12	51	9
Major medical expense	..	47	43	4		
Supplementary	..		32			
Comprehensive	..		11			

PROTECTION	TOTAL	INSURANCE COMPANIES			FORMAL PAID SICK LEAVE PLANS [3]	OTHER [4]
		TOTAL [1]	GROUP POLICIES	INDIVIDUAL AND FAMILY POLICIES		
Loss of income	48	36	24	15[2]	11	1

[1] Totals eliminate duplication among persons protected by more than one kind of insuring organization or more than one insurance company policy providing the same type of coverage. [2] Individual policies only. [3] Persons with formal sick leave plans but without insurance company coverage. [4] Includes union-administered plans and employee mutual benefit associations.

SOURCE: Health Insurance Institute, *Source Book of Health Insurance Data 1965*, pp. 12, 14, 16, 18, 20, and 22 (data for 1964).

General Medical Expense · Policies providing protection in case of general medical expense are the most popular kind. They include hospital, surgical, and regular medical expense policies. These policies are actually prepayment or medical budgeting plans for the more expensive common disabilities. They generally cover a large part of the costs of an appendectomy, pneumonia, or simple fracture; and there is a high likelihood that the family will collect on its policy over a period of several years. Four-tenths of the persons covered by each of these kinds of policies are the primary insured persons, usually the earners, and the rest are their dependents. Among persons with hospital insurance, 93 percent also have surgical insurance, and 72 percent have regular medical insurance.[9]

Hospital expense policies provide benefits toward hospital charges for room and board, for the operating room, and for certain items such as X-rays and medicines. More persons—151 million—are covered by hospitalization insurance than by any other type of health insurance. About four-tenths of these persons are covered by insurance company group plans, generally purchased at the place of employment. Four-tenths are insured by nonprofit organizations, primarily Blue Cross.

While plans differ, a plan may provide benefits for 30 days of hospital care for each hospital stay, if successive stays are separated by at least 90 days. Coverage may include the hospital bill for a semi-private room and meals, general nursing care, operating rooms, and other specified items. The group rate for a nonprofit plan may approximate $50 a year for an individual or $120 for a family. The nongroup rate may approximate $60 for an individual or $130 for a family.

Surgical expense policies pay benefits according to a set schedule which lists the maximum amount of benefits for each type of surgical procedure, up to about $400–$500. A large number of people—141 million—are covered by surgical expense policies. Almost half of these people are covered by insurance company group plans. About four-tenths are insured by the major nonprofit organizations, primarily Blue Shield.

Regular medical expense policies pay benefits toward physicians' fees for non-surgical care given in the hospital, home, or at the doctor's office, and some provide benefits for diagnostic X-ray and laboratory expenses. Sometimes these benefits are included in hospital and surgical expense policies. About 109 million people have regular

9 *Source Book of Health Insurance Data 1965*, pp. 19 and 23 (data for 1964).

medical expense insurance. Four-tenths of them have insurance company group policies. Almost half have policies with the major nonprofit organizations.

A plan may provide for surgical care according to a stated schedule up to $350, and for limited amounts of medical care for a maximum of 30 days for each hospital stay, and for some other expenses. The group rate for a nonprofit plan may approximate $30 annually for an individual and $80 for a family.

Major Medical Expense · Policies offering protection against major medical expense were introduced on a nationwide basis in 1951, and have increased greatly in popularity as their advantages have become evident. These policies help pay the heavy medical expenses caused by catastrophic or prolonged illness or injury, such as that caused by a calamitous accident, polio, heart disease, or cancer. Such protection is true insurance rather than a medical budgeting plan, since it helps to cover high costs that are extremely unpredictable. The likelihood of collecting for major medical expense is not great over the family life cycle, which means that this feature *per se* can be low cost.

A simple (or "stripped-down") policy for major medical expense may require the insured to pay the first $500 or $1,000 of expense in a year or for an illness. This is the deductible amount. Then the policy pays benefits for additional costs of various types of medical treatment at a rate of 75–80 percent, and the insured pays the remaining costs—the coinsurance feature. There may be a "corridor" after expenses have reached a stated amount, such as $3,000, at which point the insured pays the next $100 or so himself. Benefits are received up to the maximum stated in the policy, usually $5,000, $10,000, or higher.

The deductible amount, the coinsurance feature, and the corridor are expected to deter the careless use of medical services. The cost of the insurance is lowered by a bigger deductible amount, a larger corridor, and a larger coinsurance portion paid by the insured. A higher maximum increases the cost only slightly since few disabilities cost more than $10,000 for medical expense.

Major medical expense coverage may be purchased in three ways—as a policy covering major medical expense only, after a high deductible; as a supplementary feature to basic hospital and surgical expense policies; or as a comprehensive policy that makes payments after a small deductible amount, such as $50, which means that the policy covers both general medical expense and major medical expense.

About 47 million people are covered for major medical expense under policies issued by insurance companies, mostly as group policies. Four-tenths of the covered persons are the primary insured persons, and the rest are their dependents. The policies are generally supplementary to basic hospital and surgical expense policies, but some are comprehensive policies that make payments after a small deductible amount. Some of the individual and family policies cover major medical expenses only, after a large deductible amount. Additional persons are covered for major medical expense by supplemental features of Blue Cross-Blue Shield policies or by independent plans.

Benefits under one comprehensive plan written by an insurance company for a large group may be summarized briefly as folllows:

KINDS OF EXPENSES	HIGH OPTION RECEIVES	LOW OPTION RECEIVES
Hospital room and board	100 percent of the first $1,000 of allowable expenses each year, plus 80 percent of any balance.	100 percent of the first $500 of allowable expenses each year, plus 75 percent of any balance.
Other hospital, surgical, and medical expenses	80 percent of allowable expenses over first $50 each year.	75 percent of allowable expenses over first $50 each year.
Maximum benefit (lifetime)	$40,000 per person. Plus automatic annual restoration of $2,000 per person.	$15,000 per person. Plus automatic annual restoration of $500 per person.

Allowable expenses, including a semiprivate room in a hospital, are explicitly defined, and excluded services and supplies are stated. Annual costs paid by the employee and employer are as follows:

INSURED PERSONS	HIGH OPTION PREMIUMS		LOW OPTION PREMIUMS	
	EMPLOYEE	EMPLOYER	EMPLOYEE	EMPLOYER
Earner only	$ 82	$ 44	$34	$34
Earner and family	204	107	81	81

Loss of Income · Insurance against loss of income pays benefits to employed persons during the time they are ill or makes specified payments for certain dismemberments. About 36 million persons have such insurance. A policy paying $200 a month for a maximum of

2 years after a waiting period of 30 days may cost about $80 a year at 30 years of age, but higher amounts at later ages.

In addition, 11 million workers are employed under formal sick leave plans which help to meet the same type of need. Such plans are especially helpful when unused sick leave can be accumulated toward a time of greater need.

Selecting Health Insurance · In choosing health insurance, the family should first purchase protection against the most *disastrous risk.* For those with a moderately good income and some savings, the cost of pneumonia or an appendectomy would be unpleasant, but not disastrous, whereas a medical bill for $3,000 or $10,000 would be a catastrophe. For a poor family with low income and no savings, a broken arm might be a disaster; and it would have to seek charity for a greater expense.

Risks that are very improbable, such as the costs of polio, are not worth insuring against separately, although they may be included in "package" policies, such as those for major medical expense, with small additional cost. Risks that are very probable, such as expenses for check-ups, immunization, and flu, may cost twice as much through insurance as by direct payment because of the company's costs of handling the policy and making payments.

The individual needs to purchase health insurance while he is young and healthy since it may be difficult or very expensive to purchase when he is unwell or approaching 60. Coverage for maternity care generally needs to be purchased at least ten months or a year before need. Some policies exclude certain other types of coverage for the first three or six months. Some plans exclude chronic disabilities which the insured has when he purchases the policy. Those reaching 65 years of age may want to purchase health insurance to supplement their Medicare benefits during later years.

Health insurance purchased through a group policy that is negotiated by the employer with an insurance company or with Blue Cross-Blue Shield is generally much cheaper than when individually purchased because of economies in the group purchase and subsidy from the employer. However, such a policy may be lost when the employee leaves the job or retires. Since he may be unable to purchase a private policy at that time, it is highly desirable that such group policies be *convertible* to individual policies in case of need.

The health insurance policy should be *noncancellable*, that is, the insurance company should be unable to cancel it during the year or during an illness because the insured has shown a provoking tendency to be disabled. The policy should also be *guaranteed renewable* to age 65, even though the annual premium may increase with the years because of the individual's advancing age or increasing costs of medical care services. Otherwise, the individual may find that he is without insurance at the time that he needs it most. The policy may cover *accidental bodily injury*, that is, injury as the result of an accident (an unforeseen and unintended event); but it may be restricted to *accidental means* which is much more difficult to prove.

In selecting the company from which to buy health insurance, one should check its reliability, the service it gives in terms of speed and amount of payments, and the helpfulness of the agent at a time of difficulty. The buyer should see that the company is admitted to sell insurance in his state; and it may be wise to learn if it can sell in New York State with its stringent controls on insurance.

The buyer should check the benefits-premium ratio of the company which shows how much it pays out to policy holders as contrasted with what it requires for the costs of doing business. An idea of the costs of operating health insurance organizations can be obtained from Table 12–6. Health insurance benefits received from insurance companies totalled 69 percent of the premiums paid them in 1964. Benefits amounted to higher proportion of premiums on medical expense policies and to lower proportions on loss of income policies. The difference is partly because group policies constitute a higher proportion of medical expense coverage than of loss of income coverage. Benefits were about 85 percent of premiums on group policies, but 42 percent on individual and family policies. Benefits from the nonprofit organizations amounted to 94 percent of the premiums paid them.

A number of suggestions have been made for the improvement of health insurance. It would be more effective if it encouraged preventive medical care and covered mental illness, general medical care that is nonsurgical and nonhospitalized, and nursing home care, to reduce hospitalization for the chronically ill and the aged. Removal of the limits on time and maximum amounts on major medical expense policies would greatly increase their usefulness.

Furthermore, it is desirable that the practices of the insuring organizations and of the persons managing medical care discourage unnecessary use of hospitals and other medical services or increases in surgical and medical fees which result in increases in insurance premiums for all. Differences in rates for insured and uninsured persons complicate the picture. If insured persons are charged twice as

TABLE 12–6. Health Insurance Premiums Paid by the Public to Insurers and Benefits Received from Insurers

ITEM	PREMIUMS PAID (BILLIONS)	BENEFITS RECEIVED (BILLIONS)	BENEFITS AS PERCENT OF PREMIUMS
Insurance companies, total	$6.8	$4.7	69
Hospital expense[1]	4.9	2.3	74
Surgical and medical expense[1]		1.3	
Loss of income	1.8[2]	1.0[3]	55
Group policies	4.2	3.6	85
Hospital, surgical, and medical expense[1]	3.3		
Loss of income	.9[2]		
Individual and family policies .	2.5	1.1	42
Hospital, surgical, and medical expense[1]	1.6		
Loss of income	.9[2]		
Blue Cross, Blue Shield, and other hospital-medical plans[4]	4.3	4.0	94
Hospital expense[1]		2.8	
Surgical and medical expense[1]		1.3	

[1] Includes major medical expense.
[2] Includes accidental death and dismemberment premiums paid.
[3] Excludes accidental death and dismemberment benefits received.
[4] Includes independent and medical-society approved or -sponsored plans.
SOURCE: Health Insurance Council. Quoted by Health Insurance Institute, *Source Book of Health Insurance Data 1965*, pp. 33–44 (data for 1964).

much as the uninsured, their health insurance results in personal savings only when the bills are large, as the following comparison shows:

ITEM	MEDICAL BILL FOR INSURED PERSON		
	$100	$500	$2,000
Payments by the insured person	$190	$270	$ 570
Deductible amount	50	50	50
Coinsurance at 20 percent	10	90	390
Cost of comprehensive health insurance, earner only, group, (not subsidized)	130	130	130
Payments by the insurance organization on behalf of the insured person	40	360	1,560
Comparable medical bill for uninsured person	50	250	1,000

QUESTIONS

1. How important are the costs of medical care to families?
2. Why has the percentage of income spent on medical care been increasing?
3. How variable are the costs of medical care from one family to another? Through time? How are the costs related to family income and size? To age and sex of the individual?
4. What is the incidence of acute conditions among various age groups? Of chronic conditions?
5. What items are included in the term "medical care"? How costly are some of them?
6. What public programs help to cut the family's needs for medical care?
7. Discuss what the family can do directly to cut its medical needs.
8. In what ways can the family prepare financially ahead of time for the costs of medical care?
9. If its preparation ahead of time is not sufficient, what can the family do when it needs emergency medical care?
10. Describe and compare the various types of health insurance.
11. Obtain copies of some health insurance policies and compare their features.
12. What specific suggestions would you make to the family that is involved in selecting health insurance?

SUGGESTIONS FOR FURTHER READING

Health Insurance Institute. *Source Book of Health Insurance Data.* New York, latest edition.
U. S. National Center for Health Statistics. *Vital and Health Statistics: Data from the National Health Survey.* Public Health Service Publication No. 1000, Series 10, latest reports.

"All things that are,
Are with more spirit chased than enjoy'd."
—THE MERCHANT OF VENICE

Other Expenditures / 13

- HOUSE FURNISHINGS AND
  EQUIPMENT
- HOUSEHOLD OPERATIONS AND
  UTILITIES
- RECREATION
- OTHER CATEGORIES

A third of disposable income of consumers goes for the remaining categories of expenditure, although they are relatively small individually. More than half of this total amount is spent for house furnishings and equipment, household operations, utilities, and recreation.

HOUSE FURNISHINGS AND EQUIPMENT

Five percent of consumer income goes for house furnishings and equipment, including household textiles, furniture, floor coverings, major appliances, small appliances, and housewares such as china and kitchen and cleaning equipment. (Excluded are expenditures for television, radio, phonographs, musical instruments, and related items.) Expenses for house furnishings and equipment increase with income and include costs for items for establishing a home, expansion, and replacement, as the case may be.

In planning purchases of furnishings and equipment, the family considers its needs today and in the future as affected by family size, stage of the life cycle, and activities. It takes into account the likelihood of moving to other dwellings and the frequency and distance of such moves. Family standards and income are basic to the final determination of expenditures.

In selecting furnishings and equipment, the family needs to learn to recognize quality and judge its relationship to price. Items such as tables and couches that can be used in different rooms or for different purposes have greater usefulness for many families. In selecting equipment, the family needs to decide the size and special features that are essential and those that are unnecessary luxuries. The family may want to consider the purchase of used equipment and furniture and of unfinished furniture. Such purchases may be especially wise during the early period when the family is moving frequently. A family that has imagination and taste combined with some ability at carpentry and sewing may save considerably by constructing some of its own furniture and slipcovers or by refinishing used furniture.

Young couples need to accumulate funds toward their beginning purchases and for additional purchases when their family expands. As a start for their thinking, a list of furnishings and equipment for establishing a home was priced in a recent mail-order catalog. The items were classified as basic, additional, and for further expansion as follows: [1]

BASIC ITEMS		ADDITIONAL ITEMS	
$100–$400	Range, gas or electric	$60–$220	Couch
$160–$500	Refrigerator	$50–$200	Two easy chairs
$20–$100	Table	$30–$110	Chest for bedroom
$10–$70	Two chairs	$30–$100	Vacuum sweeper
$70–$100	Kitchen utensils	$60–$260	Washer
$20–	China, glassware, tableware	Variable	Curtains, drapes, table linens
$70–$200	Bed frame, mattress, springs	Variable	Rugs
$60–	Basic household linens (sheets, towels, etc.)	FURTHER EXPANSION	
		Variable	Multiples of items above
$40–	Basic cleaning tools (broom, iron, etc.)	$60–$200	Dryer
		$70–$200	Sewing machine
		$130–$220	Dishwasher
$550–	Total	$150–$300	Freezer

Ownership of large equipment is widespread in this country. More than eight-tenths of households own a refrigerator, seven-tenths

---

[1] Adapted from "What Does It Cost to Establish a Home," by Sanna Black and Helen Bell, Pennsylvania State University Extension Service, 7 pp., processed.

own a washing machine, and three-tenths own a clothes dryer. In addition, some households live in rental apartments or houses that include certain pieces of equipment in the unit or in community rooms. Clothes dryers, air conditioners, and dishwashers are increasingly popular. About 3 percent of households purchase a refrigerator or washer in a calendar quarter, and 3 percent or more expect to purchase a refrigerator, washer, or dryer within the next six months. The percentages of households are as follows: [2]

ITEM	OWNED ITEM, OCT. 1966	PURCHASED ITEM, JULY–SEPT. 1966	INTENDED TO PURCHASE ITEM WITHIN NEXT 6 MONTHS
Refrigerator	84	3	3
Washing machine ..	71	3	5
Clothes dryer	29	1	3
Air conditioner	21	2	2
Dishwasher	11	1	1

Purchase of major equipment necessitates planning ahead to accumulate cash or to buy on instalments, since most family incomes can support only a limited amount of instalment payments at one time without strain. Equipment and furnishings do not last forever, though one prefers to think so. How much money will be needed and when will it be needed? Future prices of equipment are not predictable, but some data are available as general guides as to when new equipment will be needed. These data indicate the present service-life expectancy of major items, that is, the number of years that the average owner uses a given item, whether or not its service potential is completely exhausted. Although figures differ from one family to another because of differences in the equipment and in the family situation, the averages are generally helpful.

Average service-life expectancy under one owner ranged from 14 to 16 years for a number of major items purchased new. These include gas and electric ranges, electric refrigerators, freezers, electric clothes dryers, tank vacuum cleaners, and wool rugs for the living room (Table 13–1). Thus a family that purchased these items at about the same time may later wish to replace them the same time. Some items, such as electric washing machines, have a shorter expectancy, whereas electric sewing machines and upright vacuum cleaners have a longer expectancy. No significant differences in ex-

[2] U. S. Bureau of Census, *Current Population Reports*, Series P–65, No. 16, 1966.

pectancy were found between residence or regional groups. However, it is possible that family income and family size and composition affect expectancy. Scattered data intimate that equipment purchased with a house may have a shorter expectancy than when purchased separately.

Since different items of home furnishings and equipment continue in service from a short time to approximately 25 years, on the average, perhaps the family should count on an annual depreciation or replacement of about 15 percent on the outstanding balance. In an emergency, however, the sale price of used items may be much less than such a depreciation rate indicates. Furniture and equipment once moved into the home become "used" and may sell that first year for as little as half the purchase price. Winter is likely to be a poorer

TABLE 13–1. Service-Life Expectancy Under One Owner of Selected Items of Household Equipment and Furnishings[1]

ITEM	NEW WHEN ACQUIRED (YEARS)	USED WHEN ACQUIRED (YEARS)
Ranges:		
Electric	16	8
Gas	16	9
Refrigerators, electric	16	8
Washing machines, electric:		
Automatic and semi-automatic	11	5
Wringer and spin-dryer	10	6
Clothes dryers, electric	14	..
Vacuum cleaners:		
Upright	18	8
Tank	15	..
Sewing machines:		
Electric	24	16
Treadle	..	13
Living room wool rugs[2]	14	10
Toasters:		
Automatic	15	8
Nonautomatic	7	4
Freezers	15	11

[1] Estimate for the individual item based on latest data collected between December 1957 and May 1961 by the Bureau of the Census in conjunction with its Current Population Surveys.

[2] Limited to rugs 8 x 10 feet or larger, including wall-to-wall carpeting. Includes only the period of service in the living room.

SOURCE: J. L. Pennock and C. M. Jaeger, "Household Service Life of Durable Goods," *Journal of Home Economics*, January 1964, pp. 22–26. Reprinted with permission of the American Home Economics Association.

time for resale of expensive furnishings and of power equipment for the lawn and home workshop. For example, one couple sold slip-covered club chairs at $10 each, straight backed chairs at $8, and lamps at $7. A new coffee table with leather top, purchased for $60, sold for $20. Hurried sale may prevent the family from realizing reasonable amounts even for prized antiques.

HOUSEHOLD OPERATIONS AND UTILITIES

Four percent of consumer income goes for household operations, including telephone and telegraph, supplies for laundry and cleaning, household paper supplies, domestic service, postage and writing materials, and a wide variety of other small items. Expense for household operations increases with income, but declines in importance.

Since a third of total consumer expenditure for household operations goes for telephone service and four-fifths of households have telephones available, the family that needs to cut expenses will consider what is necessary in the type and amount of such service, and if extra conveniences and beauty are worth the additional cost.

Savings may be made on other items of household operations by a variety of methods. Use less expensive types of cleaning and laundry supplies, such as diluted white vinegar to clean tile, rubbing alcohol to clean windows, washing soda to cut grease. Purchase inexpensive brands (when acceptable) on sale in the cheapest size and kind of container that is practicable. Avoid waste in use of soaps, paper products, and other items. Avoid damage to furnishings and equipment, and make repairs at home when feasible.

Decisions on saving on some items of household operations are more complicated. For instance, employment of a worker to do the housework or care for the children may enable a family member to take a paid job that pays better. Or consider the laundry and cleaning problem. Money may be saved by use of coin-operated dry cleaning machines rather than commercial dry cleaning services, as long as items are steam-pressed to destroy bacteria. Use of coin-operated laundry machines is generally cheaper than commercial laundry service or ownership of home laundry equipment when few loads are laundered in a week, unless extra transportation cost absorbs the savings. Of course, time savings, convenience, standards, and preferences are also important in deciding on methods to use.

Almost 4 percent of consumer income goes for fuel, light, refrigeration, and water. As income increases, expense for utilities increases, but declines in importance. The climate, the size and construction of the house to be heated or cooled, the size of the family and its use of equipment are important in setting the level of expenses for utilities. Fuel bills may be cut by use of the less expensive type in the community. All utility bills may be controlled by the family's care to avoid wasteful use.

Family preferences or efforts to save in other budget areas by home laundry, home preparation and freezing of foods, home sewing, home care and repair of the auto, home recreation and use of television—all increase expenses for utilities as well as for equipment. Thus we see that expenses for utilities and household operations are closely related to decisions in other budget areas and cannot be considered in isolation.

RECREATION

Almost 5 percent of consumer income goes for recreation, including televisions, radios, phonographs, musical instruments, admission to movies, sports events, concerts, plays, expenses for participant sports, hobbies, pets, and play equipment. The expenditure on recreation would bulk larger if it included transportation, food, and lodging for recreational travel, as well as food and other items for entertainment, and fabrics and wood used for the pleasure of constructing objects. With increased income, expense for recreation increases in amount and tends to increase in percentage.

Approximately a fifth of total consumer expenditure listed for recreation is devoted to televisions. The Census Bureau reported in October 1966 that 92 percent of households owned one or more televisions; 5 percent had purchased one in the previous calendar quarter; and 6 percent planned to purchase one within the next six months. The 1960 Census showed a fabulous increase in televisions and in multiple ownership since 1950, contrasting with a decline in prevalence of radios, as follows:

ITEM	PERCENT OF OCCUPIED HOUSING UNITS	
	1950	1960
Televisions	12	87
1		77
2 or more		10
Radio	96	91
1		57
2 or more		35

The necessity of planning ahead for the purchase and replacement of televisions is clear. Service-life expectancy under one owner was estimated in 1960 as 11 years for new sets and 6 years for used sets. These included television sets alone or in combination with radios or record players, but excluded portable and color sets. Technical advances may further decrease service life as families seek the latest improvements.

Worthwhile recreational activity expands the individual's personality in ways that are not possible in his working hours and helps build interests for his later years. In his recreation he has an opportunity to be independent, creative, active or receptive, perhaps successful, and, at least, to work off his aggressions in a socially acceptable manner. In terms of cultural interests, recreation helps to round out experience by developing the sensory, social, technological, intellectual, aesthetic, and empathetic interests—whichever are most needed.

Inexpensive recreation of high quality can be provided at home by entertainment of friends, roller skating and gardening, tearing down and rebuilding motors, carpentry, reading, painting, or playing the piano. Radio and television can expand and deepen interests at low cost, if wisely managed. Free and low-cost community facilities, such as parks and recreational areas for nature study and active sports, adult education in the creation or appreciation of art and music, museums, libraries, free concerts—all provide unparalleled opportunities. In addition, there are church, community welfare, and political activities that are worthwhile.

It is also desirable to consider the advantages of travel in this country or abroad. The potential expansion of one's understanding is enormous. Although such trips require time and money, many families could travel more extensively if they appreciated the special opportunities for personal development and were, therefore, willing to watch daily expenditures.

OTHER CATEGORIES

Let us look briefly at the remaining categories of expenditure, each of which took a relatively small proportion of disposable income of consumers. The figures on national aggregates from the Department of Commerce are as follows:

3 percent for alcoholic beverages
2 percent for tobacco

2 percent for personal care
1 percent for private education
1 percent for religious and welfare activities
1 percent for reading
5 percent for other items

Gifts and Contributions · Gifts and contributions include expenditures for religious and welfare activities listed above as well as gifts of clothing, food, and other items or of money used for such purposes which were entered under the specific categories in the national aggregates. The Survey of Consumer Expenditues showed that families and single consumers averaged a total of about 5 percent of income for gifts and contributions of all types—money and nonmoney—to relatives not living with the family, to other persons, and to religious, charitable, health, and cultural organizations.

In addition, some families gave whole or partial support in the family home to needy relatives. For instance, the SCE showed that 8 percent of husband-wife families had present in the home some persons other than their own children. These extra persons were likely to be grandchildren or elderly parents. An additional 14 percent of husband-wife families included some children of their own who were 18 years old or over.

Considering average income and other types of expenditures, questions might be raised as to whether appropriate amounts are contributed to needy persons and welfare organizations. Each family does well to consider whether it would obtain more satisfaction by aiding others than by purchasing additional goods and services for itself.

Many elderly parents could use aid if freely offered. A survey of persons 65 years old and over showed their modest incomes and asset holdings (largely in a nonfarm home) as follows: [3]

MARITAL STATUS	MEDIAN MONEY INCOME, 1962	MEDIAN VALUE OF ASSETS, 1962*
Married couples**	$2,875	$11,180
Nonmarried men	1,365	2,900
Nonmarried women	1,015	3,285

* Excludes cash value of life insurance, equity in annuities or retirement plans, and value of autos and personal effects.
** Includes couples with head or wife 65 or over.

[3] "Findings of the 1963 Survey of the Aged," *Social Security Bulletin,* March and November 1964.

Both income and assets decline with greater age, and finally the widowed mother may have to live with her children. The elderly who live with relatives have lower incomes than those living alone, according to the following Census data: [4]

MARITAL STATUS AND LIVING ARRANGEMENT	MEDIAN MONEY INCOME, 1959	PERCENT OF ALL AGED PERSONS[*]
Couples, living alone	$2,670	42
Couples, with relatives present	2,400	15
Nonmarried, alone or with nonrelatives	1,010	21
Nonmarried, living as head, with relatives	840	7
Nonmarried, living as relative of head	520	15

[*] Includes persons 65 and over and spouses of persons 65 and over. Noninstitutional population.

In many cases, the relatives living with elderly couples or nonmarried persons contribute sizably to the support of the elderly.

While average cash contributions to elderly parents are small, contributions to married children may be sizable. One study found $500 (including $200 for the wedding) as the median total value of the contributions that families made to their newly married child during the first year of marriage.[5] This equalled 7 percent of median income of the parental families. Contributions decreased during the second and third years of the child's marriage to 3 percent of parental income, or $200 median for the nine-tenths of parents giving. The study showed that goods were more frequently given than services or money, and that the dollar value of goods was higher. High amounts of contributions were associated with high economic level and a feeling that families should contribute. Other writers have pointed out that contributions toward their newly married children may at the same time serve to increase teen-age marriages, population growth, and feelings of dependency.[6]

Schorr concludes that adult children in the United States do not usually make cash contributions to their parents, but frequently

[4] 1960 *Census of Population*, "The Income of the Elderly Population."

[5] A. B. Clark and J. Warren, *Economic Contributions Made to Newly Married Couples by Their Parents*, Cornell University Agricultural Experiment Station, Memoir 382, 1963, 24 pp.

[6] See M. B. Sussman and L. Burchinal, "Parental Aid to Married Children: Implications for Family Functioning," *Marriage and Family Living*, 1962, pp. 320–332.

assist their adult children.[7] He summarizes the situation as follows: "It seems likely that it is chiefly the middle-aged parents who are giving to their children, but the *reason* that they give continues into their old age. That is, an American parent is ambitious for his children and grandchildren, as they are for themselves. He is reluctant to take money if he feels it interferes with meeting their own needs. Even if he is not quite so ambitious for his children, he wants to feel independent despite some sacrifice in his standard of living."

Education and Reading · Personal expenditures for education and reading materials take only 2 percent of disposable personal income, contrasted with 6 percent for alcoholic beverages, tobacco, and personal care. Even when all public and private expenditures on education, including capital outlays, are totalled, the amount exceeds by only a tenth the spending on alcohol, tobacco, and care. The latest complete figures may be summarized as follows: [8]

ITEM	BILLION DOLLARS	ITEM	BILLION DOLLARS
Alcoholic beverages	11.3	Education (including	
Tobacco	7.4	capital outlays)	27.9
Personal care	6.2	Subtotal	27.9
Subtotal	24.9		
		Public libraries	
Funeral and burial	1.6	(including	
Pari-mutuel net receipts .	.6	capital outlays)	.3
Jewelry and watches	2.3	Reading materials	
Grand total	29.3	(personal spending) . .	3.9
		Grand total	32.1

When we go farther, we find that total expenditures on education, public libraries, and personal purchases of reading materials are just about a tenth above personal spending for alcohol, tobacco, personal care, funeral and burial, pari-mutuel net receipts, and jewelry and watches. At this point in time, review of these individual and social decisions seems highly desirable.

While average personal spending on education and reading materials is small, expenses for a child in public schools may total

[7] A. L. Schorr, "Filial Responsibility and the Aging," *Journal of Home Economics,* 1962, pp. 271–276. Reprinted with permission of the American Home Economics Association.

[8] *Statistical Abstract of the United States, 1966* (data for 1962).

$200 or more a year, in addition to costs of clothing and lunches, if a child takes part in various activities. Expenses for a student in college are much greater: Annual tuition and fees may range from about $500 to $2,000, depending on the college attended. Books and supplies may average $200. Clothing and personal expenses may be moderate or high, depending on the individual situation. If the student lives away from home, room and board costs may approximate $800–$1,000. In addition there is the cost of transportation for two or more round trips from home. A student who attends a public college in his home town and lives at home may be able to minimize expenses at $1,000–$1,200 for the academic year. But one who attends a leading private college away from home may require $3,000 for tuition and room and board alone.

Tuition and other college costs have been increasing, and some predictions are that they will increase about 50 percent in ten years. The family needs to plan for future costs for college for each child, and the annual costs during the years when some children are in college. For instance, a family with three children born two years apart would have one in college for four years and two in college for four years. Savings may be made ahead of time by the parents and by the children. During college, the students may earn part of their expenses or the parents may contribute out of their earnings, particularly if the mother takes a paid job or changes to full-time employment. Scholarships, gifts, and loans are also used.

Average costs of college were estimated at about $1,550 a year by the University of Michigan Research Center in 1960. Half of the families with children in college used money that had been saved for the purpose; and in a fifth of the families, the mother took a job to help meet the costs. On the average, the expenses were met as follows: [9]

Parents' contribution	$ 950
Student's earnings	360
Scholarships	130
Other sources	110
TOTAL	$1,550

It is understandable that only 40 percent of the children in families with incomes between $5,000 and $7,500 go to college. Probably

[9] University of Michigan Research Center, *How People Pay for College*, a study made for the U. S. Office of Education, 1960, 160 pp.

many of those children make sizable contributions to their own support, or depend on scholarships, gifts from relatives, or loans.

A survey by the Association of American Medical Colleges indicated that the parents and relatives of a medical student contributed 82 percent of the average cost of $11,642 for his four years of professional training. It is not surprising, therefore, that 43 percent of all medical students came from families with annual incomes over $10,000.[10]

Special Occasions · Many cultures subscribe to the idea that a person deserves special honor at three or four times in his life—at birth, coming of age, marriage, and death. A family with a low or moderate income sometimes spends a disproportionate amount on such occasions, perhaps as compensation for the privation of daily living. Since these events are highly charged with sentiment, the extended family and friends need to consider ahead of time the wisdom of elaborate ceremonies in contrast with alternate uses of the money.

Might a sizable part of the money that is spent by the family for entertainment and by relatives and friends for luxury gifts at birth and coming of age be more thoughtfully placed in a fund for the child's education? A wedding costing the family a thousand dollars or more might be celebrated more simply and the excess money used to help the young couple buy necessary furniture. Money spent on elaborate wedding gifts that will be stored in the parents' attic for many years might be used to purchase necessary items for establishment of a home.

Even death costs money and therefore cannot be excluded from the discussion. The family needs to determine what expenses are necessary to abide by state laws and religious rules. What additional customs does the family deem essential? Considering the subject ahead of time may restrain the family from prodigal use of its resources at a time of grief. It is possible to have a decent burial at a much lower price than many people pay. The service, casket, and memorial can be simple. The necessity of being interred, returned to the home community for burial, and placed in a lot with perpetual care should be weighed carefully. It is worth considering a simple burial and using the remainder of the insurance money or other resources to support the family or establish a memorial for charitable or other purposes.

[10] Association of American Medical Colleges, Education Research Service, 1960.

QUESTIONS

1. What is the importance for family living of the items discussed here?
2. How can one save money on each of the categories?
3. How can one enrich the family's experience by better planning?
4. How does the service-life expectancy of equipment affect financial plans?
5. Work on a plan to adapt the list of basic and additional furnishings and equipment to your own needs.

SUGGESTIONS FOR FURTHER READING

Consumers' Research. *Consumer Bulletin,* buying guide, latest issues.

Consumers Union. *Consumer Reports,* buying guide, latest issues.

Ehrenkranz, Florence and Inman, Lydia. *Equipment in the Home.* New York: Harper and Row, 1966.

Household Finance Corporation. *Money Management: Your Equipment Dollar.* Chicago, latest edition.

——. *Money Management: Your Home Furnishings Dollar.* Chicago, latest edition.

——. *Money Management: Your Health and Recreation Dollar.* Chicago, latest edition.

U. S. Department of Agriculture. *Consumers All: The Yearbook of Agriculture 1965.* Washington, D.C.: Superintendent of Documents, 1965, pp. 81–149 and 214–338.

U. S. Department of Agriculture, Washington, D.C. Single copy of latest edition of following publications free from the Department as long as free supply lasts.

Washington Machines . . . Selection and Use. G–32.

Sanitation in Home Laundering. G–97.

Part Three

Your Investments

and

Long-Run Protection

"As hard to come as for a camel
To thread the postern of a small needle's eye."
—King Richard II

The Family's
Savings Program / 14

- SIZE OF FAMILY SAVINGS
- ACCUMULATED WEALTH OF CONSUMERS
- THE FAMILY'S BALANCE SHEET
- CARE OF FINANCIAL RECORDS
- INVESTMENT OBJECTIVES

Families make savings to provide for future needs—certain or uncertain, specific or general. They accumulate funds for future necessities, emergency expenses, and large purchases in the near, intermediate, and far future. These funds are invested in a variety of ways including savings accounts and government bonds, Social Security, life insurance, annuities, and business ownership (in addition to real estate, which has been discussed). Wills are used to distribute estates among heirs. Before studying the individual types of investments, it is desirable to consider the family's savings program in general so that each part may be seen in perspective.

SIZE OF FAMILY SAVINGS

The Department of Commerce estimates that in recent years the nation's consumers are saving about 5 percent of their disposable personal income.[1] The proportion is the same as in 1929, although disposable income per person is 80 percent higher in dollars of constant purchasing power. While consumers save in good times, they

[1] U. S. Department of Commerce, *Survey of Current Business*, July 1966 and August 1965.

draw on savings in bad times to meet their expenses. At the bottom of the depression in 1933, net dissavings totalled about 2 percent of disposable personal income. On the other hand, consumers can be induced to save large amounts under unusual conditions, as at the peak of the war in 1944 when they saved about 25 percent of disposable income.

Studies of family expenditure patterns indicate that the proportion of income saved varies considerably with family characteristics. Other conditions being equal, the proportion saved is generally higher for those with higher incomes, smaller families, and for those living on farms.[2] The proportion saved is higher for households headed by a person 45–64 years old than for younger or older households because of higher income per person due to declining family size and because of the imminence of retirement. In other words, savings are made when the family is under lessened pressure to spend and increased pressure to save.

Savings Plans · When and how much a family should save is determined by its own personal situation. Current income must first cover current needs. At times, current income is more generous in relation to basic needs, thus facilitating saving. Periods of general economic prosperity and high employment give families good opportunities. Early in the marriage before children are born and later when they are grown are generally the easiest periods in the family life cycle. Smaller families and those with higher incomes generally find less pressure on current income than do their opposite numbers, thus have greater opportunities for saving without large sacrifices of current living.

How much a family should save is also determined by its valuation of its future needs and of other resources that will be available for meeting them. What needs does it see arising in the future—medical care, necessities when the father is unable to earn, education for the children? How seriously it values each of these future needs affects importantly how heavily it will weigh current expenditures. Strangely enough, the elderly are more likely to overvalue the future, when they have so little of it; and the young, who have so much of it, to undervalue it.

At the same time, the family may already have considerable financial resources in investments and insurances for meeting future needs, or it may expect that they will be met by other means. Perhaps the family intends that each child have a college education, but

2 U. S. Bureau of Labor Statistics and U. S. Department of Agriculture, *Survey of Consumer Expenditures 1960–61*.

expects him to win a scholarship, work his way through college, or be financed by a kindly aunt or grandparent. As for their own old age, the parents may be making compulsory contributions to retirement programs, expect their children to support them, or hope to inherit money.

Thus, the family's savings program is dependent on its current needs in relation to current income, as compared with future needs in relation to resources expected to be available at that future time.

Saving Objectives · Saving objectives differ considerably by stage of the life cycle, according to the Survey of Financial Characteristics of Consumers, the most comprehensive ever made. Young consumer units (families and single consumers) mentioned two primary objectives of saving—to buy a home and to provide for children's education—and a lesser objective, to provide for emergencies (Table 14-1). Those headed by persons 35-44 years old saved primarily to provide for children's education and secondarily, to provide for emergencies and for old age. Those 45-54 years old concentrated on saving to provide for old age, but also to provide for children's education and for emergencies. Among those 55-64 and 65 and over, the primary objective was to provide for old age and the secondary was to provide for emergencies.

A variety of additional objectives for saving were mentioned by a tenth or less of any age group: buy durable goods, acquire financial independence, take a vacation or trip, build own business, increase income, provide an estate, and help children establish a household. Further analyses of the Survey showed that some of these objectives were clearly related to the economic level. Savings to build their own business, to increase income, and to provide an estate were mentioned most frequently by certain groups with high income or high accumulation of wealth, as follows:

SAVING OBJECTIVE	PERCENT MENTIONING WAS TWO OR MORE TIMES THE PERCENT FOR ALL UNITS	
	AT 1962 INCOME LEVEL	AT ACCUMULATED WEALTH LEVEL
Build own business	$25,000–$99,999	$25,000–$99,999 $500,000 and over
Increase income	$15,000–$24,999 $50,000–$99,999	$50,000–$99,999 $500,000 and over
Provide estate	$10,000 and over	$50,000 and over

TABLE 14–1. Saving Objectives of Consumer Units

SAVING OBJECTIVES	PERCENT OF AGE GROUP MENTIONING SPECIFIED OBJECTIVE*					
	ALL UNITS	UNDER 35 YEARS	35–44 YEARS	45–54 YEARS	55–64 YEARS	65 YEARS AND OVER
Buy home	18	40	19	15	8	4
Provide for children's education	29	39	51	32	12	4
Provide for emergencies	32	27	34	31	33	34
Provide for old age	41	17	32	53	59	47
Buy durable goods	7	13	10	6	3	2
Acquire financial independence	11	12	12	11	13	7
Take vacation or trip	5	8	4	7	5	2
Build own business	3	5	3	3	2	2
Increase income	2	2	3	2	2	2
Provide estate	3	1	4	3	4	4
Help children establish household	1	1	. .	1	. .	. .
Other	14	17	11	12	14	15
No objective mentioned	13	10	11	13	11	22

* Percentages may add to more than 100 because some consumer units mentioned more than one saving objective. Age of head is basis for grouping consumer units (families and single consumers).

SOURCE: Dorothy S. Projector and Gertrude S. Weiss, *Survey of Financial Characteristics of Consumers,* Board of Governors of the Federal Reserve System, 1966, p. 146 (data as of December 31, 1962).

Saving to provide an estate was mentioned by 71 percent of those with incomes of $100,000 and over and by 33 percent of those with accumulated wealth of $500,000 and over. Understandably, these high economic levels mentioned infrequently that they saved to provide for emergencies. On the other hand, among consumer units with incomes below $3,000, three-tenths mentioned no saving objective, which seems reasonable.

ACCUMULATED WEALTH OF CONSUMERS

Median wealth of consumer units (families and single consumers) was about $6,700, according to the Survey of Financial Characteristics of Consumers. About 26 percent of consumer units had less than $1,000, 35 percent had $1,000–$9,999, 34 percent had

$10,000–$49,999, and 6 percent had $50,000 or more (Table 14–2). The wealth figure included assets less the debt secured by the assets. Only 10 percent of young consumer units had wealth of $10,000 or more, whereas 57 percent of the preretirement units had as much. Wealth of $10,000 or more was owned by only 28 percent of units with incomes of $3,000–$4,999, contrasted with 69 percent of units with incomes of $10,000–$14,999. Unfortunately, equities in annuities, retirement plans, and life insurance had to be omitted from the estimates.

Accumulated wealth of consumer units was primarily a function of past savings, since only 1 in 20 reported that inheritance accounted for a substantial portion of their assets (Table 14–3).

TABLE 14–2.   Size of Wealth* of Consumer Units

GROUP CHARACTERISTIC OF CONSUMER UNITS (FAMILIES AND SINGLE CONSUMERS)	PERCENTAGE DISTRIBUTION OF CONSUMER UNITS BY SIZE OF WEALTH				
	ALL UNITS	UNDER $1,000	$1,000–$9,999	$10,000–$49,999	$50,000 AND OVER
All units	100	26	35	34	6
Age of head:					
Under 35	100	50	40	10	..
35–44	100	23	41	33	5
45–54	100	18	30	45	7
55–64	100	16	28	44	13
65 and over	100	19	31	40	9
1962 income before taxes:					
0–$2,999	100	43	33	24	1
$3,000–$4,999	100	40	31	25	3
$5,000–$7,499	100	18	46	30	5
$7,500–$9,999	100	9	36	50	5
$10,000–$14,999	100	3	29	55	14
$15,000–$24,999	100	..	13	50	37
$25,000–$49,999	100	..	..	13	87
$50,000–$99,999	100	..	..	1	98
$100,000 and over ...	100	..	..	..	100

* Assets less the debt secured by the assets. Because of the difficulty of family estimate, the figures excluded equities in annuities and retirement plans and the cash surrender value of life insurance. Excluded from the calculation were those debts not secured by a specific asset, such as instalment debt (other than automobile), noninstalment debt, and charge accounts. Debt on life insurance policies was also excluded.

SOURCE: Dorothy S. Projector and Gertrude S. Weiss, *Survey of Financial Characteristics of Consumers*, Board of Governors of the Federal Reserve System, 1966, p. 98 (data as of December 31, 1962).

TABLE 14-3.   Inherited Assets in Relation to Total Assets

GROUP CHARACTERISTIC OF CONSUMER UNITS (FAMILIES AND SINGLE CONSUMERS)	PERCENT OF GROUP THAT INHERITED STATED PORTION OF ITS TOTAL ASSETS	
	SMALL PORTION	SUBSTANTIAL PORTION
All units	12	5
Size of wealth (selected groups):		
$1–$999	5	..
$5,000–$9,999	12	6
$25,000–$49,999	16	9
$500,000 and over	24	34
1962 income before taxes (selected groups):		
$3,000–$4,999	9	3
$5,000–$7,499	12	4
$50,000–$99,999	12	14
$100,000 and over	9	57
Age of head:		
Under 35	8	1
35–44	9	3
45–54	12	4
55–64	17	7
65 and over	12	9

SOURCE: Dorothy S. Projector and Gertrude S. Weiss, *Survey of Financial Characteristics of Consumers,* Board of Governors of the Federal Reserve System, 1966, p. 148 (data as of December 31, 1962).

However, inheritance was much more important for those with large wealth, for those with high income, and for units headed by older persons. For example, among those with wealth of $500,000 and over, 34 percent had inherited a substantial portion of their assets and 24 percent had inherited a small portion.

Past savings of the consumer unit depended importantly on its income history—its length and level. The close relation between accumulated wealth and income history is seen when age of the head of the consumer unit and the unit's current income are used jointly as an estimate of the family's income history. The accumulation was smallest when the earning period was short and the income level was low; and the accumulation was largest when the earning period was long and the income level was high. For example, $600 was the median wealth of young units with incomes of $3,000–$4,999, whereas

TABLE 14–4. Median Wealth of Consumer Units at Selected Income
Levels

AGE OF HEAD OF CONSUMER UNITS (FAMILIES AND SINGLE CONSUMERS)	ALL INCOMES	MEDIAN WEALTH AT SELECTED 1962 INCOME LEVELS—			
		$3,000–$4,999	$5,000–$7,499	$7,500–$9,999	$10,000–$14,999
All ages	$ 6,700	$ 3,000	$ 6,700	$12,100	$17,700
Under 35	1,000	600	2,800	4,000	6,800
35–44	6,700	2,800	6,900	13,600	17,900
45–54	11,000				
55–64	13,200	8,000	16,200	22,000	27,900
65 and over	10,000	15,600	25,000	32,200	48,100

SOURCE: Dorothy S. Projector and Gertrude S. Weiss, *Survey of Financial Characteristics of Consumers*, Board of Governors of the Federal Reserve System, 1966, pp. 98–99 (data as of December 31, 1962). Medians estimated by the present writer on the basis of published distributions.

$27,900 was the median wealth of preretirement units with incomes of $10,000–$14,999 (Table 14–4).

At each important income level, young units had smaller accumulations of wealth than did older units. At the $5,000–$7,499 income level, young units had median wealth of $2,800 whereas preretirement units had $16,200. At the $7,500–$9,999 income level, young units had median wealth of $4,000, contrasted with the $22,000 of preretirement units. At these income levels, many older units also had sizable equities in annuities, retirement plans, and life insurance.

Composition of Wealth · Certain types of wealth, such as liquid assets, automobiles, and homes, are commonly owned, whereas equity in investment assets, a business or profession, and miscellaneous assets are infrequently owned. Out of 100 consumer units covered by the Survey (Table 14–5):

79 held some liquid assets
73 had equity in an automobile
57 had equity in their own home
31 had investments such as stocks, marketable bonds, and real estate
17 had money in a farm or nonfarm business or profession in which they were active in management
8 had such miscellaneous assets as beneficial interest in trust and nonmortgage loans to individuals

TABLE 14–5. Composition of Wealth of Consumer Units

ITEM	TOTAL WEALTH	OWN HOME [1]	AUTO-MOBILE [1]	BUSINESS, PROFESSION [2]	LIQUID ASSETS [3]	INVESTMENT ASSETS [4]	MISCELLANEOUS ASSETS [5]
Percent of group with equity in specified assets, by size of wealth:							
All groups	:	57	73	17	79	31	8
$1–$999	:	9	74	3	70	4	3
$1,000–$4,999	:	54	76	8	78	14	6
$5,000–$9,999	:	78	77	16	85	30	7
$10,000–$24,999	:	84	82	19	96	42	11
$25,000–$49,999	:	80	88	38	97	64	15
$50,000–$99,999	:	72	89	54	98	89	15
$100,000–$199,999	:	86	93	53	100	93	16
$200,000–$499,999	:	84	84	57	97	95	12
$500,000 and over	:	81	79	66	100	99	52
Percent of total wealth in specified assets, by size of wealth:							
All groups	100	27	3	18	13	33	5
$1–$999	100	10	48	2	34	4	2
$1,000–$4,999	100	48	16	3	26	6	1
$5,000–$9,999	100	59	8	9	17	6	1
$10,000–$24,999	100	55	5	9	16	13	1
$25,000–$49,999	100	37	3	19	18	21	2
$50,000–$99,999	100	21	2	24	16	36	2
$100,000–$199,999	100	17	2	17	14	48	1
$200,000–$499,999	100	9	1	24	7	56	3
$500,000 and over	100	4	.	23	4	50	18

*[See footnotes on facing page]

At higher accumulations of wealth, an increasing proportion of consumer units have some equity in investment assets, business or profession, miscellaneous assets, and liquid assets. The proportion with some equity in an automobile or an owned home increases generally, but declines at the highest levels of wealth.

As the accumulation of wealth increases, the proportion of wealth devoted to various assets changes decidedly. With increased size of wealth—
    A decreased share is in automobiles and liquid assets.
    An increased share is in business and investment assets.
    The share in homes first rises, then declines.
For example, when accumulated wealth is $1–$999, it is comprised of—
    48 percent in the automobile
    34 percent in liquid assets
    18 percent in all other assets
When wealth is $5,000–$9,999, it is composed of—
    59 percent in the home
    17 percent in liquid assets
    24 percent in all other assets
But when wealth amounts to $25,000–$49,999, it is composed of—
    37 percent in the home
    21 percent in investment assets
    19 percent in business or profession
    18 percent in liquid assets
     5 percent in all other assets

In addition, 51 percent of all consumer units have investment in life insurance, 15 percent have retirement plans, and 1 percent have individual annuities. Since most families start with few financial assets and 94 percent of all consumer units have less than $50,000, the detailed discussion in succeeding chapters will emphasize the types of assets held most commonly by those with modest accumulations of wealth.

[Footnotes for Table 14–5 on preceding page]
1 Market value less mortgage debt on specific item.

2 Farm and nonfarm, at book value.

3 Checking accounts, savings accounts, and U. S. savings bonds (at maturity value).

4 Equity in publicly traded stock at market price, other marketable securities at par value, mortgage assets, real estate at market value, business not managed by unit at market value, and company savings plans.

5 Beneficial interest in trust, nonmortgage loans to individuals, and other assets.

SOURCE: Dorothy S. Protector and Gertrude S. Weiss, *Survey of Financial Characteristics of Consumers*, Board of Governors of the Federal Reserve System, 1966, pp. 21 and 110 (data as of December 31, 1962).

THE FAMILY'S BALANCE SHEET

The family's balance sheet consists of a list of its total accumulated assets (what it owns), financial liabilities (its debts or what it owes), and the calculation of its net worth. The assets included on the balance sheet are cash items, investment items, and salable durable goods owned by the family, with ownership evidenced by appropriate legal papers or possession. The liabilities are debts that are also evidenced by legal papers or other promises to pay. Net worth, indicating the net financial position of the family, is simply the difference between total assets and total liabilities and is not ordinarily found in any one financial asset. In case of decease of the family heads, assets could be sold, debts paid, and the remainder of the estate (net worth) divided among the heirs.

The financial assets and liabilities recorded on the balance sheet are realized ones, not simply potential ones. In other words, financial assets do not include personal assets such as education, skills, and wealthy relatives that may eventually result in income and savings. Assets include only the realized results of former income, other receipts, and savings. Nor does the liability section of the balance sheet include personal liabilities such as poor health and indigent relatives that may eventually reduce income or cause withdrawals of savings. Needless to say, an individual's morality and personal development, which may be great social and personal assets or liabilities, have no place on the balance sheet.

The purpose is not to minimize the importance of personal characteristics or of potential financial assets or liabilities, but simply to recognize that they cannot be exchanged for cash today and, therefore, cannot be valued in dollars and cents on the family's balance sheet. For the young couple, these nonfinancial assets may constitute almost all of its assets; the preretirement couple may find that its nonfinancial liabilities comprise the largest part of its liabilities.

The family's balance sheet summarizes its financial situation at a given point in time—as of January 1 or July 1 of the present year, or at another date more appropriate for the family. It shows what the family owns and what it owes today. The situation might be quite different in another month. The balance sheet differs fundamentally, therefore, from the family's budget of expected income and expenditures for a month or year, or its record of them. The budget and record both deal with income and expenditures over a period of time, whereas the balance sheet deals with an accumulation at a point in time.

Use of the Balance Sheet · The family's present balance sheet indicates its current financial resources available in emergencies such as illness and unemployment, as well as the size of its accumulation toward other goals. The balance sheet shows the size and kind of estate to be divided in case of death, separation, or divorce.

Study of its current balance sheet may cause the family to re-evaluate its investments to be certain that there is sufficient liquidity for cash needs of the near future, sufficient variety of types of investments to hedge against possible future inflation and depression, and that each individual investment is the best possible for its purpose.

Periodic construction of the family's balance sheet on the same date each year indicates growth or decline in net financial position from one year to the next and may cause the family to revise its goals or its current spending. If the growth is greater than anticipated or "necessary," the family may consider enlarging its savings objectives or expanding current consumption. If the growth is less than desired, the family may revise its plans for use of savings or change its budget in order to enlarge savings.

A change in net worth may be owing to a number of reasons. For instance, an increase of $500 may arise because of savings made or liabilities decreased, an increase in durable goods, general rise in the value of investments during an inflationary period, or unusual increase in the value of a specific investment. A decrease in net worth by $300 may be caused by withdrawals of savings or increases in liabilities, ordinary depreciation of durable goods, general decline in value of assets during a depressed period, or unique loss in value of a particular asset.

In other words, a family may make savings during the year out of its current income and still have no higher net worth at the end of the year. At the same time another family may spend all of its current income during the year and still have an increase in net worth by year's end. It could be discouraging.

Construction of the Balance Sheet · A simplified example of a family's balance sheet is presented in Table 14–6 to indicate the wide variety of items to be listed and the calculations to be made. Some families have a greater variety of items than does this hypothetical family, and some have multiples under a single heading.

First, it should be noted that assets have been divided into six classes from "quick" or most liquid assets to least liquid, least salable ones, as follows:

Cash and cash forms, e.g., cash and checks on hand
Loans, e.g., notes owned
Securities, e.g., mutual fund shares
Business investments, e.g., business and equipment
Real estate, e.g., own home
Household goods, e.g., automobile.

Liabilities have been divided into four classes (also on the basis of the time element), from debts requiring early payment to those extending over the longest period of time, as follows:

Current bills outstanding, e.g., charge accounts
Loan balances, e.g., bank
Instalment payment balances, e.g., automobile
Mortgage balances, e.g., home.

After entering the amounts for each item, it is desirable to calculate subtotals for each of the six classes of assets and four classes of liabilities in order to study the situation. For instance, this family has $1,200 in cash and cash forms opposed to owing $300 on current bills and $400 on instalment payment balances—therefore, it is in a good position to pay its short-term and intermediate debt. In fact, cash and checking account balances are just equal to current bills outstanding. At this time the family might consider using some of its cash forms to complete some instalment payments if it is receiving a decidedly lower rate of interest than it is paying.

Some of the specific asset and liability items are directly related to each other: for instance, the owned home is valued at $12,000 and has a mortgage of $10,000. Others, such as corporate stocks, have no directly related liabilities in this example.

Assets total $16,700, liabilities total $10,700, and, therefore, net worth is $6,000. In this case one can see to some extent where the net worth (or net ownership) actually is, since this may be a helpful concept for the student:

$900 in cash and cash forms
$1,000 in securities
$2,000 in real estate
$2,100 in household goods.

Valuation of Assets · This hypothetical balance sheet was constructed easily. But the family's balance sheet involves the much more serious problems of including all assets and valuing each one

TABLE 14–6. The Family's Balance Sheet [January 1, This Year]

ITEMS	AMOUNTS	TOTALS
ASSETS		$16,700
Cash and cash forms		1,200
Cash and checks on hand	$ 100	
Cash in safe deposit box	. . .	
Checking account balances	200	
Savings account balances	500	
U. S. Government bonds	300	
Cash receivable	. . .	
Prepaid expenses	. . .	
Savings and loan shares	. . .	
Credit union shares	. . .	
Cash value of insurances	100	
Loans		. . .
Notes owned	. . .	
Mortgages owned	. . .	
Securities		1,000
Investment company shares	. . .	
Corporate bonds	. . .	
Corporate stocks	1,000	
Business		. . .
Business and equipment	. . .	
Farm business and home	. . .	
Real estate		12,000
Own home	12,000	
Other buildings, lots	. . .	
Household goods		2,500
Automobile	800	
Furnishings and equipment	1,500	
Jewelry, furs, clothing	200	
Stocks of food	. . .	
LIABILITIES		$10,700
Current bills outstanding		300
Charge accounts	100	
Other (doctor, taxes, etc.)	200	
Overdue and unpaid	. . .	
Loan balances		. . .
Bank	. . .	
Life insurance	. . .	
Personal loan company	. . .	
Relatives, friends	. . .	
Instalment payment balances		400
Automobile	200	
Furnishings, equipment, etc.	200	
Mortgage balances		10,000
Home	10,000	
Other real estate	. . .	
NET WORTH		$ 6,000

properly. Certain assets, such as cash and checking account balances, and all liabilities are simple to value for the balance sheet; but some asset items are more difficult.

U. S. Government bonds might be listed at purchase price or at redemption value. Other paper assets, such as corporate stocks, may be listed at original purchase price or at current sale price—which may be quite different figures. Durable goods, such as the home and automobile, may be carried on the balance sheet at original purchase price less depreciation, replacement price less depreciation, or the current sale price. The choice of method may affect the figures on the balance sheet.

The proper valuation method depends on the purpose, and there are many purposes for constructing a balance sheet or parts of it. For instance, the insurable value is replacement price less depreciation; the proper value for personal property tax purposes depends on legal requirements. For present liquidation or division of an estate or for consideration of revision of investments, the current sale price of each item should be entered. The most conservative method is whichever gives the lowest value, item by item.

A simple method that disregards unrealized profits or losses and is useful if one is satisfied with his current investments and durable goods, expecting to keep them some time, is as follows:

> Original purchase price for paper assets.
> Original purchase price less depreciation for durable goods—
>> House: Depreciate 3 percent a year on the outstanding balance.
>> Furnishings and equipment: Depreciate 15 percent a year on outstanding balance.
>> Automobile: Depreciate 32 percent of original price at end of first year, 18 percent second, 11 percent third, 10 percent fourth, 8 percent fifth, 6 percent sixth.

Reserves · Once it has calculated net worth, the family needs to see that its reserves for various purposes are developing as planned by dividing net worth among the following purposes that are appropriate to that family:

> Repair of home, automobile, furnishings, and equipment
> Emergencies not covered by insurance (unemployment, etc.)
> Replacement of automobile
> Replacement of furnishings and equipment

Purchase of a home
Vacation travel
Education of children
Retirement
General or unspecified

When the net worth has been separated into reserves for the various purposes, it may look smaller than at first glance, and there may be little in the general or unspecified category that might cause one to worry about plans for it.

Contingent Assets · In addition to its salable financial assets, a family may have a large number of contingent assets—that is, assets that become available only in a specified eventuality and are contained in insurance protection of various types. Here we are dealing with the specific dollar protection provided, not the cash surrender value which is only fractional. Important contingent assets of families are as follows:

Automobile insurance, all types
Health insurances, all types
House insurances
Insurances on furnishings, personal effects, personal liability
Social Security
Life insurance
Annuities
Retirement programs

Although only the cash surrender value of any insurances can be listed on the balance sheet, it is clear that these items may make a tremendous difference to the family in specified emergencies. Or, to put it another way, a family having such contingent assets is in much stronger financial position than without them.

CARE OF FINANCIAL RECORDS

Proper care and safekeeping of its financial records can be of utmost importance to the family. Certain highly valuable papers need to be kept in a safe deposit box or other equally safe place. In addition, records of these papers need to be kept in a separated place—at home or in another place. It is generally advisable that both husband and wife have some understanding of the different items involved.

The family should keep the following papers in a safe deposit box or other safe place:

> All legal evidences of ownership of all assets, including savings passbooks, U. S. Bonds, stock and bond certificates, deeds and titles to property. It is important to go through the list of family assets recorded on the balance sheet to be certain that all relevant papers are included.
>
> All legal evidences of debt and its cancellation, including notes, mortgages, income tax returns, tax receipts, cancelled checks, and other important receipts. The list of liabilities on the balance sheet and memory of discharged obligations will aid in completing these materials.
>
> All insurance policies, including automobile, health, home, furnishings and equipment, liability, life, annuity, and retirement, whether group or individual policies.
>
> Other important items such as—

Birth certificate for each member	Social Security card for each member
Marriage certificate	
Divorce and support papers	Armed forces papers
Wills (perhaps at lawyer's office)	Diplomas
Immigration papers	Licenses
Naturalization papers	Registrations
Passports	Credit cards
Family health records (immunization, etc.)	Family's balance sheet
	Household inventory

The family also needs to keep at home or in another place separated from the legal evidences themselves the following items:

> Record of location of evidence of ownership and all needed details on all assets, including a record of the amount and all other information for identification.
>
> Record of location of legal evidence of debt and its cancellation and needed details on all liabilities and repayment schedules.
>
> Record of location of all insurance policies and of essential data on each policy, including the protection, beneficiaries, premium amounts and dates, insurance company.

Record of essential data on all other items and where the items themselves are kept.

Additional records, including the location of the family's safe deposit box, its number, location of the keys, in whose name it is held; the family's budget and record of income and expenditures.

INVESTMENT OBJECTIVES

While the home, business and professional assets, and insurance with cash surrender value are purchased primarily for their use value, these assets, as well as liquid assets, investment assets, and miscellaneous assets help the family meet the following major investment objectives:

Liquidity—the ready convertibility of the investment into cash without loss, as needed in an emergency.

Safety—safety of the principal that has been invested with assurance that it will be returned intact at time of need.

Simplicity—an investment that requires limited knowledge or attention from the individual investor.

Income—a return on the investment in the form of interest, dividends, or profits which meets family needs for a steady income or its hopes for a high income.

Hedge against inflation—growth in value and dollar return in an inflationary period which compensate for the declining value of the dollar.

Capital gains—an increase in resale value of the investment which may be due partly to restricted income payments through the years.

Tax status cover—an investment which minimizes current taxes on investment income, achieved through tax-free investments or those that re-invest earnings rather than make high current income payments.

Because no one type of asset is likely to meet all of the above objectives, some of which are antithetical, the family has to select a few related objectives and concentrate on them or diversify its assets. In addition, diversification helps protect the accumulation of assets since some can profitably be liquidated when others cannot be and since the value is not completely dependent on one type of asset. To aid the family in considering various assets, each common type will be discussed in some detail in the succeeding chapters with regard to its major characteristics, including its ability to meet important investment objectives.

QUESTIONS

1. How have personal savings varied as a proportion of disposable income through the last 40 years?
2. Which families tend to save the largest proportion of their income at a particular time and why?
3. How much should a family save?
4. What are major objectives of saving at each stage of the life cycle? What are additional objectives? How do saving objectives differ with economic level?
5. How large is accumulated wealth of consumers? How is wealth defined here? How important is inheritance?
6. Show how past savings are related to the income history of the consumer unit.
7. How frequently are various types of assets owned by consumers? What changes occur with increased accumulations of wealth?
8. As the accumulation of wealth increases, how does the proportion of wealth devoted to various assets change?
9. Explain the meaning of the family's balance sheet in general terms.
10. What use can the family make of its balance sheet?
11. Why may an increase occur in the family's net worth? A decrease?
12. What items might appear on a family's balance sheet? Classify.
13. What is the reason for the order of items on the balance sheet?
14. What methods of valuation are possible for items on the balance sheet? Which method is preferable?
15. What is the meaning of a "reserve"? Give examples.
16. What are contingent assets? What is their importance to the family?
17. Which financial records need to be kept in a safe deposit box or other equally safe place?
18. What financial records need to be kept at home or in a separated place from the items in safe-keeping? Why?
19. Explain each of the important investment objectives. Can they all be achieved in one investment? Which one?

20. What is meant by diversification of investments? What are the possible advantages? Disadvantages?

SUGGESTIONS FOR FURTHER READING

Board of Governors of the Federal Reserve System. *Survey of Financial Characteristics of Consumers*. Washington, D.C., latest reports.

Household Finance Corporation. *Money Management: Your Savings and Investment Dollar*. Chicago, latest edition.

U. S. Department of Commerce. *Survey of Current Business*, latest issues.

Savings Systems and Savings Bonds / 15

- · CHECKING ACCOUNTS
- · BANK OPERATIONS
- · SAVINGS ACCOUNTS
- · U. S. SAVINGS BONDS

Liquid assets in checking accounts, savings accounts, or U. S. savings bonds are held by eight-tenths of all consumer units, making liquid assets the most commonly owned form of assets. Virtually all units with accumulated wealth of $10,000 or more hold some liquid assets. While liquid assets comprise more than a tenth of total consumer wealth, they become relatively less important with increases in wealth. Liquid assets amount to a third of the wealth of those with $1–$999, but to only 4 percent for those with wealth of $500,000 and over.

CHECKING ACCOUNTS

Checking accounts are the most liquid form of asset other than cash. Six-tenths of all consumer units have checking accounts, and the proportion increases with amount of wealth (Table 15–1). While half of those with $1–$999 have checking accounts, almost all with wealth amounting to $50,000 or over have checking accounts. Those with more wealth hold larger amounts in checking accounts, but these accounts comprise a decreasingly important share of their wealth. For example, checking accounts represent 15 percent of the

TABLE 15–1. Composition of Liquid Assets of Consumer Units, by Selected Size of Wealth

ITEM	ALL UNITS	SIZE OF WEALTH			
		$1–$999	$5,000–$9,999	$25,000–$49,999	$500,000 AND OVER
Percent of group with equity in liquid assets	79	70	85	97	100
Checking accounts	59	47	65	80	99
Savings accounts*	59	39	63	82	70
Commercial banks	37	23	37	55	47
Mutual savings banks ..	8	7	5	14	25
Savings and loan associations	20	6	21	42	18
Credit unions	11	10	14	11	5
U. S. savings bonds	28	11	32	42	30
Percent of total wealth in liquid assets	13	34	17	18	4
Checking accounts	2	15	4	2	1
Savings accounts*	9	15	10	13	2
Commercial banks	3	7	4	4	1
Mutual savings banks ..	1	2	1	3	..
Savings and loan associations	3	3	4	5	..
Credit unions	1	4	1	1	..
U. S. savings bonds	2	5	3	3	..

* Includes small amount not specified as to type.

SOURCE: Dorothy S. Projector and Gertrude S. Weiss, *Survey of Financial Characteristics of Consumers,* Board of Governors of the Federal Reserve System, 1966, pp. 21, 114, 118, 122 (data as of December 31, 1962).

wealth of those with $1–$999, but only 1 percent at wealth of $500,000 and over.

A checking account makes it possible for a family to transfer funds by drawing a personal check, which greatly simplifies payments, provides receipts, and diminishes the necessity for carrying large sums of cash. The family may prefer one or more checking accounts or a joint account with two people able to draw checks. Which is most convenient depends on the business methods of the couple using it.

Particular care should be taken to make out a check correctly and see that there are no blank spaces on the line and no blank lines which might be filled in, to the drawer's loss. Check stubs are filled in completely to avoid overdrawing the account and to identify any checks that are lost. The bank statement and cancelled checks are reviewed for accuracy when they are received from the bank; and cancelled checks should be kept at least six years as proof of payment.

A check is generally endorsed at the bank by the person receiving it and deposited in his account. However, he may wish to mail it to his bank for deposit or give it to another person in payment. In either case he uses a "restrictive" endorsement on the back of the check such as:

For deposit only		Pay to order of
Peoples National Bank	*or*	Bernard Brown
Aaron Adams		Aaron Adams

Most checking accounts are at banks that belong to the Federal Deposit Insurance Corporation, an agency of the Federal government, that insures each deposit account to a maximum of $15,000 and pays the depositor in case of bank failure. No interest can be paid on checking accounts under the rules of the Federal Reserve System and the FDIC. Furthermore, charges are generally made for the checking service on a per-check basis or on the minimum monthly balance, since the service may cost the bank more than it can earn by lending the excess funds. In terms of investment objectives, then, checking accounts are generally superior in liquidity, safety, and simplicity, but do not help meet other objectives.

Related Services · In addition to allowing the person to draw checks on his account, the bank will for a small fee help him in other ways to transfer funds. *Certified checks* are personal checks that are guaranteed by the bank on which they are drawn and therefore are more acceptable to the recipient. *Cashier's checks* are drawn by the bank on itself and *bank drafts* are drawn on the bank's funds in another bank—both are most acceptable to the recipient. A *bank money order* can be purchased for making payment with the particular advantage of a receipt for the sender. In addition, banks sell *traveler's checks* that are useful to those away from home or faced by emergencies.

Two additional services of banks should be noted. The family may rent at a nominal charge a safe deposit box for the safekeeping of valuable papers and other items. If the box is owned jointly, either person has access to it. However, the box is generally sealed for tax purposes when one owner dies. This may be a disadvantage to the survivor and indicates the desirability of keeping the will at another place, perhaps a lawyer's office. Since the box can be entered only during banking hours, certain insurance papers and other items that might be needed quickly should be kept at another place. Keeping valuable papers of another person in one's box may cause complications, particularly if the box owner dies suddenly.

An additional service of the bank is in selling and redeeming U. S. savings bonds as an agent of the Government. For this purpose the bank carries an account in the name of the Government, makes additions to it when bonds are purchased and subtractions from it when bonds are redeemed, for which it receives a small fee from the Government.

BANK OPERATIONS

Since banks are extremely important in the family's financial transactions, it is useful to have a basic understanding of their operations. A bank accepts deposits, keeps some cash on hand for current payments, keeps reserves at other banks and the Federal Reserve Bank, making loans and investments with the excess.

Demand deposits, known to individuals as checking accounts, are created by the deposit of money or by bank loans. Demand deposits constitute eight-tenths of the effective money supply of the country since a large part of payments are made by this means rather than by the use of cash. Time deposits are also made at banks in the form of savings accounts and certificates of deposit. Bank accounts are owned primarily by individuals, partnerships, and corporations, but also by states and their political subdivisions, the Federal government, and other banks.

Banks make primarily real estate loans, commercial loans, and loans to individuals; banks invest generally in marketable securities of the U. S. government. A bank could provide complete safety for all deposits by keeping them in the vault and charging for the service. Otherwise the bank provides safety by selecting high-quality loans and investments. The interest received on these items and the charges made for certain services enable the bank to pay its expenses, interest on time deposits, and dividends to stockholders.

The combined assets of all U. S. banks consist of the following: [1]

TYPES OF ASSETS	PERCENT OF ASSETS DECEMBER 31, 1965
Total assets	100
Cash, balances with banks, collection items ...	14
Securities	26
U. S. government obligations	15
Obligations of States and subdivisions	9
Other securities	3
Loans and discounts	57
Real estate loans	22
Commercial and industrial loans	16
Loans to individuals	11
Other loans	8
Bank premises, other assets	3

There are about 14,300 banks in the country with total deposits of about $400 billion. Most of these banks are classified as "commercial," that is, specializing in demand deposits and commercial loans, whereas 3 percent of the banks are mutual savings banks, specializing in savings accounts and real estate loans, although they also have checking accounts.

Of the commercial banks, a third are national, that is, have charters from the national government and "national" in the bank's title, and two-thirds are state chartered. All national banks by law, and a sixth of the state banks belong to the Federal Reserve System and are subject to its regulations with regard to investments, interest payments, reserves, check clearance, etc. These banks total 44 percent of all banks with 71 percent of all bank deposits, obviously including the largest banks.

All Federal Reserve members are required to belong to the Federal Deposit Insurance Corporation, and many state nonmember banks and mutual savings banks have joined voluntarily. Thus the FDIC includes 97 percent of all banks with 97 percent of all bank deposits. FDIC regulation and supervision of insured banks are similar to those of the Federal Reserve System. Figure 15–1 presents a diagram of the organization of the banking system to clarify the relationships, which are summarized as follows:

[1] *Federal Reserve Bulletin.*

TYPE OF BANK	PERCENT OF ALL BANKS	PERCENT OF ALL BANK DEPOSITS
All banks	100	100
Commercial banks	97	86
National banks	34	47
State banks	63	39
FR and FDIC ...	10	24
FDIC only	51	14
Not FR or FDIC .	2	1
Mutual savings banks	3	14
FDIC	2	12
Not FR or FDIC .	1	2

Check clearance is simple in a local situation, but involves more steps when the two banks involved are distant from each other. The system can best be seen by assuming that only one check is drawn and cleared during a day. Mr. Brown draws a check on his account at Bank B for $100 to pay his rent to Mr. Jackson who then deposits it in his account at Bank J. Bank J sends the check to the local clearing house where Bank B pays Bank J, probably by check. Bank B receives Mr. Brown's check and deducts the amount from his account. Bank B thus has a decrease of $100 in its deposit liabilities and a like decrease in its cash assets. Bank J has an increase of $100 in its deposit liabilities and a like increase in its cash assets.

To enlarge understanding a bit, suppose that Mr. Brown draws a check on Bank B in Boston for $50 payable to Mr. Rollins in Richmond who deposits it there in his account at Bank R. Bank R then sends the check to the Federal Reserve Bank in Richmond where its deposit is increased by $50; and the deposit of the Federal Reserve Bank of Boston is decreased by $50. The check is forwarded to the Boston Federal Reserve Bank which decreases the reserve of Bank B by $50. The check then goes to Bank B which decreases Mr. Brown's account by $50. Thus Bank B has a $50 decrease in its deposit liabilities and in its cash assets. But Bank R has an increase of $50 in its deposit liabilities and its cash assets.

The steps in the process might have been greater if the bank receiving the check for deposit was a nonmember, nonclearing bank of the Federal Reserve or located in Roanoke rather than Richmond. In actual practice, many checks are deposited each day at each bank and the bank will finally pay only net clearance debts. Settlements between Federal Reserve District Banks are made through the Inter-district Settlement Fund in Washington.

FIGURE 15–1.   Organization of the United States Banking System

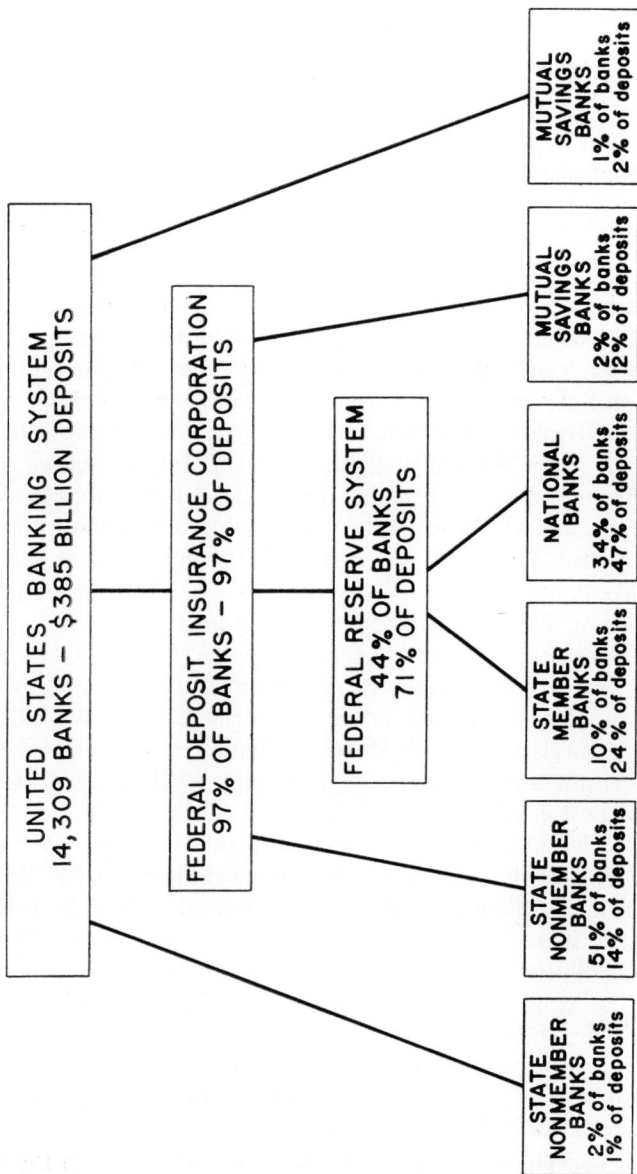

UNITED STATES BANKING SYSTEM
14,309 BANKS – $385 BILLION DEPOSITS

FEDERAL DEPOSIT INSURANCE CORPORATION
97% OF BANKS – 97% OF DEPOSITS

FEDERAL RESERVE SYSTEM
44% OF BANKS
71% OF DEPOSITS

MUTUAL SAVINGS BANKS
1% of banks
2% of deposits

MUTUAL SAVINGS BANKS
2% of banks
12% of deposits

NATIONAL BANKS
34% of banks
47% of deposits

STATE MEMBER BANKS
10% of banks
24% of deposits

STATE NONMEMBER BANKS
51% of banks
14% of deposits

STATE NONMEMBER BANKS
2% of banks
1% of deposits

SOURCE: *Federal Reserve Bulletin* (data as of December 31, 1965).

SAVINGS ACCOUNTS

Some type of savings account is owned by 59 percent of all consumer units. Ownership of savings accounts generally increases with size of wealth, but decreases for the groups with most wealth. These savings accounts are at commercial banks, mutual savings banks, saving and loan asociations, and credit unions. Nine percent of consumer wealth is held in savings accounts. While the average dollar amount in savings accounts increases with size of wealth, the proportion of wealth held in this liquid form is quite small at high levels of wealth.

The various types of savings accounts provide a high degree of liquidity, safety, and simplicity, along with some earnings on small and irregular amounts of savings. Under normal conditions money may be withdrawn from regular savings accounts without notice, although notice of one to six months may be required under the specific regulations of the institution for a given type of account. Most deposits in banks and savings and loan associations are insured up to $15,000 by agencies of the Federal government. But it is the responsibility of the individual to ascertain the situation at his own institution and to take this into account in making his decision.

Interest payments, sometimes called "dividends," differ from one institution to another, depending on the individual situation and on regulations, both of which change from time to time. Maximum rates that may be paid on certain types of deposits are set by agencies of the Federal government for institutions in which they insure deposits. The purpose is to prevent the institutions from competing for savings by paying excessive rates of interest to the detriment of quality in their selection of loans and investments.

In general, small and irregular deposits that may be withdrawn shortly from regular savings accounts pay lower rates of interest than do lump sums, such as $1,000, placed in savings certificates of deposit for a year or other set period. The larger the proportion of real estate loans among the institution's loans and investments, the higher the rate of interest it is usually able to pay in normal times. Where maximum legal interest charges on home mortgages and actual rates charged are higher, as on the West Coast, institutions are able to pay higher rates on savings.

Types of Accounts · Almost 4 out of 10 consumer units have *savings accounts at commercial banks*. Consumers hold 3 percent of their total wealth in such accounts. A regular savings account is evidenced by a passbook showing deposits and withdrawals, and withdrawals are ordinarily made without notice. The first $15,000 of each account is insured in those banks that belong to the Federal Deposit Insurance Corporation—which includes most commercial banks holding most deposits.

Commercial banks are owned by the stockholders and operated for profit. For the 13,800 commercial banks, a quarter of the dollar amount of loans and investments is in commercial and industrial loans—their single most important type—and a sixth is in real estate loans. The interest rate paid on regular savings accounts currently approximates 3 percent or up to 4 percent a year, depending on the bank and the type of deposit. Certificates of deposit may be used for large deposits, generally $1,000 or more, for a set period such as a year. The interest rate on these is currently about 5 percent, but rates up to 5.5 percent a year may be negotiated under some circumstances.

Only 8 percent of consumer units have *savings accounts at mutual savings banks*. One percent of consumer wealth is held in these accounts. Savings accounts are evidenced by passbooks, and withdrawals are ordinarily made without notice. The first $15,000 of each account is insured in those banks that belong to the FDIC—which includes two-thirds of these banks holding five-sixths of deposits in such banks.

There are only about 500 mutual savings banks in the seventeen states that permit them, but they have 14 percent of the nation's bank deposits, mostly in savings accounts. Mutual savings banks are owned by their depositors, and the directors serve without pay. Real estate mortgages comprise eight-tenths of their loans and investments. The "dividend" rate to the depositors may be 4 to 5.5 percent a year, depending on the length of time for which the money is deposited.

A fifth of all consumer units have *savings and loan shares* in a savings and loan or building association. These savings comprise 3 percent of consumer wealth. Regular accounts are evidenced by a passbook and withdrawals may ordinarily be made without notice. Seven-tenths of these associations, holding most of the savings, belong to the Federal Savings and Loan Insurance Corporation which insures each member's savings to a maximum of $15,000[2] and pays the share owner in case of failure of the association. This corresponds to the FDIC protection for a bank deposit.

For the 6,200 savings and loan associations, generally owned

---

[2] Federal Home Loan Bank Board, quoted in *Statistical Abstract of the United States 1966*, pp. 463–464.

by their members, these savings are the source of capital. Loans on real estate mortgages comprise about nine-tenths of their loans and investments. Current "dividends" approach 5 percent a year, and higher rates are paid on savings certificates for large sums for a year or more.

Eleven percent of consumer units have *credit union shares*. They comprise 1 percent of consumer wealth, but higher proportions at low levels of wealth. Savings may be withdrawn at any time. Safety of the money is maintained by regulations and by the personal relationships of the group, since they are usually fellow employees of a single company. There are approximately 22,000 credit unions, with about 17 million members.[3] Half are federal and half are state chartered. Shares can be purchased only by those who are eligible to join the organization, and loans are made to the members mostly in small amounts for personal purposes or for automobile purchase. Credit union interest charges generally cannot exceed 12 percent a year which is modest for personal loans. Shares in credit unions pay currently about 5 percent a year in "dividends," and generally are prohibited from paying more than 6 percent.

Earnings on Savings · The actual earnings on a savings account or certificate depends not only on the stated rate of interest, but also on related regulations:

> *How often* is interest compounded?
> The more frequent the compounding, the higher the annual return on $100 at a given rate of interest. Thus, daily compounding results in a higher return than does annual compounding at a stated rate of 4 percent.
> *On what amount* is interest paid?
> Interest for the month may be paid on money deposited by the first of the month, by the 10th of the month, or even by the 20th, as a special inducement. A full month's interest may be paid on sums withdrawn in the last three working days of the month. On the other hand, interest may be paid only on multiples of $100 in the lowest balance at any time during the calendar quarter, with no interest paid on any amount that has been on deposit for less than the full previous calendar quarter, and a charge of a dollar made on accounts deposited for less than three months. Specific requirements as to minimum amounts,

---

[3] Department of Health, Education, and Welfare, quoted in *Statistical Abstract of the United States 1966*, p. 465.

minimum balance to be maintained, or minimum time should be studied for any effects on earnings.

On savings certificates of deposit, certain additional questions are pertinent:

When does the certificate *mature?*

If the certificate matures in 6 months to 2 years, it may be impossible to renew it or secure another at an equally high rate of interest. Thus, a certificate with longer maturity may be more valuable at a lower rate of interest for the person who wants to hold it several years.

What happens if the certificate is *redeemed before maturity?* On a high yield certificate (or bond, as they are sometimes called) paying 5 percent compounded annually, the rate may go down to 3.5 percent. On a lower yield certificate with interest compounded quarterly, the certificate may be redeemed after the quarterly payment with no interest loss. Some big banks make their certificates of deposit negotiable so that a depositor who needs his money before the certificate expires can sell it to a securities dealer at a slight loss of yield.

Accumulation of Savings · Interest earned on savings is a decided aid to the family in accumulating funds. At a modest rate of 1.5 percent compounded annually, $100 grows to $135 in 20 years, $181 in 40 years, and $244 in 60 years (Table 15–2). Or in 60 years, $100 accumulates to $589 at 3 percent or $1,868 at 5 percent. In other words, it takes more than 45 years to double $100 at 1.5 percent, less than 25 years at 3 percent, and less than 15 years at 5 percent. If one withdraws his interest each year, he receives a much smaller sum, particularly over the long run and at higher interest rates, as follows:

ITEM	ANNUAL INTEREST RATE		
	1.5 PER-CENT	3 PER-CENT	5 PER-CENT
First 10 years' accumulation (maximum)	$116	$134	$ 163
Sum saved	100	100	100
Simple interest (withdrawn regularly) ...	15	30	50
Interest on interest (foregone)	1	4	13
Total 60 years' accumulation (maximum) ...	244	589	1,868
Sum saved	100	100	100
Simple interest (withdrawn regularly) ...	90	180	300
Interest on interest (foregone)	54	309	1,468

This illustrates both the power of interest and of interest on interest.

TABLE 15–2. Accumulated Amount of $100 at Compound Interest, 5 to 60 Years

YEARS INVESTED	INTEREST RATE COMPOUNDED ANNUALLY		
	1.5 PERCENT	3 PERCENT	5 PERCENT
5	$108	$116	$ 128
10	116	134	163
15	125	156	208
20	135	181	265
25	145	209	339
30	156	243	432
35	168	281	552
40	181	326	704
45	195	378	899
50	211	438	1,147
55	227	508	1,464
60	244	589	1,868

If you can place $100 a year in savings, you can create a tidy sum in a working lifetime. At 1.5 percent compounded annually, you would accumulate $2,347 in 20 years, $5,508 in 40 years, and $9,766 in 60 years (Table 15–3). Or in 60 years, $100 invested annually accumulates to $16,795 at 3 percent and $37,126 at 5 percent. A sizable part of the accumulation in the long run and at higher rates of interest is interest and interest on interest as the following comparison indicates:

ITEM	ANNUAL INTEREST RATE		
	1.5 PERCENT	3 PERCENT	5 PERCENT
First 10 years' accumulation	$1,086	$ 1,181	$ 1,321
Sum saved	1,000	1,000	1,000
Simple interest	82	165	275
Interest on interest	4	16	46
First 20 years' accumulation	2,347	2,768	3,472
Sum saved	2,000	2,000	2,000
Simple interest	315	630	1,050
Interest on interest	32	138	422
First 60 years' accumulation	9,766	16,795	37,126
Sum saved	6,000	6,000	6,000
Simple interest	2,745	5,490	9,150
Interest on interest	1,021	5,305	21,976

While the rate of interest and compounding are important in the accumulation of funds, it is clear that savings accounts generally

TABLE 15–3. Accumulated Amount of $100 Saved Annually for 5 to 60 Years at Compound Interest

YEARS INVESTED	INTEREST RATE COMPOUNDED ANNUALLY		
	1.5 PERCENT	3 PERCENT	5 PERCENT
5	$ 523	$ 547	$ 580
10	1,086	1,181	1,321
15	1,693	1,916	2,266
20	2,347	2,768	3,472
25	3,051	3,755	5,011
30	3,810	4,900	6,976
35	4,628	6,228	9,484
40	5,508	7,766	12,684
45	6,457	9,550	16,769
50	7,479	11,618	21,982
55	8,580	14,015	28,635
60	9,766	16,795	37,126

fail to provide capital gains. Nor do they provide a tax shelter or a hedge against inflation. Any capital gains on savings accounts, in the form of interest on interest, are usually minor because such savings are left intact for short periods and modest rates of interest are actually paid. At the same time, interest earned is subject to income taxes each year, whether the interest is withdrawn or not. Since the dollar amount of the principal amount saved remains constant as inflation progresses, savings accounts do not serve as a hedge against inflation.

U. S. SAVINGS BONDS

A quarter of consumer units own some U. S. savings bonds, and 2 percent of consumer wealth is invested in them. Consumers hold about $50 billion worth of these bonds today.

Individuals and families buy savings bonds in Series E and H at present.[4] Savings bonds may be owned by any individual or organization except a commercial bank and are registered in the name of the owner or two co-owners or an owner with a beneficiary. Thus

---

[4] Series A to D bonds were on sale prior to May 1941 and all had matured by May 1951. Series F and G bonds were issued May 1, 1941, to April 30, 1952, when they were withdrawn from sale. Series J and K were issued on May 1, 1952, and withdrawn from sale April 30, 1957.

they cannot be transferred, sold, or used as collateral for loans. Bonds will be replaced in case of loss by giving notice to the Bureau of the Public Debt in Chicago of the serial numbers, issue dates, names, and addresses on the bonds.

Investments in U. S. savings bonds are liquid after the first few months, completely safe since they are backed by the full taxing and borrowing power of the Government, simple to manage, and provide some earnings. While interest earned is subject to Federal income taxes, it is exempt from state and local income taxes.

Although U. S. savings bonds have many advantages, they do not serve as a hedge against inflation. Their dollar amount remains constant, except for any accumulated interest, but the value of a dollar decreases in inflation. An extreme example is that of a Series E bond bought for $75 in 1941 and redeemed for $100 in 1951. In the meantime the price level of consumer goods increased by three-quarters so that the $100 received bought only as much as $57 would have bought in 1941. In November 1966 when the same bond could be redeemed for $165, the accumulated amount would buy as much as $74 bought in 1941 since prices had more than doubled.

Series E Bonds · Series E bonds have been continuously on sale since May 1, 1941. They are sold in maturity value denominations of $25, $50, $75, $100, $200, $500, $1,000, and $10,000 at a price set at 75 percent of maturity value—from $18.75 for a $25 bond up to $7,500 for a $10,000 bond. No one may obtain more than $20,000 maturity value of these bonds in a year. Series E bonds are sold by banks, savings associations, and other local sales agencies, including the Payroll Savings Plan at places of employment. These bonds are redeemable at a stated value at the option of the owner, without advance notice, any time after two months from the issue date. Bonds issued since December 1, 1965, mature in seven years from the date of issue.

Series E bonds are accumulation bonds—that is, the interest accumulates in the bond rather than being paid out regularly. Interest accrues through increases in redemption value at the end of each six months from the issue date and currently approximates 4.15 percent per year compounded semiannually when held to maturity. Since interest accumulates at low rates at first, it is generally advisable in case of necessity, to cash bonds most recently purchased and keep those that are accumulating interest at a higher rate.

Redemption values and interest rates are as follows on $100 bonds currently issued:

PERIOD HELD	REDEMPTION VALUE	INTEREST RATE FOR PREVIOUS HALF YEAR
Less than ½ year	$ 75.00	0
½ year	75.84	1.1
1 year	77.28	1.9
1½ years	78.80	2.0
2 years	80.40	2.0
2½ years	82.08	2.1
3 years	83.84	2.1
3½ years	85.68	2.2
4 years	87.56	2.2
4½ years	89.48	2.2
5 years	91.44	2.2
5½ years	93.44	2.2
6 years	95.52	2.2
6½ years	97.68	2.3
7 years	100.00	2.4

All E bonds have a 10-year automatic extension privilege at a straight 3¾ percent a year compounded semiannually upon their maturity values, beginning May 1, 1961. Redemption values of some older issues of $100 bonds (purchased for $75) are as follows:

DATE OF PURCHASE	REDEMPTION VALUE, NOV. 1966	MONTH OF FURTHEST MATURITY	REDEMPTION VALUE WILL BE
May 1941	$165	May 1971	$199
Dec. 1948–May 1949	128	Dec. 1978–May 1979	215
Dec. 1952–Mar. 1953	117	Aug.–Nov. 1972	151
June–Nov. 1958	100	May–Oct. 1977	158

While interest is subject to Federal income taxes, the reporting of interest on Series E bonds may be deferred until the year in which the bonds are cashed. These bonds can thus serve as a tax cover by being held until income is subject to lower tax rates, for example, after retirement or during other periods of low income or high medical expenses.

Series H Bonds · Series H bonds went on sale June 1, 1952. They are sold at par in denominations of $500, $1,000, $5,000, and $10,000. No one may obtain more than $30,000 worth of these bonds in a year. Series H bonds are issued only by the Federal Reserve Banks and the U. S. Treasury. Local banks and other financial institutions accept and forward applications for bonds. These bonds are redeemable at par at any Federal Reserve Bank or the U. S. Treasury at the option of the owner after six months from the issue date, on one month's written notice. The bonds mature in ten years.

Series H bonds are current income bonds, with interest being paid every six months by check at the rate of approximately 4.15 percent compounded semiannually, when held to maturity, with a lower rate in the early years and a higher rate later. The amounts of checks on a $1,000 bond are as follows:

ITEM	INTEREST CHECK
First check (after 6 months)	$11.00
Next check (1 year)	19.40
Next 18 checks	21.50

All H bonds issued by January, 1957, have a 10-year automatic extension privilege after maturity.

Marketable Securities of Governmental Bodies · While a large number of consumer units own U. S. savings bonds, only 1 percent own marketable securities of the U. S. Government, and a smaller proportion hold marketable securities of state and local governments. The percentage of consumer units owning some marketable securities (bonds, notes, certificates, or bills) of governmental bodies, by size of consumer wealth, according to the Survey of Financial Characteristics of Consumers, is as follows:

SIZE OF WEALTH	U.S. GOVERNMENT SECURITIES	STATE AND LOCAL GOVERNMENT SECURITIES
All units	1	..
$1–$24,999	..	..
$25,000–$49,999	1	..
$50,000–$99,999	1	3
$100,000–$199,999 ...	8	2
$200,000–$499,999 ...	13	15
$500,000 and over	18	41

Since marketable securities of governmental bodies are held by few families, and these are largely in upper economic levels, we will note them only briefly.

Marketable securities of the U. S. Government are held largely by U. S. Government agencies, banks, corporations, and state and local governments. Some are held by trust funds, as well as by wealthy individuals. Marketable securities include a variety of items ranging from short-term Treasury bills to long-term bonds. These securities are bought and sold regularly on the market at varying prices. Currently, the yield is about 5 percent on various taxable securities. A special attraction of state and municipal bonds to wealthy persons is that such bonds are exempt from federal income taxes.

QUESTIONS

1. How widely are liquid assets owned by consumer units? Why?
2. What are the advantages of having a checking account?
3. What particular cautions should be noted in the use of a checking account?
4. What is the FDIC? How does it serve depositors?
5. What additional services do banks provide families?
6. In general terms, how does a bank operate? What is the importance of its operations to families?
7. How does a bank make a profit?
8. How widespread are the operations of the FDIC?
9. What is the importance to the family of some knowledge of check clearance?
10. Compare savings accounts at commercial banks, savings accounts at mutual savings banks, savings and loan shares, and credit union shares with regard to liquidity, safety, interest payment, and operation of the institution. What is the importance of the FSLIC?
11. What specific regulations determine the earnings actually made on savings?
12. What effect does interest have on the accumulation of savings? Contrast short and long run. Contrast a low interest rate with a higher rate.
13. What are general advantages of U. S. savings bonds?
14. Describe Series E savings bonds. What unique advantage do they have for certain investors?
15. Describe Series H savings bonds and their particular advantage.
16. Who hold marketable securities of governmental bodies?
17. Discuss the ability of liquid assets to serve as a hedge against inflation.

SUGGESTIONS FOR FURTHER READING

Board of Governors of the Federal Reserve System. *Federal Reserve Bulletin*, latest issues.

————. *Survey of Financial Characteristics of Consumers*, latest reports.

U. S. Bureau of the Census. *Statistical Abstract of the United States*. Chapter on banking, finance, and insurance, latest edition.

U. S. Treasury Department. *Current Income Series H Savings Bonds*, latest edition.

————. *Information About Series E Savings Bonds*, latest edition.

Social Security / 16

- SIGNIFICANCE OF SOCIAL
  SECURITY TO FAMILIES
- BENEFITS UNDER OASDI
- THE MEDICARE PROGRAM
- FINANCING SOCIAL SECURITY

Nine out of ten working people are now building protection for themselves and their families under the Social Security program, more properly called Old-Age, Survivors, Disability, and Health Insurance. This program has been developed from the contributory old-age retirement system, called Old-Age Insurance, for the nation's workers in industry and commerce that was included in the Social Security Act of 1935.

In 1939 the Act was expanded to provide benefits for dependents of retired workers and for dependent survivors of deceased workers. In 1956 benefits were added for disabled workers, and in 1958 for dependents of disabled workers. Thus the program developed into Old-Age, Survivors, and Disability Insurance. In 1965 the Medicare program was added for elderly persons. Since the passage of the Social Security Act, the section on social insurance has been amended eleven times, most recently in 1965.

Attention will be focused on these features of the Social Security program since they are important to most families through their life cycle. But the broad Social Security program includes some additional features that should be mentioned. The original Social Security Act of 1935 provided for grants-in-aid to the states for aid to the needy through old-age assistance, aid to the blind, and aid to dependent children when states had programs that met certain requirements. The various states thereafter generally established approved plans. To these was added aid to the permanently and totally disabled in 1950.

The original Act also included a tax on employer payrolls for unemployment insurance, with provision for an offset of 90 percent of the tax for employers covered by approved state laws. By June 1937, all states had passed such laws. In addition, the Act provided for grants-in-aid to the states for services for maternal and child health, crippled children, and child welfare.

SIGNIFICANCE OF SOCIAL SECURITY TO FAMILIES

Benefits are payable under the Old-Age, Survivors, and Disability Insurance program to the retired earner and his dependents, to the dependent survivors of a deceased earner, and to the disabled earner and his dependents, when all requirements for eligibility are met. Potential benefits to the family are great and are standard throughout the country.

If a man has been earning and paying Social Security taxes on $4,800 a year, he would receive $136 a month in the event of his disability, or, if he has a wife and children, the family may receive as much as $309 a month. If the earner dies, his widow and two children would receive $306 a month. If the worker survives and his earnings continue at the $4,800 level, he may retire at 65 and receive $136 a month as long as he lives. His elderly wife will receive an additional $68. If the earner should die first, his widow will receive $112 a month for the remainder of her life.

The Medicare program, which provides hospital insurance and medical insurance for persons 65 and over, is particularly important for the elderly who may lose their group health insurance when they retire and may find private insurance too expensive to purchase on their reduced incomes. At the same time, their need for medical care is likely to grow as age advances.

Thus Social Security provides a floor of protection on which to build a private insurance and investment program. The disability and survivorship features provide protection for the young family; the retirement and survivorship aspects and Medicare protect the family in old age. In spite of expanding benefits under the program, private savings and private purchases of protection from insurance companies have increased greatly. Undoubtedly these increases are partly a function of increased incomes. But it is likely also that protection under Social Security has awakened the public to potential contingencies and has encouraged the building of private insurance and investment programs to supplement Social Security benefits.

Social Insurance · Social Security is not charity, but is an insurance program to which the earner contributes during his earning years. There is no "means" test for eligibility for payments—that is, the recipient of benefits may have any amount of savings and investments and gift income.

Social Security is a social insurance program which differs importantly from private insurance. For instance, a private insurance company contracts to make specific payments in case of specified eventualities, such as $10,000 in case of the individual's death. For this promise, the company charges an annual premium that remains constant thereafter on permanent insurance. Costs are directly related to benefits to be paid in each event. A contract for double benefits generally costs somewhat less than twice as much each year. Benefits are paid to the insured or his estate, regardless of whether he has dependents.

Under social insurance, specifically OASDI, the annual payment (tax) is determined by law as a percentage of income earned, up to a stated maximum. Benefits received (in relation to taxes paid) in each eventuality favor those whose need is presumed to be greatest —those who earn low incomes; those who are young when they are disabled or die; those who attained retirement age with limited opportunity for coverage under the program; and those who have dependents.

For instance, a person who is disabled or retires having averaged $800 a year in covered occupations receives $44 a month, whereas a person who averaged $4,800 receives $136. Full disability and survivor benfits are available for those, most likely young or elderly earners, who have been taxed a short period for Social Security. Retirement benefits are available to those who reached retirement age by 1957 after 1½ years of coverage under Social Security, whereas those reaching retirement age in 1991 or later must have been covered at least 10 years. Most regular earners will have been covered 30 or more years by the time they retire.

Benefits are related importantly to the number of eligible beneficiaries under the law. A man covered for 10 years at an average of $4,800 a year and dying at age 35 would leave no Social Security estate (except the lump-sum death benefit) if he had no dependents. But if he left a widow and two young children, they would receive $306 a month as long as the children were dependent.

As a result of all of these differences, one person might have paid maximum Social Security taxes throughout a long working life and never receive any monthly benefits from Social Security or build any Social Security estate, whereas another person might have paid low taxes and receive large benefits personally or for his dependents. The importance of social insurance is then its potential benefit in relation to presumed need of the earner and his dependents. In no way does Social Security create a generalized estate that the earner may withdraw early or may dispose of as he wishes after his death.

Self-Supporting Program · The Social Security program is self-supporting, depending on current and past tax payments of employees, employers, and self-employed persons accumulated in the Trust Funds. Presumably workers' wages could otherwise have been increased by the amount of employers' taxes. Since the program is self-supporting, the bigger the program, the bigger the tax that has to be paid: The more eventualities covered by the program, the larger the monthly benefits available, and the shorter the period for establishing eligibility for benefits—all of these perforce increase the tax required. As the public seeks wider benefits and Congress enlarges the program, it is important that consideration be given to whether the program will become excessively burdensome, particularly to earners of moderate and low incomes, all of which is taxed without any exemptions. For example, total OASDHI taxes currently paid on behalf of a worker are $264 (a very important amount) when he earns $3,000, $581 (a sizable amount) when he earns $6,600, but no more than $581 when he earns $15,000, or any amount over $6,600, as follows:

HUSBAND'S INCOME	OASDHI TAXES PAID BY—			TOTAL OASDHI TAX
	EM-PLOYEE	EM-PLOYER	BOTH	AS PERCENT OF TOTAL INCOME
$3,000, wages	$132	$132	$264	8.8
$6,600, wages	290	290	581	8.8
$15,000, wages	290	290	581	3.9
$15,000, interest income .	0	0	0	0

As Social Security benefits have expanded, there has been a decrease in the number of needy persons receiving old-age assistance, and small rise in the number receiving other types of public assistance, since more people have become eligible for Social Security benefits as earners or their dependents. These assistance programs for the needy are supported by general revenues of the federal and state governments. In general, the change to Social Security means that earners of higher incomes and those living on investment income make little contribution to the support of the country's needy, other than those who are unemployed for long periods and the medically needy. In 1966 when some $20 billion in OASDI and hospital insurance taxes were paid on the first $6,600 of earnings at a rate of 4.2 percent by the employee, 4.2 percent by the employer, and 6.15 percent by the self-employed, the same amount could have been collected by a flat 3.5 percent tax on aggregate personal incomes.

BENEFITS UNDER OASDI

It is essential for the family's welfare that application for benefits be made without delay at the local Social Security office in the event of the earner's disability, his death, or his approaching 65 or 72 years of age. Benefits will not be paid without an application being made and back payments cannot be made for more than twelve months.

Application for benefits must be accompanied by the earner's Social Security card, his birth certificate or other acceptable proof of his age, and by the marriage certificate and children's birth certificates if benefits are claimed for the earner's dependents. Applications should be made even though all needed materials are not presently available. In case of a disability claim, a medical report form is to be filled in.

Insured Status · In determining insured status, the Social Security Administration counts the earner's "quarters of coverage"—that is, the number of calendar quarters in which he paid Social Security taxes on his income. The quarters are January to March, April to June, July to September, and October to December. An earner is considered covered in a quarter in which he earns $50 or more in an occupation covered by Social Security. A self-employed person or farm worker receives four quarters of coverage for a year in which he earns $400 or more. An earner who pays taxes on the maximum taxable earnings in a year is considered covered for four quarters, even if the money is earned in the first quarter.

Whether the earner and his dependents are eligible for any benefits depends on the earner's being currently or fully insured. The calculation of insured status simply determines whether any payments can be made on the earner's account, but does not determine the size of the payments.

The earner is *currently insured* if he has 1½ years of coverage under Social Security within the three years immediately preceding his death or entitlement to retirement benefits.

The older earner is *fully insured* when he retires or dies if he has been covered by Social Security a minimum period. Some examples of the number of years of coverage required are as follows:

EARNER REACHES 65 (62 IF A WOMAN), OR DIES	REQUIRED YEARS OF COVERAGE
In 1957 or earlier	1½
In 1967	4
In 1971	5
In 1979	7
In 1991 or later	10

Certain workers born before 1892 can qualify for benefits with less than 1½ years under Social Security. From time to time, the quarters of coverage necessary for certain elderly persons to become insured have been lowered.

If the earner is disabled or dies before reaching 65 (62 if a woman), he is fully insured:

(1) If he has been covered 10 years, at which point he is fully insured for life.

(2) Or, if he has one quarter of a year of coverage (earned any time after 1936) for each year that has elapsed since 1950 and up to the year of disability or death. In counting the years since 1950, omit all years previous to the one in which the earner reached 22. But in any event, there must be at least 1½ years of coverage.

Old-Age Insurance · Since the minimum retirement age has been lowered from 65, an earner may retire at 62 years of age with monthly benefits for himself and certain dependents if his insured status is as follows:

MONTHLY PAYMENT TO—	EARNER'S STATUS AT RETIREMENT
Retired earner, 62 or over	Fully insured
His wife, 62 or over	Fully insured
His wife, caring for his child who is under 18 or disabled and entitled to benefits	Fully insured
Dependent children	Fully insured
His dependent divorced wife, 62 or over	Fully insured
Dependent husband, 62 or over, of a retired woman earner	Fully *and* currently insured

A dependent child is one who is:

> Unmarried.
> Under 18 years of age; or
> 18 or over and severely disabled before reaching 18 and continuing to be disabled; or
> Between 18 and 22 years of age, if a full-time student.

Survivors Insurance · Certain survivors of a deceased earner may receive benefits if the earner's insured status is as follows:

MONTHLY PAYMENT TO—	EARNER'S STATUS AT HIS DEATH
His widow, caring for his child who is under 18 or disabled and entitled to benefits	Fully *or* currently insured
Dependent children	Fully *or* currently insured
His widow, 60 or over	Fully insured
His dependent divorced wife, caring for his child who is under 18 or disabled and entitled to benefits	Fully *or* currently insured
His dependent divorced wife, 60 or over	Fully insured
Dependent parents, 62 or over	Fully insured
Dependent widower, 62 or over, of a deceased woman earner	Fully *and* currently insured
Lump-sum death benefit (to estate)	Fully *or* currently insured

The requirement of being fully *or* currently insured is clearly the least restrictive, and the requirement of being fully *and* currently insured is most restrictive. This last combination is set for a dependent husband as evidence that the woman earner has been supporting him. On the other hand, it is presumed that a wife has been supported by her earning husband.

Disability Insurance · A disabled earner is one under 65 years of age who, because of a physical or mental condition, is unable to engage in *any substantial* gainful work and whose disability is expected to continue for at least 12 months or to result in death. Payments may begin for the seventh month of disability. Until 1960 a disabled earner had to be at least 55 years old to receive benefits.

If the disabled earner is fully insured *and* has been covered by Social Security in five of the ten years immediately preceding the disability, the following persons are eligible for monthly benefits:

> Disabled earner
> His wife, caring for his child who is under 18 or disabled and entitled to benefits
> His wife, 62 or over
> Dependent children
> His dependent divorced wife, 62 or over
> Dependent husband, 62 or over, of a disabled woman earner.

Under certain conditions, disability benefits are reduced for workers who are eligible for Workmen's Compensation. But the total benefits to the earner and his family are never less than the Social Security payment alone would be.

The Woman's Situation · A woman earner becomes eligible for benefits at retirement or disability as does a man. Her dependent children and parents become eligible for benefits in the same way as do a man's dependents. Her dependent husband, however, is eligible only if extra requirements are met, as previously noted.

Many women quit paid work temporarily or permanently to rear families. Amounts are added to their Social Security accounts at any time they return to paid work. Even though a woman is no longer employed, certain benefits may be paid, depending on the insured status required:

> If she was employed for 6 consecutive quarters—
> She is currently insured for the succeeding 1½ years.
> If she was employed for 10 years—
> She is fully insured for life.

She is currently insured for the next 1½ years, if 1½ years of her coverage were at the end of her employment.

She is insured under the disability provisions for the next 5 years, if 5 years of her coverage were at the end of her employment.

A woman earner who becomes eligible for benefits on her own account as well as on the account of her husband who is retired, disabled, or deceased, selects the higher benefit amount but does not receive both benefits.

A wife or widow receives benefits on her husband's account after his disability, retirement, or death only if she has in her care his child who is under 18 or disabled and entitled to benefits, or if the woman is elderly—62 years old or over for a wife or 60 for a widow. Therefore, there may be a period when the woman receives no benefits—from the time the youngest child reaches 18 until the wife reaches the advanced age.

Widows who remarry after reaching 60 years of age are eligible for whichever benefit is larger—that based on the retirement benefit of the former husband or a wife's benefit based on the account of the present husband. Monthly payments to the wife (or dependent husband) of a person entitled to old-age or disability payments generally cannot be made until the marriage has been in effect at least one year, unless the couple are parents of a child.

A divorced wife of a deceased earner receives benefits on her previous husband's account—

If she has in her care his child who is under 18 or disabled and entitled to benefits, *and*

If the previous husband was making, or supposed to make under a court order, a substantial contribution to her support.

A divorced wife at age 62 or a surviving divorced wife at 60 is entitled to benefits at the time the worker becomes disabled, entitled to retirement benefits, or dies—

If they had been married at least 20 years, and

If the previous husband was making, or supposed to make under a court order, a substantial contribution to her support.

At any time, remarriage of a divorced wife disqualifies her for benefits on the previous husband's account, but does not disqualify his dependent child in her care. The woman then becomes eligible for benefits on the account of her present husband.

Earning While Receiving Benefits · Through the years, the law has been amended to permit higher earnings while receiving Social Security benefits. At present the monthly benefits to a person receiving retirement or survivors insurance benefits are unaffected by his current earnings—

> If he earns no more than $1,500 a year.
> If he neither earns wages of $125 nor performs substantial services in self-employment in a given month.
> If he is 72 years old, no matter how much he earns.

Otherwise, his benefits are reduced if he earns more than $1,500 in a year under the following general rule:

> $1 in benefits to the earner (and his family) is withheld for each $2 earned from $1,500 to $2,700;
> In addition, $1 in benefits is withheld for each $1 of earnings over $2,700.

The earnings of a person who is receiving benefits as a dependent or as a survivor affect only his own benefits and do not stop payments to other members of the family. On the other hand, the earnings of a retired earner affect family benefits, and substantial earnings by a disabled worker stop family benefits.

Earnings from work of any kind, whether or not it is covered by Social Security (except tips of less than $20 a month with any one employer) are counted in figuring whether benefits must be withheld. Total wages and all net earnings from self-employment are added together in figuring earnings for the year.

Income from investments and gifts is not counted as earnings from work. Thus, Social Security benefits are not affected by income from savings, investments, pensions, and insurance, and from royalties received after age 65 because of copyrights or patents obtained before age 65.

If the retired earner works after he starts receiving benefits, and if his added earnings will result in higher benefits, his monthly benefit will be automatically refigured after the end of each year.

Amount of Benefits · The amount of benefits to be paid in case of retirement, disability, or death of the earner is based on the worker's average yearly earnings covered by Social Security. Average earnings are calculated by:

> (1) Counting the number of years after 1955 and up to, but not including, the year the earner is disabled, dies, or reaches 65 (62 for women). A young person may omit the years previous to the one in which he reached 22. But in any event, the total must be at least five years.
>
> (2) Selecting an equal number of years after 1950 when covered earnings were highest; and
>
> (3) Averaging earnings for the selected years.

The calculation is made by the Social Security Administration when application is made for benefits. Previous to that time, the earner may be interested in estimating his benefits. For the young person earning a maximum amount under Social Security, his calculation after 2 years of work would be as follows: $\dfrac{6,600 + 6,600}{5} = \$2,640$ average yearly earnings. After 5 years, the yearly average would, of course, be $6,600, and would continue at this average as long as he is regularly covered for $6,600 a year.

If he, or she more likely, should retire from paid work after 10 years, the average yearly earnings for Social Security benefits would thereafter decline as follows:

$$10 \text{ years later: } \frac{6,600 \ (10)}{10 + 10} = \$3,300$$

$$25 \text{ years later: } \frac{6,600 \ (10)}{10 + 25} = \$1,886$$

The earner who is disabled or who retires at 65 receives the basic benefit—the primary insurance amount. Benefits to individual persons are the following percentages of the basic benefit:

PERSON	PERCENT
Disabled earner	100
Earner who retires at 65	100
Earner who retires at 62	80
Dependents of retired or disabled earner:	
Wife, with child in her care	50
Wife, starting benefits at 65 or over	50
Wife, starting benefits at 62	37.5
Dependent child	50
Dependent husband, starting benefits at 65 or over	50

Dependents of deceased earner:
    Widow, with child in her care 75
    Widow, starting benefits at 62 or over 82.5
    Widow, starting benefits at 60 .... 71.5
    Dependent child 75
    One dependent parent, at 62 or over 82.5
    Both dependent parents, at 62 or over (each) 75
    Lump-sum death payment (not over $255) 300

The actual amount payable to each person is, however, smaller in some cases because the law sets limits on the total monthly benefit payable. Early retirement or early acceptance of dependents' benefits by a wife or widow results in permanently reduced monthly benefits. However, the total amount over the long run is about the same.

Examples of monthly benefits to certain individuals are given in Table 16–1. For instance, if annual earnings average $4,800, a couple retiring at 65 receives $204 a month, or a widow and two children receive $306. The maximum amount payable to a family is $309. At average earnings of $3,600, the retired couple receives $168, and the widow and two children receive $240. In future years as workers achieve average yearly earnings of $6,600 under Social Security, maximum monthly benefits to a disabled or retired earner will increase to $168, and maximum benefits to a family will be $368. On the other hand, if average annual earnings taxed under Social Security have been $800 or less, the disabled or retired earner receives $44 a month, and maximum benefits to a family are $66.

Social Security benefits have some special advantages. In the first place, these benefits are not subject to Federal income tax. This means that they are valuable even to the person with high investment income. Furthermore, the amount of monthly benefits payable in the various eventualities has been increased occasionally through the years for those already on the rolls as well as those becoming eligible for benefits in the future. In January 1940, when benefits were first payable, a retired earner with average annual earnings of $3,000 covered by Social Security received $41 a month, whereas today, if he still survives, he receives $102. Although the first increase in benefits was made in 1950, the increases have fairly well compensated for the increased cost of consumer goods since 1940.

THE MEDICARE PROGRAM

On July 1, 1966, nearly all persons 65 and over became eligible for "Medicare," which comprises two kinds of health insurance— hospital insurance and medical insurance.

TABLE 16–1.   Examples of Monthly Cash Benefits Under OASDI

BENEFICIARY	AVERAGE YEARLY EARNINGS AFTER 1950				
	$800 OR LESS	$1,800	$3,600	$4,800	$6,600
Earner retired at 65	$44	$ 78	$112	$136	$168
Disabled earner	44	78	112	136	168
Wife's benefit at 65 or with child in her care	22	39	56	68	84
One child of retired or disabled worker	22	39	56	68	84
Widow 62 or over	44	65	93	112	139
Widow under 62 and 1 child	66	117	169	204	252
Widow under 62 and 2 children	66	120	240	306	368
One surviving child	44	59	84	102	126
Two surviving children	66	117	169	204	252
Maximum family payment ..	66	120	240	309	368

SOURCE: U. S. Department of Health, Education, and Welfare, Social Security Administration, *Social Security*, OASI–35, 1966.

Hospital Insurance · Most elderly persons are automatically covered for the Hospital Insurance. Those who are 65 or over and are entitled to Social Security or Railroad Retirement Act benefits are automatically eligible for Hospital Insurance. Others should inquire at their local Social Security office since nearly everyone who reaches 65 before 1968 is eligible for the program. Those who reach 65 in 1968 or later and are not eligible for monthly cash benefits under the retirement programs will need some work credit to qualify for Hospital Insurance benefits.

The Hospital Insurance plan will pay the cost of covered services for the following hospital and posthospital care:

Up to 60 days in a hospital (except for the first $40) and all but $10 per day for an additional 30 days during each spell of illness. (There is a lifetime limit of 190 days on payments for treatment in mental hospitals.)

Up to 20 days in an extended care facility, and all but $5 per day for an additional 80 days for each spell of illness.

Up to 100 home-health visits by nurses or other health workers from a home-health agency (but not doctors) in the 365 days following release from a hospital or from an extended care facility.

80 percent of the cost of out-patient diagnostic tests in a hospital (after the first $20) for each 20-day period of diagnostic testing.

Medical Insurance · Elderly persons must enroll within a specified period to be eligible for the Medical Insurance plan. All are free to do so. Enrolling during the quarter immediately before one is 65 provides protection at the earliest possible date. Those who wait to enroll after they are 65 may have higher premiums to pay.

The enrollee pays a premium of $3 monthly, with the Federal Government matching this amount. The rate may be adjusted after 1967 if medical and other costs covered by this insurance program rise. The Medical Insurance may be dropped later if the enrollee desires.

The Medical Insurance plan will pay 80 percent of the reasonable charges for the following services after the first $50 in each calendar year:

Physicians' and surgeons' services, no matter where the services are received—at home, in the doctor's office, in a clinic, or in a hospital.

Home-health services even if the person has not been in a hospital—up to 100 visits during a calendar year. This is in addition to the 100 visits provided under the Hospital Insurance program.

A number of other medical and health services, such as diagnostic tests, surgical dressings and splints, and rental of medical equipment.

FINANCING SOCIAL SECURITY

OASDI and Hospital Insurance are financed by compulsory taxes paid by current earners and their employers and by self-employed persons. Taxes under the Federal Insurance Contribution Act, first levied on January 1, 1937, are deducted by the employer from the worker's wages, then forwarded along with his equal contribution to the District Director of Internal Revenue. The self-employed person with net earnings of $400 or more in a year reports his earnings and pays his tax when he files his individual income tax return. As long as a person has earnings that are covered by the law, he pays taxes regardless of his age or whether he is receiving Social Security benefits.

Wages and self-employment income on which the worker has been taxed for Social Security are entered on his own Social Security record. The record is used to determine eligibility for benefits and the amount of cash benefits. The worker should check on his account from time to time to see that his earnings are being credited to the record. The earner keeps the same Social Security account number for life, but any change in name is to be indicated on a new card.

The maximum amount of earnings that can count for Social Security and on which FICA taxes are paid is $6,600 starting in 1966. However, the maximum taxable amount has been increased through the years from the $3,000 base when payments were first made under FICA, as follows:

$3,000 a year in 1937–50
$3,600 in 1951–54
$4,200 in 1955–58
$4,800 in 1959–65
$6,600 in 1966 and thereafter

Any earnings over the maximum for a given year cannot be used to figure benefit payments. Each employer is to deduct taxes currently on the first $6,600 of earnings by the worker. If the employer accidentally deducts taxes for additional earnings, the worker should apply to him for a refund. On the other hand, if an earner has more than one employer so that taxes have been deducted on a total of more than $6,600 in a year, the worker claims a refund of the excess contributions on his income tax return for that year. FICA taxes are not refunded for any other reason.

The tax rates for OASDI and Hospital Insurance in 1967–68 total 4.4 percent to be paid by the employee and an equal amount by his employer. The rate totals 6.4 percent for the self-employed person. Rates are scheduled to increase in the future. As the Social Security program has been expanded through the years, tax rates have advanced from the 1 percent paid by both employees and employers in 1937–49. A small part of the present rate is for the Hospital Insurance, as the following contribution rate schedules show:

PERCENT OF COVERED EARNINGS

ITEM	FOR OASDI	FOR HOSPITAL INSURANCE	TOTAL
For employees and employers (each):			
1967–68	3.90	.50	4.40
1969–72	4.40	.50	4.90
1987 and after	4.85	.80	5.65
For self-employed people:			
1967–68	5.90	.50	6.40
1969–72	6.60	.50	7.10
1987 and after	7.00	.80	7.80

Social Security taxes paid are divided according to formula and credited to three separate trust funds:

Federal Old-Age and Survivors Insurance Trust Fund,
Federal Disability Insurance Trust Fund, and
Federal Hospital Insurance Trust Fund.

The enrollees' premiums along with the Government's matching contributions are placed in the Federal Supplementary Medical Insurance Trust Fund. Money in each fund is used to pay benefits and administrative expenses for the specific purpose and may be used for no other purposes.

Any money not required for current benefit payments and expenses is invested in interest-bearing securities of the U. S. Government to guarantee security of the Trust Funds. At the end of 1965, the Federal Old-Age and Survivors Insurance Trust Fund totalled about $18 billion and the Federal Disability Insurance Trust Fund totalled about $2 billion. Of course, no payments had been made into the other two trust funds at that time. Current benefits and expenses of these funds are met largely from current receipts of the Funds.

Kinds of Work Covered · Almost every kind of employment and self-employment is now covered by Social Security and subject to FICA taxes. Originally, only earnings in business and industry were covered and taxed. However, some occupations are covered only if certain conditions are met. While details may be obtained from the local Social Security office, the conditions may be summarized briefly as follows:

Farm operators and ranchers with net earnings from self-employment of $400 or more in a year are covered.

Clergymen may elect to be covered by Social Security by filing a waiver certificate with the Internal Revenue Service indicating their desire to be covered as self-employed persons.

In *family employment*, work done by a parent as an employee of his son or daughter in the course of their trade or business is covered by the law, but domestic work for them is not covered. Work done for a parent by a child who is under twenty-one is not covered. Also not covered is any work performed by a wife or a husband for the spouse.

A *domestic worker's* cash wages for work in a private household are covered by the law if they amount to $50 or more from one employer in a calendar quarter. The employer makes the earnings report and forwards the taxes.

Employees who receive tips amounting to $20 or more in a month with one employer must give the employer a written report of the amount within the first 10 days of the following month and have taxes withheld on them.

Employees of nonprofit organizations operated exclusively for religious, charitable, scientific, literary, educational, or humane purposes, or for testing for public safety, may be covered by Social Security if the organization files a certificate with the Internal Revenue Service waiving its exemption from the payment of Social Security taxes, and if the employee also signs a form indicating his desire to be covered. Thereafter, new employees of the organization are automatically covered. But if an employee of a nonprofit organization earns wages of less than $50 in a calendar quarter, the wages for that quarter are not covered.

Employees of state and local governments may be covered under voluntary agreements between the individual state and the Federal Government.

Farm employees are covered by Social Security if they earn $150 or more in cash during the year or do farm work for the employer on 20 or more days during a year for cash wages figured on a time basis. Household workers employed on a farm operated for profit are also covered under these rules.

Employees of the Federal Government who are not covered by their own staff retirement system are covered by Social Security.

For active duty in *military service*, Social Security coverage is credited for base pay after 1956 and for $160 a month to most veterans who served between September 15, 1940, and the end of 1956.

Earnings in *railroad employment* are reported to the Railroad

Retirement Board and not to the Social Security Administration. However, if the worker has less than 120 months of railroad service when he retires or is disabled, his earnings for railroad work after 1936 are considered in figuring his retirement or disability benefits under Social Security.

American *citizens working abroad* for American employers are covered by Social Security.

Earnings are taxed for Social Security under the preceding rules even though the worker is currently receiving Social Security benefits as a retired earner, a survivor, or a dependent.

Not covered by Social Security are agricultural workers temporarily admitted to the United States for this purpose and foreign exchange visitors doing work for which they were admitted.

QUESTIONS

1. What type of social insurance of importance to most families was included in the Social Security Act of 1935? What major types have been added?

2. What other features are included in the broad Social Security program?

3. How important is the Social Security program to families?

4. What are the particular aspects of a social insurance program?

5. What is the significance of the fact that the Social Security program is self-supporting?

6. When should application for benefits be made? How?

7. How does the earner achieve a currently insured status?

8. How will you achieve a fully insured status? Your father?

9. What is the importance of the earner's insured status in the event of his old-age retirement, death, or disability? What additional requirements are set for disability benefits?

10. What is the woman's situation under Social Security?

11. Can an OASDI beneficiary earn while receiving benefits?

12. What is the importance of average annual earnings covered? How is the calculation made?

13. What proportion of the basic benefit do major beneficiaries receive?

14. What are the monthly benefits to the earner and the maximum to the family at average yearly earnings of $6,600? At 800 or less?

15. Describe the two features of the Medicare program—Hospital Insurance and Medical Insurance.

16. How is the Social Security program financed?

17. What kinds of work are covered?

18. Evaluate Social Security in terms of the family's investment objectives.

19. What types of changes have been made in the program through the years? What changes are currently being considered?

20. What is the relationship of FICA taxes to the individual's income tax return?

21. Why is no sum for Social Security placed on the family's balance sheet of its assets and liabilities?

22. Obtain a copy of recent amendments to Social Security Law and study them for any significant changes.

SUGGESTIONS FOR FURTHER READING

U. S. Department of Health, Education, and Welfare, Social Security Administration.
    Characteristics of State Public Assistance Plans Under the Social Security Act. Washington, D.C., latest revision.
————. *Social Security.* Washington, D.C., OASI–35, latest revision.
————. *Social Security Bulletin,* latest issues.
————. *Social Security Handbook.* Washington, D.C., latest edition.

Life Insurance / 17

· SELECTING LIFE INSURANCE
· PLANNING THE FAMILY'S LIFE
INSURANCE PROGRAM

Americans own about 400 million life insurance policies providing about $1 trillion of protection. Two-thirds of the population has some coverage. Among husband-wife families, the husband is insured in 9 out of 10 that include children under 18 years old, and in 8 out of 10 without children (Table 17–1). The family head is insured in 6 out of 10 other families including single consumers.[1]

The amount of insurance coverage is highest for husbands with children. Among insured husbands in husband-wife families, 54 percent have insurance coverage of $10,000 or more when they have some children under 18, and 41 percent have $10,000 or more coverage when they have no children. Only 18 percent of the insured heads in other types of families have $10,000 or more of life insurance.

Life insurance coverage increases with income. Among husband-wife families with the husband under 65 years of age, 71 percent of husbands own life insurance when income is under $3,000, but 94 percent or more when income is $5,000 and over (Table 17–2). The average amount of coverage for the insured husbands increases from $3,800 at the lowest income level up to $67,000 when income is $15,000 or more.

Other family members are much less frequently insured than are family heads, and for smaller amounts. Out of six families, three have all members insured, two have some members insured, and one has no member insured. Coverage varies greatly among age groups:

[1] Unless otherwise noted, data used are generally from the *Life Insurance Fact Book 1966*, supplemented by 1965 and 1964 editions, by the Institute of Life Insurance.

TABLE 17–1. Life Insurance Coverage of Family Heads

| ITEM | HUSBAND IN HUSBAND-WIFE FAMILIES | | HEAD IN OTHER TYPES OF FAMILIES INCLUDING SINGLE CONSUMERS |
	WITH CHILDREN UNDER 18 YEARS OLD	WITHOUT CHILDREN UNDER 18 YEARS OLD	
Percent of family heads insured	89	80	64
Percent distribution of insured heads by amount of life insurance owned: total	100	100	100
Under $1,000	3	3	18
$1,000–$4,999	21	38	54
$5,000–$9,999	22	18	10
$10,000–$22,999	35	27	13
$23,000 and over	19	14	5

SOURCE: A national consumer survey conducted in 1965 for The Prudential Life Insurance Company. Quoted by the Institute of Life Insurance, *Life Insurance Fact Book 1966*, p. 8.

it fluctuates from about half of children under 18 for an average of about $1,300 for the insured children, to more than three-quarters of persons 35–44 for an average of about $8,800, to about half of persons 65 or older for an average of $2,700.

Life insurance is purchased as a protection against financial loss because of a person's death. Insurance is a method of *risk-sharing* by which a large group of people place money in a common fund from which payments are made to those individuals who suffer loss. Fundamentally, insurance provides *protection* against an unpredictable loss by the payment of a known charge (premium) in advance. While the death of any individual is unpredictable, deaths among a large group are predictable so that each person's contribution to the fund can be calculated. Some life insurance polices include a savings feature as well which results in a loan value and cash surrender value.

SELECTING LIFE INSURANCE

In selecting life insurance, a family needs to consider the characteristics of the various plans, the types of life insurance, factors affecting costs, and nonforfeiture values.

TABLE 17–2.   Life Insurance Coverage of Selected Types of Persons

CHARACTERISTICS OF PERSONS	PERCENT INSURED	MEAN AMOUNT OWNED BY INSUREDS
Husband under 65 in husband-wife families, by personal income of family head:		
All incomes	89	$11,400
Under $3,000	71	3,800
$3,000–$4,999	87	6,000
$5,000–$8,999	96	11,600
$9,000–$14,999	95	22,000
$15,000 or more	94	66,600
All persons	64	4,700
Husband in husband-wife families	86	10,600
With children under 18 years old	90	12,600
Without children under 18 years old	80	7,600
Head of other families of 2 or more persons	73	3,700
Wives	59	2,100
Other household members under 18 years old	53	1,300
Other household members 18 or older	62	2,800
Single consumers	57	4,200
All persons, by age:		
Under 6	50	1,300
6–13	54	1,400
14–17	57	1,300
18–24	67	3,600
25–29	74	6,800
30–34	73	7,700
35–44	78	8,800
45–54	75	7,200
55–64	70	4,800
65 or older	52	2,700

SOURCE: A national consumer survey conducted in 1960 by the Life Underwriter Training Council and the Life Insurance Agency Management Association. Quoted by the Institute of Life Insurance, *Life Insurance Fact Book 1966*, p. 9 and *Life Insurance Fact Book 1964*, p. 9.

Plans of Life Insurance · Life insurance is purchased under four quite different plans—term, straight life, limited payment life, and endowment—or under plans that offer a combination of these basic plans. The present discussion focuses on the fundamental features of these plans, although various minor features are frequently added in practice.

TABLE 17-3. Approximate Annual Premiums per $1,000 of Life Insurance for Selected Plans, by Age at Issue to Males [Nonparticipating premiums for ordinary life insurance purchased in units of $1,000]

PLAN	ANNUAL PREMIUM FOR POLICY ISSUED TO MALE AT AGE—				
	20	30	40	50	60
1-year term*	$ 8	$ 8	$11	$16	$34
5-year term*	8	8	11	18	38
10-year term*	8	9	13	22	44
Term to age 65*	11	13	17	24	38
Straight life	16	20	27	37	57
20-payment life	24	29	36	47	63
20-year endowment	47	48	50	54	64

* Convertible to permanent insurance. Renewable at end of term at premium for attained age, up to age 65.

The *term plan* provides benefits at death if death occurs within a specified term, thus is similar in nature to property and automobile insurance. Like them, it provides protection with no savings feature, thus has no cash or loan value. Mortgage insurance or credit insurance is actually term insurance that decreases as the amount of the mortgage or other debt decreases, and is referred to as decreasing term insurance.

The term plan is the least expensive of all plans per $1,000 of insurance at the age at purchase. But the premium increases at successive renewal dates, from approximately $8 at age 20 and $9 at age 30 up to $44 at age 60 for a ten-year term plan (Table 17-3). The term chosen may be one year, five years, ten years, or longer, or to age 65, with a level premium throughout the term.

The chief advantage of a term plan is that it permits a young family with a limited amount to spend for life insurance to have maximum protection while the children are young. For instance, $100 a year provides about $12,500 in protection while the father is under 30, $11,100 from 30–39, and $7,700 from 40–49. This plan permits other persons also to maximize protection for a brief period of time when it becomes necessary. The major disadvantage of the plan is the increasing cost with advanced age so that $100 a year buys only $2,300 of protection at age 60—but perhaps the need for protection has declined proportionately.

It is generally desirable that the family select a term plan that is convertible into permanent insurance at the request of the insured and is renewable at the end of the period without a new medical examination, since advancing age may make it more difficult to pass the examination. Being examined by one's own doctor before seeking a policy is usually desirable in order to avoid establishing a poor health record with the insurance company. Furthermore, it is probably advisable for the family to buy several policies in $1,000 or $5,000 units, depending on family circumstances, rather than one large policy, so that the family may later drop one policy if it wishes. *NO* Families carrying large amounts of insurance may carry their policies in $10,000 units, and make savings on the larger sizes.

Some insurance companies prefer to sell term plans because of their restricted liability and greater profitability when interest rates are low, but other companies prefer to avoid term plans, partly because buyers misunderstand the plans. The insurance salesman may find term plans easier to sell because of the low initial premium. But, since his commission is generally a percentage of the premiums, he makes less money by selling $10,000 of insurance on a term plan than on the other plans.

The *straight life plan* is purchased in a stated amount for the whole life, with a constant premium payable throughout life, as determined at the age at purchase. For example, a $1,000 policy purchased at age 20 costs about $16 a year for life, or, at age 30, $20 a year for life. This plan has the particular advantage of relatively low cost which does not increase as age advances, thus allowing a family to keep a relatively large amount of insurance in force.

For $100 annual premium a person can buy about $6,200 worth of insurance at age 20 and keep it in force thereafter for the same payment. Of course, even this charge may become burdensome after retirement, which encourages selection of a variant that is paid-up at age 65.

During the early years of policy ownership, the premium includes some savings in addition to current protection so that reserves are built up and invested to meet the excess expenses of the later years. For instance, a policy purchased at 20 years of age costs about $16 per $1,000 whereas protection only (in a term policy) costs $8. Keeping the same policy in force thereafter means that at age 50 the annual premium just covers current protection; but at age 60 the premium is about half of the cost of current protection. Total premiums by age 60 are somewhat greater than the total protection cost, but by age 70 total premiums are less, as follows:

ITEM	APPROXIMATE TOTAL PREMIUMS FOR AGES—				
	20–29	20–39	20–49	20–59	20–69
Straight life purchased at age 20	$160	$320	$480	$640	$800
Protection cost* . . .	80	170	300	520	960
Additional payment .	80	150	180	120	−160

* Based on approximate cost of 10-year term plan.

The *limited payment life plan* is a whole life plan with benefits payable at death which requires level premium payments for only a limited period of time, such as 10, 15, or 20 years (or until death, if it occurs earlier). After the limited period, the policy is paid-up—an advantage to the individual wishing to complete payments while earnings are high.

A $1,000 policy purchased at age 20 costs about $24 a year for 20 years or, at age 30, about $29 a year for 20 years. As a result, $100 annually spent on life insurance at age 20 provides only $4,200 of protection for the family, contrasted with about $11,100 under a term policy to age 40.

The annual premium for the limited payment plan includes a large amount of savings as prepayment of future premiums. It is in the later years of life that gains accrue from the early purchase of a limited payment plan. Total premiums by age 60 are somewhat less than total protection cost, but by age 70 total premiums are only half as much, as follows:

ITEM	APPROXIMATE TOTAL PREMIUMS FOR AGES—				
	20–29	20–39	20–49	20–59	20–69
20-payment life purchased at age 20	$240	$480	$480	$480	$480
Protection cost	80	170	300	520	960
Additional payment .	160	310	180	−40	−480

The *endowment plan* includes life insurance for the term of the policy with the face value of the policy being paid at the insured's death or at the end of the period, whichever occurs first. Thereafter the life insurance is cancelled.

The endowment feature is a special advantage when a sum is wanted for education or another purpose at a future time, if the family will not otherwise accumulate the savings. An endowment policy for a child's education might better be purchased on the father's life than on the child's, unless the plan contains a payor clause so that premiums cease at the death of the person paying for the insurance.

A 20-year endowment plan for $1,000 may be purchased at age 20 for an annual premium for 20 years of about $47, and little more up to age 50. This means, then, that $100 used annually for life insurance premiums provides about $2,100 worth of protection at age 20, and almost the same amount up to age 50. This contrasts greatly with the protection purchased for $100 annual premium on the other plans, as follows:

PLAN PURCHASED AT AGE 20	PROTECTION FOR $100 ANNUAL PREMIUM AT AGES—		
	20–29	30–39	40–49
10-year term (renewed regularly)	$12,500	$11,100	$7,700
Straight life	6,200	6,200	6,200
20-payment life	4,200	4,200	4,200 (no premium)
20-year endowment (new plan purchased at age 40)	2,100	2,100	2,000

The premiums for an endowment plan are level throughout the payment period and involve a very large amount of savings—almost $40 a year to age 50—in order to accumulate, with interest, the endowment amount of $1,000 at the end of the 20 years. Since this plan is primarily used to force savings, total premiums paid by any age are a great deal more than the protection cost, as follows:

ITEM	APPROXIMATE TOTAL PREMIUMS FOR AGES—				
	20–29	20–39	20–49	20–59	20–69
20-year endowments purchased at ages 20, 40, and 60	$470	$940	$1,440	$1,940	$2,580
Protection cost	80	170	300	520	960
Additional payment .	390	770*	1,140	1,420*	1,620

* $1,000 cash endowment receivable at ages 40, 60 (and 80), if death does not precede.

Several plans have been developed as combinations of these basic plans to meet special needs or encourage purchases. A *family income policy* is a combination of a straight life plan with decreasing term insurance. For instance, at death of the insured $10 monthly income is paid for the remainder of a 20-year period commencing at the date of issuance of the policy and the $1,000 face value is paid at the end of the period. This policy may cost about $20 a year if issued at age 20, and $16 a year after age 40 when the family income feature is dropped. For a slightly higher premium, the face amount is payable at death. Alternative plans provide for income during the remaining part of 10, 20, or 30 years after issuance of the policy.

A *family policy* includes insurance for all family members and is purchased in sizable units such as $5,000 which includes $5,000 straight life for the husband, perhaps $1,500 term insurance for the wife, and $1,000 term insurance for each child, including those born after the policy is issued. Such a policy costs less than when several policies are purchased separately.

A *modified life policy* starts as a term policy, then automatically converts to a straight life policy perhaps 3 or 5 years later. The beginning premium is not so low as for a term policy and the later premium is not so high as for a straight life policy purchased at the later age.

Types of Life Insurance · Insurance as an institution providing protection against financial loss developed in the seventeenth century in a London coffeehouse owned by Edward Lloyd where marine insurance was sold. From that simple beginning, Lloyd's of London grew into a world-wide organization insuring against nearly all kinds of hazards, and the insurance business developed into a tremendous and important one throughout the world.

The United States now has about 1,700 legal reserve life insurance companies, contrasted with about 500 at the end of World War II, and one company in 1759. Nine-tenths of these companies are *stock companies* owned by stockholders who receive any profits. A tenth of the companies are *mutual companies* that are owned by their policyholders. The mutual companies, generally older and larger than the stock companies, hold about seven-tenths of the assets of all U. S. life insurance companies and account for about six-tenths of the insurance in force.

About 94 percent of all life insurance in force is purchased from legal reserve life insurance companies as ordinary, group, credit, and industrial life insurance. While the amount of such life insurance protection has almost quadrupled in recent years, the amount of group and credit insurance has increased much more than average, whereas industrial insurance has increased little, as follows:

TYPE OF LIFE INSURANCE	AMOUNT IN 1965 AS MULTIPLE OF 1950
Total legal reserve life insurance	3.8
Ordinary	3.3
Group	6.4
Credit	14.6
Industrial	1.2

Ordinary life insurance, usually purchased privately by the individual, provides over half of all life insurance protection (Table 17–4). Nearly all life insurance companies have some ordinary life insurance in force. Ordinary life insurance is generally issued in amounts of $1,000 or more, and policies average $4,700. Premiums are cheapest when payable annually, but may be paid semi-annually, quarterly, or monthly by check or in person at the insurance company's office. A medical examination is required before the policy is issued.

Almost four-tenths of ordinary insurance is owned under a

TABLE 17–4. Types of Life Insurance in Force in United States

INSURER AND TYPE OF LIFE INSURANCE	COVERAGE		POLICIES		AVERAGE SIZE OF POLICY
	AMOUNT IN BILLIONS	PER-CENT	NUMBER IN MILLIONS	PERCENT OF COMPANY POLICIES	
Total	$959	100	..	..	..
Legal reserve life					
insurance companies ...	901	94	320	100	..
Ordinary insurance ..	498	52	107	33	$ 4,660
Group insurance	306	32	61	19	5,050
Servicemen's Group					
Life Insurance ..	28	3	3	1	10,000
Credit insurance	57	6	63	20	900
Group policies	49	5	..	..	..
Individual policies .	8	1	..	..	..
Industrial insurance .	40	4	89	28	450
Other insurers	59	6	..	..	..
Veterans insurance ..	39	4	6	..	6,600
Fraternal insurance ..	16	2	..	..	..
Savings bank insurance	2	..	..	..	..
Assessment and other					
insurance	1	..	..	..	..

SOURCE: Institute of Life Insurance, *Life Insurance Fact Book 1966,* pp. 5, 17, 22, 102–103 (data for 1965).

straight life plan, over a tenth under limited payment, a tenth under term, less than a tenth under endowment, and three-tenths under various combination plans. Through the years, straight life has maintained its place as the most popular single plan of ordinary life insurance. Term and combination policies now constitute twice as large a proportion as in 1950, whereas limited payment and endowment constitute about half as large a proportion. Approximate premiums on the various plans considered earlier were for ordinary life insurance since it is the most important type.

Group life insurance has grown in importance so that it provides about a third of total life insurance protection today. Policies average $5,000. Group life certificates are issued under 233,000 master contracts of insurance companies, usually with employers for the benefit of employees, though some are with unions, professional associations, and other groups. The employer generally withholds regular amounts from the workers' pay, sometimes adds additional amounts, and forwards the total payment to the insurance company.

No medical examination is required, other than that for employment. The policy is usually a term plan, and the amount may be limited to one or two times the worker's annual earnings up to a stated maximum. Some policies may be converted to permanent insurance when the employee leaves the company or to a reduced amount on his retirement. Some policies provide coverage for dependents of the primary insured person. Because of the various economies in issuance of group life insurance, the premium may be as low as $7 per $1,000 of protection.

Some life insurance companies have no group insurance in force, whereas others have large amounts. Metropolitan Life accounts for about a fifth of the group coverage in force and Equitable Life, Prudential, Travelers, and Aetna together account for an additional half.

Servicemen's Group Life Insurance, the largest single master contract ever written, went into effect in 1965. This plan provides automatic coverage of $10,000 of group life insurance for each person on active duty in the uniformed services. While the plan is supervised by the Veterans Administration, it is underwritten by the legal reserve life insurance companies.

Credit life insurance, the newest type, has grown greatly as many lenders have come to require it. The insurance is used to repay debt in case of the borrower's death while he still owes money on an instalment purchase or home mortgage. These policies, providing 6 percent of total life insurance protection, average $900. Thus credit life insurance provides limited insurance protection for the individual family.

Credit life insurance is term insurance that decreases in amount as the loan is repaid. This insurance is usually purchased through a lending agency that has a master contract with an insurance company, though some policies are purchased individually. A 15-year policy for $1,000, purchased individually, may cost about $7 at age 30, with the face amount of insurance declining from $1,000 at the beginning of the first year to about $100 at the beginning of the 15th year. Short terms, such as 3–5 years, and group purchase both operate to lower costs.

Standard rates are $1 per $100 of credit insurance per year in Maryland, according to the State Insurance Commissioner. About 55¢ of the premium dollar is rebated to the lender in the form of a commission. Insurers are chosen by the lenders who are frequently agents or have a direct interest in the insurance company. In Washington, D.C., the maximum legal rate is 49¢ per $100.[2]

Industrial life insurance is issued in small amounts with premiums collected weekly or monthly at the family's home by the insurance agent. No medical examination is required, and term insurance is not generally available. For these reasons, the cost per $1,000 of total insurance protection is considerably higher than under ordinary life insurance. While the weekly premium for a $500 policy purchased at age 20 may range from about 22¢ to 59¢, depending on the plan of insurance, the total premium paid in a year for total protection of $1,000 (in two policies of $500 each) ranges from $23 to $61 as follows:

PLAN OF INSURANCE	POLICY ISSUED AT AGE		
	10	20	30
Straight life	$17	$23	$30
20-payment life	30	38	47
20-year endowment	60	61	64

Industrial policies comprise 4 percent of all insurance in force, but a considerably higher proportion of total policies. Their average size of $450 indicates that they are small burial policies, frequently issued on each member of a family. Purchase of industrial life insur-

2 Bart Barnes, "Maryland Warned to Forestall U. S. Action: Credit Insurance Curb Urged," *The Washington Post*, June 8, 1967, p. H 1.

ance has increased little as workers seek larger policies and are able to obtain group life insurance at the place of employment. Metropolitan Life and Prudential account for a third of industrial insurance in force. Many life insurance companies have no industrial insurance in force.

Six percent of total life insurance is carried by other insurers than legal reserve life insurance companies. The major part is *veterans life insurance*. This includes U. S. Government Life Insurance covering veterans of the first war; participating National Service Life Insurance issued to servicemen during and following World War II, and nonparticipating NSLI for those who entered the Armed Forces after 1950 and some veterans whose disabilities made private life insurance unobtainable. These policies are inexpensive for eligible persons, and generally should be maintained if possible.

Savings bank life insurance has more than doubled in the past ten years. This insurance, written by savings banks in Connecticut, Massachusetts, and New York, comprises a small part of all insurance in force. Policies are purchased and premiums paid at the bank which reduces the costs and premium rates. Families that have a convenient savings bank and that can develop their own insurance programs may save considerably by checking the plans available.

Fraternal life insurance is issued by lodges, societies, and fraternal organizations to their members. The amount has increased modestly in recent years. There is also some amount of insurance in force with *assessment associations*, mutual aid groups, and burial societies, but the amount has declined during recent years. In addition, some retailers act as self-insurers when they include credit life insurance in instalment contracts.

Determination of Premium Rates · The annual premium that an individual pays for life insurance depends on the plan of insurance that he chooses, the type and amount of insurance, and the person's age, sex, occupation, and health. Underlying these individual differences are three basic factors determining costs of life insurance: mortality rates, earnings rates, and operating expenses.

The *mortality rate* is the death rate expected next year and each succeeding year of the contract for the group to which the individual belongs. The likelihood of death in a given year is predictable for the group with considerable accuracy on the basis of a large accumulation of death statistics, but is not predictable for any specific person. The rate is higher for men than women, for the aged, for those in poor health, and those in dangerous occupations. Persons who are in exceptionally good health and in safe occupations may get preferred risk policies at reduced rates when purchasing sizable policies.

The age-adjusted death rate in the United States has dropped almost half from 1.44 per 100 population in 1915 to .74 in 1964. The decrease from 1935 to 1955 was particularly large with the spreading use of the sulfas and antibiotics. The mortality rate is now very low except in the first year of life and in the later years. Death rates are especially low for children and for young adults during the years that they have young children in the home. This means that premium rates for life insurance can be much lower than during the later years of life. Not until age 50 for men and 60 for women does the annual death rate reach 1 in 100 (Table 17–5).

The death rates may be used to estimate the likelihood of the deaths of young parents before their children are grown. Roughly

TABLE 17–5. Death Rates in the United States [Rate per 100 population in age group]

AGE	MALE	FEMALE
All ages	1.11	.82
Under 1 year	2.87	2.19
1–4 years	.11	.09
5–9 years	.05	.04
10–14 years	.05	.03
15–19 years	.13	.05
20–24 years	.18	.07
25–29 years	.18	.09
30–34 years	.21	.12
35–39 years	.30	.19
40–44 years	.46	.28
45–49 years	.75	.42
50–54 years	1.23	.64
55–59 years	1.90	.94
60–64 years	2.82	1.45
65–69 years	4.36	2.28
70–74 years	6.05	3.57
75–79 years	8.62	5.85
80–84 years	12.98	10.02
85 years and over	22.46	20.11

SOURCE: U. S. National Center for Health Statistics, *The Facts of Life and Death*, Public Health Service Publication No. 600, Revised 1965, p. 11 (data for 1963).

speaking, among men who are now 25 years old, approximately 1 percent will be dead by age 30, probably leaving some preschool children; an additional 2 percent will be dead by age 40, probably leaving school-age children; and an additional 6 percent will be dead by age 50, probably leaving teenagers or older children. Among women who are now 25 years old, less than 0.5 percent will be dead by age 30, an additional 2 percent by age 40, and an additional 4 percent by age 50. While death is unlikely during the child-rearing years, the financial effects on family support can be disastrous.

The death rates may also be used to estimate the likelihood of death of their children. Roughly speaking, among boys born alive, approximately 3 percent will be dead by age 1, and an additional 2 percent will be dead by age 20. Among girls born alive, about 2 percent will be dead by age 1, and an additional 1 percent by age 20. After the first year of life, then, the child's remarkable recuperative powers almost assure his attainment of adulthood.

The influence of the mortality rate alone on premium costs may be seen by a self-insurance plan: A thousand 20-year old men might decide to insure themselves for $1,000 of 10-year term insurance. Since 18 of them will be dead by age 30, if they are an average group, benefits will total $18,000. This will require annual premiums of about $2 a person for the ten years.

The mortality rate affects premium rates also as it affects expenses for supplementary benefits that insurance covers, such as the payment of double indemnity for accidental death and the cessation of premiums at the death of the person (other than the insured) who is paying the premiums. Morbidity rates affect the costs that must be covered when premiums cease at the disability of the person paying the premiums.

The *earnings rate* on invested funds also is important in determining the premium. The higher the earnings rate, the lower the necessary premium. Costs of insurance plans, such as endowment and limited payment that include large savings during the early years, can be lowered considerably by a high earnings rate.

Assets of life insurance companies total $159 billion, almost four-tenths as much as the assets of all banks in the country. About four-tenths of the assets of life insurance companies are invested in real estate mortgages and four-tenths in corporate bonds. Interest rates have been rising so that the net rate of return on total invested assets now approaches 5 percent. The rate, which was in 1947 at the lowest point for this century, has changed from time to time, as follows:

YEARS	APPROXIMATE RATE
1915–1932	5%
1933–1939	4%
1940–1954	3%
1955–1963	4%
1964–1965	5%

The company's *operating expense* is another important factor determining premiums. These expenses include commissions to agents, home and field office salaries, medical fees, and rents. Operating expense is affected by the type of insurance sold (e.g., group contrasted with industrial), the efficiency of the individual company, and the amount of new sales of insurance, since costs of commissions and issuance of new contracts are higher than costs of maintaining old contracts. Premium rates are also affected by the vigor of price competition in the industry, as in any field. Selling competition among insurance companies is obvious in aggressive salesmanship and special features added to policies, but rate-cutting on a like policy is less obvious.

Over half of the income of life insurance companies goes for policy benefits, a quarter is invested, and less than a quarter is used for various expenses. The use of the life insurance company income dollar is estimated as follows:

Total income, 1965	100¢
Premiums	78¢
Net investment earnings and other income ..	22¢
Use of income	100¢
Benefit payments in year	53¢
Additions to invested funds	25¢
Operating expenses	17¢
Taxes	4¢
Dividends to stockholders	1¢

Premiums for life insurance are stated in two ways—as participating and nonparticipating. Policies with *participating premiums* account for about two-thirds of all life insurance in force. For these policies, a set premium is paid by the policy holder at the beginning of the year and a "dividend" received by him at the end of the year if there is a difference between the premium charged and actual experience of the company during the year. Policies with *nonparticipating premiums* have no dividends payable. To simplify the earlier comparison of approximate premium rates on various plans of life insurance, nonparticipating premiums were used since the final rate would be the same as the stated premium.

In purchasing life insurance or other insurance, the family is wise to limit its shopping for premium rates and policy terms to insurance companies that rate high in safety. It is advisable to check with the State Insurance Department to see that the company is licensed to do business in the state, if there is any question about the possibility. It is helpful to know if the company is licensed to sell in New York State which has more stringent regulation of insurance companies than many other states. A company that has remained in business some years and has an established reputation has thus shown continued ability to pay claims. A large-sized company has a greater opportunity to diversify risk among a large number of policy holders and among different types of investments than does a small company.

Nonforfeiture Values · Sizable numbers of life insurance policies in force are terminated by lapse or surrender each year, indicating the importance of a family's understanding its prerogatives in such an event in order to avoid losses. About 5 percent of ordinary life insurance policies are voluntarily terminated annually, with a higher rate for policies in force less than 2 years and a lower rate for those in force 2 years or longer. Higher rates of voluntary terminations would be expected on industrial insurance, fraternal insurance, and assessment and similar types because of the characteristics of the policyholders and of the insurance.

Voluntary termination is higher in depressed periods when families use the cash values of their insurance for emergency funds and cut family expenses by dropping policies. Even in prosperous periods, overpurchase of insurance leads to lapses of policies. There may be a temptation to concentrate on the immediate rather than long-run situation since the commission rate for salesmen is generally much higher in the first few years that the policy is in force than in the later years.

Life insurance policies with a savings feature build a cash surrender value out of the excess premiums (over the protection cost) and accumulated interests on them. The policy states the surrender charge and the amount of the cash surrender value at the end of each year, with none for the first few years while the cost of selling is being written off. Obviously, the larger the savings feature and the longer the period of premium payments, the larger will be the cash or loan value of a policy. Of three $1,000 plans purchased at age 20, the cash value 10 years later may approximate $75 on a straight life plan, $150

TABLE 17–6.   Approximate Cash or Loan Values per $1,000 of Ordinary
Life Insurance, Nonparticipating

ITEM	AGE AT ISSUE OF POLICY		
	20	30	40
Straight life plan:			
At end of 10th year	$ 75	$ 125	$ 175
At end of 20th year	200	300	375
At 65 years of age	600	550	475
20-payment life plan:			
At end of 10th year	150	200	275
At end of 20th year	400	525	625
At 65 years of age	700	700	700
20-year endowment:			
At end of 10th year	425	425	425
At end of 20th year	1,000	1,000	1,000

on a 20-payment life plan, and $425 on a 20-year endowment (Table
17–6). Term policies, involving no savings, generally have no cash
surrender value.

The nonforfeiture values of a policy are in terms of its value
in cash or insurance if the policy is dropped because an individual
person cannot or does not choose to continue premium payments. He
may take the cash surrender value of the policy. He may continue the
policy by borrowing on its loan value to pay the premiums. He may
take extended-term insurance providing the original amount of protection for a specified term. Or he may take a paid-up policy on the
original plan for a reduced amount. In the two latter choices, the cash
surrender value is used to buy as much insurance as possible.

The choice of nonforfeiture value that the family makes is
related to its reason for surrendering the policy. For instance, a $1,000
straight life plan bought at 20 years of age would have roughly the
following values 20 years later:

$200 cash surrender or loan value;
$1,000 of insurance on straight life plan by continuing present
policy about 12 years through borrowing on cash value to
make premium payments;[3]

---

[3] If the loan has not finally been repaid at the time that the policy comes due or
is surrendered, the loan plus accumulated interest charges will be subtracted from the
face value or cash surrender value, as the case may be.

$1,000 of insurance on extended term plan for about 20 years
(paid-up); or

$450 of insurance on a whole life plan in a paid-up policy.

If the family no longer needs the insurance or if it has great need for cash, it will take the cash surrender value. If the family hopes that it can later make premium payments and retain the old policy, it will borrow on its loan value in order to continue the policy in force. After about twelve years, the cash surrender value will have been absorbed by this method. The extended term policy guarantees as large an amount of insurance for a longer period. The paid up whole life plan guarantees a much smaller amount of insurance permanently.

When the family wishes to change to a smaller or larger policy or another type of policy, it should first try to convert its old policy to the new one in order to avoid a new medical examination and to avoid the first year or so when a new policy has no cash value. Premium rates may also be lower by conversion. If conversion is not possible, it is most prudent to obtain the new policy before surrendering the old one.

PLANNING THE FAMILY'S LIFE INSURANCE PROGRAM

Average expenditure on personal insurance totalled about $300 for all urban families and single consumers in 1961, according to the Survey of Consumer Expenditures. Almost half went for life insurance and almost half for Social Security with small amounts for other types of personal insurance. The proportion spent on insurance generally increased somewhat with income. But families at a given income level spent about the same amount whether they had few or several members.

How Much Should a Family Buy? · Facts about life insurance are only a starting place for the family in determining how much life insurance to buy. How much depends on its *need* for life insurance compared with its *ability* to pay for it.

The family's need for life insurance is determined first by the *necessary expenses* of the family after this person's death. Expenses include the burial expenses and final medical expenses for any member and, for some members, the replacement of his or her contribution to family support from his earnings or services in the home. In specific terms, money is needed for the readjustment period, rearing the children, support of the widow thereafter, and perhaps for inheritance and estate taxes in order to conserve the estate. The amount needed depends on the number and ages of the dependents that the individual would leave, their health, the family's standard of living, including the level of education considered necessary, debt left at his death, and the present price level and future changes in it.

It must be admitted that the financial loss to the family is unequal at death of different members. Death of a child or elderly member necessitates burial expenses and perhaps final medical expenses, but probably reduces family expenses over a longer period— and it certainly does not reduce family income. The mother's services are generally considered essential in a home with young children; therefore, money to help replace her services for a few years is particularly useful. Generally speaking, the bulk of insurance should probably be placed on the husband's life in order to replace his earnings, at least partially. Furthermore, insurance purchased on the life of other members may be jeopardized by the husband's death unless the insurance contains a payor clause, providing that it becomes paid-up at the death or disability of the person paying for it.

The family's need for life insurance also depends on *other resources* that will be available for meeting necessary expenses after the person's death. The family may carry a large amount of job-required insurance, such as Social Security and group insurance. Veterans insurance or Workman's Compensation may be provided. The family may have sizable savings in cash funds and savings bonds and investments in the home and other assets on which it can draw in case of death. The family may be able to pay the necessary expenses from income of other earners. For instance, the father's income may pay death expenses for the child, or money may be borrowed. The mother and older children may take jobs if the father dies. Or the family may have wealthy relatives or other sources of help.

Various methods simultaneously may be part of the family's financial plan. While the death of the father is not likely to occur during the child-rearing years, the family realizes that it might occur and buys some insurance as a protection against the great financial loss. In addition, it makes some investments in other directions, perhaps in a home, from which it could withdraw its equity if necessary. At the same time, the parents may realize that the father's death would require further adjustments, with a cut in the family's level of living and the mother taking a paid job or being forced to seek some family assistance, particularly while the children are small.

Unfortunately, the family's need for life insurance may be high, but its ability to pay for it may be low because of the size of *income* in relation to necessary *current expenses*. The proportion of a given income spent for current consumption is affected by the size of the income and by the size and composition of the family, its standard of living, and its valuation of present needs contrasted with future needs. Also the family may consider that a sizable part of its funds not needed for daily expenses should be used for *other types of insurance* (than life insurance) and for other *savings and investments* such as:

Other types of insurance—
Auto insurance against liability or damage to the asset.
Health insurance against medical costs and decreased earnings.
Property insurance against loss or damage to the house and furnishings, and householder's liability.
Annuities and retirement plans because of declining earning capacity in old age.
Savings and investments for—
Large desirable expenditures such as education of children, vacations, purchase of household equipment, auto, home.
Emergency expenses not covered by insurance, such as ordinary repairs, medical care.
Periods of increased costs when children or aged parents are supported or when price levels increase.
Periods of decreased earnings not covered by insurance or incompletely covered, such as those due to disability, unemployment, maternity leave, decreased rates of pay or profit, or decreased return on investment.

The first approach to any financial hazard is the use of particular care, personal and public, to prevent its occurrence. Individual care in daily living as well as traffic safety programs and other public programs help prevent premature death. Beyond that, a family may decide to ignore a particular hazard, feeling that it is extremely unlikely to occur, its cost would be slight, or that pressure on income makes specific protection impractical. Few families can afford all the insurance they need, so must select protection against the most disastrous events that are likely to occur. Of course, some persons with both high need for insurance and the ability to pay for it do purchase little insurance because of carelessness or disregard for the possibility of death.

Since high needs for life insurance are not always matched by high ability to pay for it, a family should generally purchase no more than it can afford to keep in force over a period of time. Life insurance can provide protection only if it is in force at the person's death. Frequent purchase and surrender of policies defeats the purpose while raising insurance costs because of the absence of a cash surrender value during the first few years.

As changes occur through time in the need for life insurance and ability to pay for it, the family should revise its insurance program to keep it up-to-date for the current situation. Purchase of several policies rather than one large one enables the family to drop one occasionally as it becomes desirable. By the time of retirement, when the need for protecting young children and the middle-aged wife has passed, the parents may take the cash value of their policies in the form of an annuity for their old age.

Developing a Program · The first step in developing a life insurance program is to estimate the income necessary for family support after the person's death. Supposing the Whipple family with husband and wife 30 years old and three small children currently spends $5,000 a year for living. They might estimate that the widow and children could live at about the same level on $5,000 a year while the children are young and on $6,000 when education costs increase (Table 17–7). The widow alone might require $2,500 or less thereafter.

The second step is to estimate sources of income for family support after the earner's death. For most families, Social Security benefits provide a sizable part of this family income—approximately $3,600 a year in this case while the children are under 18 years old. The family objective might be, then, to supplement this amount with $1,000 annually from insurance and investments. Current earnings by the widow and children would supply additional amounts, or the level of living may have to be reduced.

Using Table 17–8 to estimate the estate necessary at the husban's death to supply $1,000 for final expenses and burial plus income of $1,000 annually to the widow and children thereafter, we find that the amount declines from approximately $20,000 at age 30 to $15,000 at age 60. But this estate may be provided partly from savings and investments. If the family accumulates about $300 a year in cash value of a company retirement plan, home, and other investments, the life

TABLE 17–7. Example of Development of a Family Life Insurance Program [1] [Family of husband and wife, age 30, and 3 young children that currently spends $5,000 a year for consumption]

ITEM	AGE OF FAMILY HEAD			
	30	40	50	60 [2]
Annual income for widow and children .	$ 5,000	$ 6,000	$ 2,500	$ 2,200
Minimum Social Security benefits .	3,600	3,600	..	1,200
Current earnings by widow & children	400	1,400	1,500	..
Insurance and investments	1,000	1,000	1,000	1,000
Estate needed at stated age to provide $1,000 final expenses and $1,000 annual income thereafter	20,000	19,000	17,000	15,000
Cash value of company retirement plan, home, and other investments	1,000	4,000	7,000	10,000
Life insurance estate needed	19,000	15,000	10,000	5,000
Plan for life insurance estate at death of husband	19,000	15,000	12,000	12,000
Group life insurance (term plan) .	6,000	6,000	6,000	6,000
Ordinary life insurance:				
Straight life plan	6,000	6,000	6,000	6,000
10-year term plan	3,000	3,000	..	..
10-year term plan	4,000	..	..	..
Life insurance estate at death of wife to provide $1,000 final expenses and $3,000 annual income for remaining years before age 35:				
5-year decreasing term plan	14,000 [3]	..	..	..
Approximate annual cost of insurance .	251	186	150	150
$6,000 group life insurance	42	42	42	42
$6,000 straight life plan	108	108	108	108
$3,000 10-year term plan	24	36	..	..
$4,000 10-year term plan	32	..	..	..
5-year decreasing term on wife . . .	45	..	..	..

[1] Assumes all amounts in terms of present price levels; Social Security benefits at present amounts based on average taxed earnings of $4,800; future income discounted at 5% annually; lower premiums for life insurance purchased in units larger than $1,000; term insurances renewable and convertible.

[2] Approximate situation if husband and wife live to retire at 65:

Annual Social Security benefits to husband and wife	$2,400–$3,000
Cash value of savings	$ 15,000
Company retirement plan and other investments	$ 12,000
Cash value of $6,000 straight life insurance plan	$ 3,000
Husband's group life insurance in force (annual premium about $40) . .	$ 2,000
Annual Social Security benefit to elderly widow	$1,300–$1,700

[3] Providing about $14,000 when wife is 30.0 years old; $12,000 at 31.0; $9,000 at 32.0; $7,000 at 33.0; $4,000 at 34.0; and zero at 35.0.

TABLE 17–8. Present Value to Family of Annual Income of $1,000 Received for 1 to 60 Years

YEARS OF INCOME	DISCOUNTED AT ANNUAL INTEREST RATE OF	
	3%	5%
1	$ 971	$ 952
2	1,913	1,859
3	2,829	2,723
4	3,717	3,546
5	4,580	4,329
10	8,530	7,722
15	11,938	10,380
20	14,877	12,462
25	17,413	14,094
30	19,600	15,372
35	21,487	16,374
40	23,115	17,159
45	24,519	17,774
50	25,730	18,256
55	26,774	18,633
60	27,676	18,929

insurance estate needed declines from $19,000 at age 30 to $5,000 at age 60.

To provide the necessary life insurance estate, the husband will purchase the maximum group insurance policy (assumed to be $6,000 in this case), probably at his place of employment, and will carry the maximum amount of veterans life insurance for which he is eligible (assumed to be none for this husband). To these he may add privately purchased ordinary life insurance, part as permanent insurance and part in term plans to be dropped when no longer necessary, as follows:

$6,000 straight life plan—in force until retirement;
$3,000 10-year term plan—in force from age 30–49;
$4,000 10-year term plan—in force from age 30–39.

Because the loss of the mother's services while the children are small would be a calamity for this family, a 5-year decreasing term plan on her life might be added at age 30 to provide $1,000 for final expenses plus the equivalent at her death of $3,000 yearly income for the remaining years if her death occurs before she is 35. The cash receivable would thus decline from about $14,000 when she is 30 to about $4,000 when she reaches 34, and to zero when she reaches 35.

From time to time through the years, the family will review the program to see that it remains practicable. If the husband lives to retirement at 65, the husband and wife will receive about $2,400–$3,000 annually in Social Security benefits. The husband's life insurance needs will be small thereafter if savings have accumulated as planned to about $12,000. His group life policy may be reduced to $2,000 for the same annual premium; and he may use the $3,000 cash value in the straight life policy for retirement income. After the husband's death, the widow alone will receive about $1,300–$1,700 annually in Social Security benefits.

Settlement Options · At the death of the insured, the policy benefits may be paid to the beneficiary in a lump sum or in four other basic ways, as follows:

The *interest* option provides that the lump sum be left with the insurance company to a certain date or until the beneficiary requests it, with the interest accumulating or being paid annually. On a $10,000 policy at 2½ percent interest, $250 could be paid annually or left to accumulate to the payment date.

The *amount* option provides a stated amount of money each month until the money and interest are paid out. For a $10,000 policy, monthly payments of $100 could be made for a little beyond 9 years.

The *time* option provides a monthly income for a specified period of years. The $10,000 policy would provide an income for 20 years of $53 a month.

The *lifetime income* option provides a regular income for the beneficiary's remaining lifetime. The monthly amount is related to the age at which payments start, and is about $50 for a woman 62 years old with payments starting immediately on a $10,000 policy.

The method of payment of policy benefits may be determined by the purchaser and set forth in the policy. If this is not done, the beneficiary may, at the time of settlement, decide on an optional method on a supplementary contract, rather than a cash settlement. It should also be noted that one of these options might be chosen for use of the cash surrender value of the policy at retirement or earlier, generally resulting in higher returns than by purchasing an annuity with the cash value.

The interest option is most useful to the beneficiary who does not have high present need for funds, but expects to have higher needs later or wishes to conserve the estate for others. The lifetime income option is generally most useful to a beneficiary who is older, unless the insurance amount is very large. For the widow left with young children, the amount and time options provide a stated amount of income for a stated period so that it cannot be dissipated by careless use or unwise investments.

However, these four options introduce an element of inflexibility into policy benefits which does not exist when a lump sum payment is received. The beneficiary may need funds immediately to pay funeral and final medical expenses for the insured. There may be unanticipated needs of the beneficiaries through the years due to medical care, education, or a rising price level which make it highly desirable to use more than a specified amount. When the options pay 2½–3 percent interest, more may be earned by investing in savings bonds and other equally safe forms. Early repayment of the home mortgage and other debts may result in considerable savings of interest. Generally speaking, when the total estate is modest, the insurance amount should be paid in a lump sum, with the beneficiary instructed ahead of time about the necessity for care in its use.

Certain life insurance policies, such as the family income policy, may provide that the face value of the policy be paid at the end of the income period, some years hence. If it is important to obtain the face amount of the policy at death, the beneficiary accepts the face amount discounted for the number of remaining years. If income payments are receivable only 5 years, the face amount of $1,000 is discounted to $863 (at 3 percent interest) receivable at death; but the amount is only $554 at death if income payments are receivable 20 years (Table 17–9). The present value is even less under a 5 percent rate of discount.

Life Insurance as an Investment · Only the cash value of a life insurance policy is entered on the family's balance sheet of assets and liabilities and needs to be considered as an investment. This sum is reasonably liquid since it can be obtained as a loan or cash surrender value. The investment is generally safe because of the methods of operation of insurance companies and regulation of them in many states, although the buyer needs to beware of unreliable operators. Investment in life insurance is simple in comparison with many other types. The lump-sum death benefit is generally not subject to federal income taxes. However, earnings on funds invested in life insurance

TABLE 17–9. Present Value to Family of Sum of $1,000 Received 5 to 50 Years Hence

YEARS BEFORE SUM IS DUE	DISCOUNTED AT ANNUAL INTEREST RATE OF	
	3%	5%
5	$863	$784
10	744	614
15	642	481
20	554	377
25	478	295
30	412	231
35	355	181
40	307	142
45	264	111
50	228	87

are relatively low. Obviously, investment in insurance enjoys no capital gains and is not a hedge against inflation.

QUESTIONS

1. How widespread is ownership of life insurance policies?
2. Why is life insurance purchased? What is the fundamental feature of all insurance?
3. Differentiate among the following plans of life insurance: the term plan, the straight life plan, the limited payment life plan, and the endowment plan. What are the particular advantages of each?
4. Describe a family income policy, a family policy, and a modified life policy. What is the particular advantage of each?
5. How does ordinary life insurance differ from group insurance? Credit insurance? Industrial insurance? What companies sell these types?
6. What types of life insurance are sold by other insurers than legal reserve life insurance companies? How important are these?
7. What is the most important type of life insurance? Describe it in detail. What plans are most commonly sold under this type?
8. What factors affect the premium rate that is paid for life insurance by a specific person?
9. What are the three basic factors determining premium rates?
10. Differentiate between participating premiums and nonparticipating.

11. What is the meaning of nonforfeiture values of life insurance? What are the various types? Who would choose each?

12. How do cash or loan values of life insurance policies grow?

13. How much do families spend on life insurance?

14. How much life insurance should a family buy?

15. On whose life should the family buy insurance? Why?

16. What steps are taken in developing a life insurance program for a family?

17. Analyze and criticize the program developed for the Whipple family.

18. Construct a program for a hypothetical family that is quite different than the Whipple family.

19. What is the meaning of the present value of future income? Why is it important?

20. What settlement options are available for proceeds of a life insurance policy at death? What is the advantage of each?

21. What are the special advantages of taking the proceeds in a lump sum?

22. What is the meaning of the present value of a lump sum received in the future? What is its importance?

23. How well does life insurance meet each of the major investment objectives? Is this the major purpose of insurance?

SUGGESTIONS FOR FURTHER READING

Flitcraft Incorporated. *Flitcraft Compend.* New York, latest edition. Data on life insurance companies and premium rates for different policies.

Huebner, Solomon S. and Black, Kenneth, Jr. *Life Insurance.* New York: Appleton-Century-Crofts, 1959, 6th ed. (or later edition when published).

Institute of Life Insurance. *Life Insurance Fact Book.* New York, latest edition.

Maclean, Joseph B. *Life Insurance.* New York: McGraw-Hill, 1962, 9th ed. (or later edition when published).

"Therefore my age is as a lusty winter,
Frosty, but kindly."
—As You Like It

Retirement Annuities / 18

- · PLANNING AHEAD FOR
  RETIREMENT INCOME
- · DECIDING ON RETIREMENT
  BENEFIT PLANS

The necessity of financial planning for old age is emphasized by the high likelihood of living beyond the earning years. Among men who are now 25 years old, about 68 percent will be living at age 65, 41 percent at age 75, and 14 percent at age 85. Of the women who are now 25 years old, about 80 percent will be living at age 65, 57 percent at age 75, and 24 percent at age 85.

Persons who have already attained 65 years of age have an even greater chance of surviving to advanced age. Among men who have attained age 65, 60 percent will be living at 75, and 20 percent will be living at 85. Of the women who have attained age 65, 72 percent will be living at 75, and 30 percent at age 85. To think in terms of older grandparents now 75 years old, 34 percent of the men and 42 percent of the women will attain 85.

The length of the retirement period is also important. Average remaining lifetime at 65 years of age is now 13 years for white men and 16 years for white women (Table 18–1). Average remaining lifetime at 65 years of age for nonwhites is almost as great—12 years for men and 15 years for women. These figures are 1 year longer for white men, 2 years longer for nonwhite men, and 4 years longer for women, both white and nonwhite, than at the beginning of the century. The great increase in life expectancy in this century, about which we hear, has been effected with small extension of life for the elderly, sizable extension for young adults, but great increases in expected lifetime of the newborn because of the radical decline in deaths among infants and young children.

Thus, expected lifetime at birth, now 68 years for white males and 74 years for white females, is 19 years longer for males and 23 years longer for females than at the beginning of the century. Life expectancy at birth is currently 7 years shorter for nonwhites than for whites, presumably due to poorer average living conditions and medical care. However, life expectancy at birth has increased decidedly more for nonwhites than for whites during this century, and is now 28 years longer for nonwhite males and 32 years longer for nonwhite females than at the beginning of the century.

We might also note that the female is more durable than the male, and increasingly so. Life expectancy at birth is greater for females than for males, and the difference has increased since the beginning of the century for both whites and nonwhites. Life expectancy at age 65 is also greater for women than for men, and, again, the difference has increased since the beginning of the century for both whites and nonwhites.

An important method of providing money for the later non-

TABLE 18–1. Average Remaining Lifetime at Selected Ages

ATTAINED AGE	REMAINING LIFETIME			
	WHITE MALE	WHITE FEMALE	NONWHITE MALE	NONWHITE FEMALE
0	68	74	61	67
1	68	75	63	68
10	60	66	55	60
25	46	52	41	45
35	36	42	32	36
45	27	33	24	28
55	19	24	18	21
65	13	16	12	15
75	8	9	9	11
85	4	5	5	6

SOURCE: U. S. National Center for Health Statistics, *The Facts of Life and Death*, Public Health Service Publication No. 600, Revised 1965, p. 22 (data for 1963).

earning years is through retirement annuities. An annuity provides an annual or monthly benefit payment to the annuitant from a stated date for a fixed number of years or until his death. The worker purchases an annuity contract to provide income for himself in his old age when he can no longer earn, whereas he purchases life insurance to protect his dependents in case he should die during his earning years while he is supporting them.

Although most people purchase annuities to provide income during the retirement years, some with special needs purchase annuities that will make regular income payments to themselves or others during earlier years. A medical examination is not necessary for the purchase of an annuity unless the contract has a life insurance feature added, since the insurance company has no interest in selecting the healthiest people for this type of contract. However, there may be some tendency for self-selection by the most vigorous. Because of their greater longevity, women pay higher rates for annuities.

PLANNING AHEAD FOR RETIREMENT INCOME

Families plan ahead in a variety of ways for retirement income. Savings are made during the earning years and invested in savings accounts and savings bonds, an owned home or other real estate, corporate stocks and bonds, and in an owned business. The accumulation at retirement is then used for support in the later years. A few elderly persons manage to live on their current investment income received as interest, rents, dividends, and profits, and thus maintain their principal intact. Others sell assets from time to time as necessary to supplement current income.

About 70 million employed persons, more than nine out of ten, are covered by Social Security. Of the 50 million who have previously worked and established wage credits, 11 million are retired workers currently receiving monthly benefits. In addition to Social Security, a large proportion of workers are now covered by employer pension plans, and many individuals purchase private annuities.

Employer Pension Plans · About 36 million persons are covered by employer pension plans, including 8 million under public plans of state, local, and federal government and railroad retirement systems, and 28 million under pension plans of private employers (Table 18–2). Private pension plans are a phenomenon of the last 30 years when employees sought fringe benefits and employers sought to de-

TABLE 18–2. Number of Persons Covered by Pension Plans and Annuities

TYPE OF PLAN	MILLIONS OF PERSONS
Total under pension plans	36
Public pension plans	8
Private pension plans, noninsured*	21
Private pension plans, insured	7.0
Group annuities	5.8
Deposit administration	3.4
Deferred annuity	2.3
Other pension plans	1.4
Individual policy pension trusts	.8
Other plans	.6
Total with insured private annuities	1.7
Individual annuities	1.1
Supplementary contracts	.5

* Not underwritten by an insurance company. Insured plans and annuities are underwritten by an insurance company.

SOURCES: Institute of Life Insurance, *Life Insurance Fact Book 1966*, pp. 32–36; *Social Security Bulletin*, April 1966; Annual Reports of Civil Service Commission and Railroad Retirement Board and Census of Governments (data as of end of 1965).

crease rates of labor turnover. The number of persons covered by these plans is now 7 times the 4 million covered in 1940.

Private pension plans include pay-as-you-go, reserve, individual employer, multi-employer, union-administered, and nonprofit organization plans, and railroad retirement plans supplementing the Federal railroad retirement program. Employers make the total contributions to the majority of plans. Of the three-fourths of private pension plans that are not underwritten by a legal reserve insurance company, employers make 88 percent of the contributions and employees make the remainder. Of the one-fourth of the plans that are underwritten by insurance companies, employers make 80 percent of the contributions. Employer contributions are a much smaller proportion under many public pension plans.

Employers are not taxed on the sums they contribute to pension funds—that is, the sums are treated like wages, other labor costs, and other costs of production. The worker is taxed on the sum that he contributes. While the worker pays taxes on retirement income from the employer's contribution, the retired worker is usually in a low tax bracket at that time, so pays lower taxes than if he had received the amount in wages while he was working. Employer contributions to private pension plans are labor costs to the company and presumably could be paid in current wages at no greater expense. Such contributions are, then, deferred wages. Many employers who prefer pension plans because they help to reduce labor turnover obtain mixed benefits—reduced turnover among older workers, but small reduction among younger.

Many private pensions are financed largely on a pay-as-you-go basis out of company profits or union receipts during the worker's retirement years. In such cases, workers may be disappointed in their retirement benefits when plants close, companies fail, or union membership declines. Accumulated reserve funds now average about $2,600 per covered worker under noninsured plans and $3,700 under insured plans. Since many plans are fairly new and there are many young workers, these sums are expected to be larger at the time of retirement. However, consideration needs to be given to whether adequate assets are maintained toward future benefits. Concern for safety of these funds has resulted in proposals for Federal reinsurance of private pension plans, along the lines of the Federal Deposit Insurance Corporation, with employers paying a special premium for this reinsurance, as do banks. The portion of the fund that is held in securities of the employer company is of particular significance since the company's decline or failure may result in decline in pension rights as well as loss of employment.

Insured pension plans of private employers are handled in several ways. Deposit administration group annuity plans cover almost half of all people under insured pension plans. In such plans, a single fund is set up for all employees in the pension group and, as each employee retires, money is withdrawn from the fund to purchase an annuity for him. Deferred group annuity plans cover about a third of persons under insured plans. This method provides for the purchase of a paid-up annuity benefit each year for each worker. About a tenth of persons are covered by individual policy pension trusts, frequently used by smaller firms and involving the purchase of a whole life or endowment policy for each employee.

A study of private pension plans showed that the normal retirement age in most plans is 65. Many plans require a minimum of 10 or 15 years of service in order to receive any monthly benefits at retirement. Amounts of benefits to be paid generally vary with years of service and sometimes also with rates of compensation. Under many plans, private benefits are reduced by all or part of Social Security benefits receivable, so that Social Security provides the greater part of retirement income. Private plan benefits commonly begin to approach the amounts of expected Social Security benefits only for workers with high earnings and long service.[1]

Benefits to the survivors of a worker who dies before retirement differ considerably under various plans. There may be no benefits if it is a noncontributory plan, that is, the worker has made no direct contribution. Or a sizable amount of life insurance protection may be receivable, if purchased along with the investment in a pension. Or a refund may be made of the worker's direct contribution to the pension plan with, in some cases, modest interest added or cash-surrender charge deducted.

Benefits vary from plan to plan for workers who leave an employer before retirement age because of disability, individual discharge, mass layoff, or movement to other jobs. If the worker has not met the minimum service requirement of 5 to 15 years for retirement benefits, he has no such benefits due from this company when he retires at a later date. At the time of separation he generally receives the total amount of his own direct contributions to the pension fund, sometimes with a small amount of accumulated interest. Any contribution that his employer has been making on his behalf is lost to him forever.

Only when the employer's contribution is "vested" in the employee does the worker have a claim on it, in cash or retirement benefits, at early death or early separation from the company. Some pension plans provide for partial vesting after 10 or 15 years on a job; others provide for vesting only at the time of retirement. A very few pension plans provide for immediate full vesting. A special case is that of the nonprofit Teachers Insurance and Annuity Association which provides for instant vesting of all employer contributions toward a pension for the teacher. However, many teachers are not covered under this system, and many who are presumably covered move into and out of teaching.

Workers are extremely mobile today as they seek better opportunities or are forced to seek new jobs because of rapid technological changes and other reasons. Average service on one job of about 5 years means that a worker may have 8 employers during a working lifetime. While he may have been continuously covered under various pension plans, he may thus fail to qualify for a pension from any of

[1] Donald J. Staats, "Normal Benefits Under Private Pension Plans," *Monthly Labor Review*, July 1965, pp. 857–863. Analysis of reports filed with U. S. Department of Labor by private pension plans covering more than 25 workers on plans current in Winter, 1962–1963.

his employers.[2] Estimates that only a third to a half of those covered by private pension plans will actually benefit at retirement have resulted in a proposal for "portable" pensions so that the workers may carry his pension rights with him from employer to employer. Another proposal is for a "clearinghouse" that would record the pension credits in years of service and contributions by the worker and his several employers, and would make the single monthly payment due at his retirement. Social Security is the one fully portable pension system available to the worker today.

Private Annuities · About 1.7 million persons are covered by insured private annuities, two-thirds of them purchased as individual annuities and one-third resulting from supplementary contracts that provide income from the proceeds of life insurance. Regular income is one of the options that may be selected when death benefits are receivable from life insurance; or the cash value of a life insurance policy may be converted at retirement or another date into an annuity.

An annuity may be purchased by *instalment payments* over a period of years with benefits *deferred* for a stated time or to a stated age. An annuity purchased for a *lump sum* may make *immediate* benefit payments or deferred payments, according to the contract selected.

The deferred annuity may include certain benefits before the annuity benefits start, in case the annuitant dies or wishes to withdraw his money earlier. However, a *true deferred annuity* starts benefits at the stated time, but has no cash or loan value and no death benefits earlier. Obviously it is the cheapest kind for a given amount of annuity benefits, but few people would be willing to accept the risk of loss of premiums. A *retirement income annuity* has a cash or loan value before annuity benefits start, as well as a death benefit payable if death occurs earlier. The amount equals the premium payments, less a loan charge or cash-surrender charge.

A *retirement income policy* includes a sizable amount of life insurance benefit at death before retirement, usually about $1,000 per $10 of monthly annuity, as well as a cash or loan value equal to the premiums paid (less a charge) before benefits start. Obviously, it provides more benefits than do the true deferred annuity and the

---

2 Median years on the current job increase with age to 12 years for men 45–54 and 16 years for men 55 and over, and 16 years for single women workers 45 and over. See Harvey R. Hamel, "Special Labor Force Report: Job Tenure of Workers, January 1966," *Monthly Labor Review*, January 1967, pp. 31–37.

retirement income annuity, so that its cost is higher, other circumstances being equal.

DECIDING ON RETIREMENT BENEFIT PLANS

When the worker approaches retirement age he is able to select the annuity contract most appropriate to his current circumstances and probable future. The worker takes into account his current dependents and other beneficiaries, as well as various financial resources for his retirement years. Foremost for most workers is an estimate of the minimum amount of Social Security benefits receivable for the husband and wife together and for either one alone. If they own a home, they may continue to live in it, and draw on current income or principal from any other investments they have. Or they may convert part of these assets into cash to purchase a private annuity, and may convert the cash surrender value of life insurance policies into an annuity, since the primary need is now for retirement income for the earner and wife rather than protection of young children.

Workers who have the self-discipline to make regular savings and investments during the earning years may gain considerably by purchasing an annuity for a lump sum at the time of retirement rather than by instalment payments during the earning years on a private annuity or pension plan. Interest and other earnings on personal investment are higher than the 1–3 percent rates generally received on instalment payments. Furthermore, personal investments in noncash forms are likely to rise in value with rising price levels, whereas instalment investments in retirement plans do not.

Supposing a man has a total of $20,000 at retirement. Investing it at 4 percent provides an annual income of $800 permanently, assuming that the principal remains intact. While income is modest, the special advantage is that he may draw on his invested capital as needed for unusual expenses, such as medical. Or he may use the $20,000 to purchase a fixed contract providing income of about $1,300 a year for 20 years. This involves a payment of both interest and principal so that there are no benefits remaining if he lives longer than the 20 years.

However, he may use the $20,000 to purchase a straight life annuity that pays him about $1,800 annually as long as he lives, with no payment after his death. The life annuity has the particular advantage over private investment and a contract for a fixed number of

FIGURE 18–1. Features of Annuities

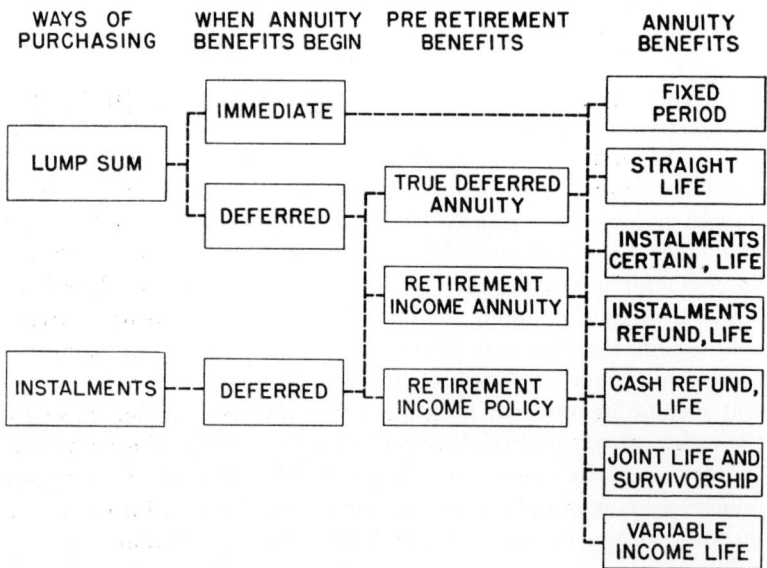

WAYS OF PURCHASING	WHEN ANNUITY BENEFITS BEGIN	PRE RETIREMENT BENEFITS	ANNUITY BENEFITS

```
                        ┌──────────────┐                                          ┌─────────────┐
                  ┌─────│  IMMEDIATE   │──────────────────────────────────────┐   │   FIXED     │
┌──────────────┐  │     └──────────────┘                                      ├───│   PERIOD    │
│   LUMP SUM   │──┤                        ┌────────────────┐                  │   └─────────────┘
└──────────────┘  │                    ┌───│ TRUE DEFERRED  │──┐               │   ┌─────────────┐
                  │     ┌──────────────┐│   │    ANNUITY     │  ├──────────────┼───│  STRAIGHT   │
                  └─────│   DEFERRED   │┤   └────────────────┘  │               │   │    LIFE     │
                        └──────────────┘│                       │               │   └─────────────┘
                                        │   ┌────────────────┐  │               │   ┌─────────────┐
                                        │   │  RETIREMENT    │  │               ├───│ INSTALMENTS │
                                        └───│ INCOME ANNUITY │──┤               │   │CERTAIN, LIFE│
                                            └────────────────┘  │               │   └─────────────┘
                                                                │               │   ┌─────────────┐
┌──────────────┐        ┌──────────────┐   ┌────────────────┐  │               ├───│ INSTALMENTS │
│ INSTALMENTS  │────────│   DEFERRED   │───│   RETIREMENT   │──┘               │   │ REFUND,LIFE │
└──────────────┘        └──────────────┘   │ INCOME POLICY  │                  │   └─────────────┘
                                           └────────────────┘                  │   ┌─────────────┐
                                                                               ├───│ CASH REFUND,│
                                                                               │   │    LIFE     │
                                                                               │   └─────────────┘
                                                                               │   ┌─────────────┐
                                                                               ├───│JOINT LIFE AND│
                                                                               │   │SURVIVORSHIP │
                                                                               │   └─────────────┘
                                                                               │   ┌─────────────┐
                                                                               └───│  VARIABLE   │
                                                                                   │ INCOME LIFE │
                                                                                   └─────────────┘
```

years of insuring that the annuitant cannot outlive his income, at the same time that it provides maximum permanent income. For most people, a combination of methods is most desirable with some money held in private investments that can be converted into cash in case of unforeseen need and some money placed in a life annuity that they cannot outlive. Of course, retirement benefits from Social Security and employer pension plans count as life annuities.

Selection of an annuity involves several decisions, including purchase by a lump sum or instalments, of an immediate annuity or of a deferred annuity which generally provides some preretirement benefits before annuity benefits begin (Figure 18–1). Finally, the purchaser of an annuity selects the contract under which annuity benefits are to be paid: an annuity contract for a fixed period, a life annuity providing a fixed income, or a life annuity with a variable income.

Annuity Contract for a Fixed Period · A contract for regular income payments during a specified number of years may be purchased from a life insurance company and from some banks under a savings payout plan. The annuitant receives the regular income as long as he lives and his beneficiary receives it for the remainder of the fixed period of years. Thereafter, no benefits are receivable since the principal and accumulated interest have been paid out. Approximate annual income per $1,000 invested in a fixed contract varies from $506 for 2 years to $47 for 30 years, as follows:

YEARS OF BENEFITS	ANNUAL INCOME PER $1,000 (AT 2½% INTEREST)
2	$506
5	210
10	111
15	79
20	63
25	53
30	47

Annual income from a fixed contract is enlarged by a shorter payout period, a higher rate of interest applied to the invested funds, and, obviously, a larger sum invested. Such a contract may be made with income payments starting at any age that one desires. If benefits are deferred, annual income will be larger. Death benefits from life insurance may be taken under this type of contract.

Life Annuity With Fixed Income · The life annuity pays a regular income from a stated date or age until the death of the annuitant. The premium charged for a life annuity depends on life expectancy, the earnings rate on investments of the insurance company, and the costs of operating the company. Because women have greater life expectancy, costs of a life annuity of a given amount are higher for them. The various life annuity contracts differ in the amount of retirement benefits and in the payments made after the death of the annuitant.

The *straight life annuity* begins regular benefits at a stated age and continues them until the death of the annuitant, when all benefits cease. An individual might receive benefits for only a month or for a long period of years, depending on how long he lives, and no benefits are paid on this contract thereafter. Since this is a simple life annuity with no additional features, it is the cheapest type. A straight life annuity of $10 a month starting at 65 years of age costs a man about $1,400 in a single premium at age 65 (Table 18–3). The annuity costs about half as much if purchased in instalments over 40 years because of the accumulation of interest.

The straight life annuity is generally most useful to the indi-

TABLE 18-3. Approximate Premiums for Life Annuity of $10 per Month for Male at Age 65, by Age at Issue of Contract

TYPE OF LIFE ANNUITY	LIFE ANNUITY OF $10 A MONTH AT AGE 65			APPROXIMATE IMMEDIATE LIFE ANNUITY PER MONTH FOR $10,000 PREMIUM AT AGE 65
	SINGLE PREMIUM AT AGE 65	ANNUAL PREMIUM TO AGE 65 FOR CONTRACT ISSUED AT AGE—		
		25	45	
Straight life	$1,400	$18	$51	$72
Instalments certain or guaranteed:				
10 years	1,500	19	54	67
20 years	1,900	24	69	53
Instalment refund	1,600	21	58	63
Cash refund	1,700	22	61	59
Joint life and survivorship*	1,700	22	61	59

* Payable until death of second spouse; wife same age as husband at time of purchase.

vidual who has no one else to support and wishes to maximize his annual income while he lives, even though he leaves no estate for a beneficiary. For a total premium of $10,000, he can secure a monthly income of $72 as long as he lives. The larger annual income is possible through use of the individual's premiums and the interest on them, plus the excess premiums of those who die early, that is, before receiving benefits equal to their premium payments. The extra premiums of those who die early are thus used to support fellow annuitants who live long, rather than being left to a beneficiary or making extra profits for the insurance company.

The *instalments certain or guaranteed annuity* provides benefits from a stated age to death of the annuitant and, if the annuitant dies early, regular payments to a beneficiary for the remainder of the guaranteed period, likely to be 10 or 20 years. The instalments certain annuity is slightly more expensive than a straight life annuity if the guaranteed period is only 10 years, but is a third more costly for a 20-year guarantee. The instalments certain annuity is particularly useful to the individual who has special responsibilities to meet over the next 10 or 20 years after his retirement (such as the education of children), which he will meet out of the annuity if he lives, or during the guaranteed period if he dies earlier.

The *instalment refund annuity* provides income during the lifetime of the annuitant and, if he dies early, regular instalments continue to his beneficiary until total benefits equal his total premium payments. This type, therefore, provides some protection for beneficiaries and costs less than the annuity with a 20-year guarantee. It has the advantage of insuring that the annuitant or his beneficiary will receive at least as much as he has paid for the annuity.

The *cash refund annuity* makes benefit payments during the lifetime of the annuitant and, if he dies early, pays his beneficiary a lump sum equal to the difference between total benefits and total premiums. Since the refund is paid in a lump sum, it costs somewhat more than an instalment refund annuity where further interest earnings are accumulating.

The *joint life and survivorship annuity* pays benefits to a couple as long as either spouse lives. It is about as costly as a cash refund annuity; but the cost is lowered if the contract provides that benefits be reduced to two-thirds or one-half on the death of one spouse. When both spouses have died, there are no further benefits, regardless of how long they have lived. This type of annuity is particularly useful for a couple wanting to insure that income continue to the end of the life of both partners.

Life Annuity With Variable Income · Since a conventional life annuity pays a fixed amount each year until death, it cannot compensate for rising prices of consumer goods during a future inflationary period or for generally rising levels of living with increased productivity of the economy. The average man who purchases an annuity at age 65 has 13 years to watch his retirement income decline in value if long-term trends continue. A woman has longer. Furthermore, a man who purchases a private annuity at age 25 or places part of his current earnings or deferred earnings in an employer's pension plan has 46 years, on the average, to watch the erosion of value of his early investments.

Reserve funds of conventional annuities underwritten by insurance companies and trusteed pension accounts managed by commercial banks are placed largely in real estate mortgages, corporate bonds, and government obligations where earnings are moderate and fixed over a long period. The purpose has been to secure the funds against losses that might result from investment in securities that vary in income and in resale value.

In recent years over half of the states, including New York, have amended their regulation of insurance companies to permit them to sell *variable annuities*, usually group polices only. Premiums received by the insurance company are invested in corporate stocks or in a combination of stocks and bonds. Growth stocks are likely to be favored over the long run.

The purchaser of a variable annuity buys *variable units*, rather than a stated annuity amount as under a conventional contract. During retirement years, annuity benefits are based on the number of variable units that have been purchased in instalments over the previous years or in a lump sum. Each unit is given a value based on the relationship of value of the investment (in appreciation of stocks plus dividends on them) to the original investment. The annual benefit is computed by multiplying the number of units by the value of each unit.

Since the benefit from a variable annuity may be high in good years and low in bad years, this type should be purchased only by those who understand its nature and the vicissitudes of the stock market. Most useful, perhaps, is a fixed annuity plan to provide a set income for retirement years combined with a variable annuity to provide additional income during inflationary and growth periods. The individual family in making its decision needs to take into account the amount and nature of its other sources of income for retirement years—Social Security, cash forms, owned home, corporate stocks. The variable life annuity shares the unique advantage of all life annuities in that benefits are receivable throughout the remaining lifetime, whereas the individual might outlive his income from private investments or a contract for a fixed number of years.

QUESTIONS

1. What is the likelihood of a young adult living to retirement? What is the expected lifetime of those now sixty-five years old? How important are those expectations to financial plans?

2. How does the purpose of a retirement annuity differ from the purpose of life insurance?

3. What are the various ways that families accumulate funds ahead of time for their retirement years?

4. How widespread are employer pension plans today? Who contributes to these funds? When?

5. What are the special advantages to workers of employer pension plans?

6. What features of employer pension plans are of special importance to workers?

7. Why do people purchase private annuities from insurance companies?

8. Clarify each: lump sum or instalment purchase; immediate and deferred annuity. What is the particular advantage of each?

9. Differentiate preretirement benefits under the true deferred annuity, the retirement income annuity, and the retirement income policy.

10. At the time of retirement, what factors does the worker take into consideration in selecting the method of payout of annuity benefits?

11. Explain the annuity contract for a fixed period. What are the important advantages and disadvantages?

12. Why is it important to retain some investments in forms other than annuities?

13. What is a life annuity with fixed income? How does it differ from an annuity contract for a fixed period?

14. Compare the following life annuities: straight life, instalments certain, instalment refund, cash refund, and joint life and survivorship. Include special advantages of each.

15. Explain the development of variable annuities. What are their particular advantages? Particular disadvantages?

16. Consider retirement annuities in terms of the general investment objectives.

17. Construct a retirement income plan for a hypothetical couple 65 years old with a realistic accumulation of financial assets and physical disabilities.

18. Construct a retirement income plan for an unmarried person of sixty-five.

SUGGESTIONS FOR FURTHER READING

Bernstein, M. C. *The Future of Private Pensions.* New York: Macmillan, 1964.

Flitcraft Incorporated. *Flitcraft Compend.* New York, latest edition. Data on premium rates for different annuity plans.

President's Committee on Corporate Pension Funds and Other Retirement and Welfare Programs. *Public Policy and Private Pension Programs.* Washington, D.C.: Superintendent of Documents, 1965.

U. S. Bureau of Labor Statistics. *Labor Mobility and Private Pension Plans: A Study of Vesting, Early Retirement, and Portability Provisions.* Washington, D.C.: Superintendent of Documents, 1964.

——————. *Special Labor Force Reports,* latest reports.

——————. *Unfunded Private Pension Plans.* Washington, D.C.: Superintendent of Documents, 1964.

Investments
in / 19
Business

- · INDEPENDENT BUSINESS
- · CORPORATE STOCKS AND BONDS
- · THE PURCHASE OF STOCKS
- · INVESTMENT COMPANIES
- · INVESTMENT OBJECTIVES

Investments in business are made in independent businesses and corporations, and through investment companies, each method having special advantages. Business investments are not commonly held by families and single consumers, with only a sixth of consumer units having some equity in an independent business or profession, less having some common stocks, and a small proportion having shares in investment companies.[1]

Among eleven million business enterprises, 80 percent are sole proprietorships, 8 percent active partnerships, and 12 percent active corporations. While independent businesses comprise nine-tenths of the total number, corporations make eight-tenths of the sales and earn six-tenths of the net profits, as follows: [2]

---

[1] Board of Governors of the Federal Reserve System, *Survey of Financial Characteristics of Consumers*, 1966 (data for December 31, 1962).
[2] Treasury Department, Internal Revenue Service, *Statistics on Income*, 1963, U. S. Business Tax Returns.

ITEM	ALL	SOLE PROPRIE- TORSHIPS	ACTIVE PARTNER- SHIPS	ACTIVE CORPORA- TIONS
Percent of:				
Number of enterprises	100	80	8	12
Business receipts	100	15	6	79
Net profits	100	27	10	63

These data may be considered in another way—independent businesses do two-tenths of the business and make almost four-tenths of the profits.

Business tax returns give some indication, also, of the small average size of independent businesses, as contrasted with corporations, and their small net profits, as follows:

ITEM	SOLE PROPRIE- TORSHIPS	ACTIVE PARTNER- SHIPS	ACTIVE CORPORA- TIONS
Average business receipts.. ..	$19,900	$79,300	$761,800
Average net profits	2,600	9,400	40,900

INDEPENDENT BUSINESS

According to the Survey of Financial Characteristics of Consumers, 17 percent of all consumer units have equity in a farm or nonfarm business or profession in which they are active in management. Included are sole proprietorships, partnerships, and closely held corporations whose shares are owned entirely by an individual or family or other small group and are not publicly traded.

A tenth of consumer units headed by a person under 35 years of age have equity in their own business or profession, as do two-tenths of those 35–64 years old and a tenth of older units. Three percent of all consumer units consider building their own business as an important objective for making further savings. This includes 5 percent of units with a head under 35 years old, 3 percent at 35–54, and 2 percent at 55 and over.

Ownership of assets in their own business or profession is common among wealthier consumers. Two-thirds of those with incomes of $25,000–$100,000 have equity in such assets, and a third of those with incomes of $100,000 and over. Half of consumer units with accumulated wealth of $25,000 or more have equity in a private business or profession.

TABLE 19–1. Owner's Equity in Own Business or Profession [Mean equity for those having some equity]

AGE OF HEAD OF CONSUMER UNITS (FAMILIES AND SINGLE CONSUMERS)	MEAN EQUITY AT SELECTED 1962 INCOME LEVELS (BEFORE TAXES)—					
	ALL INCOMES	$7,500–$9,999	$10,000–$14,999	$15,000–$24,999	$25,000–$49,999	$50,000–$99,999
All ages	$23,000	$13,000	$19,000	$39,000	$ 97,000	$396,000
Under 35	8,000	5,000	15,000	..	..	..
35–54	24,000	11,000	20,000	29,000	91,000	502,000
35–44	20,000	..	..	..	..	..
45–54	28,000	..	..	..	..	..
55–64	29,000	27,000	18,000	61,000	104,000	304,000
65 and over ..	29,000	..	..	..	113,000	416,000

SOURCE: Dorothy S. Projector and Gertrude S. Weiss, *Survey of Financial Characteristics of Consumers,* Board of Governors of the Federal Reserve System, 1966, pp. 110–111, (data as of December 31, 1962). Means estimated on the basis of published data.

Generally speaking, an owner's equity in his business or profession increases with his age and with his income level (Table 19–1). When these two factors operate together, owner's equity averages $5,000 for young units with incomes of $7,500–$10,000, but equity averages over $100,000 for preretirement units with incomes of $25,000–$50,000. Clearly, the older owner has had more time for building equity. The relationship between income and equity is mutual, with higher income enabling the person to build his business, and higher equity resulting in higher income.

The concentration of an owner's financial interests in his business enterprise is indicated by the increase in owner equity in direct proportion to increases in the size of total wealth. The average owner's equity in his business approximates about half of the total in all assets—including the home, liquid assets, and investment assets, in addition to business equity.

Of the 9 million sole proprietorships, 37 percent are in agriculture, forestry, and fisheries (mostly agriculture); 24 percent in the services; 20 percent in wholesale and retail trade (largely retail); and 19 percent in all other industries. Of the active partnerships, totalling less than one million, 28 percent are in wholesale and retail trade (largely retail); 25 percent in finance, insurance, and real estate; 19 percent in services; 14 percent in agriculture, forestry, and fisheries; and 14 percent in all other industries.

Establishment of a sole proprietorship or small partnership is a common way of practicing certain professions such as medicine, dentistry, and law, and is frequently used also in accountancy, architecture, construction, fine and applied arts, and insurance and real estate where the major capital investment is in the worker's specialized education and experience rather than in plant and equipment. Many skilled craftsmen such as barbers, beauticians, shoe repairmen, and auto mechanics, establish independent shops with modest investment for marketing their skills.

While funds for necessary facilities and family support during the early period are required for establishment of a professional practice or craft shop, the necessary funds for facilities, equipment, and stocks are multiplied in fields such as agriculture, wholesale and retail trade, and manufacturing where the independent enterprise competes with many large concerns with heavy capital investment. Thus, a major handicap to the establishment of an independent enterprise for many people is the requirement of sizable funds.

In addition to the owner's equity, borrowed funds and credit are used when they can be obtained. Such additional funds are generally obtained more easily by an established business than by a new enterprise. A major cause of low income and failure of independent businesses is that they are undercapitalized. Failure rates are especially high among businesses less than five years old which account for half of all failures, according to Dun and Bradstreet. The large number of failing businesses with liabilities of less than $25,000 indicates the small size of many of them.

Surveys show lower average income for families dependent on self-employment earnings than for those dependent on wages and salary. Families with self-employment income only report average incomes of $5,800 in nonfarm self-employment and $3,800 in farm business, contrasted with a $7,000 average for wage and salary employees (Table 19–2). The nonfarm self-employed and the wage and salary workers average about $1,000 more income when they have additional income from investments and transfer payments, but farm operators average almost $1,000 less, probably due to semi-retirement.

Such data raise questions as to why families operate independent businesses when average incomes are lower than for employed people. First, the possibility of errors in reporting must be noted, especially for self-employed families that may overlook various cash receipts since they generally hire a cost accountant only for the preparation of tax returns.

An important reason for operating an independent enterprise is the greater opportunity for high income for those with superior

TABLE 19-2. Family Income in Self-Employment and Employment [Median money income before taxes]

ITEM	TOTAL	EARNINGS					NO EARNINGS
		WAGES OR SALARY ONLY	SELF-EMPLOYMENT INCOME ONLY			WAGES OR SALARY AND SELF-EMPLOYMENT INCOME	
			TOTAL*	NONFARM ONLY	FARM ONLY		
Median family income:							
Earnings only	$6,900	$7,000	$5,200	$5,800	$3,800	$6,700	..
Earnings and other income (transfer and investment) ..	7,800	7,900	5,300	6,800	3,000	8,700	..
Other income only	2,400	..	..	..	..	..	$2,400
Percent of families	100**	72	7	4	2	13	..
Earnings only	48	38	3	2	1	7	..
Earnings and other income (transfer and investment)	44	34	4	2	1	6	..
Other income only	8	..	..	..	..	..	8

* Includes a relatively small number of families reporting both nonfarm and farm self-employment income.
** Includes a relatively small number of families reporting no money income, not shown separately.
SOURCE: U. S. Bureau of the Census, *Current Population Reports*, Series P–60, No. 51, 1967, p. 27, (data for 1965),

FIGURE 19–1. Income Distributions of Self-Employed Families and Wage and Salary Families

FAMILIES WITH

SELF-EMPLOYMENT
INCOME ONLY

WAGES AND SALARY
INCOME ONLY

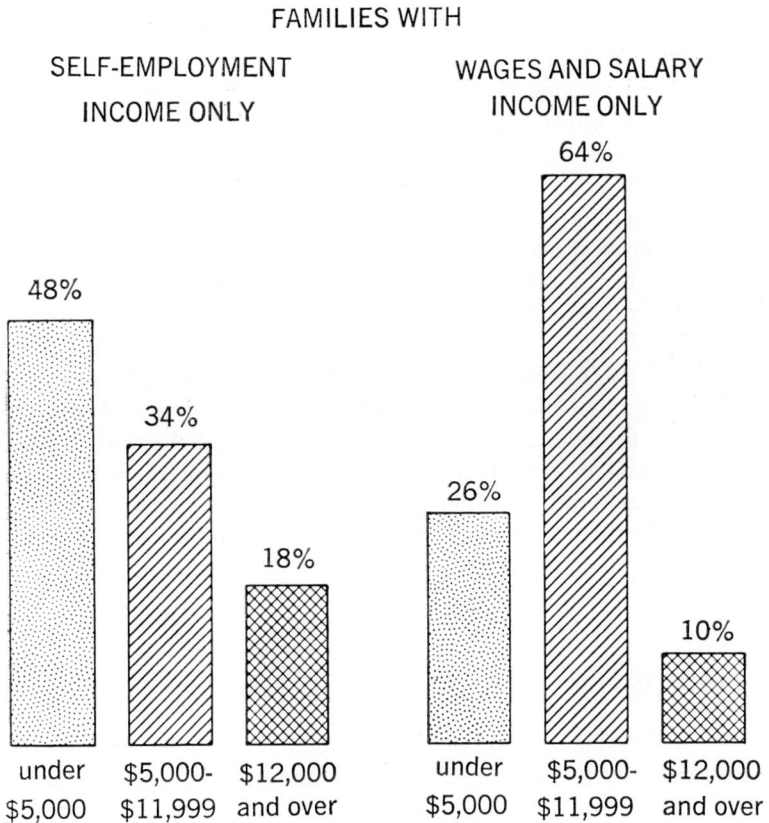

SOURCE: U. S. Bureau of the Census, data for 1965.

ability and vigor. The proportion with incomes of $12,000 and over is almost twice as large among families with self-employment income only as among those with wages and salary only—18 percent compared with 10 percent (Figure 19–1). At the same time, the self-employed generally accept more risk of earning low incomes and unstable incomes from year to year than do wage and salary workers in normal times.

Of course, some self-employed families with constant low incomes continue to operate independent enterprises because of ignorance of other opportunities or because they are earning the most they can. Family members can assist part-time in the family business when they could not obtain convenient paid work. Some operators lack the skills required for paid jobs, are aged or handicapped, or would otherwise be unemployed. They operate part-time or subsistence enterprises—they can "live off the farm" or "eat out of the store."

In addition, an independent enterprise offers special nonfinancial advantages that the operators recognize and employed workers envy. Chief among these are independence in decisions and hours of work, special incentives in working for oneself, the adventure of developing new lines of endeavor, and the achievement of building an enterprise. For elderly and financially independent persons, operation of a business may be chiefly an interesting activity. Those people who prefer to live on a farm or in a small community may operate a business because of the lack of paid employment locally available.

Nonfinancial advantages and potential financial advantages are considered by operators of independent business. Required is a realistic appraisal of personal qualifications, owned capital and opportunities for credit, the competitive situation, and alternatives available. Investment in their own business provides many owners with much greater returns on their funds and on their own services than they could otherwise obtain. Others could earn more on their funds by investing them in other ways, and could earn higher or more stable incomes as employees than as owners.

CORPORATE STOCKS AND BONDS

Thirty-one percent of all consumer units own some type of investment asset, including the most common type—publicly traded stocks, owned by 16 percent (Table 19-3). The percentage owning various investment assets is as follows:

ASSETS	PERCENT OWNING
Any investment assets	31
Publicly traded stock	16
Common stock	14
Mutual funds and other investment companies	5
Preferred stock	1
Share in investment clubs	1
Marketable securities other than stock	3
Mortgage assets	4
Investment real estate	11
Business not managed by unit	4
Company savings plans	4

TABLE 19–3. Investment Assets of Consumer Units, by Size of Wealth

ITEM	ALL UNITS	$1–$999	$1,000–$4,999	$5,000–$9,999	$10,000–$24,999	$25,000–$49,999	$50,000–$99,999	$100,000–$199,999	$200,000–$499,999	$500,000 AND OVER
Memo: Percent of consumer units with specified size of wealth	100*	16	19	16	23	11	4	1	1	..
Percent of group with equity in—										
Any investment assets	31	4	14	30	42	64	89	93	95	99
Publicly traded stock	16	2	6	14	21	31	57	74	76	88
Investment real estate	11	..	4	8	14	29	43	35	42	43
Percent of total wealth of group in investment assets	33	4	6	6	13	21	36	48	56	50
Mean equity in—										
All investment assets	$ 7,000	..	$ 200	$ 400	$2,100	$ 7,500	$24,600	$64,100	$169,100	$628,300
Publicly traded stock	3,700	..	100	100	600	2,500	11,900	31,700	96,800	420,700
Investment real estate	1,600	..	100	200	900	3,100	8,300	15,500	20,200	75,500
All other	1,700	..	100	100	600	1,900	4,400	17,000	52,000	132,100
Mean equity for those having some equity in—										
Investment assets	22,600	$400	1,200	1,500	4,900	11,700	27,600	69,000	177,900	634,600
Publicly traded stock	23,300	300	900	1,000	2,700	8,100	20,800	42,800	127,400	478,100
Investment real estate	14,300	..	1,300	2,100	6,400	10,700	19,300	44,200	48,100	175,500

* Includes 10 percent with no wealth, not listed separately.
SOURCE: Dorothy S. Projector and Gertrude S. Weiss, *Survey of Financial Characteristics of Consumers*, Board of Governors of the Federal Reserve System, 1966, pp. 21, 98, 114, and 118 (data as of December 31, 1962). Mean equity for those having some equity estimated from published data.

Only those groups with total wealth of $25,000 or more have sizable equity in all investment assets or in publicly traded stocks, specifically. Stock equity averages $2,500 at $25,000–$50,000 wealth, or $8,100 for the 31 percent having some stock. Averages are higher for those with more wealth, as are also the proportion owning stock. For instance, those with wealth of $50,000–$100,000 average $11,900 in stock equity, or $20,800 for the 57 percent owning some. In passing we might note the importance for wealthier groups of investment real estate, including residential units and office buildings.

The concentration of consumer units with less than $25,000 total wealth on equity in their own home and liquid assets illustrates one of the prerequisites for investment in the stock market by most families. A conservative approach entails sufficient investments in other forms to protect the family in case of loss on stocks. Included are sizable amounts in cash forms to provide for emergencies and for early uses, such as the purchase of durable goods or vacation expenses, so that securities will not be sold precipitously, perhaps at a loss. Many families other than those living in a metropolis also consider that a sizable equity in home ownership or a mortgage-free home is a prerequisite to investment in corporate securities. In all cases the family should be protected by sufficient amounts of life insurance, health insurance, and retirement income annuities.

A related financial requirement is that the nonprofessional investor have a secure income from other sources, earnings or other, to provide for regular living expenses for the family before risking investment in securities. The young person with no family responsibilities is in a generally good position to take risks since he has years ahead in which to earn income and recover any losses. Also, an older person after his children are reared may feel that he can risk some of his funds, though he has less time to recover losses out of future earnings. During the period of maximum responsibility while a family is being reared, the parents may feel that a risky investment is undesirable since it may be the children's education that is risked.

An individual or family considering the purchase of corporate securities needs to evaluate also its personal qualifications for taking the risks involved. The proper temperament is a foremost requirement. Is the person calm enough to live with the ups and downs of the stockmarket without becoming unduly optimistic or depressed? Does he enjoy the thrill of taking risks? Does he have confidence in his own judgment, and is he flexible about changing his mind when conditions change? Many people should not invest in corporate securities simply because they are not temperamentally suited to the venture.

Furthermore, there is a need for knowledge and time to give to investing in securities. Of course, one may obtain assistance from a broker or other specialist but the purchaser makes the final decision, requiring some knowledge of general business conditions, the industry, the company, and the position of his security in the company's capital structure. The purchaser must also be willing to give some time to regular evaluation of his securities, buying and selling as conditions indicate. Some people feel that they lack sufficient knowledge and the time to acquire and put it to use because of the importance to them of other interests—their home, business or profession, or other.

Investing or holding funds in any way is never riskless. The company may fail; the going rate of interest in the economy may change; or the purchasing power of the dollar may change. A speculator generally looks for a large, quick profit by frequent buying and selling of securities, which requires considerable effort. An investor concentrates on longer holding of investments from which he hopes to make at least a moderate profit, although a large one is highly acceptable. Since few families own corporate stocks and bonds, our discussion will be relatively brief, considering the complexity of the subject. The purpose is to provide an introduction to a detailed study for those who consider such investments to be appropriate for their situation.

Corporate Enterprises · Of the 1.3 million active corporations, 30 percent are in wholesale and retail trade; 29 percent in finance, insurance, and real estate; 14 percent in manufacturing; 12 percent in services; 7 percent in construction; 4 percent in transportation, communications, electric, and gas; 2 percent in agriculture, forestry, and fisheries; and 1 percent in mining.

While corporations account for only a tenth of the total number of business enterprises, they account for eight-tenths of business receipts (Table 19–4). Only in manufacturing, finance, insurance, real estate, wholesale trade, and mining do corporations constitute a quarter or more of the total number of business enterprises. However, corporations account for practically all business receipts in manufacturing and in the transportation, communications, electric, and gas group; and for two-thirds or more of total business receipts in all of the other major industry groups except services and agriculture, forestry, and fisheries.

TABLE 19–4. Corporation Share in Industries

INDUSTRY	NUMBER (IN THOUSANDS)		CORPORATION SHARE (PERCENT)		
	ALL BUSINESS ENTER- PRISES	ACTIVE CORPORA- TIONS	NUMBER OF ENTER- PRISES	BUSINESS RECEIPTS	NET PROFITS
All industries	11,383	1,323	12	79	63
Manufacturing	408	182	45	97	96
Finance, insurance, and real estate	1,115	375	34	84	75
Wholesale and retail trade[1]	2,497	403	16	71	40
Wholesale	505	138	27	83	54
Retail	1,940	257	13	62	33
Mining	63	15	24	86	102[2]
Transportation, communication, electric, gas[3]	380	56	15	93	91
Construction	848	96	11	66	19
Services	2,521	164	7	44	6
Agriculture, forestry, and fisheries	3,491	23	7	18	3

[1] Includes business not allocable to individual industries.
[2] Net loss exceeded net profits of other types of business organizations.
[3] Includes sanitary services.
SOURCE: U. S. Treasury Department, Internal Revenue Service, *Statistics of Income, 1963, U. S. Business Tax Returns* (data for 1963).

A corporation is a legal entity owned by its shareholders who have limited liability for its debts—limited to the loss of their investment. As a legal entity, a corporation pays taxes on its earnings before dividends are distributed to stockholders. A corporation is operated by a management group that is hired by the shareholders, specifically by those with sufficient shares and interest for control. For most persons who have relatively few shares in a company, share ownership entails no part in the management of corporate enterprise, in contrast with ownership of an independent enterprise which generally requires active management.

A chief advantage of the corporate form is the right to sell ownership shares widely and thus obtain funds for large-scale production. Corporations sell stock at the time of incorporation to obtain funds for building facilities and starting operations, and may sell stock later for expansion. In addition, corporations borrow long-term funds by selling bonds, borrow short-term money from banks, and buy supplies on credit. Most sales of corporate stock involve resale of stock by previous owners through the organized stock exchanges rather than sales of newly issued stock which supply new funds to the corporations. However, resale prices of its stocks are important to the corporation since they may affect its ability to float new issues and obtain loans.

Corporate Bonds · About 2 percent of consumer units hold some corporate bonds. A corporate bond signifies a loan to the company and places the bondholder in a creditor position. The bond states a fixed interest paid regularly on its face value, perhaps 3 percent or 4 percent a year on a $1,000 bond, and prior to any payment of dividends. The bond usually has a maturity date when the principal is due. Some bonds allow redemption by the corporation before the maturity date.

Mortgage bonds are secured by liens on the company's property—all of it or specific items. *Debenture bonds* are unsecured promises which leave the bondholder in the same position as other general creditors of the company. These bonds are successfully issued by corporations with a high credit rating. *Income bonds* pay interest only when sufficient profit is earned. If interest is not paid, it may accumulate and be payable at a later time. *Convertible bonds* are convertible into shares of common stock on specified terms.

Prices of bonds fluctuate less than for stocks because of their more stable yield. Prices fluctuate around the face or maturity value: When a bond is purchased at below 100, it is purchased at a discount and therefore has a higher actual return than the interest rate stated on the bond. A rise in interest rates in the economy causes sales at discount. But a bond purchased for more than 100 is purchased at a premium and has a lower actual yield than stated. A fall in the going rate of interest will bring premium prices.

Average annual return on a $1,000 3 percent bond due in 20 years and purchased at 90 can be approximated as follows:

$$\frac{30 \ (\text{annual interest})}{900 \ (\text{purchase price})} = 3.33\% \text{ current yield.}$$

$$\frac{100 \ (\text{extra receipt at maturity})}{20 \ (\text{years to maturity})} = \$5 \text{ annual increase in value.}$$

$$\frac{30 \ (\text{annual interest}) + 5 \ (\text{annual increase in value})}{950 \ (\text{average value of bond which grows from 900 to 1,000})} = \frac{35}{950}$$

$$= 3.68\% \text{ average annual return.}$$

If the same bond was purchased at 110, the calculations would be:

$$\frac{30}{1100} = 2.73\% \text{ current yield.}$$

$$\frac{100}{20} = \$5 \text{ annual decrease in value.}$$

$$\frac{30-5}{1,050} = 2.38\% \text{ average annual return.}$$

Preferred Stocks · A share of stock, preferred or common, represents part ownership of a company which is evidenced by a certificate having no maturity date. The stock may have a stated *par value* which is carried on the company's books, but does not determine the price of the stock since it may sell above or below par. Dividends are declared by the company's board of directors when circumstances and company policy warrant it. As a result, dividend payments fluctuate from time to time.

Only 1 percent of consumer units own any preferred stocks, probably due to a widespread opinion that they offer neither the stable income prospects of corporate bonds nor the high income possibilities of common stocks. Preferred stocks are, first of all, preferred as to assets—that is, the owners of these stocks are entitled to receive the par or stated value of their stocks before any distribution of assets among the common stockholders if the company fails or is liquidated. However, all creditors have a prior lien on company assets at such a time.

Preferred stocks are also preferred as to earnings, that is, they have a fixed prior claim on earnings of the company when dividends are voted by the board of directors out of after-tax income. The stated dividends must be paid on preferred stocks before any can be distributed to common stocks. Many preferred stocks are *cumulative*, meaning that any dividends not paid in past years must be paid before dividends can be paid on common stocks. A few preferred stocks are *participating*, that is, when dividends are distributed, they receive a minimum fixed amount; then they share to some extent with common stocks in further dividends paid.

Preferred stocks are usually *nonvoting* stocks. Many preferred stocks are *callable*, that is, they can be purchased at a fixed price at the option of the company, which gives the management considerable flexibility in financial arrangements. Some preferred stocks are *convertible* into shares of common stock under specified conditions. When preferred can be converted into common at lower than the market price of common, the right is a valuable one which is reflected in a higher price of preferred and consequently a lower yield on the investment.

The return on preferred stock is usually stated as about $4 or $5 a year on $100 par value. The yield is likely to be somewhat more than on bonds when dividends are paid, but less than on common stocks in prosperous periods. Because of the greater stability of dividends, prices fluctuate less on preferred stocks than on common stocks.

Common Stocks · Fourteen percent of consumer units own common stocks—the most popular type of investment assets. Common stock is in the residual ownership position, with final claim on the company's profits or on its assets at liquidation after the claims of all creditors, bondholders, and preferred stockholders have been satisfied. Common stock usually has voting rights, allowing the stockholder to participate in management of the company by voting directly or by assigning his proxy to another who will vote. Ownership is evidenced by a stock certificate that may be sold and that represents a pro-rata share in assets, earnings, and voting rights.

The common stockholder carries the ultimate risk, which means that he has greatest opportunity for profit if the company prospers and greatest chance of loss if it fails. The return on stocks is highly variable from one company to another and through time. While an individual company does not necessarily follow market trends, general trends provide a good overall picture. Yields on stocks were high during the 1940's and early 1950's, causing some analysts to consider stocks undervalued in relation to current dividends (Table 19–5). Dividends during recent years average about 3 percent of the current price of stock. Persons who bought their stocks at lower prices than the current ones find their actual return on investment much higher, whereas those who bought at higher prices have a lower return.

Obviously, average purchasers of stock today are less interested in current yield than in the growth of capital value, and the prospect for higher dividends and resale value in the future. When both dividend income and capital gains were considered in a large study, the average earnings on common stocks listed on the New York Stock

TABLE 19–5. Common Stock Yields and Price Indexes for Selected Years

YEARS	DIVIDEND YIELD (PERCENT)*	YEAR	PRICE INDEX OF COMMON STOCKS (1941–43 = 10)			
			TOTAL (500 STOCKS)	INDUSTRIALS (425 STOCKS)	PUBLIC UTILITIES (50 STOCKS)	RAILROADS (25 STOCKS)
1900	5	1900	6	3	24	19
1926	5	1926	13	10	24	33
1929	3	1929	26	21	59	46
1932	7	1932	7	5	21	9
1933–36	4	1933	9	8	20	13
1939	4	1939	12	12	16	10
1941–42	7	1942	9	9	8	9
1945–46	4	1945	15	15	17	18
1949–50	7	1950	18	18	20	16
1951–53	6	1953	25	25	24	23
1955–58	4	1955	40	42	31	33
1959–66	3	1959	57	61	44	35
		1960	56	59	47	30
		1964	81	86	70	45
		1965	88	93	76	47
		1966	85	91	68	46

* Aggregate cash dividends divided by aggregate value of stocks in the group.
SOURCES: Dividend yields 1900–1936 by Cowles Commission. Dividend yields 1939–66 and price indexes of common stocks reprinted with permission of Standard & Poor's Corporation.

Exchange was 9 percent compounded annually between 1926 and 1960, or 15 percent between 1950 and 1960.[3]

The price of a stock is determined by demand and supply which reflect the opinions of all people buying, selling, and holding the stock as to its value. Their opinions are based on a multitude of attitudes and events, including earnings and dividends, of the past, present, and future, which they think will affect the stock. As a result, the prices of common stocks vary in the long run and sometimes within a few hours.

Prices of 500 common stocks show great growth in this century, to 14 times their average prices at the beginning. Prices also

[3] Lawrence Fisher and James H. Lorie, *Rates of Return on Investments in Common Stocks*, Center for Research in Security Prices, Graduate School of Business, University of Chicago, 1963.

show tremendous short-term variation. The total index fell almost three-quarters between 1929 and 1932. The index rose slowly through the 1930's and the 1940's, and only in 1953 did it approach the level of 1929. Thereafter the spectacular rise resulted in a doubling of the 1929 index by 1959–60, and a tripling of the 1929 index by 1964–66. Stock prices changed much more than did prices of consumer goods which fell only a fifth from 1929 to 1932 and did not quite double from 1929 to 1966.

However, an index constructed on the value of a wide range of stocks does not indicate the trend of any individual stock which may be better or worse than average, nor does it mirror a special type of stocks. For example, the index for industrial stocks in 1964–66 was 4 times their 1929 level, whereas the index for public utility stocks was only slightly above their 1929 level and that for railroad stocks was about equal their 1929 level, as follows:

YEARS	PRICE INDEXES AS MULTIPLE OF 1929 INDEX			
			PUBLIC	
	TOTAL	INDUSTRIALS	UTILITIES	RAILROADS
1959–60 average	2.2	2.8	0.8	0.7
1964–66 average	3.3	4.2	1.2	1.0

Stocks are generally classified into several general types. *Cyclical* stocks, such as those of automobiles, steel, and building materials, generally do better than average in prosperity periods when their products are in high demand. *Defensive* stocks, on the other hand, generally do better than average in periods of declining business. These generally include utilities, gold mining, habit-forming products, and food manufacturers and food chains. *Blue chips* generally pay the maximum return consistent with least risk and include securities such as those of American Telephone and Telegraph and United Shoe Machinery. *Growth* stocks are those in growing companies. They may pay relatively low current dividends because the company's earnings are retained for expansion and improvement. The companies and industries change as some mature and new ones develop. At the extreme are *speculative* stocks which have an uncertain though highly interesting future.

THE PURCHASE OF STOCKS

Before purchasing corporate securities, the individual needs to determine whether he has met the qualifications, personal and financial, for stock purchase. Next, he needs to consider how these securities will fit into his total investment program.

Selecting Stocks · When he comes to the actual purchase of stocks, the prospective investor takes account, first, of general business conditions and future trends to determine the general desirability of stock purchase at this time, realizing what such changes will mean to the value and return on his investment. Next, he selects an industry in which to invest by determining the size and future trend of demand for its products, the cyclical or stable nature of demand, the effects of the international situation on its demand or on the cost and availability of raw materials, and labor conditions in the industry.

The purchaser selects a company in which to invest by considering its position in the industry, the strength of its management, its past record of sales, earnings, and dividends, future prospects, and its aggressiveness in improving its products, developing new ones, and expanding its markets. Finally, he determines the specific characteristics of the security he is considering, its advantages, disadvantages, price, and the place it occupies in the company's financial structure.

Fortunately, the investor can obtain help in making these decisions by use of the financial services that provide weekly reports on general business conditions, industry conditions, companies, and particular stocks. Babson's Reports, Moody's Stock Survey, United Business Service, Standard and Poor's Outlook, and Fitch's Survey provide materials for subscribers. Advice and assistance are also available from brokers and their market letters, financial magazines, trust departments of banks, and investment counsellors. Help may also be obtained by studying the published financial statements of corporations and the investment portfolios of institutional investors. A reputable advisory service is cautious about telling the investor exactly what to do, since no service can assure the results of security purchase.

The Broker and the Stock Exchange · The broker executes buying and selling orders for his customers. These orders are usually placed by telephone, but may be placed personally or by letter. After checking on the current price, one may decide to buy (or sell) 100 shares on a market order to be executed immediately at the best price available when the order reaches the floor of the Exchange; or a limit order may be placed, limiting the price to be paid (or accepted) and the time allowed to fulfill it.

The order is wired to the New York headquarters of the brokerage firm and telephoned to its booth on the floor of the Exchange. Then one of the firm's brokers goes to the trading post (one of eighteen on the floor) at which that stock is bought and sold along with about eighty others. There bids and offers are made and the broker concludes the purchase (or sale) at the best price he can get or within the set limits. The results of the transaction on the floor are telephoned to the firm's headquarters in New York from which a wire is sent to the individual's broker giving him the details.

A bill is sent the investor showing what was purchased, the price paid, commission due, postage or tax due, and total amount owed. Payment must be made within four business days. The stock certificate is then registered in the buyer's name and is transferred to him or held in the vault of the broker where it is available for future selling orders.

An order for less than 100 shares is called an odd lot which is purchased from an odd-lot dealer on the Exchange. For the service, he makes an extra charge. The broker's commission varies with the amount of money involved. The total cost of buying odd lots may approximate 3 percent of the market price, which takes a sizable share of the first year's dividends. Constant buying and selling of securities may thus result in very limited profits or even in losses.

The securities of more than 1,100 major companies are listed on the New York Stock Exchange where buying and selling is done in an open auction market between 10 a.m. and 3:30 p.m. on Monday through Friday. The Exchange is a very large area in a building at the corner of Wall and Broad Streets in New York City and is well worth a visit. The Exchange consists of 1,366 members who have seats (memberships) on the Exchange. A broker who is not a member of the Exchange has an order executed by a member and may charge the investor a small commission above the regular commission that he pays the member broker. Other major exchanges include the American Stock Exchange, Midwest Stock Exchange, and Pacific Stock Exchange.

Many securities are not listed on an exchange and are bought and sold "over-the-counter" by telephone. In general, unlisted securities are those of small companies not known nationally, but also include stocks of banks and insurance companies as well as U. S. Government bonds, municipal bonds, and the securities of many large companies. A broker who is a member of the Exchange will also execute buying and selling orders on unlisted securities.

Although it is not recommended for ordinary investors, some

large investors buy stocks "on margin," that is, make an initial cash payment of less than the total amount. Minimum margin requirements are set by the Board of Governors of the Federal Reserve System up to 100 percent of the purchase price and vary from time to time, depending on its judgment as to inflationary conditions. Buying on margin makes it possible for the investor to purchase a larger number of stocks by spreading his equity more thinly. However, if the price should fall, he might be forced to sell stocks in a falling market in order to retain ownership of some.

Market quotations as they appear in newspapers are interesting reading for the investor and others. Take, for example, the following quotations for a hypothetical company:

—1967—			DIV.	SALES IN 100's	OPEN	HIGH	LOW	LAST SALE	NET CHG.
HIGH	LOW								
42¾	34½	ABC	2	137	40	40¼	39⅞	40⅛	+⅜
(1)	(2)	(3)	(4)	(5)	(6)	(7)	(8)	(9)	(10)

The two figures before the company's name show that the highest price paid for the stock so far in 1967 was $42.75 and the lowest price was $34.50. Item 4 after the company's name shows that the last dividend declared was $2 a share. Item 5 shows that 13,700 shares of the stock were traded on the preceding day. The first transaction was at $40 (Item 6); the highest price was $40.25 (Item 7); lowest was $39.875 (Item 8); and the last sale was at $40.125 (Item 9). The last price of the day was 37.5¢ higher than the last price of the preceding day (Item 10).

Dollar Cost Averaging · Determining exactly when to buy and sell securities is an important problem for the investor. Many small investors simply buy in prosperity periods when they have excess funds and are feeling optimistic about the future, and sell in depressed periods or emergencies when money is needed for family living. But this method is a poor guarantee for success. As was pointed out earlier, money for emergencies of all types should be held in other investment forms in order to avoid precipitant sales of stocks in an unfavorable market.

Exclusive of emergency needs for cash, in deciding whether to hold or sell an investment, the individual considers what can be gained in an alternative investment. Will the alternative pay as well or better in dividends and capital appreciation? What price has to be paid for it? Will it better meet other investment needs of the family?

The easiest way to make money is to "buy low and sell high," but few know when either point has been reached. Since it is difficult or impossible to determine the "right" time to buy stocks, various formulas have been constructed by analysts, and the simple method of "dollar cost averaging" has been developed for long-term investment. It involves the investment of a specific sum of money in the stock at regular intervals, whether the stock price is high or low. Thus the investor is able to purchase more when the price goes down and less when it goes up.

Investing $1,000 annually in a stock at fluctuating prices might give the following results:

YEAR	PRICE PER SHARE	SHARES PURCHASED
1	$100	10.0
2	90	11.1
3	80	12.5
4	90	11.1
5	100	10.0
		54.7

Thus, 54.7 shares would be obtained for the $5,000 and they would have a sale value today of $5,470. However, if the price of the shares had continued to decline to $70 in the fourth year and $60 in the fifth year, they would currently be worth only $3,876 although the investor has a total of 64.6 shares. Thus a permanent decline may result in magnification of the loss.

A stock with an early decline and a later rise shows better results from dollar averaging than does one with an early rise and later decline. Many examples of the advantages of the method are drawn from the experiences of the recent 20 or 30 years when stock prices were generally advancing, as seen earlier in studying the indexes. However, a 5- or 10-year period starting in 1925 might have shown quite different results.

In order to encourage purchases of stocks by individuals who have small excess funds each month, the monthly investment plan is provided by many brokers. The plan allows an individual to invest a stated amount each month in the stock of his choice, sometimes buying more and sometimes less, depending on the price. The plan may also provide for the use of dividends to buy additional shares of stock.

It should be noted that $50 invested each month, however, will result in higher commission rates, and probably the odd-lot charge also, which may total 6 percent.

Diversification · Diversification may be achieved by investing in different industries, companies, or kinds of securities. Different types of diversification are advantageous at different stages of the business cycle. Diversification minimizes the risk of investing since low returns on one security may be balanced by better returns on another. However, it is clear that an investment placed in a company that pays good returns is better than the same amount divided among several companies with varying earnings.

Trying to diversify with a small investment involves the special expenses of odd-lot buying as well as the difficulty of following the progress of each one of the investments. A better way of diversification is to do it through the years by the purchase of $500 worth of stock of one company this year and a similar amount in another company next year. Furthermore, diversification is possible through purchase of the securities of an investment company.

INVESTMENT COMPANIES

Instead of investing directly in the stocks and bonds of operating companies, one may invest indirectly in them through the purchase of shares of an investment company in the business of making investments in operating companies. By purchasing shares of an investment company, the individual obtains part ownership of its portfolio of securities and receives dividends based on its earnings on investments. Five percent of consumer units own shares in mutual funds or other investment companies.

Purchase of shares of an investment company provides much greater diversification of investments than the small investor is able to attain directly. This diversification may be in security, industry, company, or geographical location and although the risk may be diminished, it is by no means eliminated. An investment company also provides professional management of the fund at a lower cost than one would pay privately. The company depends on a skilled management and outside counsellors to provide continuous supervision of its portfolio, including the selection of securities and the timing of their purchase and sale.

Fees must be paid annually to the management of the fund before the distribution of dividends. Fees have traditionally been set at 0.5 percent a year on the market value of the fund's assets (investments). The Securities and Exchange Commission report published late in 1966 suggests that the fees are too high in many cases. Furthermore, the Fisher and Lorie study published in 1963 found no evidence that mutual funds select stocks better than would be done by the random method.

Some investors make greater gains or better satisfy their own needs by direct investment in stocks than by indirect investment through investment companies. Also, the large number and great variety of investment companies may cause as much difficulty for the individual in selecting an investment company as in selecting an operating corporation in which to invest directly.

Closed-End and Open-End Companies · *Closed-end* investment companies, such as Consolidated Investment Trust, Lehman Corporation, and Tri-Continental Corporation, have a fixed number of shares outstanding, sold at the formation of the company or its later enlargement. Their shares, many of which are listed on the stock exchanges, are for sale from those who own them through a broker at the usual commission for buying or selling stock. Prices of a company's shares are determined by supply and demand for them and reflect to some extent the value of its assets (portfolio of securities) as does the price of any stock.

Open-end investment companies, usually called *mutual funds*, are more common than closed-end companies, having shown remarkable growth in numbers and invested funds in the last 20 years. They include companies such as the State Street Investment Corporation and the DeVegh Mutual Fund. Ordinarily new shares of stock in these companies are readily available for purchase directly from the company or through licensed dealers, and shares are redeemed by the company at any time. The price of a company's shares is determined as the appropriate proportion of the net asset value of the portfolio of securities it holds. Since this changes from time to time, the price also changes.

In addition to the purchase price, there is usually a "loading charge" of about 9 percent at purchase of shares in a mutual fund. Thus the broker makes a greater commission than on the sale of listed stocks of active corporations or closed-end investment companies. This high loading charge is a special disadvantage to the investor.

For the first two years of ownership of new shares, the investor will probably have little net return from the investment by the time he has subtracted acquisition costs (excepting any appreciation of stock value). A ceiling of 5 percent on commissions was proposed in the SEC report.

The front-end load plan of a few mutual funds is an extreme plan that the SEC recommended be eliminated. This plan usually requires an investor to sign up for 10 years of regular purchases, then deducts the total 10-year sales charge from his investment during the first year. The charge, which may absorb half of his first year's investment, is lost if the individual has to cancel the plan later. At the other extreme are 60 mutual funds, called no-load funds, that make no charge at purchase.

Because of the loading charges at purchase and of a possible small redemption fee when stocks are sold back to the company, mutual funds are not generally recommended for short-time investment. On the other hand, mutual funds have a special advantage in that small investments can be made at any time in regular or irregular amounts, similar to the monthly investment plan of stockbrokers, which gives the benefits of dollar averaging.

Investment Policy · Investment companies differ in their emphasis on capital gains, current income, and other objectives. The individual therefore needs to see that the company's objective corresponds to his own. The investment company may diversify its investments in different ways. For example, a *growth* fund aims at long-term capital gains by investment in various common stocks. A *growth with income* fund places greater stress on annual earnings. An *income with growth* fund stresses income even more. A *balanced* fund places equal emphasis on growth and income, and invests in common stocks, preferred stocks, and bonds. *Income* funds emphasize current earnings. There are also some *preferred stock* funds and *bond* funds.

The capital of the investment company may come only from common stocks (true of open-end companies formed since 1940) or from preferred stocks and bonds in addition. If the company's investments are mostly in common stocks and it has a mixed capital structure for obtaining funds, there is a greater fluctuation in the dividends and value of its common stock. Common stock has greater earnings during good times and smaller during poor times because of the primary lien of the fixed charges on preferred stocks and bonds.

As in the purchase of securities of operating corporations, the individual needs to study the investment objectives, type of fund, capital structure, strength of management, and past record and future prospects of the investment company. Annual comparisons that provide useful information include *Investment Trusts and Funds from the Investor's Point of View* by the American Institute of Economic Research and *Investment Companies* by Arthur Wiesenberger and Co.

INVESTMENT OBJECTIVES

The Survey of Financial Characteristics of Consumers found that consumer units owning investment assets have a wide variety of investment objectives. About half mention each of these: a safe, steady return; growth of capital through appreciation; and safety of capital (Table 19–6). Frequently mentioned also are maximum current cash return, liquidity or marketability, and minimizing income taxes. The chief investment objective of consumer units is a safe, steady return for four-tenths, growth of capital through appreciation

TABLE 19–6.   Investment Objectives of Consumer Units Owning Some Investment Assets * [Percentage of consumer units mentioning investment objectives **]

INVESTMENT OBJECTIVE	SPECIFIED OBJECTIVE MENTIONED	CHIEF OBJECTIVE MENTIONED
All objectives	***	100
Safe, steady return	56	39
Growth of capital through appreciation	50	30
Safety of capital	45	10
Maximum current cash return .	23	12
Liquidity or marketability	15	1
Minimizing income taxes	6	2
Other	8	5

* Investment assets include publicly traded stock, marketable securities other than stock, mortgage assets, real estate, business not managed by unit, and company savings plans.

** Thirty-one percent of consumer units had some investment assets, and seven-tenths of these mentioned one or more investment objectives.

*** Percentages add to more than 100 because some consumer units mentioned more than one objective.

SOURCE: Dorothy S. Projector and Gertrude S. Weiss, *Survey of Financial Characteristics of Consumers*, Board of Governors of the Federal Reserve System, 1966, pp. 142–143 (data as of December 31, 1962).

TABLE 19–7.   Major Investment Objectives of Consumer Units Owning Some Investment Assets, by Age of Head

INVESTMENT OBJECTIVE	PERCENT OF CONSUMER UNITS WITH HEAD AGED—				
	UNDER 35	35–44	45–54	55–64	65 AND OVER
Specified objective mentioned	*	*	*	*	*
Safe, steady return	40	49	51	65	67
Growth of capital through appreciation	63	68	52	42	31
Safety of capital	29	41	44	54	47
Chief objective	100	100	100	100	100
Safe, steady return	20	30	34	54	50
Growth of capital through appreciation	46	48	33	15	16
Other	34	22	33	31	34
Addenda:					
Percent owning investment assets	19	31	37	39	31
Percent mentioning investment objective	12	22	27	30	22

*Percentages add to more than 100 because some consumer units mentioned more than one objective.

SOURCE: Dorothy S. Projector and Gertrude S. Weiss, *Survey of Financial Characteristics of Consumers,* Board of Governors of the Federal Reserve System, 1966, pp. 110, 142–143 (data as of December 31, 1962).

for three-tenths, safety of capital for a tenth, maximum current cash return for a tenth, and another objective for a tenth.

Investment objectives differ decidedly by age. Among consumer units headed by a person 35–44, seven-tenths mention growth of capital through appreciation, five-tenths mention a safe, steady return, and four-tenths mention safety of capital (Table 19–7). On the other hand, among groups 55–64 years old, seven-tenths mention a safe, steady return, five-tenths mention safety of capital, and four-tenths mention growth of capital through appreciation. The chief investment objective of those under 45 years old is growth of capital through appreciation, whereas the chief objective of those 55 and over is a safe, steady return.

The various types of investment in business need to be compared with other types of investment in regard to their general likelihood of fulfilling the various investment objectives. First, we may consider *liquidity* or marketability. The organized exchanges provide a ready market for corporate stocks and bonds and investment company shares; mutual fund shares are readily redeemed. However, liquidity in the sense of ready convertibility of an asset into cash without loss is generally low for investments in independent business, corporate stocks and bonds, and investment companies (as well as in investment real estate and variable annuities), though it may be fairly good for top-grade corporate bonds. In general, one cannot depend on a ready market for these investments at their full value at the moment one needs cash—one may have to wait a while for the proper time or the right buyer to come along. As a result, the family needs to have funds available to meet its need for liquidity in cash forms and near-cash forms such as savings accounts, U. S. savings bonds, and cash value of insurances.

Safety of the principal is not high for investments in business. Safety is generally least for investments in independent business and common stocks (as well as real estate), better for preferred stocks and investment companies (and variable annuities), and best for corporate bonds. Blue-chip stocks are better than other stocks in this respect. Safety of principal is provided most simply by holdings of cash forms and near-cash.

Simplicity of planning and supervising the investments is not a strong point of investments in business, with independent business requiring most extreme effort in this direction, and corporate stocks needing considerable effort (as does real estate). Investments in preferred stocks, bonds, and investment companies (as well as variable annuities) are generally somewhat simpler. But the simplest are cash and near-cash.

Steady income is most easily achieved through corporate bonds among the various types of investments in business, as well as from blue-chip stocks. Savings accounts and savings bonds are superior in this respect, though the income is moderate. *High income*, on the other hand, is most likely to come from investments in independent business, common stocks, and investment real estate, though extremely low income is also most likely to come from them. More moderate and steady income is generally expected from preferred stocks and investment companies, as well as variable annuities.

A *hedge against inflation* is most available through an independent business or common stocks, preferably cyclical or growth stocks. Investment companies (and real estate and variable annuities) generally provide a good hedge. Preferred stocks and corporate bonds do not serve well in this capacity. Near-cash forms do not serve at all.

Capital gains possibilities are greatest for investments in independent business and common stocks, particularly growth stocks, and less for investment companies and preferred stocks. Corporate bonds and near-cash forms have no possibility of capital gains.

Tax status cover is provided by tax-free state and municipal bonds and certain Federal issues as well as by growth stocks that retain earnings and forego dividends until a later date when the taxpayer is in a lower tax bracket. The profits from sales of corporate stocks and bonds (and investment real estate) that have been held more than six months are taxable at the capital gains rate which is lower than the rate on income for a high-income family. U. S. savings bonds and annuities also allow postponement of income taxes which are levied only upon receipt of earnings.

QUESTIONS

1. How important are independent businesses in the economy?
2. What types of consumer units are most likely to have investments in an independent business or profession?
3. What are the important advantages of investment in independent business? What disadvantages?
4. What types of consumer units have sizable investments in corporate stocks?
5. What qualifications should a person or family have before investing in corporate securities?
6. Differentiate between corporate stocks and bonds. Between common stocks and preferred stocks.
7. What are the special advantages of the corporate enterprise over an independent business?
8. How do corporate bonds differ from one another?
9. What are some special characteristics of preferred stocks?
10. What has been happening to yields on common stocks and why?
11. How have the indexes of common stock prices changed from period to period? Why?
12. Differentiate among the following types of stocks: cyclical, defensive, blue chips, growth, and speculative.
13. How does the individual select stock?
14. What are the functions of the broker and the stock exchange?
15. Explain dollar cost averaging. What is its advantage? Disadvantage?
16. Explain diversification. What is its advantage? Disadvantage?
17. What is an investment company? How does it operate?

18. What are the special advantages of investment companies to the individual investor?

19. Distinguish between closed-end and open-end investment companies. What are the advantages of each?

20. Describe the investment policies of investment companies? What is the importance to the family?

21. What are important investment objectives of consumer units?

22. Compare the various types of business investments with regard to meeting the investment objectives. Consider also the usefulness of other types of investment.

SUGGESTIONS FOR FURTHER READING

American Institute of Economic Research. *Investment Trusts and Funds from the Investor's Point of View.* Latest edition.

Amling, Frederick. *Investments: An Introduction to Analysis and Management.* Englewood Cliffs, N. J.: Prentice-Hall, 1965.

Arthur Wiesenberger and Co. *Investment Companies.* New York, latest edition.

Ball, Richard E., ed. *Readings in Investments.* Boston: Allyn and Bacon, 1965.

Dowrie, George W., Fuller, Douglas R., and Calkins, Francis J. *Investments.* 3rd ed.; New York: Wiley, 1961.

Fisher, Lawrence and Lorie, James H. *Rates of Return on Investments in Common Stocks.* Center for Research in Security Prices, Graduate School of Business, University of Chicago, 1963.

Plum, Lester V., Humphrey, Joseph H., Jr., and Bowyer, John W. *Investment Analysis and Management.* Homewood, Ill.: Irwin, 1964.

Securities and Exchange Commission. *Public Policy Implications of Investment Company Growth.* Washington, D.C.: Superintendent of Documents, 1966.

Small Business Administration. *Establishing and Operating Your Own Business.* Washington, D.C.: Superintendent of Documents, latest edition.

Wills
Distributing / 20
Property

- A LEGAL WILL
- RELATED TAXES

Anyone who has struggled to earn money, save some, and invest it wisely wants to assure that any estate remaining at his death is conserved and distributed where it will do the most good.

A person who dies without leaving a valid will is said to have died *intestate*. The distribution of his estate is then determined by the laws of descent and distribution. Thus, by not making a will, one decides to distribute his property according to state law. In the event that there is no will and no relatives recognized by the state, the estate reverts to the state by the process of *escheat*.

State law may distribute the estate as the decedent preferred, or it may not. For instance, a man of moderate means may wish that his estate go directly to his widow to help in caring for their young children, or to care for the widow if the children are self-supporting. However, in the absence of a valid will, in a number of states his widow would receive only a third of the estate if he left two or more children, regardless of their ages (Figure 20–1). Even if there were no children, his widow would receive all of the estate only if he left no surviving parents (in Ohio) or no relatives as close as an uncle or aunt (in Pennsylvania). The individual who wants to "let the law make my will" should ascertain what kind of will the law of his state has made for him, then see if it fits his family situation.

Catherine Marshall tells in her book *To Live Again* some of

FIGURE 20–1. Examples of Distribution of Estate to Surviving Spouse When There is No Will

OHIO

CHILDREN

ONE CHILD
- SPOUSE ½
- CHILD ½

TWO OR MORE CHILDREN
- SPOUSE ⅓
- CHILDREN ⅔

NO CHILDREN

PARENTS
- SPOUSE ¾
- PARENTS ¼

NO PARENTS
SPOUSE ALL

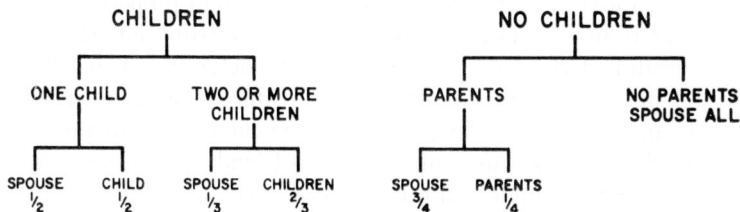

PENNSYLVANIA

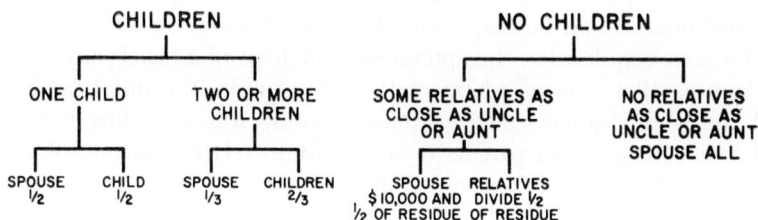

CHILDREN

ONE CHILD
- SPOUSE ½
- CHILD ½

TWO OR MORE CHILDREN
- SPOUSE ⅓
- CHILDREN ⅔

NO CHILDREN

SOME RELATIVES AS CLOSE AS UNCLE OR AUNT
- SPOUSE $10,000 AND ½ OF RESIDUE
- RELATIVES DIVIDE ½ OF RESIDUE

NO RELATIVES AS CLOSE AS UNCLE OR AUNT
SPOUSE ALL

MARYLAND

CHILDREN
- SPOUSE ⅓
- CHILDREN ⅔

NO CHILDREN

PARENTS
- SPOUSE ½
- PARENTS ½

NO PARENTS
- SPOUSE $4,000 AND ½ OF RESIDUE
- BROTHERS + SISTERS DIVIDE ½ OF RESIDUE

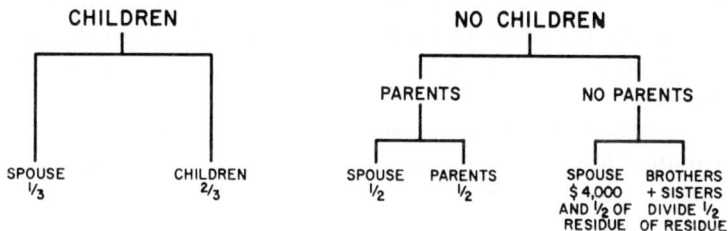

the special problems that arose when her husband, Peter Marshall, chaplain of the U. S. Senate, died without a legal will. His checking account was frozen, since it was in his name, so that she could not draw money for daily necessities. His safe deposit box was sealed, containing his insurance policies, which deferred collection on them. According to the law of the District of Columbia, a third of his estate went to his widow and two-thirds to the young son. Therefore, she undertook to have a court name her the administratrix of her husband's estate, which is usually a costly procedure. And each year she was required to file a financial accounting with the court of the property held by her as guardian of her son's estate.

A LEGAL WILL

Advantages · There are several major advantages that may be gained by making a legal will. The first is the distribution of property in ways that differ from the state law of descent and distribution. The *testator* (creator of the will) has the power to determine *who* will receive his property: he may omit some individuals who would receive property under the state law, or he may avoid having his property revert to the state. He may make gifts to friends and relatives who would receive none under state law, and he may make gifts to charities, churches, schools, hospitals, and foundations that are not possible under state distribution.

In addition, he may determine to whom his property will be distributed should he and some of his beneficiaries die as the result of a common disaster, thus preventing the heirs of a beneficiary from claiming that person's share of the estate under the intestate law. A husband who has willed his property to his wife may thus prevent it from going to her parents or more distant relatives in case of the spouses' deaths due to a common disaster.

The testator also has the power to determine *how* his property will be distributed among his beneficiaries. He may divide it in proportions that differ from those of state law. He may decide that certain persons or institutions should receive specific items such as heirlooms, the home, or the business. He can decide when the distribution is to be made—immediately, at a given age, or regularly through the years.

The testator can set up conditions to be met before the distribution is made. He may want to give the net sum or have only the income paid to the beneficiary, depending on his conception of the needs and managerial ability of the recipient. He can set up a trust fund for a beneficiary by turning over a fund to a trustee (person or organization) that will administer it as instructed. At the death of the first beneficiary, there may be subsequent ones. Such a trust fund has the advantages of conserving the capital fund so that it is not used up too quickly and avoiding subsequent federal estate taxes.

By leaving a legal will, the testator is able to appoint a guardian for his minor children and thus avoid an expensive court-appointed guardian. Also, he can appoint the executor he prefers for his estate, rather than depending on a court-appointed administrator. With a legal will, settlement of the estate may be simpler, speedier, and less costly. Also, it may be possible to save on taxes by the method of distribution.

Characteristics · A legal will has been written by a testator of sound mind, generally 18 years of age or over, whose will meets the requirements of state law. His signature is at the end, followed by the signatures of the necessary two or three witnesses. A *codicil* is a document that supplements or amends a will; however, the will might more safely be revised to include its terms if there is any chance for misunderstanding. Both husband and wife should make a will rather than having a joint will.

Certain limitations exist on the distribution of property in a will. A will cannot redistribute life insurance that is payable to a beneficiary nor property that is held jointly with the survivor, who becomes the owner. Property may be held jointly in the following ways:

> Tenants-by-the entirety—
>> In case of death, property rights go to the survivor.
>> Neither husband nor wife can sell or dispose of his part without the other's consent.
> Joint tenants—
>> In case of death, property rights go to the survivor.
> Tenants-in-common—
>> Each has an undivided fractional share of ownership.
>> Each can sell or will his share.

In Maryland and many other states, the words AND—OR may be misunderstood.

> If the deed to the property is worded Allan *AND* Beatrice Clark, it is assumed that this is the same as tenants-in-common.
> If the word OR is used, it is considered to be the same as joint tenants.

Other limitations exist on the distribution of property. A will cannot disinherit a spouse who may elect to take an intestate share or dower or curtesy right. In general, the wife has a dower right amounting to a third interest in her husband's property; and the husband has a similar type of curtesy right in his wife's property. In general, one cannot set up a perpetual trust, except for charitable purposes. The distribution of the property must be construed to be in the public interest, thus prohibiting gifts for revolutionary purposes or to prevent an individual from marrying.

The advice and assistance of a lawyer are most important in drawing up a legal will that gives careful consideration to various situations. For a person of modest means, the cost may be about $25. The will may be left in the lawyer's safe. If the spouse is appointed executor, he or she will need a lawyer's assistance in probating the will; or the lawyer may be appointed executor.

The executor or court-appointed administrator may be the husband or wife, or a lawyer or trust company which receives a fee fixed by state law. The executor's job is to see that the will is probated (that is, approved by the court as a valid last will), assemble all assets, pay all debts including taxes, locate heirs, distribute the remainder to them, and make a report of his acts as executor. This job can be quite lengthy and time-consuming. The executor is aided if there is a "letter of last instructions" that includes the place of safekeeping of valuables and valuable papers along with, perhaps, any burial instructions.

Planning Property Distribution · In planning the distribution of his property before or after his death, an individual needs to think carefully about several relevant matters. Just what amount and kind of property does he have to distribute? This requires a careful listing and valuation of the different types. The list excludes any proceeds from life insurance or company pension that are payable to a beneficiary, property held jointly with ownership devolving on the survivor, as well as Social Security benefits, which are determined by federal law.

Next the owner needs to consider his own need for the property before his death. If he needs it in his business or to support himself in his old age, he may be unwise to give it away ahead of time and depend on the recipient to take care of his needs. A spouse who is later divorced or a son who becomes involved in the struggle to support his young children may not be sympathetic to the later needs of the donor.

Then the testator must consider the needs of others for whom he has financial responsibility. Who are they? What are their financial needs? What are their personal abilities for earning money and managing it? A man's primary responsibility is to his widow and any dependent children. After their needs are met from his estate or other sources, he gives consideration to the needs of his parents, other relatives, friends, and public causes.

If the testator has only modest means, he may feel that his total private estate should go directly and immediately to his wife to allow her maximum flexibility in its use since future needs and costs are unpredictable for the support of herself and any dependent children. On the other hand, if he leaves a large estate and a widow with little experience in the broad aspects of money management, he might consider it wiser that part of the funds be paid to her in a regular monthly amount to assure permanent support of her and any dependent children.

While planning the distribution of his property, the testator needs to keep in mind state laws governing its distribution as well as Federal and state tax laws that affect the net amount of property and allow savings by certain methods of distribution.

It is desirable that the will be reviewed regularly to assure that it is up-to-date. Certain changes make such a review highly necessary: a change of the testator's residence from one state to another means that the will must abide by the laws of the state of new residence. A change in property owned may mean that provision can be made for fewer persons or for more. Death of a beneficiary or birth of additional beneficiaries may require revision in the will. For instance, if a will was written before the birth of a child to a testator, in some states that child may take his intestate share, which may be a third or a half of the estate. Review and possible revision of the will may also be necessitated by changes in state laws affecting distribution of property, as well as any changes in state and Federal tax laws.

RELATED TAXES

The several states and the Federal government impose certain taxes on the right to distribute and inherit property. It is desirable to understand the relevant laws since these taxes reduce the amount received by beneficiaries and tax savings may be made by the choice of methods of property distribution. Few persons have the privilege of paying Federal estate and gift taxes, but many meet the requirements for paying state inheritance taxes. Our purpose is to sketch briefly the types of taxes that concern a testator.

State Inheritance Taxes · The state ordinarily levies an inheritance tax on the recipient of property. The exemption and tax rate are determined by the amount of property received and the degree of relationship between the beneficiary and the deceased. For instance, the spouse of the deceased usually has a larger exemption, sometimes as high as $75,000, and pays a lower tax rate than do more distant relatives.

State laws differ decidedly with regard to exemptions, tax rates, and property taxed. For example, the Pennsylvania inheritance tax allows no exemptions, but levies a rate of 2 percent on the inheritance of the spouse and children and 15 percent on others. There is no tax on the inheritance of property jointly owned by the surviving spouse and on the beneficiary's receipt of life insurance proceeds.

While most states levy an inheritance tax, New York has an estate tax, and Ohio levies both an inheritance and estate tax. Nevada has neither. Gift taxes are also levied by certain states—California, Colorado, Louisiana, Minnesota, North Carolina, Oklahoma, Oregon, Rhode Island, Tennessee, Virginia, Washington, and Wisconsin, and also Puerto Rico.

Federal Estate Tax · The Federal estate tax is levied on the net taxable estate of the decedent. The gross estate includes the value of all personal and real property (except that outside the United States), as well as life insurance owned by the decedent and jointly held property in proportion to the joint owner's contribution to its purchase. The gross estate is subject to the deduction of all debts, legal fees, and executor's fees for the calculation of adjusted gross estate.

Furthermore, bequests to charitable and other tax-exempt organizations, a basic exemption of $60,000, and the marital deduction are subtracted before calculating the net taxable estate. The marital deduction provides that half of the adjusted gross estate, presumably already belonging to the surviving spouse, may be left to that spouse without the imposition of Federal estate taxes, if all legal requirements are met. Finally, credit is given within stated limits for various death taxes paid to a state.

The calculation for an estate of $200,000 might be as follows:

Gross estate	$200,000
Less debts, fees	50,000
Adjusted gross estate	$150,000
Less marital deduction	75,000
Less charitable bequests	10,000
Less basic exemption	60,000
Net taxable estate	$ 5,000

The tax rate is graduated to a higher rate on a larger net taxable estate as follows:

NET TAXABLE ESTATE	ESTATE TAX
$ 5,000	$ 150
50,000	7,000
100,000	20,700
1,000,000	325,700

Federal Gift Tax · One way of escaping high Federal estate taxes is to make annual gifts to the beneficiary, so long as they are not made "in contemplation of death" (generally within the preceding three years), since the gift tax rate is lower and the base is different than for the federal estate tax.

Gifts to charitable and other tax-exempt organizations are exempt from gift taxes. In addition, an individual may give away his property at the rate of $3,000 a year to each beneficiary exempt from federal gift taxes. Also, the donor has one lifetime exemption totalling $30,000. A husband and wife may elect to consider a gift as if each had made half, thus paying a lower tax rate on the taxable portion. There is a marital deduction of one half of the value of the gift applicable against a gift made to a spouse, before applying the annual and lifetime exemptions.

To illustrate the tax advantage of gifts over inheritances, a mother may give each of her two children $15,000 in a lump sum (thus using her lifetime exemption) and $3,000 a year without paying any gift taxes. If the father's lifetime exemption and annual exclusion are also used, each child could receive $30,000 plus $6,000 a year without the parents having to pay any gift taxes. If the parents have $500,000 that they wish to give their two children, they might do it over 30 years with no gift tax and a gross Federal estate tax of only $1,600 by the following method:

Gifts to Mary:	
Mother's lifetime exemption	$ 30,000
Annual exemption of both parents for 30 years	180,000
Gifts to John:	
Father's lifetime exemption	30,000
Annual exemption of both parents for 30 years	180,000
Total gifts	$420,000
Gift taxes	0
Adjusted gross estate at parents' death	$ 80,000
Less basic exemption	60,000
Net taxable estate	$ 20,000
Gross Federal estate tax	$ 1,600

However, if the parents had died together and had left the estate to their children, the Federal estate tax would have been much higher, as follows:

Adjusted gross estate	$500,000
Less basic exemption	60,000
Net taxable estate	$440,000
Gross Federal estate tax	$126,500

The Federal gift tax is graduated according to the amount of net taxable gifts that year as follows:

NET TAXABLE GIFTS	GIFT TAX
$ 5,000	$ 112
50,000	5,250
100,000	15,525
1,000,000	244,275

QUESTIONS

1. What happens to an estate if an individual dies without a legal will?
2. What advantages may be gained by a legal will?
3. What are the specific characteristics of a legal will?
4. What limitations generally apply to the distribution of property in a will?
5. Describe the work of the lawyer; the executor.
6. What matters does the testator need to take into account in planning the distribution of his property?
7. Differentiate between an inheritance tax and an estate tax.
8. Describe state inheritance taxes in general.
9. Describe the federal estate tax.
10. Explain the rules of the federal gift tax.
11. How may taxes be saved by making gifts during life?

SUGGESTIONS FOR FURTHER READING

Brosterman, Robert. *The Complete Estate Planning Guide,* New York: McGraw-Hill, 1964.

J. K. Lasser Tax Institute and Ralph Wallace. *How to Save Estate and Gift Taxes,* 1964.

Wormser, René A. *Wormser's Guide to Estate Planning,* Englewood Cliffs, N. J.: Prentice-Hall, 1958.

Index